Savannah Fluß

daß Wayßen auch Witwen Hayß. Y auch Publique Platz aber dato noch nicht eingezuimet K Sechs Zehen Julii Meine
ut steht, u: von ferne der Statt ein ansehen macht als wäre sie verpalißadiert M Nieß Weyde. N Gärten Osten West Y
Alt Eben-Ezer zwey Stund von dem Neuen Eben-Ezer. U eine See W Burgburg zwey Stunden von Eben-Ezer N
mende Vornehme u: Reiche Leuthe aufbehalten. Z. Maaß-Stab von 300 Fuß wornach der Plan der Statt angegeben

Halle and Augsburg, 1747). A tinted copy is in the De Renne Collection, University of Georgia Library.

Detailed Reports on the

Salzburger Emigrants

Who Settled in America . . .

Edited by Samuel Urlsperger

JAMES EDWARD OGLETHORPE

Detailed Reports on the Salzburger Emigrants Who Settled in America . . .

Edited by Samuel Urlsperger

VOLUME THREE, 1736

Translated and Edited by
GEORGE FENWICK JONES
and
MARIE HAHN

*WORMSLOE FOUNDATION PUBLICATIONS
NUMBER ELEVEN*

UNIVERSITY OF GEORGIA PRESS
ATHENS

In Memory of

ELFRIDA DE RENNE BARROW

Author, Scholar, Patron of the Arts

 *Contents*

FIRST PART

SUPPLEMENT

Erste
CONTINVATION
der ausführlichen Nachricht
von denen
Saltzburgischen
Emigranten,
die sich in America niedergelassen haben.
Worin die
Tage-Register
der beyden Saltzburgischen Prediger zu EbenEzer in Georgien vom
17 Iul. 1734 bis 1735 zu Ende, mit einigen hierzu gehörigen
Briefen enthalten sind:
Nebst einem gedoppelten Anhang
Bestehend
1) In einer im August 1735 zwischen Ihro Excellentz Herrn Jonathan Belcher,
Ritter, General-Capitain und Gouverneur en Chef in Neu-Engeland
und einigen Indianischen Nationen zu Deerfield gehaltenen Conferentz;
So denn
2) In M. Nathan. Appelletons, bey der Ordination des Herrn Johann Sargent, unter den Indianern von Houssatonoe bestellten ersten Dieners des
Evangelii zu Deerfield in Neu-Engeland den 31 August 1735 gehaltenen
Predigt,
Und
einer Vorrede
herausgegeben von
Samuel Urlsperger,
Des Evangelischen Ministerii der Stadt Augsburg Seniore und Pastore
der Haupt-Kirchen zu St. Annen.

HALLE,
In Verlegung des Wäysenhauses, MDCCXXXVIII.

First
CONTINUATION
of the detailed report on the

SALZBURGER EMIGRANTS

Who have settled in America.

Wherein are contained
The Daily Entries
of the two Salzburger Pastors at Ebenezer in Georgia from 17 July
1734 to the end of 1735, together with some pertinent letters:

in addition a double appendix
consisting of

1) a report on a conference held in August, 1735, by His Excellency Mr. Jonathan Belcher, Knight, Commander-in-Chief, and supreme Governor of New England, with several Indian nations at Deerfield;

also

2) A sermon by Mr. Nathan Appleton, preached at the ordination of Mr. John Sargent, the first servant of the Gospel to be sent to the Indians of Houssatonic, who was ordained at Deerfield, New England on 31 August, 1735,

and a Preface
published by

Samuel Urlsperger
Senior of the Protestant ministry in Augsburg
and Pastor of the Main Church of St. Anne.

Halle
Published by the Orphanage Press, MDCCXXXVIII

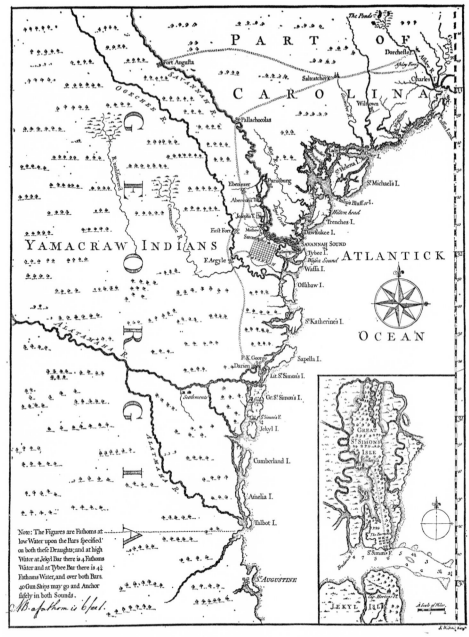

From an original in the De Renne Collection, University of Georgia Library. It is supposed to have been drawn during the period 1741–1743. It has been reproduced in several publications, including Urlsperger's *Ausführliche Nachrichten, 13te Continuation, Erster Theil* (Halle and Augsburg, 1747).

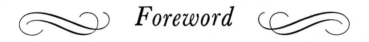
Foreword

THE Wormsloe Foundation is a non-profit organization chartered
on December 18, 1951, by the Superior Court of Chatham County,
Georgia. In the words of its charter, "The objects and purposes of
this Foundation are the promotion of historical research and the
publication of the results thereof; the restoration, preservation, and
maintenance of historical sites and documents and the conduct of
an educational program in the study of history in the State of
Georgia, and in states adjoining thereto."

As its first important activity, the Foundation has begun the
publication of a series of historical works and documents under the
title of "Wormsloe Foundation Publications." They consist of important manuscripts, reprints of rare publications, and historical
narrative relative to Georgia and the South. The first volume appeared in 1955, written by E. Merton Coulter, the General Editor
of the series, and entitled *Wormsloe: Two Centuries of a Georgia
Family*. This volume gives the historical background of the Wormsloe Estate and a history of the family which has owned it for more
than two and a quarter centuries.

The second publication of the Foundation was *The Journal of
William Stephens, 1741–1743*, and the third volume was *The Journal of William Stephens, 1743–1745*, which is a continuation of
the journal as far as any known copy is extant. However, there
is evidence that Stephens kept his journal for some years after
1745. These volumes were edited by the General Editor of the
Wormsloe Foundation series and were published in 1958 and 1959,
respectively.

The fourth volume of the series was the re-publication of the
unique copy of Pat. Tailfer et al., *A True and Historical Narrative
of the Colony of Georgia . . . With Comments by the Earl of Egmont*. This volume is in the John Carter Brown Library of Brown
University. In this publication there appears for the first time in
print the comments of Egmont. With the permission of Brown
University, this volume was edited by Clarence L. Ver Steeg of
Northwestern University, Evanston, Illinois.

The fifth volume in the series was the long-missing first part of
Egmont's three manuscript volumes of his journal. It was edited by

Robert G. McPherson of the University of Georgia. This volume contains the journal from 1732 to 1738, inclusive, and is owned by the Gilcrease Institute of American History and Art, Tulsa, Oklahoma, which gave permission for its publication.

In 1963 the Foundation published its sixth volume, *The Journal of Peter Gordon, 1732–1735*, which was edited by the General Editor of the series. Gordon came to Georgia with Oglethorpe on the first voyage; he began his journal on leaving England. The original manuscript was acquired in 1957 by the Wormsloe Foundation, which presented it to the General Library of the University of Georgia.

The seventh volume in the series was *Joseph Vallence Bevan, Georgia's First Official Historian*. It is a departure from the nature of the five volumes directly preceding, which are documentary. It was written by the General Editor, who brings to light a historiographer who was appointed Georgia's first official historian by the state legislature.

The eighth volume, *Henry Newman's Salzburger Letterbooks*, begins a series within the general series, for it is to be followed by several volumes of translations of the Urlsperger Reports (*Ausführliche Nachrichten* . . . , edited by Samuel Urlsperger, Halle, 1735ff, and dealing with the Georgia Salzburgers). This volume was transcribed and edited by George Fenwick Jones of the University of Maryland, who also will edit future volumes of the Salzburger translations.

The ninth volume of the Wormsloe Foundation Publications is the first of several volumes of the Urlsperger Reports in translation to be published in this series. It appeared in 1968. The second volume of the Urlsperger Reports (being the tenth volume in the general series) was published in 1969, edited by George Fenwick Jones, as was the first, and extends over the years, 1734–1735. The present volume, which is the third in the Urlsperger series and the eleventh in the general series, covers the year 1736. It was translated and edited by Professor Jones of the University of Maryland with the assistance of Marie Hahn of Hood College.

E. MERTON COULTER
General Editor

Introduction

THE first two volumes of these *Detailed Reports* tell how the first group of Georgia Salzburgers gathered in the South German city of Augsburg in August of 1733, established a Lutheran congregation, and journeyed to Georgia, first on foot and then by boat down the Rhine to Rotterdam and thence by ship to Dover and across the Atlantic to Charleston and, finally, to Savannah, where they landed on March 12, 1734. Settling some twenty miles northwest of Savannah at a spot they named Ebenezer, the Salzburgers reported initial satisfaction before confronting the hardships of disease, isolation, and barren soil. Encouraged by optimistic reports from Ebenezer, a second group of religious exiles from Salzburg departed from Augsburg via the same route as the first, except for a spectacular sojourn in London, and arrived at Ebenezer in January, 1735.

The secular affairs of the first group, or transport as it was called, had been entrusted to Baron Philipp Georg Friedrich von Reck, a charming and enthusiastic, but totally inexperienced, young commissary of twenty-three years. Spiritual affairs were entrusted to Johann Martin Boltzius, a teacher at the Orphanage School of the Francke Foundation in Halle, who, together with his assistant and colleague Israel Christian Gronau, was ordained at Wernigerode on their way to join their congregation at Rotterdam. Von Reck left Georgia soon after Ebenezer was settled and returned to Europe with utopian descriptions of the Georgia paradise,[1] to which he intended to return for good.

Upon von Reck's departure, Boltzius was required, or enabled, to assume secular as well as spiritual authority; and it is uncertain whether he really welcomed or resented this burden, because he himself does not seem to have been clear on this point. In his conscious mind he detested such distraction; for he was a true Halle Pietist at heart and only wished to do his Christian duty, bring souls to Jesus, and keep his own house in order. But, because souls cannot live without bodies, at least not in this life, he was committed to look out for his flock's physical welfare too; and his statements and actions make it difficult to ascertain whether he assumed his secular role reluctantly, or whether it was the Old Adam who inspired his strenuous and successful efforts to preserve his worldly authority.

After Boltzius had ruled his little theocracy wisely and well for more than half a year, it was joined by the second transport under the commissary Jean Vat, a citizen of Biel in Switzerland, who expected to take charge of all secular affairs in Ebenezer. Friction was bound to occur, yet Boltzius seems to have shown great restraint and even to have defended Vat at first from the accusations of some of his transport and of a fellow-passenger named Andreas Gottfried Dietzius, who accused him of misappropriating benefactions given to the Salzburgers in London.[2] During the first half of 1735 Boltzius had nothing to say about Vat and his conduct; yet by 24 September he confided that Vat hated him and was mistreating the Salzburgers.[3]

This volume of the *Detailed Reports* relates the continued rivalry between the spiritual and secular leader. This took a new turn upon the arrival of a third transport, again under the conduct of von Reck: for the two commissaries naturally collided at once and thus enabled Boltzius to play one off against the other. We see how Boltzius spoke kindly, even if sometimes condescendingly, of von Reck while speaking more and more openly and mordantly of Vat. For the benefit of those who have not read the introduction to Volume II of the *Detailed Reports*, it should be mentioned that those passages in the present volume set off by brackets were deleted by Samuel Urlsperger, the senior minister of the Lutheran Church in Augsburg and spiritual father of the Georgia Salzburgers, in his edition of the *Detailed Reports*,[4] which he published in order to edify his public and dispose them to support the exiles in Georgia.

To appreciate the in-fighting between the three leaders at Ebenezer, one should also read Boltzius' *Secret Diary*, in which he recorded those observations and conclusions he found too intimate to appear in the official reports.[5] Fortunately, we now have not only Urlsperger's expurgated edition, the only source known to previous Georgia historians, but also the deleted portions of Boltzius' original reports, which have been restored to this translation, and also his *Secret Diary*. These sources are further supplemented by von Reck's journal, in which he described his activities in Ebenezer and his journey to St. Simons Island.[6] Incidentally, the deleted sections of Volume I of the *Detailed Reports*, which were inaccessible when the volume appeared, have now been made available in a University of Maryland master's thesis by William Holton Brown,[7] who has carefully transcribed Boltzius' original and unexpurgated entries. An English translation, which is appended to the present volume, furnishes a valuable supplement to Volume I of these *Reports*.

Whereas the *Detailed Reports* stress Boltzius' disagreements with the two commissaries, it scarcely reveals his larger struggle with Oglethorpe, the founder and governor of the colony.[8] The *Secret Diary*, on the other hand, tells how Boltzius soon realized that Ebenezer had been badly located and that the settlement was doomed to failure unless it were removed to a more fertile and accessible area. Oglethorpe opposed the removal because it would admit a mistake and because it would remove the Salzburgers from the place where they were of most military value. Luckily, Boltzius was astute enough to see through all Oglethorpe's specious arguments and to stand his ground, whereupon Oglethorpe backed down and agreed to the removal to the Red Bluff, some five miles away, albeit with a few face-saving gestures such as having the new town retain the name of the old and thus give the appearance of continuity. In reading these reports, one must therefore observe the shifting use of the name Ebenezer. The name first designated the old settlement, while the new settlement was called Red Bluff or New Ebenezer; but it was gradually applied to the new town, and the first settlement became known as Old Ebenezer.

Arriving with the second transport, Vat found Ebenezer in a deplorable condition. Many of the original settlers were dead, most of the survivors were sick and in rags, and the land had not yet been cultivated or even surveyed and distributed. Being a pragmatist rather than Pietist, he could not endorse Boltzius' preachments that God was chastising His children for their own good and that all these tribulations were part of His divine plan. Although Boltzius says little about his efforts, Vat seems to have started right in to improve the situation despite a serious infection of his eyes; and his clear and factual reports to the Lord Trustees were probably a decisive factor in their eventual approval of Boltzius' request to move the settlement,[9] even if, according to Boltzius, Vat later sided with Oglethorpe against the removal.[10]

The strife between Vat and Boltzius was the fault of the Trustees, who had failed to define their respective authority. Vat had been allowed to believe himself in charge of all physical matters, while Boltzius considered himself still wholly responsible for the first transport. When Vat gave orders to the first Salzburgers, they continued to consult Boltzius before complying; and thus Vat felt his authority undermined. By January of 1736, when the present volume begins, the breach was complete, as we see by Boltzius' complaint of the 14th of the month to Thomas Causton, the mayor of Savannah. Boltzius' complaints indicate that Vat was a scapegoat for Oglethorpe, who let the poor Swiss transmit his disagreeable orders. For example, the "amazing and unheard of" guard duty, against which Boltzius protested on 2 March, was certainly the brain-child of the warrior Oglethorpe, rather than of the civilian Vat, whose lack of military experience caused him to delegate the command of the guard to the old schoolmaster Christopher Ortmann, who had once been in military service. Since the odious order of 22 February was written in English, it can hardly have been composed by Vat.

Oglethorpe, rather than Vat, would have seen the value of the military review of 2 March as a means of impressing and intimidating the Indians; and it may well have been such a display of readiness that dissuaded the Indians from attacking Ebenezer despite its exposed position. Vat's insistence upon storing so many supplies at Ebenezer instead of distributing them to the people was probably at the command, or at least at the advice, of Oglethorpe, who wished to prepare his colony for possible siege by the Spaniards. Such a reason would also explain Vat's refusal to distribute gunpowder for shooting squirrels for soup, since the gunpowder was there for shooting Spaniards, not squirrels.

As the deleted parts of Volume I of the *Reports* have revealed, Boltzius had never had a high regard for von Reck, whom he considered worldly and frivolous; yet, after a year of smoldering friction with Vat, he looked forward to von Reck's return and promised his parishioners much good from the very godly young nobleman. Von Reck arrived in Ebenezer on 7 February; and already by the 25th of that month Boltzius was praising his Christian disposition and attitude toward the congregation in contrast to that of the cruel Mr. Vat, who was opposing him in everything. The squabbles between the mature Swiss commoner and the hotblooded young Hanoverian nobleman neutralized their power, which then fell by default to Boltzius; and, as a result, Boltzius soon arrogated Vat's authority as distributor of provisions.[11]

With Vat out of the way, Boltzius was able to devote more attention to von Reck, whom he held responsible for the sad lot of the third transport. From the beginning he had objected to von Reck's readiness to accept any and everybody into his transport, not only in Regensburg, Frankfurt, and London, but even in Charleston and Savannah; for these people were not Salzburgers or even religious exiles. Christ, the converted Jew, seems to have been the only serious Christian among those picked up along the way; and it is apparent that the others had only economic reasons for going to Georgia. Boltzius often distinguished between true Salzburgers (including the "Austrians", or Protestant exiles from Upper Austria) and the irreligious late-comers.

Oglethorpe had wished the third transport to settle on St. Simons Island, where he was building the fort and town of Frederica as a bastion against the Spaniards in Florida; but the Salzburgers insisted upon joining their co-religionists in Ebenezer. Assuming that they would honor his request to go to Frederica, Oglethorpe had loaded their supplies accordingly, with the result that they all went to Frederica instead of to Savannah. Thomas Causton, the mayor of Savannah, did the best he could with what he had in the storehouse there; yet the third transport never received their due. Boltzius blamed von Reck for the lack of provisions, but he also confided that it was Oglethorpe's way of punishing the third transport for refusing to accede to his wish.[12] As late as 16 April, Henry Newman, the secretary of the Society for Promoting Christian Knowledge, seems to have thought that von Reck was going to take his people to Frederica,[13] a fact which may account for his having been permitted to pick up such a motley group on the way.

As Boltzius mentions in his entry for 25 February, Vat first enjoyed the confidence of both Causton and Oglethorpe; but von Reck seems to have annoyed Oglethorpe greatly, as Boltzius reports on 14 June. Also, von Reck had won the enmity of many of his transport when he proved unable to fulfil his promises of all this and heaven too, as we see in the case of Ossenecker, Rieser, and Ernst.[14] It was, therefore, not difficult for Boltzius to put the entire blame on von Reck, as he did by 19 June, and to divest him of his last shred of authority by 5 August. By 13 August Boltzius' victory was complete.

It is easy to see why both Vat and Boltzius took offense at the exuberant and charming, but utterly incompetent, young baron. Boltzius objected to his worldliness; yet the first example of his worldliness seems trivial enough to us. At Vat's departure on 15 July, von Reck gave him a noisy farewell (whether out of courtesy or malicious joy, we cannot say) by firing some salvos and blowing on a bugle. This was not his first offense, for two and a half years earlier he had celebrated the Hanoverian envoy's departure from Rotterdam in the same way, as Boltzius reported in his subsequently deleted entry for 4 December 1733.

More serious was von Reck's apparent land-hunger, for which he was willing, consciously or unconsciously, to exploit his transport.[15] As the impecunious scion of an old family, he craved to carve out an estate in Georgia appropriate to his noble birth; and, for this purpose, he brought with him a charter for five hundred acres of land.[16] In order to validate a land-grant in Georgia, the recipient had to cultivate a certain portion of the land within a given time, and this required much labor. This may help explain von Reck's missionary zeal in trying to procure religious exiles for Georgia, including not only legitimate Lutheran exiles expelled from Salzburg and Upper Austria, but even Moravians and Waldensians. Fortunately for the Trustees, they learned of his proselytizing efforts among the Moravians in time to prevent him from making any commitments, such as he made to Ossenecker, Rieser, Ernst, and others.[17]

Despite his similar methods, von Reck should not be confused with the usual run of *Seelenfänger,* or "soul-catchers," who were then enlisting indentured laborers for the New World on a commission basis; because he himself was thoroughly convinced of the advantages of emigrating to America, as is proved by his determination to do so. Von Reck's inconsistencies and apparent hypocrisy can be attributed to his youth and to a lack of introspection, as well as to faults inherent in young men born to the privileged orders. Even his thrashing of the Salzburger woman on 6 August would have been normal behavior in Central Europe at the time, where no nobleman would brook such effrontery on the part of a peasant woman. We should also remember that nerves were very frayed by then in Ebenezer and that the proud young nobleman had been definitively displaced by the commoner Boltzius on the very day before. In any case, it is refreshing to see how quickly the oppressed emigrants from Central Europe asserted their newly acquired rights of freeborn Englishmen.

That von Reck's failure was due to his immaturity is indicated by his later life. After returning from the Georgia debacle, he married a wellborn heiress ten years older than himself and entered first the Hanoverian and then the Danish civil service, in which he held positions of trust and responsibility to an advanced age. His younger brother Ernst Ludwig, who accompanied him to Georgia but is never named in the *Reports,* was only seventeen years of age and was, as Boltzius comments on 15 August, too shy to cause much trouble. He too survived the Georgia ordeal and returned home safely, where he attained the rank of captain in the Hanoverian army. These two young noblemen prove the German adage that barons do not emigrate (*Baronen wandern nicht aus*).

In observing Boltzius' victory over Vat and von Reck, one might consider him either a sanctimonious hypocrite or an astute diplomat; for he often contradicted himself when expedience demanded it. On 11 February he claimed credit for not letting the third transport settle at Frederica, but on 19 June he blamed von Reck for not letting them do so. On 7 June he stated that he would not approve of sending laborers to Frederica, and on 12 June he even said he would rather renounce his position as minister; yet by 23 June he was no longer opposed, provided, of course, that it was the will of God (as it turned out to be by 21 July. In this regard we should remember that Boltzius had the great advantage of being sole interpreter of the Lord's will.) Boltzius could also retract what he had previously written, for example in his letter of 9 October. But, instead of attributing these about-faces to inconsistency or lack of character, it is fairer to attribute them to an open mind, which was not too proud to change as the situation changed. For example, Boltzius was opposed to letting individual Salzburgers go to Frederica, and he agreed only with the proviso that it would be a large group accompanied by one of the pastors. Besides that, the economic situation had meanwhile worsened at Ebenezer and there was danger of actual starvation.

Boltzius did show credulity toward anyone who feigned deep religious faith. To escape his Moravian masters in Savannah, the indentured carpenter Volmar needed only to complain of their heretical views in order to make Boltzius accept him in Ebenezer, from which he promptly ran away. Boltzius' pious parishioners frequently invited him into their huts to help them with their religious scruples; then, after listening attentively and appreciatively to his solution, they would only incidentally mention their lack of medicines or other supplies.

As an orthodox minister, Boltzius had little understanding for those who differed from him in dogma. This explains his fear of the Moravians in Savannah, who were then called Herrnhuters after Count Nicolaus Ludwig Zinzendorf's estate in Saxony, where they had lived before coming to Georgia under the guidance of August Gottlieb Spangenberg.[18] Although these Herrnhuters claimed to be Lutherans in good standing, the orthodox Lutheran clergy considered them the worst kind of dissenters and innovators. Above all, Boltzius detested "natural honesty" or "bourgeois respectability," which so often deluded a man into thinking himself sanctified and sure of salvation even though he had never acknowledged his utter depravity and crawled like a poor little worm into the wounds of Jesus.[19]

Boltzius' unquestioning faith also led him into many contradictions. When the Schweigers lost their baby on 27 September, it was divine punishment for their sins; but, when the righteous Steiners lost both their babies on 20 July, Boltzius thanked God for letting them participate so soon in His glory. The same was true of Rott's death, which Boltzius recognized as divine punishment,[20] whereas similar deaths of godly people in Ebenezer were a blessed release from this vale of tears.

In view of the constant backbiting, jealousy, and gossip with which Boltzius had to contend, he can be pardoned for his almost paranoic fear of spies, enemies, accusers, and calumniators, which we see in his entry for 26 June. Since slander might well have alienated the benefactors in Europe, the Salzburgers' reputation was a matter not only of pride but of survival itself. The amazing thing is that Boltzius' Leibnitzian optimism survived all his physical hardships and spiritual tribulations. Never did he question the omniscence or omnipotence of his loving Father; and typical was his reminder to his congregation on 7 March that "it is a precious benefit from God when He leads His children not according to their own but to His will." It is to be remembered, however, that much of the sermonizing in his reports was aimed at his mentors back at Halle, who were to see that he had profited from their theological instruction.

Although we might question Boltzius' motivation in undermining the authority of the two commissaries, time was to vindicate him. In championing the removal from Old Ebenezer, he not only renounced his comfortable parsonage and well cultivated garden there but also risked losing the favor of Oglethorpe and even of the Society for Promoting Christian Knowledge, which provided his stipend. When conditions had become unbearable at Ebenezer, he had an opportunity to accept an invitation from certain Lutherans in Philadelphia to come and organize a Lutheran Church in Pennsylvania,[21] which was then the El Dorado of all emigrating Germans. Instead, Boltzius remained and toiled for more than thirty more years among his affectionate and appreciative congregation, who never doubted his love and sincerity.

Despite Boltzius' pious platitudes and theological ramblings, he was, or at least became, a keen observer of the social, economic, and political scene; and we are indebted to him for many interesting, and sometimes unique, descriptions of the flora, fauna, Indians, slaves, and settlers of early Georgia. He also gives good pictures of the early efforts in agriculture and animal husbandry and vivid descriptions of the prevalent diseases such as scurvy and malaria. Very interesting are his comments on the value of private enterprise in developing a new country, for example in entries from 29 to 31 May.

This volume begins with a foreword by Urlsperger, which introduced the edition of 1739. The reader interested primarily in the Georgia Salzburgers in 1736 might well skip over this foreword, which tells little about the Salzburgers in that year and merely anticipates Boltzius' later diary. Because the diary for 1736 was so discouraging, Urlsperger had delayed its publication until he could give some favorable news, such as the letter dated 21 January 1738, which reassured the reader that conditions were already much better than those described in the diary he was about to read.

Urlsperger's edition includes a long appendix containing von Reck's journal of his journey to and from Georgia, together with a description of Georgia and the Indians there; two German translations of letters from Jonathan Belcher, governor of Massachusetts, and Benjamin Coleman, a clergyman of that colony; and numerous letters from the pastors and congregation at Ebenezer. This appendix has been deleted for want of space, and because it adds little to our knowledge of the Georgia Salzburgers. The most pertinent part of von Reck's journal has already been published,[22] and the letters from Massachusetts do not concern the Georgia Salzburgers. Although numerous and often long, the letters from Ebenezer give little factual information that is not better covered in the diary; and therefore it has been decided that the publication of the remaining diary has a priority over that of this extensive appendix.

In the following translation, citations from the Luther Bible, when recognized, have been made to conform to the King James version, unless the wording of the latter would not fit the context. References to Biblical passages are explained in the notes only if they help clarify the context. We should remember, of course, that most of Boltzius' readers would have recognized all the references at once. The notes to the diary have been kept to a minimum by identifying all persons in the index. In consulting the index, the reader should note certain irregularities in spelling. Consonants are sometimes geminated, so that we find Kiefer—Kieffer, Schweighofer—Schweighoffer, Arnd—Arndt, and Schmid—Schmidt. Dialect variations sometimes come through as in the case of Grüning—Grining, Reck—Röck, and Gschwandl—Geschwandel.

As in the previous volume, we again wish to thank the authorities of the University and State Library of Sachsen-Anhalt in Halle, DDR, for supplying microfilms of Boltzius' diary, from which Urlsperger's deletions have been restored to this translation. We

also wish to thank the American Philosophical Society for sub-
sidizing necessary research and the General Research Board of the
University of Maryland for defraying filming and typing costs.
Above all we wish to express our appreciation to the Wormsloe
Foundation and especially its patroness, the late Mrs. Elfrida De
Renne Barrow. To her this volume is gratefully dedicated.

George Fenwick Jones   Marie Hahn
University of Maryland   Hood College

Preface

That which could not be brought out at the 1738 Easter Fair[23] is taking place this year, at which time the Second Continuation of the Detailed Reports on the Salzburger Emigrants who settled in America is being delivered to the Christian and gentle reader under Divine guidance.

This Second Continuation contains 1) an extract of the diary of the two pastors Boltzius and Gronau of what took place with them and among their congregation in all kinds of situations, and how our faithful God let them experience sometimes the sweet and sometimes the bitter for their broader training and trial; 2) the diary of Mr. von Reck,[24] which contains not only the journey of the third transport from here to Georgia and their happy arrival there, but also his return trip to Germany, where he then lived at Halle, in Saxony, as private tutor to a young Baron von Ende. In this diary there are also the extracts of two letters promised in the preface to the First Continuation, of which Mr. Jonathan Belcher, Commander-in-Chief and Governor of New England in America, wrote one and Mr. Coleman, Doctor of Theology and First Pastor in the capital of Boston wrote the other.; 3) also enclosed are the letters written by the two pastors to Germany and England in 1736 from Ebenezer; and, finally, 4) letters written to me and to others by various Salzburgers are also included. In this regard one should remember that I have let the Salzburgers' letters remain in their natural form because many people both near and far have evinced a special enjoyment in their manner of writing. Also, I have printed a few letters from the year 1737, which should otherwise have been added to the Third Continuation, so that people might know how things were in that year.[25]

Moreover, since I can well surmise what a desire many will feel to learn the spiritual and physical condition of the Ebenezer congregation during the past year 1738, I wish to impart an extract, to wit, the one immediately following, from a letter written to me from there and to impart from it a short report about the Ebenezer orphanage, which has been recently established with faith in God's care, about their amply allotted good land, about their first blessed harvest, about their present sound health, and about other internal and external advantages.

1

Extract from a Letter of the two Pastors Boltzius and
Gronau to the Editor–January 21, 1738

Oh how it strengthens us in the faith that the Lord still fulfils
His Word in us: "I shall neither forsake you nor abandon you," of
which we now have so many dear proofs with the two newly arrived
ships. His paths that He goes with us are glorious and good, as
upright souls among us now comprehend better than before and
praise God for His wondrous, indeed blessed, guidance. He has
certainly let the experience of all sorts of hardship serve to let many
die away more and more from the world and from the treacherous
temporality that is still in the flesh and to live for the will of God
and to hasten as pilgrims and strangers towards blessed eternity
and the heavenly fatherland.

The surveying of the land has proceeded so well that our dear
people now have their own land and, to be sure, have distributed
themselves among the good parcels of land around the river[26] in
such a way that each has received, as a start, a few acres of fertile
soil in addition to his garden. The few who have not yet been provided for will be supplied as well as possible. The land that the
surveyor must still select for the pastors and which, according to
his promise, should turn out to be good, will be ceded to them for
their use and enjoyment as long as they live, since we already have
as much land near the city as might be necessary for us if God ever
bestows the means to prepare it for planting and to have it fenced
in. In addition, there are still a few parcels of land in our region
that have not been given to anyone as their own, but those who
have the time and inclination can plant and use them for a few
years. God has also provided for the widows and orphans now that
arrangements have been made for them through His blessing. It is
also a blessing that, with this year's bad harvest, the people have
had such a good opportunity to earn a little money, with which
to buy both foodstuffs and clothing and also cattle. And thus we
look upon the building costs as charities that well serve the congregation, and rightly so, etc.

Extract from a Letter of the two above-mentioned Pastors
to N. N. of the same date.

Our dear God has deigned to have us build a house for our poor
and orphans in our dear Ebenezer, in which our present orphans,
together with the two poor people who were taken in with them at
the same time, have shared in the recently received blessing; and
they will be truly and diligently encouraged to gratitude toward
God and mankind for the great good they have experienced in this

wilderness and which exceeds that of other wretched children. Through unknown benefactors our wondrous God has given us some money with which we shall erect a school for the benefit of the children among us and for those of other places in the land. We made a beginning of this last fall with the erection of a spacious orphanage in the name of our good Lord God; and, since twelve orphans are already there and since four other children have also come from the neighboring city of Purysburg, they will be provided with nourishment and clothing according to their needs from the blessing that God bestows. From now on we two and the married couple appointed for that purpose will work on them both in and out of school through the Word of God and prayer, so that they may soon be led to the Lord Jesus in their tender youth. If it should please the Lord to expand and increase our little institute, which has been set up in His name and to His glory, then we hope we can take in many a poor child straying in error without supervision and care and save it from bodily and spiritual, yea, even eternal ruination. Perhaps through this institute our miraculous God will eventually prepare a way even for the poor heathen children to the beneficial healing knowledge of His Son. With all our hearts we wanted to lead all children in the entire country and in neighboring Carolina—Christians, Jews, and heathens to our dear Saviour, if He will send us the opportunity and the means for doing so. There is still room in His wounds.

Extract from a Letter of the two above-mentioned Pastors to the Editor from the 13th of February, Old Style 1738[27]
Through God's grace we observe an almost general contentment among the people. The longer they are here the better they like it; and they will like it all the more when they can finally eat their own bread. Because they do not know whether others might like it as much as they, they do not wish to persuade anyone in their letters; but, as I hear and read, some of them merely report that they are well pleased here and that they have here that which they sought, namely God's pure Word and Evangelical pastors. Perhaps our true and wondrous God will bestow something toward the church and school buildings, of which we are in the utmost need. As soon as the boards are cut, we shall, where feasible, hold services under the roof of the orphanage, just as we often gather there now, God be praised, with much blessing.

Extract of a Letter of Mr. Boltzius to the Editor from the 17th of May, Old Style, 1738.
Mr. Causton asked me to assure my listeners that he has orders

to assist upright and industrious people upon my recommendation in every way in their want; and they need not worry that restitution will be demanded from them. They should give no credence to the rumor widespread in the land that the Trustees wish to bind the inhabitants of the colony through the benefits and gradually make them slaves, etc. At the same time he proved to be very generous toward our orphanage by sending it a fine supply of beef and pork, likewise of flour, rice, and corn, also some salt and two blankets. God has helped our orphanage so much that, up to now, no child or adult, who number twenty-one persons all together, has any lack of foodstuffs and clothing. And, although there is no longer any supply of money, they have already been taken care of through the provisions received until such time as our Father bestows something again.

This spring the trees have been cut down around the orphanage and the very fertile soil has been prepared for planting; and various people in the congregation have earned something from this job as well as from a few others. With it they have paid for the twenty head of cattle which I ordered from Mr. Causton. The kingdom of our Lord Jesus Christ is certainly with us; and a few, indeed many, battle bravely and with good success under the banner of the Predecessor, Pioneer, and Sovereign.

Physically we are well, as are also the members of our congregation, as long as the Lord wishes it. No one lacks food among us, even though in the previous year little grew in this land. Through God's blessing everyone will surely hold out until the harvest; and, since the crops this year are thriving so well, we hope for a good harvest from God's bounty. As often as they can, the carpenters interrupt their field work and work on my worthy colleague's house with all their hearts, along with the other Salzburgers. I hope this will be completed in the fall.

On Mr. Oglethorpe's order, a broad and at the same time long plot has remained vacant. Our orphanage is built at its extreme end; and the remaining nice large plots are destined for the storehouse, church, school, and the two parsonages. Each of such public plots is somewhat more than an acre of land.

> Extract from a Letter of the same person to the Editor on
> the 26th of August, Old Style, 1738.

Little by little one will recognize better and better what our wise and wonderful God has done to our Salzburgers through Your Grace. Now and then I hear very beautiful testimonies, especially when they experience the power of the gospel in their conversion and the illumination of their souls. Then they confess unasked in which danger of self-deceit, of seduction, etc., they have been mired and how lucky it was for them that God led them into the deserts and yet onto a green meadow of His Word, of the Holy Sacraments, and of many physical benefits. They often ask whether or not a new transport will soon be sent here again. If God should ordain it, I truly believe no one will perish or die of hunger. We are very gratified when we think back and find that, to be sure, our God has led us into much need but has also led us out again and refreshed us in an unexpected and wonderful way. He also takes unto Himself the poorest and most wretched among us so that widows and orphans find a dwelling and set a table. From the very beginning our dear Father has provided so fatherly for this institute, which was erected in His Name and to His glory, that we can say with joy: it is not the work of a man but of the Lord. He Who began it can also continue and expand it.

Already the first year God is blessing this house with corn, beans, rice, and sweet potatoes as well as all kinds of crops that grow in the orphanage garden and field and now are being harvested little by little. Even though the same is insufficient for the maintenance of the work, it is still a beautiful blessing and a great help. The preparation of the field, the making of the fences and other work have indeed necessitated some expenses, but through this the poor among us have received an opportunity to earn something for themselves, and the orphanage will profit for many years from this work. The work on people's souls is also continuing nicely in the congregation and in the orphanage. If only it could be made possible for us not to have to concern ourselves with anything but our ministerial duties.

The authorities in Savannah do not meddle at all in our congregation and their affairs. Thus I can well see that the Trustees are pleased that our people are not just governed according to ordinary laws but rather in a Christian and best possible means; and various gentlemen who have been with us from Savannah have attested a great liking for our set-up.[28] And thus it probably would not displease the Trustees if a Christian justiciary of German blood and of the Evangelical-Lutheran religion were sent to us unasked. We both, as well as our families and our dear congregation, are still well, God be praised! The fever is of almost no importance this year. It attacks this one and that one violently, but it ceases in a few days.

Extract from a Letter of Mr. Boltzius to the Editor from
October 4th, Old Style, 1738.

I must herewith mention that the money that a dear benefactor
allotted for establishing a school has been applied to the construction of an orphanage. And, because our dear God has let us come
into some trials and tribulations up to now, I have had to use some
of the money from the poor-box for the maintenance of this work.
I can do this without harm to the congregation not only because
this institution was erected for the benefit of the Salzburgers, who
had had much profit and use from it, but also because a certain
benefactor sent a sum of money here that has actually been put at
our own disposition for some necessary use. We have preferred to
maintain ourselves as well as possible with our salary and a few
other gifts thrown in so that we can aid the orphanage in this way.

From my lost letters of January 1st of this year I repeat that
Kalcher and his wife are striving for nothing so earnestly as to save
their souls and to reconcile themselves with God and man and to
come to peace. Together with Mrs. Schweighoffer they pray and
struggle very honestly for their souls and for those of the children in
the orphanage; and our dear God also demonstrates in them that
which is in Psalm 1: "Whatsoever the godly doeth shall prosper."

Finally, I am adding the contents of the letter from October 14,
1737, which likewise got lost: "Again almost all of us have been
sick from the fever, still not as violently as in the previous year.
The site for the orphanage is exceedingly well placed, almost a
square acre of land, it lies on the right side of the town and toward
the south but still on a line with and in the territory of the town.
The clearing out of many large trees, bushes, and roots has cost a
lot of work; but now the lovely firm fence around the garden is a
credit to the city. The house itself is forty-five feet long, thirty wide,
and twenty-two high. It has three rooms, and a chamber just behind
each room, all of the same length and width, namely, fifteen feet.
The manager with his family and Mrs. Schweighoffer live in the
middle and can observe the girls on the right and the boys on the
left side day and night through certain windows. In front of the
house toward the street there is a large empty space for chickens,
cattle, and other businesses; but behind it, towards the garden,
there is a spacious kitchen with a small unheated room for cooking
which, together with the house, is set off from the garden and barn
yard by a fence. Necessary stalls and so on, separate lavatories for
married couples, girls, and boys, as well as a wash-hut and cellar
are built on this space. In the beginning we had only two boys and

two girls, at first in the doctor's residence and then in the orphanage. However, they soon increased to twelve but have not remained at that number. To this I have added a short report how much good could be done here in this country through such institutions, since there are so many orphans going astray."

This brief report shows how many false things have been spread about our Salzburgers in Ebenezer in foreign and domestic newspapers to their detriment and to the calumny of God's work. On the contrary, it shows how much matter it contains for the praise and glory of God.

May our God be highly praised because He has neither rejected the prayers that have been made for this little flock inside and outside of Europe nor turned away His goodness from shepherds and sheep. May He be praised because He lets that which is necessary for the congregation remain necessary; because He lets His Word succeed well with the souls; because His Sacraments are dispensed with blessing; because He preserves the two pastors with life and health in their extraordinarily many unaccustomed and important works, and because He helps them soon again when they have suffered hardship; because He has given them wisdom, courage, and strength to act prudently in their calling and to surmount the difficulties occurring therein in faith and with prayer, in such a way that they have become a good aroma for many near and far; because He has not given the good sheep into the hands of their enemies, but has covered them up to now with His protection; because He is still inclining to them the hearts of the most honorable Trustees, of the most praiseworthy Society that bears the name of Society for Promoting Christian Knowledge, of Mr. Oglethorpe, of Mr. Causton and many other upright Englishmen; because He has by now supplied them with as much good land as they could ever wish for; because they are becoming more and more acquainted with the land and accustomed to living in it and therefore also more stable in their health; because their Heavenly Father has sent them a good harvest last year for the first time, so that they can now eat their own bread; because He has granted them hearts grateful to Him and their benefactors for all this and much else, and, finally, because He has set up the first O R P H A N A G E in Georgia, or indeed in all the West Indies, at Ebenezer and has conferred upon it very Christian, understanding, and industrious managers. As a pious Salzburger widow from this house stated on February 15, 1738: "The ORPHANAGE here, into which I and some children came, has been built with God's help. May our dear

God be praised for not only starting this great work but also for completing it. The Lord's Name be praised and blessed from now to eternity!"

If one is wise in God and thus not inclined to distrust and belittle God's works in their small beginnings and in their progress, which is bound with many difficulties, and to find fault perhaps because of the human weaknesses manifesting themselves therein (to which kind of person one must give his own way at his own responsibility and meanwhile not hinder him from continuing swiftly in his course), such a one will be able to observe much to his edification and to the strengthening of his faith. I have written in the preface to the First Continuation: "What is still lacking (namely, of those things that Ebenezer requires), the Lord will give as He finds it good, so that shepherds and sheep themselves will learn that our God is the old God of Whom it is said: He does what the God-fearing desire and hears their crying." Now I can write: "God has already given much of what was lacking: Shepherds and sheep learn to glorify Him and say: "God is the old God: He has done what the God-fearing ones of Ebenezer and others supplicating for them in the Name of Jesus have desired and has heard their crying." Yes, I can write not only that but also this: "God has done more than we have wished from Him." A Salzburger foresaw that in faith and, therefore, wrote here in the year 1737, when things were becoming more encouraging in Ebenezer: *"That is only the beginning, it can soon become better."* But, until it became better, they were satisfied, wrote, and had others write, "that they are, and also can be, satisfied with what God is doing, because He gives them His Word, for the sake of which they emigrated, so bountifully and with so much blessing yet also grants them all necessary earthly things." But another among the Salzburgers reported: "It is truly hard work; but we work for ourselves, because the land belongs to us and we also have genuine freedom."

Moreover, we do not want to omit reporting to the gentle reader two pieces of information: the first of which is that on January 27th of this year, at the request and wish of the two pastors and their congregation and also with the gracious approval and at the expense of the most honorable Trustees, seven Ebenezer colonists departed from here in God's Name, after they had been strengthened through God's Word, and had received gifts from various benefactors both here and abroad, among whom especially the two free imperial cities of Memmingen and Lindau[29] are to be counted, and also supplied with all kinds of necessary and useful gifts, especially books, linen, Schauer balsam,[30] and suitable tools for the Ebenezer congregation. Moreover, they were blessed with a generous viaticum from the most praiseworthy Corpus Evangelicorum[31] through His Excellency, the Baron of Schönfeld, envoy of the Prince Elector of Saxony.

Among the above-mentioned colonists is the carpenter Sanftleben, who, having returned to Germany from Ebenezer a year ago in order to fetch his sister, has reported as an eye-witness the true nature of the present good circumstances of the colonists in Ebenezer in the many places where he stopped. Through his return trip to Ebenezer and by taking along his nearest relative, he really refuted the incorrect reports spread about the bad circumstances there.[32] Therefore, we now wish only that the Lord, Who up to now has been with them on their trip, may further be their pillars-of-fire so that they may arrive there in due time to the praise of God and to the great joy of their brothers and sisters in Ebenezer. This will not fail to materialize, not only because these few people themselves, among whom is a shoemaker so long wished for by the congregation, are so constituted that one can hold out good hopes for them, but also because they will bring many good things and reports with them to Ebenezer.

The second is that, because our dear God sees how He can use this Salzburger flock and especially their shepherds as an admirably good salt, He has already directed many a good heart here and there to be helpful to their need and the institutions set up for the benefit of the poor, sick, and orphans. Nor do we by any means doubt that He, whose water courses have an abundance of water, will continue to do as He began. In this respect we do not have to conceal that a midwife who belongs to the new orphanage in Ebenezer resolved to give the orphanage all the money she earned from her profession, and that she had done so.

An English preacher, Mr. Whitefield,[33] who carefully observed everything in Ebenezer and now has journeyed to England for a few months, has not only bestowed abundantly upon the orphanage from the Indies but also from London, where he gave everyone a very good and unbiased testimony about Ebenezer and preached a collection-sermon for the construction of a church, parsonage, and school-house for the Evangelical-Lutheran congregation in Ebenezer. Our true God has not allowed this to go without blessing; now I must be silent about the other gifts that have still further flowed together and whose donors the Almighty should recompense with His grace.

There are other things that should be remembered; but, since they have been mentioned in the preface of the First Continuation, we need not mention them again.

It is my innermost wish that the perusal of this Second Continuation may bring blessing in both the old and new worlds: in the old, that the readers praise God for the good that He has wrought and given in Ebenezer and follow the good examples there. And, since the spiritual life is being sowed there by them in such a way, that those readers will not refuse to let them harvest some physical blessings. In the new, that in such a way the colonists, strengthened in faith through all kinds of new evidence of Divine Providence, will be awakened to God's praise and stimulated to continue zealously in the course of their Christianity and be induced still more to pray incessantly for their benefactors, as they also do.

If I should wish something else, it is this: that the Gospel of Jesus Christ the Crucified and Resurrected, for Whose sake our colonists emigrated from their country and for Whose sake I was persuaded to give assistance to this business, may run quickly and be experienced by all listeners as divine power and wisdom and draw many, many here and from afar and persuade them to commit themselves completely to the Saviour of all the world and preserve this dear congregation, to which such a precious worthy Word is entrusted, from all impurity, disorder, division, wickedness, and sin. On the other hand, may He preserve them at all times through His mercy in true grace with the pure doctrine that leads to faith and the sanctification of life and also with the Scriptural use of the Sacraments and with upright and true ministers who administer the office of reconciliation there, as has taken place up to now, and defend them from all others most powerfully through His spirit. He Who calls the people in Ebenezer is faithful, and He will do it. Pray for them you who read this. The Grace of our Lord Jesus Christ be with us and with them, Amen. Written on the 23rd of March, 1739.

Samuel Urlsperger

Daily Register

Of the two pastors, Mr. Boltzius and Mr. Gronau
From January 1st to the end of the year 1736

The 1st of January. During the past year eleven children who actually belong to our congregation were born and christened in Ebenezer; but only four of them, two boys and two girls, are still living. Twenty-one persons, counting both adults and children, died during that year and have doubtlessly passed on into happy eternity. On this first day our kind Father in Heaven has already given us His blessing during the study of His Word. We hope that in His kindness He will never let the preaching of His gospel be fruitless during this whole year but will use it to give His children a firmer foundation in His grace, to make the timid souls come closer, and to lead the unrepentant and hypocrites to the recognition of their sins and to true conversion.

Friday, the 2nd of January. This afternoon the unmarried men came to my room, as they had been asked to do, for the purpose of preparation and communal prayer. All of them were very sincere. They as well as the others who want to go to Holy Communion, forty-one members of the congregation in all, wish to be relieved of having to carry provisions from the landing[34] tomorrow, since it is then that we intend to have our service of confession and penance. They would be tired out and not sufficiently fresh and alert for this important undertaking.

Sunday, the 4th of January. During the service a Salzburger remembered a matter he wanted to tell me for the glory of God. While the persecution in Salzburg was being openly carried on, he had clung to the Protestant religion and also had had several good books; but he had still been quite uninformed und unconverted. Yet in his very ignorance he had been so full of zeal that he would have gone into the fire rather than return to Popery from the Protestant doctrine. A burgomaster who knew him well had made him appear before him and a group of other gentlemen. They had tried to change his mind by threatening many fearful punishments, e.g. that he would be taken to the Turkish sea;[35] but, through God's mercy, he had not allowed himself to be moved. Instead, he had said openly: "It is written in the Bible: 'He who loveth his father or mother more than Christ is not worthy of Him.' " They asked him if he had sworn to the Lutheran doctrine. He answered "No", because that was not necessary: he was driven to it by his knowledge and his conscience. Thereupon all of them became very angry, cursed him, and had the bailiff throw him out and into prison.

Shortly thereafter his sponsor-in-baptism, an old gray man, came to him and tried to bring on his defection with a seemingly sound argument, saying that he had had many Bibles and had compared the Catholic, Lutheran, and Reformed faiths. After much study he had finally concluded that the Roman Catholic faith alone was the one which could bring salvation. He said he was a very old man and he should not think that he would want to go to hell. And he would not give him, his godchild, bad advice. Or did he claim to be smarter than his sponsor and many other learned men? He answered he could not do otherwise than consider the Lutheran doctrine to be the right one because his heart told him so. If this should cost him his life, he would say the Lord's Prayer and die gladly. After all the others his mother came to tempt him, trying to persuade him with tears, words, and gestures to stay. But he gave her a brief and good answer; namely, that she and he were mere human beings who lived for only a short time and that each must see to it that his soul be cared for eternally. No, he could not follow her in this, etc.

A certain young man had been there who had more enthusiasm than he. He had helped others greatly by urging them to be steadfast and by reading to them, etc. But when it came to the point of expulsion, he had preferred to defect. This example had taught him a great deal; namely, never to trust his own strength but to pray diligently and not to stop at outward knowledge. A man had had many beautiful books which made him and others well grounded in their knowledge of the Protestant doctrine; but he, too, defected and became a horrible blasphemer of truth, who did much damage with his example and his talk, etc.

Toward evening two [twenty] armed men from Savannah came here via Abercorn and brought written orders from the magistrate of Savannah to the effect that nine [two] Salzburgers should be at court in Savannah on Wednesday, at 9 o'clock in the morning, to attend the trial of a murderer. We respected this order from the authorities in Savannah, telling the people who had frequently come to our house during the evenings for their edification and prayer that, although all of us would like to be together on such a day of solemn thanksgiving and prayer, we should carry out this order because it was a necessity. The [seven] persons destined to go there should keep well guarded the treasure which God had given them today through the preaching of the gospel and their participation in Holy Communion.

Monday, the 5th of January. For several days we have had beautiful summer weather during the daytime, but the nights still have been very cold. Today it started to rain. The water in the river is so high again that it is coming back into our gardens again. If it should rain for several days, we fear that they will be completely flooded again. As is the custom, people have started about this time to plant European peas.

Tuesday, the 6th of January. [This being the feast of the Epiphany], a pious Salzburger called on me and gave me much refreshment with his edifying talk about the rich grace which God has bestowed upon him and others in this congregation. His physical needs are great, but he did not let me notice them. But, since I had learned this from another Salzburger, I tried to relieve his distress and encouraged him to tell us about further necessities in the future. Frequently one must urge these people a great deal before they will accept a gift, and they gladly live in the greatest of need because they say that they do not want to accept benefits which others may need even more.

In the morning and in the afternoon our dear listeners were reminded to give thanks with heart and mouth for the great benefit of the knowledge of Christ they have received through the gospel; and they were urged to offer heartfelt prayers for others, Christians as well as heathens, who either do not have it at all or are still very much in the dark. In order to make all of us more eager to do this duty, I used the evening prayer hour in our room partly to tell them about the pitiful circumstances of our [heathen] ancestors in Germany and also about the grace given them through the light of the gospel, as well as the great benefit bestowed upon them by the Reformation after the divine truth had again been darkened by the Popish doctrine.

At the same time I let them know that our wondrous God had already turned the light of the gospel on the poor heathens in the East Indies[36] for some twenty years and, although this encountered many difficulties and hindrances at the beginning (as is usually the case with works that are pleasing to God and are designed for the salvation of people's souls), that more than three and one-half thousand souls had been joined with our Lord Jesus through Holy Baptism since the beginning of the mission. What God has done for the heathens in the East Indies He could easily do for the heathens in the West Indies and in this country. It is our task to pray for them, to wait for this blessed time of aid with desire and patience, and follow Christ's teaching at the same time, to set a good example for everyone, including the heathens: "Let your light so shine before men, etc." Hereupon we all knelt before God and prayed with heart and mouth for ourselves and for the heathens. Through God's grace we will continue to do so after He has given us renewed awakening for it on this day. The sight of the poor heathens always drives us to compassion and prayer for them; but they come to our place only very seldom and, when they are traveling through (which occurs only very infrequently), they stay here only for the night. Without doubt they prefer to stay in places where they have an opportunity for excessive drinking and other disorderly things.

Wednesday, the 7th of January. The rainy weather is continuing intermittently, and the water in our river continues to get higher. Since the water in the Savannah River must also be high, our people will have a difficult journey. Today two men went to Abercorn to help them. They will go in a small boat, which has been built there for use with the big one. If the small boat should not be finished they will use ours, which is tied up there, so that those in the big boat will not be without help. We hear from the postman that Governor Oglethorpe did not leave London until December because he had to wait there that long for the arrival of the King from Germany.[37] Since the continuation of our diary may be necessary to our benefactors in regard to certain points, we will write several letters today and send them with the diary to Secretary Newman in London by a safe opportunity we have in Purysburg.

Thursday, the 8th of January. Some time ago it was reported in our diary that Gschwandel wanted to marry Mrs. Resch, whose husband was lost in the woods.[38] They have promised to marry each other, but they do not expect the ceremony to be held until after we have received the verdict of our benefactors in London. Perhaps one of the next ships will bring an answer to this as well as to a question we have asked Court Chaplain Ziegenhagen. We will also speak to Mr. Oglethorpe about this, because we want to exercise every possible caution in this matter. It is certainly more than likely that Resch is dead, although we have been unable to find any trace or to get the least report of him.

The wolves are continuing to do much damage to the calves in the pasture. For this reason the people are making better arrangements for their safety. It is said that they also have done a great deal of damage to large and small livestock in other places, more this year than at any other time. When the nights are cold and bright with stars, we can hear such horrible howling in the evenings all around our place that we are sure a great many of them are around.

Friday, the 9th of January. Last night we had a violent windstorm once again, which brought the cold weather back to us. We and others are of the opinion that this winter is colder than the last one, although Divine care does not let us suffer from the cold so much this time.

Saturday, the 10th of January. Although Mrs. Schweighofer has risen from her sickbed, her entire body is still without strength and her right arm without feeling. She praises her Heavenly Father with heart and mouth for having let her cross give her much spiritual good. Through Christ she has learned to know Him better as her reconciled Father; and she knows very well that He cannot do anything but good, although it may often appear bad to the weak flesh. She still suffers from occasional temptations; but they do not last long, and she knows very well that, for her, JESUS is the victor. She knows that we must struggle here until death and that the rest for which she is longing with so much patience does not come until later.

She is committing her young[39] children, who formerly caused her so much grief, to the care of the Almighty God, who does not let even a bird go hungry. I read to her the hymn: "Be contented and be still, etc.";[40] and she marked it for further study. Earlier, when she was in good health, she used to give her very best services, without pay, to the women of our place who were in childbirth. We have tried to serve her and her children with physical benefits to the best of our ability. We will soon help her to obtain a half barrel of flour for her household so that things can be prepared for the care of her body according to the custom of the Salzburgers, who prefer foods made with flour above all others.

Tomorrow, God willing, we shall speak about the Gospel of St. Luke 2: 41 ff. about the usefulness and the necessity of the rituals pertaining to divine services. We intend to show, as we have done on many other occasions, that these outward rituals are not the service God requires in the New Testament, but that they are necessary and useful, which everyone must know from experience if he has made regular use of the rituals and means offered in this congregation. At the same time I intend to apply and explain the words of Amos: Chapt. 8, vv. 4–6, 11–12.

The 11th of January.[41] On this Sunday we gave the married people a number of reminders in regard to private and public worship, using the example of Mary and Joseph from the regular Sunday gospel, Luke 2: 41 ff. We showed in detail how bad and unfortunate it is when married people are not of the same religion or of the same mind, with one of them working for his salvation in all sincerity and the other one wanting to serve the sins of the world. On this occasion we also urged the unmarried people, not only in the sermon but also during the review lesson, to pray and to be very careful in their future selection of a spouse, pointing out to them the great danger [on the contrary] of being led astray and getting lost.

When they had assembled for evening prayer in our house, I read them part of the letter printed in the 6th *Contribution to the Building of the Kingdom of God*,[42] which deals with a marriage performed in heaven. I dwelt especially on the words of a foreign teacher that are quoted in it and which are very thought-provoking. In our circumstances this matter must be treated and discussed very often; because people in this country enter into such mixed marriages as to give the effect, appearance, and sad experience that God had not given His permission and did not approve of such unequal and often objectionable marriages, which were started without Him.

The big boat with provisions arrived at our creek this afternoon. Two men brought us this news. The others will not come until tomorrow. After their arrival another ten men must go back with the large and small boats to get the rest of the provisions. On this occasion my worthy colleague will go along to Purysburg and from there on to Savannah. He will deliver the letter that was written to Mr. Causton yesterday and tend to some private matters. But first and foremost he will look for a safe means, in Purysburg or Savannah, for the delivery of our package of letters and diaries. This time we have written to the Society, Court Chaplain Ziegenhagen, Reverend Senior Urlsperger, Pastor Preck [Pran] in Augsburg, and Professor Francke,[43] giving them brief accounts of present conditions in our congregation. May God hold His hand over these letters as well as those sent earlier; and may He let them further His honor and the best interest of our beloved congregation, for Christ's sake.

The 12th of January. This morning the people brought the big boat with its cargo to the landing at our place. This made all of us very happy because it relieves them of the many difficulties they would have had in bringing the provisions from the landing to our place in a small boat. The water is high at present, and for that reason the passage of the boat was made easier.

I received a letter from an honest and rich merchant [named Eveleigh], who told me that the letters we sent him on October 28th of last year had been given shortly thereafter to a captain who was on the point of leaving for London. He also reported he had come across a little tract which was published by the late Dr. Cotton Mather, a preacher in Boston. In it he had seen such surprising reports on the beginning and progress of the Orphanage and school in Halle, which were the result of the late Professor Francke's[44] work, that it would have been unbelieveable to him if he had not known said English teacher and his honesty. He assumes that I was educated and prepared for the service of God in this school because he had read that my dear colleague and I were recommended to the Society by Professor Francke.[45] Finally, he offers in a most friendly manner to serve us in any way he can. Perhaps our wondrous God will bless this connection to do much good [at least, we shall be able to deliver our letters and diaries to this man, who has a large correspondence with England.]

At the next opportunity I intend to send him an English translation of the late Professor Francke's beautiful tract: *Christ the Core of the Holy Writ*.[46] Instead of a preface, it has a very edifying and detailed biography of the late teacher[47] in the English language. I also have on hand, in the English language, the life and character of the late Anton Wilhelm Boehm, which I shall also send him. We would like to have more of these and similar tracts which take, as it were, the historical and indirect approach in leading the mind toward spiritual reflections; for God's blessing could be multiplied with them. If someone who knows the English language well would translate the incomparably beautiful tract of Pastor Freylinghausen: *Introduction to the Study of the Passion Story*,[48] he would do something extremely useful. Perhaps a pious English preacher will do this sometime when he comes across the tract in Latin, in which language it is now available.

The 13th of January. We have started to base evening prayers on Luther's small catechism, and we pray to God to honor this simple work on young and old with His blessing. Of course, we and our listeners would like it much better if all of us could be together for such an act. But we have good reasons not to postpone it any longer. We fear that our absences will not cease after Mr.

Oglethorpe's arrival, but that we will have even more business here and there. We are using the following method: after the singing of a short hymn, the chief subject of the previous prayer hour is briefly repeated. Then the children recite several times, loudly and clearly, the part of the catechism under consideration, which also recalls the words of the catechism to the adults. This passage is catechized briefly, and its real meaning is explained and applied to the practice of godliness. The entire prayer service is scheduled to last only one half hour; and for that reason we must be very brief. In it we have the advantage of being able to take up the entire catechism at short intervals. If, on the other hand, we were to do this on Sundays, one lesson would be forgotten by the time another one was being studied. However, in the future we intend to use it also for the basis of our Sunday afternoon catechizing. What could be more important for simple listeners than to know the truths of the catechism?

As early as last Friday a man of the congregation had noticed something objectionable in somebody else. He did not want to report it at the time partly because he had scruples (he did not wish to commit the sin of calumny), and partly because he had other apprehensions. This, in turn, brought him pangs of conscience and disquiet. Today we had an opportunity to draw this matter out of him. Such knowledge is [very] necessary for our continued watchfulness. The Enemy[49] is working in our congregation to cast suspicion also on those who call on us often for the sake of their edification or in pursuit of some other good causes: whenever we speak with them privately and make representations about matters not advantageous for their Christian spirit, about which we have to be very serious at times, they are apt to fall upon this or that person whom they would like to see accused and reprimanded during the sermon, etc. We often speak against such misbehaviour with great force, both publicly and privately, explaining to the listeners that the devil is always using such tricks in an attempt to bring misunderstanding and separation between teachers and listeners and thus to prevent the very salutary private visits. In some instances people already had postponed their simple visits for fear of being looked upon as gossipers and slanderers.

When the greater part of our congregation wanted to go to Holy Communion on the 4th, we used the words from John 21: 23 and Matthew 18: 18 during the preparatory lesson to show that not only the key that absolves but also the key that binds is a precious gem and great benefit, which the Lord Jesus has given His church, but also that great damage has been done to Christendom through misuse of the former and neglect of the latter. Proper use of these two keys assumes special supervision of the listeners by the teachers. This is not practical in other places because of the many listeners and members of the church. But since our congregation still consists of few members, they should not consider such individual supervision a burden but a benefit of God. A teacher could not come under suspicion if he cares for each sheep in his flock with diligence and thoroughness. Everything is aimed at the salvation of immortal souls, for whose salvation one must employ every means and opportunity, etc., Ezekiel 3: 17 ff.

The 14th of January. This time my dear colleague was not able to stay in Purysburg to celebrate Holy Communion with the people there, as they requested. An important matter made it necessary for him to come straight home from Savannah, which he did late yesterday evening. [Various people in Purysburg, who otherwise have availed themselves of our pastoral office, have said very rude and sundry things that are annoying. Therefore we are sick and tired and fearful of conducting Holy Communion there. Nevertheless, there are still some good souls in Purysburg, whom we shall not forget.] Some of the German people in Purysburg have let us know already that they would like to live among the Salzburgers; there probably would be more if they should get better land. [However, we are not yearning for those people. Instead, we shall protest to Mr. Oglethorpe not to send to our congregation such Protestants who, to be sure, profess the gospel but do not wish to become pious. We have experienced enough vexation from such people in the past.]

If God should let our congregation come into a better material position with regard to their land, we believe many additional Salzburgers would be desirous of following their brothers to America and into the wilderness. [In reply to a letter written him by my dear colleague (See under Jan. 10th), Mr. Causton wrote an answer that we can thank God for. He does not approve Mr. Vat's behavior but rather concedes us complete liberty to hold our worship service according to the will of the Trustees. He is also very pleased that we, through God's grace, seek to employ exactness with the congregation and to prevent all libertinism; and in so doing he even rendered a fine verdict about the upright behavior of the Salzburgers. He will personally put this letter before Mr. Oglethorpe; and it can serve as an apology if Mr. Vat should present his unwarranted and unfounded complaints, as he has threatened to do. We do not want to start anything but only to remain on the defensive, and, upon demand, to inform Mr. Oglethorpe of Mr. Vat's entire behavior in this connection. This has already been translated into English from our diary.]

The 15th of January. The last rainy weather was again followed by severe cold, which is continuing. We believe that, if we had snow as in Germany, this winter would be very similar to that over there. But the working people here have the advantage of not being kept from field-work by snow. Besides, they can drive their livestock to pasture all winter long, while over there they have to feed it in stalls. During the day the sun is rather warm, thawing the ground very quickly so that they can always work it.

[Before our evening prayer hour, the soot in my fireplace began to glow up on the little roof placed there to hold back the rain. To be sure, this was very easily brushed away and thus extinguished by a man who climbed up with a broom. Presumably, however, whenever he hears about it, it will be just like water on his mill to Mr. Vat, who wants very much to hinder this construction. The fireplace has been built in German fashion so that, according to the testimony of the carpenters and masons, the house could not suffer any fire damage if only it were cleaned of soot. They have recently offered to do this, but they were hindered from doing so by their recent journeys. Instead of pine or spruce, one must select oak or some other hard wood so it will last, even though it is more difficult to get. I am as fond of the fireplace as of the house itself, and without it I would not have been able to endure this severe winter because of my weak constitution and the work I had to do.]

The 16th of January. [Last night Veit Lemmenhoffer's wife gave birth to a son under very hard and precarious circumstances. The child was very weak, and I was summoned for the baptism. At my arrival, however, I heard that it had been baptized by the midwife soon after its birth, because it had only given a few indications of life and its death was expected at any moment. I questioned the four women who were present as to the manner and means with which the baptism was carried out. Since I found everything in order, I prayed briefly with them and blessed the child. Women in childbirth are in a bad way in such cold weather. Because their huts and present little houses are still so badly protected against the cold, the women have to make do with the fire in the kitchen as best they can. This morning I learned that the child is improving little by little and already has gained strength. May God be praised!]

Today and yesterday Mr. Vat has distributed the provisions to the last Salzburgers, just as he did with the first ones fourteen days ago. This time the flour is very beautiful. It was brought from

Pennsylvania by Captain Yockley, at the order of the Trustees. One can also buy this flour for money from the store-house at a very good price.

The 17th of January. We are longing very much for the arrival of Mr. Oglethorpe. From him we not only expect definite news about the land; but at the same time we also hope to get some news from England and Germany, especially answers to the letters we sent over by Captain Thomson. Yesterday the wind became favorable but soon changed back to northwest. Today we had very beautiful summer weather during the day, but we suspect that the night will again be very cold. [Veit Lemmenhoffer informed me secretly that he as well as his kinswoman, Adam Riedelsperger's wife, had fallen into sadness and worry; because Mrs. Rheinländer had said to them that the emergency baptism, which their child received immediately after its birth, was nothing. However, I instructed him briefly in that which baptism actually consists, etc., item: that it does not have its power from the minister and can therefore also be performed by another Christian man in case of necessity. If such a one is lacking (as happened this time, because he had been sent for help in the difficult circumstances of the birth; moreover, he would have been inefficient because of his naiveté and timidity), the emergency baptism could be carried out by a Christian woman by virtue of the spiritual priesthood, using natural water and in the Name of the Father, the Son, and the Holy Ghost. Therewith, I brought to his mind the example of Zipporah and other Jewish women at the time of the Maccabees. Tomorrow, God willing, this emergency baptism shall be officially confirmed to the congregation according to the instructions of the Augsburg church agenda, because their worries will then stop.

Mrs. Landfelder, who is also called Mrs. Schoppacher because of her first husband,[50] is now used as midwife instead of Mrs. Schweighoffer; and God is granting her His blessing for her loyal service. She performed the private baptismal act but would not have done it if it had not appeared as the greatest emergency. She put off this holy action in the case of the two children of Mrs. Eischberger, who nevertheless was very weak, until I arrived at night, because there was somewhat more life in them. On this occasion, even though she had not overlooked anything, I instructed her further what to do in the future, in regard to the children and our office, in which we are ready to serve day and night.]

For some time L. [Mrs. Landfelder] has shown very fine seriousness in her Christian endeavors, proving herself very kind and eager to serve the Salzburgers although she is not a Salzburger herself.

Whoever of us learns to fear God learns quickly to live at peace with honest people. [We propose to have the confirmation of the emergency baptism on Sunday rather than another day; and we plan to do it that way in the future unless necessity demands otherwise. I had Rheinländer come to me and questioned him about his knowledge of the emergency baptism; however, I found that he did not approve his wife's thoughtless words. He had also tried by some instruction to correct her in her mistaken opinion. For a long time he lived with his family among the Presbyterians in New York. Therefore, I suspected he could perhaps have fallen into the error of the Reformed concerning such an emergency baptism.]

The 18th of January. Mrs. Burgsteiner was churched this morning with her baby, prior to the sermon. After the sermon we confirmed the emergency baptism of an infant [which was already mentioned yesterday] (that had been baptized by L. [Mrs. Lemmenhoffer] because it was born very weak).[51] This was done in the presence of the entire congregation. Most of our listeners, who had never seen such a ceremony, found it very pleasant and edifying. It is very beautifully arranged in the church agenda of Augsburg.

During evening prayer I again tried to make it easy and pleasant for the people, who had again assembled in a large number, to learn the cathechism of our blessed Luther, the study of which we started last week in the daily hour of evening prayer. The letter written by pastor Sommer about Luther's catechism, which is contained in the 5th *Contribution to the Building of the Kingdom of God*,[52] gave me an excellent opportunity for this. The listeners come to these daily meditations and studies of the truths of the catechisms just as regularly as they do to the sermons and lessons on Sunday. We are already aware that our merciful and ever faithful God has begun to bless this simple work. Some of them have become very fond of the opening words of the first commandment: "I am the Lord thy God, etc.," although they cannot find them in their catechism. Those that were printed in Halle contain the first and second commandments in their entirety, but we have only a small number of them.

The 19th of January. Our small boat returned toward evening. The big one will not follow until tomorrow. With it there came to us two women from Purysburg in order to put a boy and a girl into school here. The girl is not yet here but will come at the first opportunity and will be taken in by her sister, Mrs. Schweiger. We are still in such circumstances that we have to conduct our household as frugally and economically as possible. For this reason we are not yet in a position to take care of other children. Perhaps,

through God's blessing, a few of these matters will be changed after
the arrival of Mr. Oglethorpe. Of poor children there are not a
few whom we would like to have the opportunity of serving with
physical and spiritual works of love. The shoemaker [Reck] from
Purysburg is going home again, having used up his leather for us
and having earned a goodly sum of money. This time the poor
amongst us, who cannot make out with wooden shoes at all times,
have also been cared for. [In other respects the shoemaker is a
wretched soul, as one hears in Purysburg. On the other hand, however, he received many pangs of conscience while among us. God
grant that it may penetrate him for once! While here, he conducted
himself in an orderly, quiet, and efficient manner and often attended divine services.]

The 20th of January. Today my dear colleague went by boat to
Purysburg, where he will stay until Sunday, at which time he will
serve Holy Communion. [To be sure, the many disorders that are
the fashion among the people there hold us back; but the desire to
gain something with them even once drives us back there again.
At least they hear us a few times.] On such occasions we show the
inhabitants the advice and will of God in regard to their salvation.
This has not been entirely useless [for a few] on previous occasions.
The day after tomorrow the big boat must again go to Savannah
with ten men; it remains to be seen whether it will be the last
time this quarter. The eagerness shown by the good people during
prayer hour for the truths of the catechism can hardly be put into
words. On this occasion, now given over to the consideration of
the Ten Commandments, God shows them (as we have heard some
of them say) the abomination of their hearts and the sins of their
youth so well that they cannot thank God enough for this good
deed. The name of the Lord be praised and blessed from now until
eternity, Hallelujah!

The 21st of January. The beautiful summer weather which
started a few days ago is continuing, but at night we still have a
heavy freeze. Since previously it had been very cold for a long
period, some of them now expect an earlier spring than we had
last year; and they are getting started with planting and sowing
in their gardens. Two years ago, when we came to Charleston at the
beginning of March, we found the gardens full of good kitchen
vegetables and roots, some of which had already begun to go to
seed. This makes us suspect that the cold weather at that time did
not carry over into the spring as late as it did last year. Through
practice we are gradually acquiring experience.

[Those who recently started making shingles have given it up because they enjoy the work in the fields better, and it is also time for sowing. Here and there they prepare plots of land, although nothing yet for certain has been assigned and they do not even know whether they may keep them.]

The 22nd of January. It rained nearly all day today. Thus, the people who left for Savannah this morning in the big boat not only had a difficult trip down but will have the same on the way back; because the water will be higher and run more swiftly against them. But twice high water has given them the advantage of being able to bring the boat all the way to our place.[53] If we were to be transferred to some other place, it is hoped that we will be able to carry our belongings in this big boat easily and in a short time. To do so by land would require a long time and too much hard work.

A Salzburger from the first transport showed me an unknown variety of Indian peas which are almost square, as large as German peas, and of very good flavor. Last summer one single such pea produced a very long vine which spread out and grew very tall. He got more than one thousand peas from it. He was surprised and happy over this divine blessing and promised to share them with others in the community because the labor spent on them is rewarded more than a thousandfold. He has a good piece of land along the river but does not know how this pea came to grow on it. This same Salzburger wondered in all humility about the wondrous governance of God, under which no land had been surveyed for them in the space of two years. He said that, since God was our beloved Father, He surely meant this to be good for us. He often thought like this: if they had received their land quickly, their industry in the fields might have prevented their diligence in prayer and worship. But as it is, they had stayed together and had been enabled to gather a fine harvest in the hours of prayer, etc.

This man is one of those who came to us for private instruction in reading. God blessed his industriousness fairly well, and for that reason I made him a present today of a large Bible which he accepted with much pleasure and gratitude. We can learn from this man how much blessing it can bring when Christianity and worldly occupation are in complete harmony. He is one of the most eager when it comes to prayer and work; and God obviously blesses his labors, although he may be a despised and dumb individual in the eyes of the proud and clever. We are continuing the school for adults around the noon hour, as much as our health and the duties of our office permit. During the summer it will probably be larger, since the people cannot work during the noon hours at that time as they are now doing. It is very good when young and old can use Bibles and hymnals during public services.

The 23rd of January. Some of the Salzburgers have gone into the forest, some on foot and some on horseback, to find the cows which they had driven into the forest. They are going in hopes of finding some calves. On this occasion they came upon a very beautiful region along the Savannah River, above our creek, which is said to have much more good land than is to be found at the so-called Red Bluff or at Indian Hut.[54] They are hoping, therefore, that, if Ebenezer is to remain in its present location, some good land will be surveyed for them in this region, which is said to be two hours from our place. They are hoping so particularly because the benefactors are seeking to serve the best interests of the people. But it worries us greatly that, in case the plantations should be many miles from our place, the good people could not be at home during the entire week and thus would have few opportunities to hear the Word of God. But the Lord does what pleases Him. Through God's grace both of us will gladly adjust ourselves to all circumstances of the people and serve them with our office, be it at home or in the fields.

The 24th of January. During last night's prayer hour we repeated the seventh commandment and catechized the eighth.[55] On this occasion the conscience of some of the members of the congregation was moved [by the disgraceful sins of theft and lying, as I heard. Ruprecht Zimmerman complained to me with great distress that a few years ago, partly in Salzburg and partly in Creutzheim, by Augsburg, he had let Satan seduce him to commit these sins. He had lived in Salzburg with a farmer whose son had a key to a servant's box from which he took approximately two yards of black linen. The farmer's son gave it to him, and soon thereafter he sold it to a tailor. He also took a few creutzers[56] from his parents. He would like very much to restore it manyfold, if it were possible despite his poverty and the absence of the people, and he would not even be afraid to confess it. I advised him to confess this sin humbly and with sincere repentence to our dear God and to ask Him for forgiveness in the Name of Jesus Christ. He should also promise with an honest heart to make restitution many times to the poor whenever he received something for his work, etc. I promised to think of this and his subsequent spiritual affliction in my prayers. All this pleased him very much.

[After he left Salzburg, he was taken in in said Creutzheim by a widow named Elisabeth Meck. She took him to a young shoemaker, who not only made him work hard and gave him little to eat but also set a bad example by all kinds of wrangling and wicked doings with his young wife. For this reason it looked dangerous for his soul. Because he could see no way to run away from him, he was seized with dread and ran away to Augsburg, unbeknownst to his master and Mrs. Meck. Here he had sinned anew through great untruth by pretending to be seeking his mother, who had long since been in Prussia, etc. Soon thereafter he fell into a lasting cold fever and was taken to the poorhouse. Here he found a spiritual and physical father in a man who had been placed there to care for the sick. Ever since this time God had started the work of conversion in him. Because the name of God might have been blasphemed in Creutzheim through his malicious and deceitful behaviour, it humbled him very much. He requested me to ask forgiveness on his account from Senior Urlsperger and Burgomaster Morell, to whom he had lied soon after his arrival in Augsburg. I intend to do this at once. This young man stayed with me until I had recorded all circumstances exactly and carefully. He is very seriously concerned about his salvation. Finally, I prayed with him, and he departed with a somewhat lightened heart.]

In explaining the commandments to naive listeners we find it very necessary to talk not merely in general terms about the sins that are forbidden and the virtues that are commanded. Instead, we must be very specific about circumstances and describe to each other the rotten hordes among the Christians and the wretched attitude of the people toward God and among themselves, [to which may be added the actual bad practice in the years of ignorance and malice, etc.]

A very pious man brought me an old edition of Arnd's *True Christianity*.[57] He had borrowed it once from a Salzburger who had become a Catholic again, and he had not returned it to him for fear that the book would be burned. While he was on his way during his emigration he had derived much blessing from it. But it gave his conscience much unrest and he asked to give it to the poor, etc.

Another one confessed that he [that during his apprenticeship he had cut off some linen cloth for his own use from a whole piece. He had seen the same on his comrade and he was in great need of it, likewise that he] had won some money gambling with somebody else who is now amongst us. He would like to pay everything back now, but he is very poor. I therefore lent him one half crown from the cash box. He promised to pay it back to me in a few years or, in case of my death, to give it to the poor. If I had made him a present of this money it would have given his mind less comfort because he wanted to make restitution on his own. He had to give the money back to the other gambler in my presence, and the latter's conscience was also moved. He is poor too, therefore the restitution will be of benefit to him; otherwise it would have been given to some other poor man. [As far as the restitution of the linen cloth is concerned, I gave him the same advice as I had given to Ruprecht Zimmermann. Jeremiah 23: 2, coll. v. 22–24.]

The 25th of January. Yesterday and the day before yesterday we again had a very cold wind and freeze after a rain. Last night we heard thunder from afar. This was followed by snow, which continued intermittently during the morning. This is the first snow we have seen in America. If more and lasting snow were to fall, the people would be in great difficulty with their livestock. The small amount of hay they have been able to make from cane leaves (for the stock will not eat any other kind) has been largely used up. Besides, many cows and calves go into the forest to find their own food. All day long the wind has been very raw and violent, but no one in the congregation has let this cold weather keep him from attending public service. The air cleared toward nightfall, and it turned much colder still. A great cold wave came last year after the thunderstorm in the winter, and the same seems to be happening at this time.

The 26th of January. My dear colleague returned home by Abercorn this afternoon. The cold weather and the difficult conditions under which he has had to live in Purysburg for the past eight days have not interfered with his health or the execution of his office there. This is to be attributed solely to the mercy and fatherly care of God. Again many Reformed and Lutheran people attended the preparation hours and sermons; and some of them were very devoted listeners. Thus his journey and the celebration of Holy Communion (with our brothers-in-faith) [58] was, praise God! not entirely useless. Outwardly, it is useful in that some souls who have come into disagreements and discord are reunited on such occasions and are taught to put their external friendship on solid ground, in accordance with God's Word. They also hear on several successive occasions what they need to do to be saved. Unless it comes earlier, this can serve as the means for true conversion on the sickbed and deathbed. At that place many people die under wretched conditions of body and soul, etc. Some families are still saying that they will ask Mr. Oglethorpe for permission to move in with us at Ebenezer. [We do not wish to disobey, but we also do not want to be too helpful to anyone in this through our intercesion and effort, rather] We will leave this to Divine guidance.

The Salzburgers who are now occupied with the transportation of some of the provisions in the big boat attended the services in Purysburg yesterday.

The 27th of January. Until now, a certain person [a man in our congregation who is not a Salzburger] has always felt the power of the Divine Word in his heart and has been convinced many times of his unconverted state and of the necessity for heartfelt conversion, but he has never succeeded in putting his Christianity on the right foundation. Instead, the spirit of the flesh, which had been in hiding under the cover of good outward exercises and public respectability,[59] has shown itself occasionally in various offences. Whenever we have seized upon such criteria of his unchanged spirit and urged true penance upon him, we have always been accused of being too sharp, suspicious, partisan, etc. Last week God gave the thunder of His Word so much force that even this person's [man's] conscience was stirred to the extent that his anguish of heart made his body sick and quite wretched. Some sins against the seventh and eighth commandments,[60] which injured his conscience both in Europe and in America, have fallen on his heart like a millstone and have tormented him as much as if he were in hell. I visited him yesterday; and, having suspected him earlier as well as now in regard to the seventh commandment, I asked only a few general questions [in the presence of his wife]. Pretending they did not apply, he answered them boldly and wondered about their meaning. But his conscience was a quick witness against him. With heavy heart he told me everything today and confessed with sorrow all the injustices and sins he had committed against me and others. Before leaving yesterday I spoke about the preparation necessary for a blessed death and promised to send him some reading matter about it. It was a medical doctor's [Dr. Carl's][61] spiritual advice and instruction for the sick and the dying [which he had his son fetch]. This lesson from the mouth of a doctor urged his conscience still more to abandon his sinful ways through openhearted confession of his sins.

[Afterwards, he came to my house as well as he could in his weakness.] On this occasion I was able to tell him, and compelled to tell him, a great deal about matters that could serve to bring him salvation. I hope to God that he will not let go up in smoke the great emotion He created in his heart, but that instead He will bless His Word, as well as the tract of the late Collin about the powerful penetration into the Kingdom of God.[62] From this I gave him, to take home, the beautiful extract that is to be found in the 3rd *Contribution to the Building of the Kingdom of God*,[63] so that this person [man] will change for the better completely, as he has resolved to do with God's grace. He cannot thank God enough for having turned him to agriculture and away from the profession he learned, because in Germany it had been the custom for him and other artisans [that is to say the unconverted ones][64] to envy and cheat each other, to lie, and to despise the others' [wares and] work, etc. [According to the testimony of this person,][65] the one with the biggest talk and the smallest conscience, who took advantage of and suppressed his neighbor, always had the most customers. In the simple occupation of field work this temptation is largely non-existent.

The [His] sinful accusations and expressions, which he had directed at us at times, burdened this man [him] no little. He now sees very well that all severity used against him [and his wife] came from heartfelt compassion and love for his soul [their souls]. He now offers, after acquisition of worldly goods, of which he has none at present, to doubly repay his ill gotten gains to the rightful owners or, in case of their absence, to the poor. I have led him back to his earlier life and asked him to go over his entire life carefully [with his wife]. It is better to awaken the sins of his youth now than on his deathbed or even before the judgment throne of Christ. May GOD have mercy upon this soul and tear it away from the bonds of sin through the power of Christ's death, etc. [His wife, whom we have already had to exclude twice from Holy Communion, is a big obstacle to his conversion. He declares, however, that he now has more hope of her improvement.]

The 28th of January. Yesterday evening the Salzburgers returned from the big boat, but they had to leave the provisions at our landing because of the low water. They have been ordered to return to Savannah immediately in order to get additional provisions. Consequently, ten persons will again depart today. The little girl whose mother was here recently on her behalf has been brought to us. She will be taken in and cared for by her sister, who has married a Salzburger named Schweiger.[66] Thus we now have two children from Purysburg in our school.

This morning we two had a sensible young Salzburger show us the way to the beautiful land which is back of our landing and near our creek on the Savannah River and which had recently been praised to us so very highly. It is easy to walk there because of the dry ground. Now we have seen for ourselves this fertile region which has been praised to us earlier. We saw more than two thousand acres of land on which are to be found oak, nut, and other deciduous trees as well as grape vines as thick as your arm.

It is said that this beautiful region extends even further toward Pallachocolas. It is true that this region is to be preferred to the so-called Red Bluff and also to Indian Hut, not only because it has more good soil, but also because there are the most beautiful pastures to be found on which our peoples' cattle can seek and find plenty of food day and night.

Should God guide the heart of Governor Oglethorpe to having their plantations surveyed there, they would feel better about building their houses in Ebenezer's present location, although this is not easily done because of the many swamps. There, however, dry and level places are to be found very easily. The region appears to be more healthful than the one in which we are living now because there the land is high and is situated near better and cleaner water than that in our river. In short, no one can blame the good people for wanting this land, for it is very desirable. The two of us would gladly leave our houses and live in the worst hut for two years if only the people would get permission to move to this region. God our Heavenly Father knows best what is good for our bodies and souls, not only at the present but also in future times; and we gladly submit to His guidance and paternal will, for He will do it right.

The 29th of January. Last night we had a thunderstorm and rain which lasted through this morning. Although both of the Schweighofers are sick, and in spite of their crosses and poverty, they feel great joy at the Fatherly love and faithfulness of God which He has shown to their souls. The husband had gone as far as chapter 45, lesson II, in Arnd's *True Christianity*,[67] and he could not tell me enough about how God had comforted his heart through it. I read him a few paragraphs from it myself and took from them the subject matter for a good conversation. For some time his wife had been longing very much for blessed relief and the journey home into the real Fatherland; but as God has not yet wanted to grant her wish, she considers this postponement of His fulfilment to be a paternal chastisement. Earlier she had not wanted to die because of her unreared children, thus attempting to interfere with our dear God's care, etc. Because of its comforting content she treasures very much the hymn: "O faithful God, merciful heart, etc.,"[68] and she would like to know a more common tune so that she will also be able to sing it. Both of them can speak very edifyingly about the salutary cross of Christians from their own experience, e.g. "God's comfort tastes sweetest and best under the cross, etc.", "God our Lord carries the heaviest burden. We are nothing and would soon fall down if He did not prevent it, etc.",

"All saints have gone to heaven through the cross, etc.", "Our present conditions are not so hard, because we have the gospel; under Popery it is different, etc.", "It will not be long before all misery will come to an end, and then comes eternity, full of joy, etc." One expression in the above quoted chapter of *True Christianity* so pleased them that they laughed with joy: "Think of this, if our dear God were to come to you and promise that He would turn all the rocks in your yard into pure gold and pearls, how thoroughly would you collect your pebbles and treasure them? In the same way you must treasure your cross, your sadness, and your misery, for God will turn them into pure joy and magnificence, making them into a crown, etc." Wisdom 5:17.

They were somewhat concerned about the fact that the failings of their bodies made them a burden to other people, who had to carry their provisions up from Savannah while they did nothing, etc. Others were preparing some land for themselves, while they had to stay in bed. However, among other things I reminded them of the words from the hymn: "God, Whom I know as love, etc.,"[69] which I had read to them last Sunday and which says in the third verse: "Suffering is my task, I cannot do otherwise, now, etc. Suffering is my worship." They liked this very much.

The 30th of January. I was told about some special circumstances surrounding the emigration from Salzburg. They cannot be written down very well, but they are very useful to me because they are adding to the high regard which I have for this work of God (for GOD has proved Himself magnificently through it). It did not happen through human counsel that man and wife, children and parents, friends and relatives, who had loved one another dearly and who needed each other for mutual assistance, were willing to leave each other, while those who remained behind attempted to break the hearts of those who left with begging, crying, and moving representations. They did so partly from ignorance and respect for the authority of the clergy, and partly because love of worldly things bound them to the fatherland.

In addition, many other temptations were present: for example, neighbors who had instructed and comforted others with their good knowledge of the Protestant doctrine defected and denounced the known truth as erroneous and a heresy, etc. They used glittering words to make little of their apostasy and the public denial of their mouths, since one could be Lutheran at heart, using the case of Peter and other verses for comfort and for covering up their malice. The most trusted friends declared to the emigrants that they would gladly leave everything and seriously encourage them and others to do the same if they could be sure that the Protestant doctrine were the only doctrine of salvation, for their salvation meant everything to them; but they could not do otherwise than to consider the Catholic religion to be true. They did not want to put more faith into their own thoughts and into the words of heretics than they put into their learned teachers who certainly would not deliberately go to hell and drag so many souls with them, etc. Others treated their relatives more harshly, but they usually accomplished less than those who used the smooth methods mentioned. After one old Salzburger, who is now amongst us, had been denounced to the authorities because of his Lutheran books and doctrine, a Catholic farmer who had heard about this denunciation had asked him how he felt and whether he hated these people who denounced and accused him. He had answered joyfully: O no, I am not the least angry but thank them with all my heart; for our Saviour has said: "Love your enemies, bless them that curse you, do good, etc." This had so impressed the man that he said he would remember that because it was very unusual, etc.

Some of them also wished that all Salzburgers who had emigrated because of their love for the gospel could be far removed from the so-called Protestant people who live worse than the Papists. They wished this because, if so removed, they would not be involved in their love of the world, their low regard for the gospel, and other undesirable matters. Besides, such bad conduct is objectionable to the Catholic people in the country and strengthens them in their error that the Catholic religion, in which good works and many exercises play an important role, is preferable to the [Lutheran] freedom and impudence [which unfortunately is practiced by many so-called Lutherans in violation of the doctrine to which they confess.][70] In this manner the work that God had done in Salzburg would be darkened and blasphemed. Some of them added: Many a one would have done better and his future judgment would have been more bearable if he had remained with Popery rather than start to serve the world and sin openly among the Protestants, to the dishonor of the Name of Christ. In Salzburg they had not even wanted to use this precious name in vain in their talk and they had suffered a great deal when they refrained from using the established greeting: "Praise be to Jesus Christ in eternity, amen!" One young Salzburger wishes very much to have his old father here with him. He would gladly work for him and assume all fatiguing tasks, etc.

The 31st of January. The Lord in His great mercy has helped us through this week, yes through the first month of this year, letting us once again put part of our wretched life behind us, and letting us come a step closer to death and eternity. May He let us spend the rest of our lifetime, which His decision and providence have still left for us here, working for the salvation of our souls as well as for the souls of those that have been entrusted to us. And may He grant us so much space in this hut that we may trim our lamps and prepare us all, as wise virgins, for the Communion of the marriage of the Lamb. "O, it costs a great deal to be a Christian, etc."[71] Except for two persons, all of the members of our congregation are now in good health. The two of us also, praise God! have been able so far to tend to the affairs of our office in good physical condition. There was no lack of occasional weak spells, but our faithful Father in Heaven lets them pass by quickly.

The 1st of February. For several Sundays, and also today, a number of families have been gathering at a house where my dear colleague has been reading to them about the edifying departure of the late Pastor Mischke, recent inspector of the Orphanage at Halle. God has placed no little edification upon this. The thing we see in this blessed man's entire life, hence also in his last hours, is the very thing that matters in the Evangelical conduct of Christianity and which alone can bring rest and comfort to the heart. The examples and speeches of this beloved teacher often come back to our mind and are very useful for us in the conduct of our Christianity and our office.

We would like to receive more edifying news from Europe because God does not leave it without blessing for us and our listeners. The Salzburgers like it very much when we visit them often and spend the time of day with them in an edifying manner. On such occasions edifying news, biographies, etc. furnish the subject for useful conversations. They serve us especially well before the prayer at evening prayer service. It is a special benefit bestowed by God on our place that all of these dear people not only attend public worship without fail, showing great devotion in doing so, but also spend the entire Sunday in the greatest of outward quiet. They spend it in their little houses with singing, praying, and good conversation, so that even the strangers who have been here were very much pleased. May our dear God, who is a God of order, continue to hold His hand over us!

The 2nd of February. Last week the Salzburgers learned that wolves have killed and eaten many of the pigs which they had driven out among the oak trees. As they fear the same for the calves that are still in the woods with the cows, they have agreed to put them in with those that were brought in recently and which are now being especially herded. Once the question of their land has been settled and made certain, they will join in making arrangements for the gradual extinction of such harmful animals in our region and for the greater safety of their livestock.

The 3rd of February. This year we are experiencing the same thing we experienced last year, namely, that a great cold wave struck after the thunderstorm. It had been rather cold for several days past, but last night the cold again became more severe than it had been. This winter is outdoing the last one with its cold weather, and the cold is more persistent and lasts longer. But, because of the fireplaces which we have built, we do not feel it as much.

This morning the people returned to our landing with the big boat. They brought orders from the Commissioner [Vat] to return once again in order to get pigs for those of the last Salzburgers who did not get any the last time. In this cold weather the people have to suffer a great deal on this long and difficult trip, but so far God has [still] heard our prayers and has averted sickness and other untoward happenings. If the boat should have to go several more times in succession, our plan to have Holy Communion one week from next Sunday would once again have to be canceled. At the moment those who intend to make use of the Holy Sacrament are staying at home because of the preparation. They intend to make up for it the next time.

Earlier, a little Salzburger girl had come to us frequently in order to be instructed and edified. But she has stayed away for some time now, and today I learned the cause of this from her mother: We could not have been pleased with her earlier because she was not a pious and believing child. Therefore, she decided to pray to God until He made her believe in the Lord Jesus. For several days she had prayed earnestly and diligently in various corners here and there. At last she had come to her mother and said: "Mother, it seems to me that I now believe in the Lord Jesus and now I may again visit [N.] the pastors." Her father and mother both are very pious people who wish nothing more earnestly than to lead their children to the Lord Jesus. They have never failed to provide admonition, prayer, good examples, as well as necessary punishment. The Lord has given, and will continue to give, His blessing on their efforts because He loves the children dearly.

The 4th of February. One of those who recently had come out into the open with a confession of sins against the seventh commandment[72] brought me some money today in order to make partial restitution for his ill gotten gains. But, since he is a very poor individual who must use it for the barest necessities as well as for the care of what little livestock he has, I let him take his money back because the damage he had done to his neighbor had recently been made good by me. He took it back with humility and gratitude and promised to make restitution in the future if God should bestow some blessings on him. He told me about various matters regarding his Christian conduct, his practice of prayer, his experiences with this practice, etc. This gives me the opportunity, in connection with next Sunday's gospel, Matthew 13: 24 ff., to tell the good souls of the congregation about the pursuit of the Enemy [Satan] against which they must struggle with much prayer and wakefulness if they do not want to be cheated with something that appears to be good. The late Arnd renders us excellent service in the conduct of our office with his magnificent book about *True Christianity.* In public and in private we often recommend [to the congregation] re-reading this or that part of it which we want to be well known for the better recognition and practice of inner Christianity. So far, God has blessed this mercifully.

The late Abbot Freihaupt used excellent judgment and wisdom when he placed pertinent chapters of this magnificent book of the late Arnd at the end of each article of his thesis. However, it is probable that only very few students use them for the purpose for which they have been cited, although one can make magnificent use of them, both at the university and in the conduct of one's office. The matter presented last Sunday in connection with the regular Sunday gospel caused us to use the evening prayer for the reading of [the last part of] chapter 37, lesson II. This brought blessings also to these people. God be praised! He is a faithful God who still does very much more than we ask for and desire.

The 5th of February. Because the wolves are becoming increasingly worse, the Salzburgers are very much worried about their livestock in the forest. Consequently, they spent yesterday and today rounding up all of the cattle and putting them with the rest of the herd. When they have freedom to seek their own food they seem to gain more weight than when they are herded. The cane leaves in the swamps around our place were either eaten up last summer or were cut to make hay. For that reason the stock must be driven a long way every day in order to get to a pasture. Besides the cane, a lot of tall grass grows here which is not suitable for stock feed. It will be burned off in the spring in hopes that better grass will gradually spread. On the deciduous trees such as oaks, nut-trees, etc., we find a great deal of moss[73] (which is called tree-oakum by the people) which cattle and horses like to eat. It is said to be much softer and more tender than that in Germany; the people gather it frequently, with little trouble, in order to feed it to the stock. In an emergency it can be used for a fairly soft mattress. The people derive great benefits from the cows; the fowl and the pigs are still a burden to them because they must buy feed for them at very high prices. Thus it is that one egg costs one pence at our place, which is two creutzer in German money. One bushel of corn [and likewise a bushel of Indian beans] now costs two pence at the store-house in Savannah, and it is consumed very quickly.

The 6th of February. Knowing that the three boys whose bond of baptism was confirmed some time ago in the presence of the congregation intend to go to Holy Communion again next time, I am making them come to see me several times in order to work on them [privately]. Righteous conduct, which alone counts with Christ, is not yet to be found in them; and they have rather neglected the good which God had once started within them. They are coming to school only occasionally because they must help their parents with the fieldwork; and one of the boys [Ott, the third boy] has to work a piece of land by himself. During their visits we regularly remind them of the solemn promises they gave before the entire congregation. This has done some good, praise God! [(Bartholomeus) Rieser's boy, who still behaves the best, departed from me today with emotion and tears. His mother demonstrated much earnestness and faithfulness in Christianity and works on her children's spiritual salvation according to her ability.]

The 7th of February. This morning our dear Father in Heaven has let us partake of that which we have wished for so long. He not only let us learn that Governor Oglethorpe had happily arrived in this country, but He also gave us the pleasure and the joy of seeing Commissioner von Reck at our place in person. We received him with heartfelt love, great joy, and praise to God. And we wondered greatly as he told us in a few words about the Fatherly protection that had been given him and those with him on their entire voyage. Commissioner von Reck had the Salzburgers come to him and told them how happy he was that God had brought him back to Ebenezer. He reported that our Father in Heaven had moved the hearts of our benefactors so that they want to give them good land. Hereupon my dear colleague, Mr. Boltzius, reminded the Salzburgers in a few words of what he had read to them on the previous Sunday at his house, during evening prayer, from the last part of the thirty-seventh chapter, Book II, of *True Christianity*, namely, that it was impossible for God not to hear our prayer.

This reminder was not without blessing, as I gathered toward evening from a Salzburger who said he had been moved so greatly by it he felt like crying out loud, for this had been so unexpected that they could not imagine it. The Governor does not intend to stay in Savannah very long because he wants to take the people he brought with him up to the Altamaha.[74] Since he first wants to speak with Mr. Boltzius about our land, the latter [the dear brother] went to Abercorn today with Commissioner von Reck and Mr. Vat in order to go to Savannah from there. May our Father in Heaven Himself put into his mouth everything he is to discuss with the Governor [our dear Mr. Oglethorpe], as we have asked Him in prayer.

The 8th of February. This morning Veit Lemmenhofer's wife was churched with her infant son. God be praised for having given this weak child so much strength. When the father told me about it, I explained in a few words how we must consider children to be precious goods which God has entrusted to our care, and that we must ask Him for much grace and assistance from the Holy Ghost so that we can [rightly] bring them up to His honor. He replied that this was certainly true and that he prayed to God for it; but he regretted that he could not express himself as he would like to do. I told him that God did not judge our words but the desire of our hearts, and that He liked it best of all when we dealt with Him in prayer as a simple child.

Toward evening I visited Schweighofer and his sick wife. I found them occupied with Schaitberger, specifically with the little tract in his book which is entitled: *The Golden Art of Nourishment of the Children of God*.[75] They had been moved to read this book because they had heard that the Salzburgers were to get good land; but since they would not be able to work any of it they tried to comfort themselves with this book. He said he believed that the churchyard would be his field. And the woman said she wished nothing more than that the Lord would come soon and take her with Him. Hereupon I said: if she were ripe enough, our dear Saviour would soon come and cut her as wheat and gather her into the barn of eternal life. Here she would shine as a sun in the Kingdom of the Father, but first He wanted to make her one of the elect in the furnace of misery.[76]

The 9th of February. Commissioner von Reck brought us many letters from England and Germany. So far as I have read them, they have given me much encouragement and have been of great use to me in my circumstances. Among others, I have received a letter from Secretary Newman in which he reports that the very praiseworthy Society for Promoting Christian Knowledge has unan-

imously decided to add ten pounds sterling to my former salary.
This is a great benefit, which the Lord my God may repay a thousandfold. But I am entirely unworthy of it, for I am not in the least
the one who has worked so faithfully and hard in the vineyard of
the Lord at Ebenezer that such a benefit should be bestowed upon
me. Meanwhile it will serve me to pray even more for the benefactors and to be more serious in prayer. May God have mercy upon me
and make me very faithful in His service [so that such money is not
invested entirely in vain].

The big boat returned from Savannah today and brought pigs
for those Salzburgers of the second transport who recently did not
get any. They also brought a letter which Captain Thomson had
given them. Although it had left London later than Mr. Oglethorpe, it had arrived in Savannah a few days earlier. Among other
things, this letter brought the news that a small box of medicines
would be sent. We were very glad to hear this, and we shall call for
it at the first opportunity. Various seeds which had been sent by
the previously mentioned merchant in Charleston were brought
at the same time.

The 10th of February. Last evening my dear colleague returned,
and Governor Oglethorpe came with him because he wanted to inspect the land to which we would like to move. He would prefer
us to remain here [and therefore needs all kinds of persuasive
arguments]; but, as we are continuing with our petitioning, it
seems that his thinking is being guided by God toward our wishes.
He left this morning to inspect the land, but not the place last
mentioned. He said that this spot was impossible because it was
situated on the other side of the Ebenezer River and he had no
authority to let us move there. But he could consider the so-called
Red Bluff, where much good land is also said to be available if the
neighboring Indian Hut is included. Meanwhile, we wish nothing
more than for that to come to pass which our Father in Heaven
has ordained for us since eternity; He has done right so far, He will
continue to do well, so that we will thank Him forever.

The 11th of February. Yesterday evening I, Boltzius, returned
under God's protection from the so-called Red Bluff, where I had
gone in the company of Governor Oglethorpe and a few of our
Salzburgers. I returned to Ebenezer with heartfelt praise of God,
because with the mercy He has held over us He has placed some
blessing on the journey. [For good reasons, I have misgivings about
putting so many details in the diary; therefore, I am reporting only
this much, that our worthy benefactor The Governor] is very fond
of us both and has promised to take good care of our community.

He cannot [may not] send us to the beautiful region on the other
side of the Ebenezer River because it would be contrary to the
promise he has given the Indians to the effect that he would leave it
unsettled and reserved for their exclusive use. For that reason we
would be in danger of malicious attacks. Nor do his orders permit
him to settle the Salzburgers on the Savannah River, for the settling
of the river is reserved to Englishmen alone.[77] Besides, the Salzburgers, who do not know English, would be in danger of having
trouble with the people passing through or with those living on the
other side. But upon our urgent representations, which I had given
to him in Savannah in writing and which he asked me to repeat with
additional details, he has selected the said Red Bluff, which the Salzburgers showed him, for the location of the town. Now the people
are free to start their field work in that region if they wish, but they
must continue to live in Old Ebenezer until the Governor has written to London and received authority approving the relocation of
the town there. He believes that he will get this; but, in case of
orders to the contrary, the people would be able to keep the land
they worked there, whereas the town would have to be built on a
hill in the Ebenezer River. For this he has specific authority.

These are only trials that moderate our joy and train us in prayer,
trust in God, and patience. Although our dear Salzburgers would
have preferred to move into the recently discovered region we
mentioned several times (for which we asked orally and in writing
during the past few days), all of them are very well satisfied with
this dispensation of our Heavenly Father, who has prepared them
through His Word for this and other fates. We also hope to God
that He may keep our worthy Governor Oglethorpe in his present
intention of letting them cultivate the entire region that is called
Red Bluff and Indian Hut. Perhaps God will bless those points
about which I wrote him today [because of the unreasonable command that they build the city on an inconvenient spot on Ebenezer
Creek in case contrary orders came from London].

We believe that the Governor will not be refused anything in
London which has to do with the establishment of this colony. We
will certainly receive what God has in store for us, be it now, a
year from now, or later. He does everything right at the proper
time. When we were on Red Bluff, two Evangelical-Lutheran
families from Purysburg came to the Governor and asked that they
be accepted by the Salzburgers. They will probably get their wish,
as we have no objections. The Governor intends to let even more of
them join us, but he will not impose anyone on us against our
wishes. He [Mr. Oglethorpe] said that already a number of families

had reported to him for the purpose of moving to our place in Ebenezer. He expects to use the river for the running of a saw mill and the fenced in lands for the keeping of several hundred cattle. The work of the Salzburgers and their way of breeding livestock pleased him so much that he has decided to send a number of English boys to us to learn animal husbandry. It is now even less likely that the Salzburgers could stay in Ebenezer and support themselves through agriculture, for we have learned from the Governor that all the land across our river belongs to the Indians by contract and that the fields prepared on that side must be vacated again in their favor. Some of them have had their best land there, and we hope they will be able to make one crop there this year because everything has been prepared for planting. Incidentally, they are glad to leave their huts, houses, and the work they did here. They all confirmed this to Mr. Oglethorpe when he asked them about it through me.

My dear colleague went to Savannah this morning in order to get the things that are on a ship there for us. He took with him some matters regarding the new work to be begun by the Salzburgers and the acceptance of a number of strange people. It is fair that our Salzburgers, who so far had to suffer many trials and difficulties, should be the first to be supplied with good land. This will take a lot of land so that not much good soil will be left. Along with the Salzburgers, Commissioner von Reck is bringing a number of other German people whom he [ratione pietatis][78] has given good recommendations. It was Mr. Oglethorpe's intention to settle this third group at some other place, on the Altamaha River; and he asked me what I thought of that. I answered briefly: as I believed that these people, too, had emigrated for the sake of the Word of God, it would be contrary to the purpose of their emigration and voyage to Georgia to leave them without a pastor: for the two of us would and could not separate, etc. Upon this Mr. Oglethorpe decided to add this third group to our congregation. [Commissioner von Reck is giving his brother[79] a town lot on the Altamaha River where the city of Frederica is to be built and around which he is to appropriate his plantation. However, the Commissioner wants to take his five hundred acres in the region around Ebenezer. In doing so, I hope he lets the Salzburgers take their land first, especially since he is in no hurry. Perhaps one day the magnificent region across the Ebenezer River, that now belongs to the Indians, can become his own. For the present, this proposal pleases him.]

The 12th of February. A Salzburger woman came to me about some worldly matter; and, when she learned that there were Salzburgers in the third group, she wished that her brother and mother could be among them. But she doubted it very much because her brother, who had acquired a good knowledge of the Protestant truth from good books, had reneged in times of temptation and had drawn his mother back with him. The means which God used for the salvation of this woman was a hymn that is well known in Salzburg and which we have sung in our church on occasion in the past. It starts: "Eternal Father in Heaven, etc."[80] This hymn provided her with much edification (for it is a very magnificent hymn; and, when the singing of it was forbidden and the people were punished for it, the Popish doctrine became more suspect to her than ever before, so much so that her enemies soon noticed it. So she was ordered before the authorities and was read twenty-four points which she was to accept as her articles of faith and to which she was to swear. A light and a crucifix were already on the table: but three things had prevented her from complying and had given her courage for frank confession: 1) That the Jesuit told her and the other people present that the salvation of their souls depended on this oath; looking upon the crucifix she was reminded of the misery and pain which the Lord Jesus suffered for our souls; this made her refrain from treating the matter lightly. 2) She had heard that other wives and mothers had been required to damn their husbands, friends, and children who were Lutheran, and this seemed quite terrible to her, etc. 3) The points read to them appeared to her to be contrary to the Word of God, etc. When she was told that, with a belief like hers, she and her husband could stay in Salzburg no more easily than a stream could run uphill, she went home grief-stricken and in tears. On the way she saw an old beggar who was sitting by the road mending his floursack. He asked her the reason for her tears, and when he learned it he lightened her spirit with very comforting talk, etc. Now she is quite happy that God will give good land to our people. This happiness is quite general.

Another woman, who has the best house of all the Salzburgers, was asked how leaving this house and the prepared fields would make her feel. She answered: I am thinking about what my husband has read to me about Abraham. He was a very rich man; but God's will required that he move here and there, and he must have had to leave many things behind. Upon this I guided her thoughts to the example of the Israelites in the desert who often stopped in one place, and, as soon as they had settled themselves somewhat, God had given them the sign saying that they must move on. Thus it must be, everything must be done according to God's wish and desire; if it had been His will, we would have wanted to stay, and we will move in accordance with His will, etc. We urged her to think more diligently of the verse: "We have here no lasting abode but are looking for the future one, etc."[81]

Partly because of the rainy weather and partly because of important affairs we have not been able to have regular evening prayer since Saturday. We learned from some of the listeners today that this worried them very much. They added that it would not be good if the fields of the people were very far from Ebenezer and they would be kept from getting their daily edification: but our faithful Father in Heaven already has partially arranged for this and He will continue to take care of it. I also have presented this matter orally to Mr. Oglethorpe, and have added some additional reasons in the letter I wrote him. We hope that God's blessing will make it effective. During my private devotion my faith was strengthened when I came upon the words on page 301 of the *Treasure Chest*,[82] which I have already used for the benefit of some of the listeners.

The 13th of February. Next Monday the Salzburgers want to start work on the newly assigned place, in God's Name; and for this purpose a number of things necessary for the work have been carried there by water. But we are still wondering whether it would not be necessary first to get the Governor's confirmation, which my dear colleague will probably bring with him. The people are so eager to work the new land that we cannot help but wonder. And we would not do a favor to our boys if we did not let them go along. The Salzburgers have agreed to work together in small groups, with four to six of them converting a certain tract into fields. This is much better than having the entire congregation work in one place, in which case one is often in the way of another. Besides, one has to worry about how the trees fall, for accidents can happen very easily when so many of the congregation are together. These inconveniences are avoided by small working parties which have the advantage that they not only work together but also eat together. With the communal labor as practiced formerly, everyone had to provide for his own food; and this caused great loss of time. I was very much pleased to see that the young and strong people will be spread out among the old and weak. Otherwise the latter would come to grief and suffer disadvantage, because they could not accomplish anything.

The 14th of February. Toward evening the brother of Commissioner von Reck arrived in Ebenezer with two married Salzburgers and an old woman from Austria. As others had done before, he expressed surprise at the industry and eagerness to work which the

Salzburgers proved themselves to possess with the construction of houses, preparing of fields, and other matters. He said he had not had as good a picture of the establishments at Ebenezer, although he had had many good reports, on board ship and in Savannah, about the industry of the Salzburgers. It is possible that, after we leave it, our region will acquire the reputation of being fertile and good, particularly if our successors are permitted to plant the land for which the Salzburgers carefully collected manure and carried it there on their backs and in wheelbarrows. We ourselves have had this done regularly in our garden, just as Mr. Zwiffler, the Ortmanns, and others have gone to much trouble and work in their efforts to prepare a good piece of land. But all of these well fertilized places, most of which are on the other side of the river, would hardly produce enough crops to feed two families; and what would become of the rest with their sandy and unfertilized soil?

It is a great benefit [of God] that the people will go to another place. But to receive this benefit we have had not only to pray and fight hard, but probably will have to do so in the future, before everything is right and in good order. There are many people in the land who speak for the best interests of the Salzburgers as little as did the enemies of the Jews that came from Babylon, as written in the books of Ezra and Nehemiah. But, if God is for us (as He truly is), who can be against us? Who asks for heaps of ashes and swollen water bladders? The Almighty can soon make room for Himself and His work. Our King reigns in the midst of our enemies. He is ever with us, etc.

I have sent my letter to Mr. Oglethorpe to Abercorn twice for forwarding but have had it returned each time. On Monday, God willing, I shall send it off with our boat which, we hope, will arrive at Red Bluff tomorrow bringing my dear colleague. We hope that, while our dear Mr. Oglethorpe is reading it, God will guide his heart to continue doing what He had decided for us in His holy council. In today's evening prayer we strengthened ourselves with a consideration of the last part of the third article of our catechism by affirming our belief in a Communion of Saints which assures us, as members of this communion that has Christ as its overlord, of the intercession of the fighting and triumphant Church. The people who arrived today found a number of acquaintances amongst us and they were cordially received and feasted by them. This last transport will find many more comforts than were enjoyed by the earlier ones, especially the first one.

The 15th of February. Yesterday evening we had a thunderstorm with much lightning and rain which passed by quickly. The cold weather we have had so far seems to have abated entirely, and now the blossoms of the peach trees are beginning to show already. We had intended to have Holy Communion on this day, but the unavoidable traveling back and forth prevented the people from attending. If it is somewhat possible, it will take place this coming Sunday. We announced this today to the congregation. The people do not have full mastery of themselves in the unsettled conditions which have befallen us once again. Because the letter we wrote to Mr. Oglethorpe has not yet been delivered, as we reported yesterday, and since it must be assumed that he will leave for the Altamaha River with the first favorable wind, a few Salzburgers have decided to go to Abercorn this afternoon. From there they will use our small boat to go to Savannah in order to deliver the letter. I have also written to Mr. Causton and asked him [very earnestly] to deliver the letter to Mr. Oglethorpe and to do so at the first opportunity, in case he has already gone.

I also found it necessary to write Mr. Causton about the disadvantageous location of the small hill on the Ebenezer River on which Mr. Oglethorpe is said to have decided, after my departure, to build the new Salzburger town. I asked Mr. Causton to put in a good word for our people. It would seem at present nearly impossible to us to move the people to the Ebenezer River because 1) at that place the river is very wide and its water is almost standing still. Many cypress trees are growing in it and much filth is piled up around them. According to the experience of our people, it is much less healthy than in Ebenezer. 2) if the town were to be built here the peoples' farms would have to extend far into the distance, because the good soil only stretches along the bank in a narrow strip. Except for that, only sandy [Ebenezer] soil is to be found. If the people have to go so far away to work their farms, they not only would have to miss worship and edification during the week (which would mean almost unbearable suffering to most of them), but they also would have no one to tend their cattle and other stock at home. If the salvation of their souls or some worldly matters were to require them to stay at home for several days, their farms would be damaged either by wild animals or bad people, especially servants and negro slaves passing by, unless someone kept constant watch. I have made these points today to Mr. Causton [which, however, shall then only be delivered to him when Mr. Oglethorpe has already departed.] Everything points to the probability that the Salzburgers once again will have to suffer many trials and difficult circumstances before the change of our location becomes a fact, and we are driven in advance to pray for their relief. [As in the previous case, I do not yet wish to report the details.]

So good is our merciful God that before sending us an unusual and unexpected trial He lets us get instruction, comfort, and strength from His holy and invaluable gospel; in His great kindness He has done so this very day. In our evening prayer hour, to which nearly the entire congregation continues to come with no little eagerness, I read them the letter written by Senior Urlsperger to the congregation. It gave us many a beautiful opportunity to acquaint them anew with the ways of God with His children who do not have good days only but must go through distress and trials. This was further explained from the experiences we have had so far. I also recommended that they read the two books of Ezra and Nehemiah and showed briefly that the children of Israel, following the will and the fatherly governance of God, had gone from their imprisonment in Babylon to Canaan with orders to build the city and the temple; but they would read how difficult and miserable it had been, and how many internal and external trials they had experienced, although one would think that everything should have gone well with them because God and His Word were with them and they performed their labors according to His will and command. The application of this was easy, and I did not have to say much. I only showed them briefly that true Christian spirit and honest love for God and His Word must show themselves during trials and difficult circumstances, etc. Also that, from the beginning, God's glory was furthered more through crosses than through good days. Nor do we read in the Bible that good days will bring us to heaven, but rather the cross, sighing, tears, etc., Psalm 126. It gave all of us great strength to know that God has guided to us so many of His good servants and children who care and pray for us, which indeed is special proof of the mercy and Fatherly fondness He has for us wretched ones.

The 16th of February. Some people went to Red Bluff today, by water and by land, in order to build a shelter for the new arrivals and to make preparations for a number of things. Their eagerness to work the new land, without all fear of the fatiguing task, is really quite remarkable. It would be a shame if the good people were to be curbed in their enthusiasm by having other burdens imposed upon them. [Mr. Vat may make all kinds of proposals to Mr. Oglethorpe which, to be sure, have a good appearance, but do not redound to the peoples' welfare. I hope we shall also be heard. I worry that he will, as he has done before, brand my protests and requests as inciting the people. The Lord sees it.]

Mrs. Schweighofer had another stroke and she seems to be coming closer and closer to her happy release. Her good husband is very weak of body himself, and he has had to bear a heavy cross with the long and painful sickness of his wife. Yesterday our dear God so blessed his soul when he listened to our description of the very great magnificence of the believers after this life, that during most of the service he wept tears of joy. Now he is greatly strengthened. [May God make known to Mr. Vat how gravely he has sinned by still keeping the wine locked up that was meant for the sick and weak in the congregation. For this reason this poor woman, as we only learned today, must also suffer lack of this refreshment that seems up to now to have agreed with her body with its wretched diet.]

The 17th of February. My dear colleague returned this afternoon and brought the things that had been sent for us in addition to our salary. God be praised for the good letters that were sent to us from England and from Germany; surely the Lord will accompany them with His blessing and give us more courage and comfort in our circumstances. May He also be praised for the physical blessings He has let us have from the hands of our worthy benefactors in the form of medicines and other things necessary for our households. May He let richly flow over them in return the wells of His bodily and spiritual blessing. Our poor once again have received a rich gift from the worthy Court Chaplain Ziegenhagen, namely, thirty pounds sterling. This is a very great benefit that will bring praise and thanks to God in the future as it was done in the past, namely, whenever the needy are given something in the way of clothing or other matter. May the living God who loves mercy be pleased and satisfied with this special work of love in Christ, and may He give our dear benefactors thousandfold blessings for it! For the efforts he has made so far on behalf of the sick of the community, Mr. Zwiffler again received a present of twenty pounds sterling from the very praiseworthy *Societaet de promovenda Christi cognitione.*[83] The Lord be the rewarder for everything in time and in eternity!

This evening after seven o'clock most of the new people, accompanied by Commissioner von Reck, arrived in Ebenezer by way of Abercorn. This way had become troublesome to the dear people because of much water and the soft ground. Earlier our Salzburgers had heard some shooting in the forest, and some of them went to meet them with burning pine torches because they knew of their arrival by this sign. Their first call was at my room, and I used the occasion to remind them of the meaning of the name Ebenezer and words: "hitherto hath the Lord helped us."[84] I told them briefly what we had experienced so far, namely, many trials as well as much proof of God's fatherly care for our bodies and souls. Also, that I knew no one in the congregation who regretted the voyage from Germany into this wilderness, etc. At last I prayed with them. Thereafter our Salzburgers took them joyfully into their huts and little houses for warmth and for possible refreshment. It has turned cold again with the northwest wind which has been blowing very hard for two days.

The 18th of February. Yesterday before dark Landfelder got lost in the woods, although he had gone in only a short way in order to get hay. Signals were given at once with shooting, and some people went after him with torches. But last night they could not find him and found him only this morning. He had already gone beyond three swamps and canebreaks and was in such confusion that he did not hear the shooting and did not see the people who were approaching him. He is of the same simple nature as the lost Resch. He was able to light a fire during the night; otherwise, his health would have suffered from the cold which became very severe again during the night. God be praised for looking upon our grief and blessing the efforts of the people! Mr. von Reck found it necessary to take all the men that had arrived yesterday, as well as most of the Salzburgers, to Red Bluff in order to build a good shelter there for the women and children who are now in Abercorn. This is a day of rest for those who returned from the trip yesterday and today, having had much to suffer from the strong wind and the high water. They will go to said bluff tomorrow in the small boat because Mr. von Reck must go to Savannah as quickly as possible to arrange for provisions for the new arrivals [with which there now appear to be difficulties.] God the almighty and loving Father increases the strength and patience of the dear people.

The 19th of February. The water in our river is nearly as high again as it was in October of last year; thus our garden is flooded again. [The longer it lasts the more we regret the work that has been done in it and the costs expended.] Some time ago we sent our diary and some letters to a theology student named Zoberbieler,[85] from Switzerland, who intended to go back to Germany. But now that his departure has been delayed and Mr. Oglethorpe has assigned him new duties in regard to some Swiss who are to come here from St. Gall and other places, we are sending said package of letters to a merchant in Charleston who has been very willing to deliver letters for us on previous occasions, besides giving us proof of his fondness in other ways.

The 20th of February. After the sea voyage various ones of the new people are getting sick now that they are on land. Some of those with us have been bedridden for several days, and today two young men came from Red Bluff complaining of swollen feet and hands. They report the same of others who are still out there. Today I distributed thread, ribbons, needles, etc. to the women of the congregation. These things had been sent by Senior Urlsperger, who has a feeling of fatherly care for us; and the women cannot give enough thanks to their Father in Heaven for them. The small handkerchiefs received at the same time I gave to the girls for use as neckerchiefs, and they probably liked this better than gold or silver; on this occasion they again had many fine things to say. The unmarried men, who now are either at Red Bluff or off in the small or large boat, will get their share when they get home. The small hand towels will go to those who need them most. Things that people in Germany consider insignificant are very expensive. Our dear God will not let this additional benefit go unrewarded as we will pray to Him accordingly.

The 21st of February. Mr. Vat returned to us via Abercorn and brought the news that the surveyor was in Abercorn and wanted to go to Red Bluff. He wants two of our people to help him, and they will be sent to him today. Many [The] people in this country usually pay little [just as little] attention to the Sundays and holy days [as the heathens.] It is, on the other hand, a great blow to our people when they have to do hard labor not only on weekdays but also on the Day of the Lord, on which our merciful God wants rest to be given even to the animals, while at the same time they are being kept from hearing the Divine Word. [The authorities always call this a *casus necessitatis*].[86] Our holy God will [surely have an insight and] hear our anxious sighs. The patience of our Salzburgers would certainly make our friends marvel with us and praise God for this mercy, if they knew all circumstances as well as we do.

For the contemplation of the first petition at evening prayer I had nearly all the Salzburgers together again, for they returned today from their work at Red Bluff. The order of these petitions,[87] the first three of which are for God, His name, His kingdom, and His will, while only the four that are left are for our physical and spiritual well being, gave me a good opportunity 1) to show in general what should matter most to a Christian in this world, namely, not himself, his honor, and his comfort, but to seek the glory and the kingdom of God. 2) I showed, especially for the sake of the newly arrived people (many of whom find our ac-

comodations uncomfortable as they are not accustomed to them),
that God's name is blessed and glorified not only in good days but
just as much when crosses are borne. I explained this with some
examples of believers in the Old and the New Testament, using
also the terrible persecution of the Christians in the first century.
We also bound one another to do everything in our power with
regard to the first petition, namely, to use the holy teachings of
the gospel so that all of us would become children of God, and as
children of God would live in accordance with the holy Word of
God. Then the almighty and loving God would certainly do His
part, in fulfilment of His promise, in regard to the fourth petition
because on it depends the honor of His Name, of which He takes
such tender care here and in the second commandment. I also
warned them against underestimating or not accepting the good
emotions and feeling of the Father toward the Son, etc. Among the
newly arrived people, many of whom are sick and bloated, there
are several good souls who visited me these days, and I was able
to talk with them about many edifying matters which encouraged
their downcast spirits. [A few who have come to the transport now
and then bring along a poor testimony. They have already given
offence here *verbis et factis*.[88] With such people one will probably
have a goodly share of work and vexation.]

[The 22nd of February. After our noonday worship service Mr.
Vat gave a signal with a little bell and called all the men and women
to assemble in the church. There he read to them in German the
following points from an English proclamation that he had also
sent to me. The title reads: "Rules to be observed by the Saltzburghers & other Inhabitants at EbenEzer":

1. The Saltzburghers & other inhabitants at EbenEzer are to
work jointly every day (Sundays & holy days excepted) four hours
in the Morning & four hours in the Afternoon, during the Planting-
season & afterwards, as it shall be thought most convenient.

2. The Carpenters & such of the said Inhabitants, as may be
capable of assisting them are to work in the same manner, at all
publick Buildings; beginning with a convenient Hut for themselves; then a Store-House; and afterwards with making two large
Hutts, capable of containing all the other inhabitants.

3. All other inhabitants are to clear jointly the Ground, designed
for Gardens & Town-Lots.

4. The said inhabitants are to build a Watch-House. And six
men are to watch every night from Sun-Sett in the Evening till
day-light in the Morning; and on Sundays & holy days during
divine service time. Each man is to receive two charges of Gun-

Powder for every nightly Watching; but bullets, as occasion shall require it.

5. The present Inhabitants at EbenEzer as shall be willing to remove to the New-Town, are to leave their Houses, Hutts, Stables & all their improvements, in the state, they now are in, but they may sow & plant their respective cleared grounds, during this season & gather the produce thereof for this year.

6. The Town-& Garden-Lots are to be assigned immediately, and ascertained by Lot, after the Surveyer's Report, to each inhabitant; and He is afterwards to be build a House in a direct Line, in the midle of the Front of his Lot.

7. The first twenty Gardens on each side of the Town shall be reserved at the Disposal of the Honnble Trustees as also the eight duble Lots in the Town; Tybee[89] February 16th, 1735.

This is a true Copy from the   James Oglethorpe
Original. EbenEzer. Febr. 21th 1735.

    John Vat. Commiss. to the
    Saltzburghers.

[After he had impressed these points on the people, he wanted to hear their resolution immediately. They, however, asked him for time to think this over. He granted them this until that evening, and then he demanded a positive answer from me as well as the people. He also threatened to leave the land unsurveyed if they quibbled about even the smallest point. Besides this, he told them still other things; for example, that he was now no longer Commissioner but Secretary, in connection with which all provisions were entrusted to him. Item: that the two ministers and Mr. von Reck would attend to the external matters pertaining to good order according to the will of Mr. Oglethorpe. Item: that the second transport would receive only three-fourths of the provision; and, because the first (transport) had already had the benefit of two years of provisions, their time was up. However, it could very well be that Mr. Oglethorpe has resolved something different, as he already has done with the third transport. To be sure, he did not wish to grant them any provisions in the beginning because they refused to go to Altamaha; finally, however, it turned out better, but with conditions.

[Item: Mr. von Reck had acted against Mr. Oglethorpe's orders when he brought the new people by way of Purysburg to Ebenezer. They all should have come here via Abercorn (as many had before). Item: that it was against Mr. Oglethorpe's orders that he had already had a hut built for himself. Item: that the Salzburgers would not receive as many provisions as previously. Once more this manifesto of Mr. Vat and the proclamation of these designated points was a tremendous trial: nevertheless, with all that, the concern of our fatherly God, who makes all things well, reigned again because 1) it was very good that Mr. von Reck was not in Ebenezer but had already gone to Savannah this past Thursday accompanied by my dear colleague because of the new transport. Otherwise, there would have been collisions between him and Mr. Vat to the scandal of our congregation. 2) Our dear Heavenly Father had already prepared our dear congregation from His Word for this new ordeal.]

On the 22nd God, in His great mercy, gave the listeners a great awakening after our catechistical treatment of the second petition: "Thy kingdom come." Among other things, I showed them that our Immanuel, the friendly Saviour, is also King and almighty Ruler of the kingdom of nature, etc. And since He takes care of all creatures He will not forget us who belong to Him because of Creation as well as Salvation and Sanctification. To explain this we gave the example of Joseph and his conduct toward his brothers in Egypt, Genesis 41: 44, and chapter 45: 4 ff. But, as the kingdoms of Christ are not opposed to each other, we should take care to note that for many Christians physical care is accompanied by many trials and crosses which we must consider to be a necessary part of the goods of Christ's kingdom of mercy, etc.

We also told them they should take care not to reverse the order of the Lord's Prayer and think first of the [contents of the] fourth petition while looking upon the hallowing of the Name of God, the spreading of His kingdom of mercy, etc. as minor matters that would take care of themselves, as is being done by most Christians; this would bring only damnation instead of blessing, etc. God especially blessed the word Kingdom of Mercy so that our Jesus would have a whole kingdom full of mercy and was now offering mercy to even the greatest of sinners. The person who acquires this in the right order should not worry about his physical care: For all worldly gifts are in the hands of the Heavenly Father. They are small matters compared to the gifts of grace which shall be added unto you, Matthew 6: 33.

[After Mr. Vat had dismissed the people, two of the most intelligent ones came to me and brought the above copy with the report that they had heard from Mr. Vat there were still some points in it that I should translate because he was afraid they would become very depressed if he did it. I read it aloud twice to the two people and we all were amazed that there was nothing else in it but what he had already made clear in detail. Therefore, he must have had some secret reasons for these figments. The good people were not a little concerned about the present unreasonable demands. Because they were supposed to bring their resolution before evening, they begged me for good advice. I sighed in my heart to God that He would bestow on me wisdom and on the dear souls a large measure of patience and likewise new consolation in this current need and trial. Hereupon I said to them that now I really could not put in their mouths the resolution that they were supposed to bring to Mr. Vat because he would like to denounce me to our superiors as an instigator of the people. Nor did I know what they were capable of practicing. They wanted to think it over among themselves and pray earnestly about it, and give this as a cause for postponing the resolution.

[Meanwhile, I assured them that our benefactors, with the love they have for us, would not lay a heavier burden upon them than they could bear. Also God still lives, who is Lord of the earth and a refuge of the poor in distress and hardships, etc., which they knew from experience. Their need was frequently even more severe in previous times, yet God had given patience and finally helped them out of it. The present test was still new and thus they were not used to it. Through God's grace it would not last long. They were also familiar again with this spirit and content. One may not utter the love that our Heavenly Father has for us, His children. But as parents they could draw a slight parallel when they consider their tender parent love for their weak little children. Also, they well knew that, wherever the need is greatest, our dear God will be near with His support and indeed with true help. For it was not unknown to them how the help and majesty of God was once shown very strikingly and greatly to the children of Israel in Egypt.

[At the same time I could assure them that the Name of God was not a little extolled and praised in Europe through the previous patience of the members of our congregation. I told them that this was surely a special grace and benefit that they, otherwise despised human beings, became tools through the wise dispensation of God and that in and through them the worshipful Name of God was hallowed here and there secretly through them. All of this could hardly take place in good days. It was our duty to persist bravely in prayer; thus, we would in due time experience God's help and realize that He has given it and that whatever good we experience, even including external things, will be His work alone.

[On departing they begged me in a moving way to champion them as best I could before God and Mr. Oglethorpe. I shall do this because of my duty and the love that I bear them, in so far as the previously cited rules can be obeyed by the people or not.

[It has already been reported above how the Salzburgers were inclined to undertake the communal work, in which manner they would accomplish once again as much in the fields, according to Mr. Vat's methods. The people ask nothing more than to be treated just like other colonists and free people, as they were promised. In all good time they would like very much to do all they can with the construction of public houses and other things that have been laid upon them. Instead of a store-house they wanted to build a sturdy, well protected hut that can be locked. Then, when the time for planting is over, they sincerely offer to build such a store-house of whole timbers, as Mr. Vat has requested of them orally, as well as to dig a cellar. If it is requested, both of us would rather live in miserable huts and leave our cottages in Ebenezer immediately if only the people will be able to sustain themselves and no longer have to suffer the bitterest reproaches and perform such slave labor as hauling up the provisions on a so unsuitable boat.

[It appears as if Mr. Oglethorpe's prophecies have started to come true, namely, that many will become sick and die from the requested move. However, as he said at that time, he does not want to be blamed for it because he warned against it. But the Lord sees and hears it! At another time Mr. Oglethorpe spoke of the people's work and the night-watch quite otherwise than it stands in the rules. Therefore, Mr. Vat is probably guilty of this and other hard things and no doubt will remain there as long as necessary to build the store-house. That six men are to be held back from divine service by guard duty even on Sundays and holy days is a severe command for these dear people, who prefer the Word of God before all else. Mr. Vat already tried this in previous times but was not able to get our consent. We shall now do what we can. We want to pray and bring everything with humility before Mr. Oglethorpe orally and in writing and then be calm, through God's grace.]

We trust that our faithful God will carry His Word to victory and blessing in our listeners as He has done not only on this day but also in our evening prayer hour, for which the dear people are once again assembling in large numbers. For the praise of God I cannot keep this a secret. We sang the hymn of faith: "A Mighty Fortress is our God, etc."[90] After that, I started to read the very edifying letter which Rev. Senior Urlsperger had written to the two of us. It gave me the most wonderful opportunity to encourage the dear souls' patient acceptance of the yoke of Christ which causes, praise God!, the shedding of thousands of tears. This made me remember the words from the 103rd Psalm: "He knoweth our frame, He remembereth, etc.," and so He will not burden us beyond our capacity. This led me to the words of the 9th verse of a hymn which has been blessed for me and others on several occasions. It is: "O Faithful God, Merciful Heart, etc."[91] I read them the entire hymn. This made the entire 13th Psalm very remarkable for us, particularly the last verse: "I have trusted in Thy mercy, my heart shall rejoice in Thy salvation." In our present circumstances we should often think of this verse and its trust in divine help. Our dear God has probably inspired the worthy Rev. Senior to compose his letter to us in this manner, for we need it very much in our present circumstances of which he knew nothing at the time. May He be the rewarder for everything, and may He further awaken our worthy benefactors and friends to intercession, good advice, and assistance, all of which we need very much.

The 23rd of February. This morning I married Peter Gruber and Maria, the widowed Mrs. Moshammer, in the presence of a few members of the congregation who had been invited. Both of them are upright [very devout] people and industrious workers. My dear colleague returned home today. He did not hold morning and afternoon services in Purysburg as he had intended. Instead, he held them at Red Bluff, where there were a number of people from the third transport as well as four Lutheran people from Purysburg. Said people from Purysburg also came to Ebenezer to learn from me about all the circumstances of the Salzburgers, especially what Mr. Oglethorpe's decision for them would be in regard to Red Bluff. They intend to move to us upon permission of Mr. Oglethorpe. [I read the above rules to them, and these seemed to them just as improper as the point that the land that was to be given to them could be held only by a man and that the female sex was excluded from inheriting it after the death of the husband or father; and therefore they wished to request Mr. Oglethorpe to remit this hard stipulation before they should resolve to move here.][92]

The little son of an Austrian who came with the recently arrived people died on the trip to Red Bluff. He was two years old. Many of the new people are sick and some of them at Red Bluff are said to be in a dangerous condition; therefore, they are asking for Mr. Zwiffler. But we have no lack of sick people here. It will be necessary for one of us to go there, but first we must set a number of things in order which give both of us a great deal to do. It is again very cold at night time and the patients out in the open must suffer a great deal.

The 24th of February. Some of the pigs that were lost some months ago have now been found by the people on the other side of the Savannah River, opposite Red Bluff. It is thought that the wolves that chased them caused them to swim there. Today they also brought the last cows out of the forest. This has become necessary because all men now go to Red Bluff to work and they can no longer look after the cattle that are left in the woods. No trace has ever been found of the cattle that were lost earlier, some at the beginning in Abercorn and some later in Ebenezer. We also must give up for lost the two oxen presented to us which ran away.

The 25th of February. A young man from Purysburg who, with his brother, was born in St. Gall in Switzerland, is rendering many valuable services to Mr. von Reck and the congregation at Red Bluff, to the extent of letting his own business play a secondary role.[93] Both brothers fear God [sincerely] and they make use of our office every time we go to Purysburg. Their name is Ziebely. Sometime ago they suffered from a great scarcity of food and everybody [completely] abandoned them. [also Mr. Pury, who had promised them much in their homeland.] But God so arranged it that Mr. Causton let them have as much as they needed for their sustenance from the store-house in Savannah, as we requested. They considered this to be a special proof of the Fatherly care of God, and they will gladly pay everything back in time, especially since their parents in St. Gall are said to be wealthy people. It was my intention to go to Red Bluff this afternoon to have services after work with Mr. von Reck and the congregation; but I could not find the place where they were working and decided to get back before sundown. After much danger of getting lost I returned to Ebenezer late in the evening. This will teach me to be more careful. [Our people are pleased with Mr. von Reck's Christian disposition, which is as different from Mr. Vat's disposition and attitude toward the congregation as day is from night. He shines before them like an edifying example and attempts to make their burden as light as possible through Christian encouragement and guidance. We help him as best we can with oral and written advice; and we hope to God that He will give him truth, caution, and good reflection, which he now greatly needs, since Mr. Vat is against him in everything. Mr. Vat stands in good credit with Mr. Causton and is supported by him even in improper things. Mr. Causton also stands very well with Mr. Oglethorpe. Things still look pretty bad with regard to the provisions for the third transport: Mr. Vat will give no more than some meat and Indian corn. We are making every effort to avoid collisions between the two.]

The 26th of February. Today Mr. Vat began to distribute to the first Salzburgers those provisions which had been in arrears from the first year. Some time ago Mr. Causton had let me ask what the Salzburgers liked best and we asked for flour and corn in addition to the 800 pounds of meat. [which, however, Mr. Vat did not want to distribute until I also resigned myself in this to his one-sided methods because I had made, in all joyousness and with the approval of the congregation, a few other objections against his opinion and had given them to him in writing. Since I still have much to write to Mr. Oglethorpe about our move to the Red Bluff in addition to the many hindrances and hard circumstances still being caused us, we want to have patience in this unreasonable demand of Mr. Vat as we have done before through God's grace.

[Meanwhile, I want to incorporate my written arguments in this diary for the information of our friends and benefactors. Already two months ago he asked me whether I would be satisfied if the provisions which had been in arrears were distributed not only among those still living of the first transport but also if the portions of all those who had died without heirs were placed in the store-house, so that they would revert to the Trustees. I inquired about his actual opinion orally, and a few days after that I sent him the following treatise:

["I have wished to petition Commissioner Vat with the following points in respect to the provisions which are still in arrears for the first Salzburgers and which you are requested to consider. 1). We should have had the provisions which are in arrears this past October. At that time not only were there no provisions in the store-house but also we had no boat to travel to Savannah to inform Mr. Causton how we were suffering at the time because of a great lack of provisions. The mail had also ceased at that time. Now a few of the people who had received sufficient allowance died before this lack of provisions. They were Lackner, Fleiss, Mittensteiner, Huber and his wife and eldest daughter, and Mrs. Reuter. Now, if the portions of these dead ones were deducted and placed in the store-house, then they would get double portions. The women and children have performed no hard work[94] and have therefore not been permitted to eat as much as the men who have had to drag provisions and other things in a miserable way from Abercorn up to here. Therefore, it happened, for example, that the Hubers' little children and a few others have had no lack of food in this troublesome time. Also, those who were sick at the time, like Hans

Gruber, Braumberger, and Steiner, performed no work and were a burden to others in their illness. Why should they still participate in the provisions yet to be distributed, especially since they are no longer living? Rott usually feigned sickness and made other excuses while the provisions were being brought up. 2). Mr. Oglethorpe sent a man named Lancaster, who was supposed to bring our people's provisions and things on pack-horses to Ebenezer; Mr. von Reck dismissed this man as a good-for-nothing. Now, since the Salzburgers have done his work and the Trustees have been caused no further expenses, it would not be against the will of the bene-factors if all the few provisions were left to them without those of the deceased. Our beloved benefactors prefer to give rather than take away. 3). Those who would have received provisions in the place of their deceased wives, relatives, etc., wish to relinquish their right and let everything be distributed among those still living who belong to the past year, provided the portions belonging to the deceased are also distributed among everyone. Also, it would re-compense to some extent the very hard work that the still living unmarried men have performed for those who were sick at the time and for the wives and children who died afterwards. The 31st of December 1735.]

The 27th of February. At this time several ships will be leaving for London with which we could send letters and the continuation of our diary. But as matters regarding our move to Red Bluff are still subject to many difficulties and we cannot yet see their out-come, we will postpone it for some time. Mr. von Reck agrees with us that we should send these things in a package at an opportune time. Several members of the congregation intend to go to Holy Communion next Sunday. They have been prevented from doing so for several successive Sundays. Some of the newly arrived people also reported for this purpose but I suggested they wait till next time because we must first learn to know each other better.

The 28th of February. This morning had been selected for our service of penance and confession. The people assembled for this preparation for Holy Communion, which was based on the same verse from John 20: 22–23[95] on which I had based earlier confes-sions. We find it necessary to expound the truth of this verse frequently so that the discipline we must use will not appear strange to anyone or as a human invention, and so that all will understand that the key to the forgiveness of sins as well as St. Peter's key are precious gifts of God. At the end of the sermon I had to apply the discipline of the church, in the presence of the congregation, against someone [Ruprecht Zittrauer] who had offended the congregation last Wednesday by getting drunk once again. Praise God! this gave special emphasis to the truths of said verse which we had presented. I related briefly how he had also conducted himself previously, [twice, so far as I know, in indulging in brandy and rum-drinking, in Purysburg] and how we had used every available means for his betterment by working on him as much as we could, in public as well as in private; how it appeared once that he was sincere in wanting to change as he had promised with heart and mouth to the small assembly in which [on October 5, 1735 (vid. Diar. ibid.)] his offences [sin] had been disposed of.

This week someone had given him a bottle of rum, or brandy, in return for certain work [for Mr. Zwiffler], which gave him the opportunity for his latest excess. This has been put down as a sin before God against both the giver and the receiver, for it is also against the rules of the Trustees, hence against the worldly authority. God arranged matters so wondrously again this time that his drunkenness was made known to me so that I could make every possible effort to prevent any scandal. But in spite of this it became known to some that he had got drunk again, which grieved the good souls no little. He was one of those who reported for Holy Communion last week, and he had received many good admonitions. These circumstances made his sin all the greater.

I had him with me last evening and briefly showed him his sins once again and the scandal caused by them; and I told him that I would not admit him to Holy Communion this time or at any other time as long as he was not sincerely converted to God.[96] These private representations depressed him very much and he confessed his sorrow. But, since he had deceived me before with his good words, I could not do otherwise than take up this sad affair in today's assembly and publicly exclude him, as a rotten and dead limb, from Holy Communion and other holy acts until such time as he proves his sincere penance before the congregation which he scandalized. We also showed the duties which the members of the congregation should perform with respect to this poor man, who was thus disciplined for the sake of his eternal salvation. [He can best be used in the community for guarding the cows because he has done that from his earliest years. However, we shall see if we can change his manner of living so that we will then have more opportunity and time to work on him privately. He is still quite ignorant. He already traveled with a Salzburger transport to Prussia[97] where, however, it did not suit him. If he should not accommodate himself to real improvement through the present discipline

and commit the same excesses again, he will not be able to remain
in the community. I pointed this out to him as well as to those who
were assembled today.]

Governor Oglethorpe recently expressed his pleasure at my removing the bad R. [Rott] and his wife to some other place, because
the longer he stayed here the more disquiet and heartache he
created. This would make it seem that he would agree easily to the
removal of other disorderly people. It was the order of evening
prayer to consider the fifth petition.[98] This gave us a good opportunity to use said scandal [of Zittrauer] for the instruction and
warning of the whole congregation and to make known to everyone why we had to use our authority against this miserable man
and his annoyance. [I found this all the more necessary because
there are people in the third transport who have brought along a
bad name. We have received complaints that they are already behaving evilly to some extent.]

The 29th of February. Twenty-eight persons from the congregation went to Holy Communion at this time. One of them was
Mrs. Schweighofer, whom God had given enough strength to come
to church. She would rather receive it with the congregation than
alone. At evening prayer I read to those assembled the letter which
Deacon Degmaier had written to the congregation. I explained it
and applied it to our past and present conditions, and God did not
let this go by without blessing. Among other things, this letter
reminded them of the divine help and rescue they had enjoyed in
Salzburg and later; and I used this opportunity to show how useful
it is not to dwell upon the cross of the present but to go over one's
entire life to determine whether we have not been in various
dangers, needs, and misery, and what the outcome of all of this
has been. Since they would find that God never tried them beyond
their capacity and has given unexpected help here and there, they
should find comfort in the help they have had and should use it
to build on a firmer foundation their childlike and firm trust in
God and His fatherly care; for He is unchangeable in His love and
the fulfilment of His promises, etc.

I also told them that a number of verses from the *Treasure
Chest*,[99] which my dear colleague had shown me last week, had
brought me great comfort and joyous courage. They are on page
163, and they read toward the end: "God can do everything except
this: He cannot leave unfulfiled what He has promised." And
since we had constantly told our listeners in the past that our
faithful God would certainly fulfil His promises to them and remove one difficulty after another, I showed them how all of this

should be understood under the condition of the cross. They had also been assured of this in the letter mentioned earlier.

I asked them to show me a single example from the Bible according to which a man who took the narrow path to heaven as a child of God had been spared the cross: I could show them the opposite. To emphasize this sentence I quoted and applied to our circumstances the verses from Genesis 5: 29, and Psalm 90: 10. I also told them that it is a special blessing from God, which they have known and should recognize again from this letter, that so many good people think about our congregation. They thank God for the good in it, at the same time presenting to Him our needs and trials. Far away people do not think about other congregations in this manner, etc.; and this should give them great comfort and good courage.

MARCH

The 1st of March. My dear colleague paid a visit to a sick Austrian. He found him cheerful in God despite his miserable physical condition and inadequate care. He thanked God for having brought him here and commended all of his circumstances to our Father in Heaven who does everything well. He told me, among other things, that some people [the Herrnhuter already] had given him advice and had attempted to set him against the pastor's office, saying that it was an unnecessary matter. But he had repulsed them with the Word of God in which he had seen the teaching office mentioned. One day Mr. von Reck told me he had asked a few [among them] of these people [Herrnhuter] why they had given offence to many people by using the Lord's Prayer either only very seldom or not at all. To his surprise they had given a very poor answer to this question; and he could see very well that some of the poor people made a good impression but had a poor foundation. Another, [in London they picked up as a hired hand a carpenter named Volmar; and, because on the entire trip he] who had failed to find among them any treatment of the Word of God as is customary in our Lutheran church, but in its stead had received from them [the minister Nitchmann who accompanied them] various peculiar explanations which he had never heard before, is making efforts to get away from them. [However, Mr. Spangenberg claims five pounds sterling passage-money before he will let him depart.] At various times this man had asked him questions about matters which appeared suspicious and incomprehensible to him. For an answer he was told that he must first be converted and he would understand, but no sooner.

The 2nd of March. Mr. von Reck will write to London to notify the proper place of his happy arrival in America with the third transport. We will use this opportunity to send our diary and our address to Court Chaplain Ziegenhagen. But we would like to postpone the writing of letters to our benefactors and friends until we have definite news regarding the new arrangements for our Salzburgers, who are still subjected to a number of difficulties. [Under the entry in this diary for February 22nd I have incorporated the rules here that Mr. Vat impressed on the people in our place, and it will be necessary to set down that which I wrote to Mr. Oglethorpe on that occasion. The entire letter reads in the English language[100] thus:

[I beg yr Honourable's permission, to acquaint you humbly what happined to me and my congregation, since Mr. Vat came again to EbenEzer. He sent me word thast (last) Sonday by the Constable Mr. Zwiffler, that he were ordered by Mr. Oglethorpe to tell the people today after our Divine Service, what should be their duty in time to come, wherefore he desired me to bid all the congregation meet together in the Church. After the people were assembled, he sent one of the Saltzburghers in my House to fetch me in the Church too, to be hearer of the things, he was about to intimate. But having preached the holy Word of God in the Morning & after Noon (for my Fellow labourer was gone with Mr. von Reck to your Town) & having had other privat business with sik people, I was extreamly tired, which weak constitution hindered me from being present in this Meeting. However I suppose it was the Direction of your Honourable, he should have communicated before to me that, which should be made known to my congregation, & afterwards we would have done it joyntly. But as he fancyd formerly to have full Authority & the only Command at EbenEzer in temporal things, he fancyd it now too.

[Besides this it would have been more convenient, if he had chosen rather the Saturday or Monday for this intimation than a Sunday, since he knows very well, what pleasure it is to me & the Saltzburghers, to worship God the whole Day in privat as well as publick. But as he forced formerly the people to neglect the Days, appointed for publick worship, so he was not at all scrupulous to fill the people's minds with strange things. It would be too much trouble for you to hear all manners of mischiefs & grieves, which are caused me & our people by the wilful & rigid behaviour of Mr.

Vat, which he endeavours now, is nothing else but to grieve me & my Fellowlabourer further, & to disheartin the distressed people by commanding them several heavy things, & threatening them cruelly. The people are very willing to obey in everything, you[101] please to command, & if it is your Order, that Mr. Vat should have an absolut power over Provisions & the people, as he pretends[102] to have, I will, endeavour my self, to the utmost of my power, to encourage them to suffer all burdens with patience, which Mr. Vat will go on to lay upon their Shoulders, and then it will be but a little difference between their sufferings here, & in their native Country. However I know Mr. Oglethorpe's fear of God, His fatherly mercy towards persecuted & distressed people, and particularly his great Favour to me & my Fellowlabourer, wherefore I firmly believe, he will give Orders to tread the Saltzburghers not like Slaves, but to let them use the same Laws & Liberties with other free people in this Colony, as it was promised to them by words of mouth & writings. But as long as Mr. Vat lives at Eben-Ezer, as long must we & our congregation be disquiet by him, & he will be so difficult to perform Mr. Oglethorpe's direction, as he was difficult in performing Mr. Causton's: The particulars of which I must leave now untouched. If you should know all the particulars of the difficulties & miseries, the Saltzburghers were forced to undergo, you would certainly count the servants at Savannah happier than the free people at EbenEzer, which will pass away & be forgotten if you grant us the following petitions.

[I make now bold to address myself with some petitions to your Honourable, concerning the Rules, Mr. Vat has made known to the people last Sunday, to be observed, which my boldness, I hope will be taken in good part, by your innate Goodness & Generosity.

[1). The people are ready to work joyntly, in the Ground with all their heart, but they beg humbly leave, to use such a manner of joynt working, as is most convenient & profitable to them & their Grounds. They were intended a good while ago to work six & six in little Parties, so that every Party would have with them one, or if necessary, two of the weak & old people, which method will be, as they certainly believe, twice more profitable for clearing out the Garden-Lots, than to work joyntly so, as they were forced to do a year ago. And since some of them might be not so industrious, they would be in such little Parties strictly observed, & compelled easily to more application: wherefore they would not need such Overseers, like Slaves, as Mr. Vat spake of, but every body would work freely with pleasure of mind, & thanksgiving to God, who inclines the generous Heart of their dear Father, Mr. Oglethorpe, to let them have some liberty. Besides this every Party would endeavor, as much as possible, to overreach one another in clearing their Garden-Lots, which will be pleasant & profitable. Some people have very good assistance by their strong wives & some boys, who can't & won't work, if the work must be done joyntly according to Mr. Vat's method. I leave untouched some advantages more, which we would have, if you would shew us the favour to let the people work in the aforesaid manner.

[2]. As for the Store-House, which shall be built immediately by order of Mr. Vat, of logs or large timbers, the people are well pleased to build for the present a good Hutt with good Doors, to be lockt up, & after their work in the Ground till planting-season is done, they will be very industrious to build a Store-& Watch-House, & what else your Honourable please to command. Be pleased to let them have this Liberty, to cultivate before their grounds, & afterwards to build the aforesaid publick buildings so you will find by experience, they will by the blessing of God, gain in short time their victuals for themselves & their poultry, which to feed & breed we wanted a good deal more, than is the ordinary allowance of the Store. One of the first Saltzburghers had on the other side of our River a good spot of Ground, which produced lately, twenty bushels of Corn, besides the Indian peas, which good Crop will be produced by other Saltzburghers too, since they have leave to remove to a better soil, if their zealous industry shall not be prevented by building publick Houses & fetching Provisions with out[103] extream heavy Boat, which is built better for a standing water, than to be used in the strong stream of Savannah-River.

[3]. If the liberty is granted, to work joyntly in little Parties, they would build little Hutts, capable for containing as many people, as work, sleep, & eat together, which would be more wholesome, than if they should lodge under one or two large Hutts, which Mr. Vat urges to be build. I pass by with silence several other inconveniences in temporal & spiritual things, which would happen, if they should live so close together.

[4]. I can't forbear to wonder very much at Mr. Vat's pretence, that twenty Gardens on each side of the Town should be reserved at the disposal of the Honourable Trustees.[104] After this manner the people's Gardens should be removed a great way of (off) from the Town, & to barren pine-land too, which would be as unhappy as in our former state. The Saltzburghers have suffered in their old settlement very much, & leave now behind all their buildings & improvements, which troubles & Losts will be made good to

them, if their Lots are laid out upon good Ground on both sides of the Town, as it was yr. Honourables prizeworthy intention by shewing me the situation of the Town upon a paper. This is my Comfort too, that you was pleased to tell me at the same time, the people should begin immediately their work, after their Town & Garden-Lots were laid out, which yr. Order & promise is of greater value to me & our Saltzburghers, than all talkings of Mr. Vat. I hope therefore Dear Sir, you will give full order, for laying out all our Garden-Lots at first, that we may certainly know, what ground belongs to every owner, which we longed for a great while ago. For it is not a little tedious to them, to live so long in those uncertain circumstances, remembering very well, that not only freedom of conscience, but also good land, which should be given them immediately after their arrival, & besides this, the priviledges & liberties of the Englishmen are realy promised to them, which good things occasioned many of them, to leave their good states, they lived in by the care of many Benefactors in Germany.

[Lastly I beg the favour of yr. Honourable, to remember, that you was lately so kind as to tell me, that if four people watch every night, & one by daytime it would be enough for the present. Wherefore I humbly beseech you to allow us the said number of 4 people for watching. That six people should be to watch on Sundays & Holy-days during divine service, is only Mr. Vat's desire, who was a scandalous contemter of the holy Word of God, & endeavoured to make the people so too, but I could not consent to let the people watch on Sundays & Holy-Days for neglecting our divine service. I doubt not, but our dear Mr. Oglethorpe will let the people have this freedom, to be all present in our publick worship, as they did Lutherto,[105] except one, who is to watch.

[Let it please you to hear the order, Mr. Vat has given other time about the nightly watches. Six men were ordered with a Corporal every night: a Parol or Watch-Word was given out at Evening by Mr. Vat to the Constable Mr. Zwiffler, to carry the said Parol or Watch-Word to the Guard after the following manner: 1). The Constable with his sword on his side took along with him one armed man (called a Titing-man)[106] carying a Lantern. 2). The Sentinel was very strictly ordered to call out in germen tongue: Wer da? or, who is there? after the Constable's answer, Rounde etc. the Corporal was called by the Sentinel to order the Guard in armes. 3). Ther the Constable drew out his sword, & set it on the Corporal's breast, and so with some ceremonies more (but very strange to the poor people) the watch-word was given so, as it is in time of dangerous wars. 4). after this, two men of the watch were ordered to go Patrol every hour all the night about every Corner of the town etc. I desired him often, to abate such strange manners, which lead the young people by degrees to prophaneness, & is very tedious to the old ones, but he denied it making poor shifts till the time, he supposed Mr. Oglethorpe were come again to this Colony, then he bid the people watch without the aforesaid troubles. I intreat you, Sir, very humbly to remove all these troublesome things from the People's watching, which, I suppose, shall be introduced again by Mr. Vat. I add no more to your Honor's present trouble, besides the asurances of my being ever with great Respect etc.

[We are awaiting Mr. Oglethorpe's resolution about this. God has his heart in His hands. May He incline it according to His gracious will. I am planning to go to Savannah this coming week to give an oral explanation and argument upon demand to the written points. I also want to hear the answer and resolution. The amazing and unheard of watch-arrangement, of which I must necessarily advise Mr. Oglethorpe in this letter for future preservation, has caused us many sighs and the congregation many inconveniences. One must utilize the utmost diligence to maintain the dear people in patience.

[To explain this I find it necessary to relate those circumstances which took place between the Ortmanns and Constable Zwiffler on May 7, 1735 (as indicated there in the diary), even though at the time one would have preferred, for important reasons, to sigh secretly rather than to record them. Mr. Vat had made the old schoolmaster Ortmann tithing-man. He had to command his number of people, who were the first Salzburgers, on the watch although he was not permitted to stand watch because of his school work. Mr. Vat considered it unlawful to free anyone from guard duty except the two ministers and doctor Zwiffler. When Mr. Zwiffler wanted to fetch the patrol from Mr. Vat (according to the silly and uncustomary setup which was previously never heard of even in all of England), the old Ortmann had to carry before him for several days a lantern in his hand and a rifle in his arm like a corporal. The old man was patient when his wife let loose against him and Mr. Zwiffler with harsh words that were both disgraceful and annoying and caused no little shock in the congregation. To be sure Mr. Ortmann was not permitted to continue doing these things. Meanwhile, Mr. Vat insisted that Mrs. Ortmann repent for her behaviour and apologize; otherwise he would have to refer the matter to Mr. Causton because, he added, Mr. Zwiffler, in performing his duty, was under royal authority. Mr. Zwiffler would have done well if he had seized

her and locked her up because of her outcry and scolding so late at
night (because it was between nine and ten o'clock) . At that time
we did not yet recognize Mr. Vat's maliciousness and let him impose a deception upon us. Therefore, we employed the utmost
diligence to prevent Mrs. Ortmann's affair from playing into Mr.
Causton's hands, although she had misbehaved very badly in her
anger. To be sure, it was a mistake on our side to have endured
such a strange watch arrangement this long. But the benefactors
can see from this how we wish by all means to avoid the opportunity for clashes. I confess it has cost much prayer and work in
the congregation to keep their spirits patient and tempers even. We
always imagined that he really had, as he said, full authority as
Commissioner to arrange things in Ebenezer according to his
judgment.

[Not long after that a few Indians came to our place with one of
their chiefs and set out the following day for Savannah to fetch their
gifts. To please them, all the men at our place were called together.
They had to perform their exercises in the manner of the ordinary
militia in Germany for such a long time that it ran over into our
prayer hour. As Constable, Mr. Zwiffler should have led the command; but, since he does not understand the drill, he had to let
Mr. Ortmann, who was formerly a lieutenant, take his place. Mr.
Zwiffler was nevertheless occupied as an officer. In this way Mr. Vat
wanted to show the Indians that our people were capable of de-
fending themselves in case of emergency. The following night
more men than otherwise usual had to stand watch.]

The 3rd of March. Yesterday I went to Red Bluff, accompanied
by a pious guide. I went to edify myself with our beloved congregation and to speak with Mr. von Reck about better care for the
sick there, and other matters. [Because Mr. Vat does not wish to
distribute either flour or butter for those who are sick and suffering,
although I have offered to pay well from the cashbox, someone in
the congregation sold me both commodities, of which I have no
supply now.] Next Saturday the surveyor will go back to Savannah.
Mr. von Reck will go at the same time in order to care for the
provisions better.

Among these dear people God has given me much strength of
body and spirit. Last evening I based the prayer hour on Matthew
28: 18, "All power is given unto Me in heaven and in earth; go ye
therefore, etc. I am with you always, even unto the end of the
world." These words had been called out to me by my dear colleague as I was leaving, and they have given me much comfort and
strength in these confused conditions. The listeners were lying

around me on the ground by the fire; and I showed them as briefly as possible that, before depriving them of His visible presence and before His departure, our friendly Savior had wanted to call out to His disciples and believers a word of comfort to which they could cling during their *vita ambulatoria*.[107] Even if they had more enemies than friends in this world, they still had in Jesus the best and mightiest friend Who, like Joseph, would use all of His power and glory for the best interest of His friends and brothers because He had sufficiently proved His active love by His willing acceptance of all suffering. No matter in which corner of the earth they might be, He would see them and their condition; for He would be with them until the end of the world and could save and help in all places and at all times, for to Him was given all the power in heaven and on earth. After briefly applying that to our present migration and the difficulties connected with it, I asked them what they would have thought if they could have heard for themselves these comforting words which the Lord Jesus had spoken to His disciples before His ascension. Perhaps they would have thought that these dear people, who had been so intimately associated with the almighty, omnipresent, and extremely gracious Lord, would have nothing but good days in this world and would experience few or no trials or unpleasantness because their Lord lacked neither the strength nor the will nor the wisdom to do good for them and to help them. But I referred them to the lives of all the Apostles and also to the epistle for last Sunday, Dom. Sexages.,[108] 2 Cor. 11: 19 ff., from which they can learn that God's promises are truly fulfilled and tested under the cross: "My strength," said Christ to the suffering Paul, "is made perfect in weakness, etc."

The 4th of March. Today an Indian brought a whole deer to our house. This has not happened in a long time. His shirt was torn completely and we provided a new one for him. This fresh meat will be given to the sick here and to those suffering want at Red Bluff. I intend to go back there this afternoon. God knows the need of the people and He still knows how to help them. I am still being comforted by Jesus' saying: "All power is given unto Me in heaven and on earth, etc." He is still the Lord of the earth and the hope of the poor, etc.

The 5th of March. Last evening before prayer hour I had the Commissioner show me around the site for the houses to see what everyone had received in the lot-drawing. Everybody was satisfied with that which God had given him, and all of them praised God's kindness for it. Through God's providence it happened that Hertzog, a single man from the first group, drew a building site which makes him the neighbor of Peter Gruber, in whose house he is living now and enjoying a good deal of assistance, which he needs because of his special situation. I marvelled at this good dispensation of God in his presence and he said that I should not marvel that it happened thus; for before the drawing he had gone into the forest and had prayed to God about it. This made a deep impression on a pious man from Purysburg who was present. I asked him if he was happy about the land he had received. He was silent for a while; and, knowing that with this question I intended to remind him of the unbecoming aspects of joy over earthly things, he complained about his earthbound heart; but he also believed that the Lord who had let him have this land would also bless it for him, etc. Other people were happy to be able to hear the Word of God again. They had begun to long for it before my arrival because they needed good admonitions and awakenings to help them with their confused circumstances.

I based evening prayer on the well known words of David: "Teach me Thy way, O Lord: I will walk in Thy truth." I told them I had always found it worthy of note that in his psalms David had so much to say about the Way. The conditions of his life and suffering doubtless gave him the opportunity for this, for he had to take many a good and many a bad way, not only as the shepherd of the sheep of his father, but also during his pursuits by Saul and by his own son. He had had to suffer just like others who have to live in the desert and uncomfortable circumstances, much hardship and misfortune, neither of which did damage to his soul or his body. Instead, they gave him incomparable advantages, for the most magnificent psalms seem to have been produced and sent to God as prayers in such circumstances. But since David also had many people with him in the wilderness who lacked either provisions or comfortable shelter, beds, rest, etc., it seems likely that the hearts of these people revealed themselves in different ways. Some of them showed the good and some the bad foundation of their hearts with words and deeds, the latter, unlike David and his kind, not deriving any blessings from their cross in the wilderness because of their own guilt.

After this introduction (which was necessary because of our present conditions), I briefly discussed the words themselves and showed that it is a great misfortune in this world to be lost in a wilderness without path or guidance, but that it is great good fortune and benefit to be put on the right path. I applied this to the spiritual aspect, pointing out that going astray spiritually is much more terrible also in this respect, that one's own wits and strength or outward human help are not enough to find one's way out; as is sometimes the case with going astray physically; for it is an eternal truth which we know from the Catechism: "I believe that I cannot come to Jesus Christ, or believe in Him through my own reason or strength, but the Holy Ghost, etc." In the same way David, recognizing his impotence and unpreparedness, prayed: "Teach me Thy way, O Lord, etc." What he meant by "way" here I explained with the prayer of Moses, Exodus 33: 13, "Show me now Thy way," (coll. John 14: 6, "I am the Way, the Truth, and the Life.") To this God had given the comforting answer: "My presence shall go with thee and I will give thee rest," v. 14. All of this was given a short application and was impressed upon the listeners, who were gathered around me like a herd lying down, so that they would do in this wilderness here as Moses had done there, namely, take no step without the presence of the Father, i. e. the faithful Saviour (Hebrews 1: 3.) who promised to guide His children with His eyes, just as the children of Israel in the desert had Him for their leader by day and by night in the column of fire and smoke. Above all things, they must learn to know this magnificent Saviour and learn to follow Him in truth, for both are recorded together in David's prayer, and the truth of the first must be proven with practice of the latter: Teach me Thy way O Lord that I may walk in Thy truth, i.e. honestly and with all my heart, before God and men. On the other hand, if someone boasts of his true knowledge of Christ but does not want to walk in the truth, living instead for the world and the flesh, he is trying to walk two different paths at the same time, According to everything we know, such is impossible in physical as well as in spiritual life, 1 John 2: 4. We are saving the rest of this beautiful verse for our next meeting.

Tomorrow afternoon the people will come back to Ebenezer and stay for Sunday. For that reason neither of us will go out to them this week. They will arrange to build a small hut for us as soon as possible so that one of us can stay with them permanently. Necessity requires this in regard to physical and spiritual matters for adults and children alike. Mrs. Grimmiger, the wife of an Austrian, is dangerously sick. As this is dangerous for her nursing child, another Christian woman has been appointed for its care while she herself is given the best treatment possible. She wants to take Holy Communion, but I am finding her to be so ignorant in spiritual matters that I am amazed. I have impressed upon her only the one word "Jesus a Saviour" in its meaning and relation to our great wretchedness and misery and to His merited salvation. The surveyor is going back to Savannah tomorrow morning, accompanied by Mr. Vat and Mr. von Reck. He promises to come back as soon as possible. [For lack of an opportunity to dispatch my letter to Mr. Oglethorpe, which was already finished last week, I have just given it today to Mr. von Reck to deliver to him.]

The 6th of March. Since the new moon we again have been having a heavy freeze at night as well as mornings and evenings. This seems to have damaged the peach blossoms which had come out in large numbers. This morning we had a long and rather cold rain. During the past few days the people have built small shelters for themselves and for their tools. If nothing interferes, they will work their fields vigorously next week. Some people of both sexes have begun with that already.

[I am quite amazed that Mr. Vat warned the people again when I was outside with them not to be so bold as to build shelters but to abide by the prescribed orders. It is as clear as daylight that the new people will experience inconveniences now in the big hut that was built for them and their belongings. Should the people lie under the open sky in this changeable weather until a complete resolution ensues from my letter to Mr. Oglethorpe, then their health will obviously suffer. When they have time to build better houses they will use the present miserable ones, that were built in haste, for future stalls.]

An old and sincerely pious man requested a handkerchief to use on his sick eyes. We had two cut for him from some good linen and we also gave him some Essentia dulci ad oculos.[109] Hereupon he so praised God in a humble way that it impressed me deeply. [This dear man has previously learned to know Mr. Vat as an obstinate, pitiless man. Among other things, he has asked him for a little bed that had been given him in London for his two children. For no reasons at all Mr. Vat has kept it back to this hour and yet given the man false hope from time to time. This afternoon Mr. Vat sent a letter to me and my dear colleague by way of Mr. Zwiffler; however, we shall not open it before next Monday. We fear that he wants to stir up unrest and anxiety on this coming Sunday once more, as is his custom. My physical constitution, which is now very weak, suffers immensely whenever my spirit is provoked; therefore this discretion cannot be held against me.]

The 7th of March. Another year has passed since God let us reach Georgia after a difficult sea voyage. For that reason I announced to the congregation today that next Saturday (the amount of work to be done at this time does not permit any other day) we would celebrate our memorial and thanksgiving day and praise God for the unspeakably great spiritual and physical benefits we have enjoyed so far. We would also humbly call upon Him to guide us in accordance with His fatherly providence through the unhappy and uncertain conditions yet to come. If we did not have this festival this week we could not be all together for it, because the people will have a great deal to do the following week in transporting provisions and with other things.

As I had done for several Sundays, I used the evening prayer to let the assembled listeners hear something from the letters which Professor Francke wrote to us recently. They contain magnificent testimony of the wise and salutary ways which God has gone with His children and also with us, and they contributed much to the encouragement of our souls. I had the opportunity to mention various matters from the Word of God which they should know and practice in their present circumstances if God were to fulfil, for each of us according to his condition, the salutary intention He has with all trials. I showed them, among other things, why the cross is very heavy and almost unbearable to many people: it comes, first of all, from willfulness. If a man does not have his way with things he imagines to be useful and God disturbs his mind instead, he becomes restive and dissatisfied like a willful child; but this is a great sin against the good God, whose will and ways have the salvation of man as their only purpose. Besides, doing this places a heavy burden upon men in the form of disquiet and discomfort. They should know that only God is good and that we are bad. And it is a precious benefit from God when He leads His children not according to their own but to His will. Otherwise, they would not only experience worldly unhappiness but would also go to hell.

I asked them only to look back and they would find proof, as I had, that if here and there everything had gone according to their thinking, ideas, intentions, they would have done much damage to themselves. And many of them would thank God with me for having arranged those matters for our best interest and different from the way we had wanted them at the time. Occasionally God will make pious people atone for their lust and will, but afterwards they can always clearly see the damage it did to them physically or spiritually. It is God's intention that they should use this to warn them against willfulness from then on. People of the world consider themselves lucky and blessed when everything succeeds according to their wishes and without interference, Psalm 144: 12–14. But all the time they are going to hell, and it is more of a divine judgment than a benefit for such people if God gives them their share of worldly goods the way they want to have them.

In connection with this I reminded them of the children of high ranking and voluptuous people who seldom turn out well because they always have their way at home and because other people flatter them, etc. I continued that one of the main reasons for [much unrest and] greater suffering from the cross and from trials is that people imagine they are excluded from God's providence in these matters and are having these experiences only as the result of action by bad people, etc. But the Word of God teaches us not only that God alone is the governor and caretaker of all creatures but also that He has so enveloped His children with His fatherly supervision and care that they are carried in His body, so to speak (Isaiah. 46: 3), as in that of a mother. Their hairs are numbered and, according to the mouth of truth, not a single one of them can fall to the ground without the will of the Heavenly Father; they are the apple of God's eye; they are a signet ring on His hand; He has marked them in His hands, etc.

If it is really true that a man has become a child of God through true conversion and thus belongs to the family of God, he does not need to fret and worry about various trials; for the Father takes care of him; He takes care of animals and birds and He certainly will not and cannot forget His children. It is said: Now my soul be His and trust Him alone who has created thee: Come what may, thy Father on high has help and advice for all things. Instead of sinning by showing an attitude of anger, displeasure, scolding, etc., against the tools used for their chastisements and trials, they should pray for them in compassionate love because such enemies of God and His children are in a miserable and extremely dangerous condition, etc. The rest of the edifying letters from our worthy fathers that were written to us recently will be made known to the congregation [as much as there is to communicate to them] in similar fashion. I am encouraged to continue with them because the blessing derived from them has become known to me in my personal contacts with various members of the congregation. God be praised humbly for all of His kindness and also for the sincere and fatherly thoughts which so many good teachers and children of God have for us.

Toward evening my dear colleague visited the parents of a pious girl. He had a very pleasant conversation with them and told me many good things about it for my edification. As she had been prevented from attending public service because of her physical weakness, she has searched for and found her edification in a little known Passion-hymn which is to be found in a small Passion-book printed in Ulm. It is: "Jesus, Thou root of life for life, etc."[110] She quoted some edifying and forceful expressions from several verses and made use of them in simple and childlike fashion. For example: "Jesus! Thy death rewards my troubles, so that I kneel at the foot of the cross." Also: "His merciful and Fatherly patience cries out mercy, mercy for guilt, etc." Also: "When I pour from this spring (namely the bitter tears), I give to the angels the sweetest of wines." Also: "Fighting and winning and ruling are Thine. Believing and loving and hoping are mine." Also: "Jesus, my life, my salvation, my love, Jesus, my brother, my share, and my heart."[111]

[The 8th of March. This morning we opened the letter that Mr. Vat sent to us both last Sunday. We want to incorporate this letter in the diary so that all can see that our anxiety was no mere conjecture and that he would have again provoked us and our congregation on a dear Sunday. It reads as follows: "Rev Gentlemen, you are desired, publickly to forwarn all et every one of the Inhabitants of this Congregation at EbenEzer; that they may not meddle with removing any Provisions, or Planks, Slabs or any other things, belonging to the Store-House, unless by Order under my hand & Seal; otherwise he, or they, acting contrary to this notice, shall be prosecuted according to Law. And Mr. Zwiffler, who (as well as the Tything-men, like as other Officers of this Province, have been continued as Constable & Tything-men for one year) is hereby required & directed to appoint every Day six men for watching in this place every night, and during Divine Service on Sundays & holy Days (for the Security both of the inhabitants & of the Stores, agreeable to the Rules, prescribed under the hand of the Honble James Oglethorpe, Esq.; dated the 16th Day of February last.

EbenEzer	I am
March the 16. 1735.	your humble Servant
	John Vat,
	Commiss. to the Saltzburghs."

[Concerning the first point, namely, the provisions, planks, and slabs (or sections of the sides of the trees for boards), Mr. von Reck will learn whether some may be used in the future. We have written sufficiently to Mr. Oglethorpe concerning the other point and are now awaiting a reply. Whoever knows the considerably fatiguing work and severe circumstances of the Salzburgers, as we do, and has some love for their health, life, and progress of their effort to gain their own victuals, cannot possibly give his consent with good conscience, to these and other burdens if he has something to say about it. Hence, may we fare as God wills, to the best of our ability we intend, with humility and seriousness, to espouse the cause of our poor people who have previously been tortured to the quick.

[Mr. Vat set out for Red Bluff very early today, and we are still awaiting to see what he will do there. Some say he is bound for Purysburg, for which reason he has locked and guarded the present store-house so that no one can get any of the things that belong to our congregation. Up to now he has only kept one room locked during his absence. In it are stored wine for the sick, nails, crowbars, files and those things given by the benefactors from London to our people upon departure but which have been withheld from them. Last week he distributed the butter that was also given to him as a treat for the second transport. If Mr. von Reck is absent for longer than eight days, the people he brought along will suffer for lack of foodstuffs that are already meagre and scarce enough now. We shall let others judge if we are forced after this to borrow something from the provisions lying there to still the hunger of these poor people. The matter of provisions for the third transport is not well organized and has a very poor appearance.]

The 9th of March. For several days Schweighofer has been so weak physically that he thought his departure from this vale of tears had come close yesterday. For that reason he had my colleague put down on paper how he wanted to distribute his worldly goods among his three children after his death. Today he was a little stronger and also quite resigned to the will of the Father. Yesterday he was very much grieved over his sins but had found comfort in the verse: "Where sin has become great, mercy is greater still, etc."[112] This had given him the following thought: "If my sins were to gather over my head and go as high as the sky, the Lord Jesus will still be above them with His mercy, for He is in heaven and has all things, including my sins, under His feet, and I can say: 'All the prophets speak of Him [Jesus] (they point their fingers at Him, so to speak, and not at Mary or the Saints) and say that in His name all those who believe in Him shall have forgiveness of sins' ".

I sought to strengthen him even more in this trust in Christ and His mercy which covers all sinners, using, among others, the following words: "It is true that the grace of God in Christ is of infinite length and breadth and stretches over all poor sinners, even the greatest ones, for His kindness is a divine kindness." People also have the qualities of love, kindness, and mercy; but compared to divine love and mercy it is no more than a drop compared to the great ocean. And although all creatures can enjoy this divine kindness, it is given to none of them as plentifully and specifically as to the fallen people to whom God has given His own, only, and most beloved Son for their Saviour. "How shall He not also freely give us all things with Him?" Romans 8: 32. Besides, as he should know from the recent Sunday gospel, this good Saviour was so willing to suffer and die for us that He did not wait until His enemies came to get Him. Instead, His heartfelt desire for our salvation made Him go to Jerusalem and deliver Himself into the hands of His enemies. He is just as ready to give us the grace He achieved as He was ready to achieve it, for He says Himself: "Whoever comes to Me I shall not cast away."[113] I then told him about his fatherly love for his children, asking whether he would not have been ready to give his children what they needed if earlier he had been willing to earn everything for them by the labor of his own hands.

Yesterday and this morning a number of people from the third transport came to me from Red Bluff to tell me about the shortage of their provisions: nearly everything had been used up now that they had to give a week's provisions to the seven men who had gone to Abercorn yesterday in the big boat to get the things that are stored there under the open sky. [Since Mr. Vat has carefully locked up all the provisions in the store-house and since, because of our holy office, we would rather be patient than give an occasion for opening the door, so] since we asked about some victuals among the members of our congregation [and] found some of them willing to give from their small supply. This will be restored to them. We may be able to make it possible to purchase two or three pigs, which are to be sent out. In this connection we must consider it a special divine dispensation that the first Salzburgers recently received provisions of corn and flour, which had been in arrears since the first year and which they can now share with their suffering neighbors. My dear colleague went out today to serve the well and the sick alike with the gospel of Christ, which is for the poor, and to get information about their physical needs at the same time. My physical weakness and violent dizzyness which have plagued me for some time have made it necessary for me to take some medicines for several days. If God should bless the use of these things to give me complete recovery, as I hope, then I will go to Savannah next Monday [in order to learn what Mr. von Reck has been able to arrange about the provisions for the people he brought along. We worry that Mr. Causton has referred him to Mr. Oglethorpe and that he will, therefore, probably have to travel to the Altamaha.]

Hernberger, a tailor who arrived with the last transport, is very wretched physically. But he lets it serve him to come closer to Christ and through Him to the Father and to eternal salvation. Haberfehner's physical weaknesses are also very great. But in our efforts to serve his physical and spiritual needs we hear from him nothing but praise for God and His loving guidance into this calm. Both men have a fine knowledge of Christianity, which is not only literal but spiritual and alive. This is clearly shown by their words and deeds. There are many good souls in this group who will soon get together with the genuine members of our congregation.[114] But there are also some among them who already have given evidence of their bad habits on a number of occasions. [especially since there is no harmony among those whom Mr. von Reck picked up along the way, and the one always complains about the other. These are Grinig, the watchmaker Müller, the tanner Helffenstein, Ernst, etc. We do not yet know whom to believe. Even the old Austrian woman, Mrs. Spielbiegler, and her son have a very poor reputation.]

The 10th of March. Among other things, my dear colleague wrote me yesterday from Red Bluff that the people there would be happy if something were sent them to satisfy their hunger. The boat also arrived in order to get some food for the people and brought along some written orders which Mr. von Reck had left for his brother. [Among other things in it, the latter was commissioned to break open the store-house with force if it had been locked by Mr. Vat. This young Mr. von Reck asked for consent to this; but I told him that I would not meddle in such forceful methods of procuring provisions for the people. Thus I would give no opportunity for calumny to my enemies and no offence to my congregation, whose model I must be in word and deed, 1. Timothy 4: 12. So far, in dealing with Mr. Vat, it has always been our way to be tolerant and to serve and to conquer through suffering as suits soldiers of Christ. In this manner Mr. Vat's mind and disposition towards us and the Salzburgers, and likewise his behaviour, have become more obvious and suspicious to Mr. Causton as well as others, than if we had demanded our rights and proceeded roughly.

The young Mr. von Reck was of the opinion that he could maintain the position of his brother as Commissioner of the people to whom he had to supply foodstuffs by having the store-house broken open on his own responsibility, as he himself had done soon after arriving; and in this case I would have no reason to oppose it. Now God seems to be pointing out to us a gentle way, namely] I let it be known that the old Salzburgers would collect as much in the way of provisions as they could spare at this time. They consist of one bushel of rice, one and one half bushels of beans, two hundred pounds of flour, three bushes of corn, some salt, and two live pigs. I advised them first to make use of this blessing of God, which is flowing from good and kind hearts, and then to await God's further aid. Mr. von Reck was pleased with this proposal. He could see and hear how actively the Salzburger women were working to the best of their ability to assist the suffering people of the third transport; and this testimony of real Christian love, which works in accordance with the needs and conditions of the neighbors, made a very good impression on him.

The 11th of March. The half year old child of the sick Mrs. Grimmiger has been brought to our place for its care, because there is little opportunity for it out there. Mrs. Rieser has accepted it, and she will receive something from the poor-box for the trouble she must have with it by day and by night. She is a good and conscientious woman, and the baby will get better care from her than from the woman at Red Bluff. The father of the child brought it himself; and he could not give enough praise to the divine goodness, which he could distinctly feel through this providing for his child. Like his wife, he is still very ignorant in matters of the Christian religion; but he is truly honest, good, and eager for the salutary doctrine. I lent him the *Schaitberger*,[115] which he is to give to a certain man out there who will read to him and his wife from it because their condition does not permit them to be with us for the memorial service and for the public worship on Sunday. He cannot read himself, but he was very pleased when I told him that we would give him an opportunity to learn to. With spring on the way, people once again are being overcome by various weaknesses, most of which are attacks of scurvy and swellings. The changeable and mostly cold weather contributes a great deal to this. [Should the poor people's current miserable circumstances become more difficult, as they promise to, the new hardships and especially the spiritual distress might bring even more sickness and death. The people wish for once to come to some order and certainty concerning their land. They also want to enjoy the rights and liberties of other Englishmen in the country, as has been promised to them orally and in writing. Since they know that these are simple peasant people who have enjoyed and still enjoy many benefits, they do not have any scruples about inflicting all kinds of burdens upon them. However, God still lives and He is no respector of persons.]

The 12th of March. Schweighofer is again a very troubled and burdened sinner who cannot find comfort in his knowledge of the great wretchedness of his sins. He thinks that he is indeed the greatest of sinners and that no promises will stay with him, although he prepared his heart for them with sighs and prayer. The Holy Writ and those chapters from Arnd's *True Christianity* which formerly provided him with so much comfort and edification now seem to be against him, he says; and his prayers and sighs appear dry and without force. When he had gone to confession and Holy Communion the last time, God had given him grace so that he could recognize, regret, and deplore all his sins; and he had been able to feel distinctly the comfort of God, which told him that all was forgiven him for the sake of Christ's blood. But now he was as restive, he said, as is written in the 88th Psalm. Only this was left to him that he believed God had not abandoned him completely, for his heart still had enough strength to give himself over completely to God and to trust Him that He will still make everything right with him.

As he had also talked about the 88th Psalm with my dear colleague yesterday, I read it to him and showed him briefly that here the Lord Jesus was praying in his terrible suffering as it was His task to do penance for the sins of all men, and consequently also for his, the patient's. The Son of God had done penance for all the sins which he now felt so bitterly; and, if He still let him feel something of their repulsiveness, He did not mean any harm by it but wanted to draw him with this burden closer to Himself, the doctor and helper, so that, as a wretched and miserable one, he could be refreshed all the more later. I also read him part of the 69th and 22nd Psalms and especially applied to him those of their verses that offer and give the dearly redeemed grace of Christ to the poor and the wretched. I also gave him a number of verses from the New Testament and asked: 1) whether he knew of a single example in which the Lord Jesus had refused to accept a great sinner? 2) whether he knew a verse in which penitent sinners, no matter how great their wretchedness appeared to them, are refused the grace of God? etc. He gave a tearful and weak "No" in answer to both questions. I affirmed this and said that I could prove the opposite to him from the writings of the Old and the New Testaments, namely, that God had saved all poor sinners through Christ and had promised them grace in His order, also that He had accepted and saved the greatest of sinners and thus had given sufficient proof of His unbounded mercy through Christ. The verses were 1 Timothy 2: 4–6; Titus 2: 14; 1 John 2: 1–2; Micah 7: 18–20. The examples were Paul, who in 1 Timothy 1 had received mercy as the greatest of sinners whom God used as an example for others who are also great sinners, and Peter, who had enjoyed many exceptional physical and spiritual benefits from Christ yet had denied this faithful Saviour three times in a terrible way, with much damning and cursing; but in spite of this the Lord thought of him with great friendliness immediately after His resurrection, without giving him a single word of reproach about his grave sins, etc.

I told him that the Lord is just as friendly toward him and that he only needs to look at His promises. Of the things he reads in the Bible or hears from it he must imagine that God and Christ are standing before him and are calling these promises out to him. I also asked him what he would think if the Lord Himself were to speak to him and comfort him, and whether his heart would not be satisfied with that, telling him that he should look upon God's promises in that same way; for, when giving them, He is speaking to us. He knew the verse which I told him: "He that heareth you heareth Me."[116] Thus, if a teacher deals with souls in the name of Christ, it is as if the Lord Himself were doing it. He should look upon the present state of his heart not as a sign of anger but as one of the grace of God. To look upon oneself as a great sinner and to look upon one's sins with aversion and grief is not the work of man. He had said himself that comfort would come if only he continued sighing for it; he knew that we have an Intercessor and that his dry and weak prayer would receive the greatest force from the highpriestly prayer of Christ. God wants the kind of prayer that comes from an anguished heart. Such prayer accomplishes the most when it appears to have the least force, as he could discover in Arnd in a number of places. I read him the hymn: "Lord Jesus Christ I cry to Thee from my deeply anguished soul, etc.";[117] and I prayed with him and his wife.

Our dear listeners came home from work early today. Consideration of the seventh petition[118] was scheduled for evening prayer, and this gave me an opportunity to give them a brief introduction to the [correct] celebration of tomorrow's memorial and thanksgiving service. I briefly went over the meaning of this petition in catechitical form and then reminded them of what I had told them several times during the reading of the letters, namely, that the misfortune we have met here since our voyage has moved many pious Christians [and teachers] in London and Germany and has caused them to pray for us. I continued that God had already heard our prayers and had helped us over so many misfortunes that we must marvel at it. In doing so I led their thinking to their own special experiences and showed how this knowledge that God had saved them from so many difficulties should be put to use; 1) It should serve for the grateful remembrance of the help and benefits received, etc. 2) It should lead to childlike trust in further help: The God who has helped so far and has lightened many a burden is still alive and is still as kind, wise, and almighty as He has been since eternity. We will still have to experience many a misfortune in this life, but also much divine help, etc.; and in all difficulties we must employ no other weapons than the weapons of Jacob and all the martyrs, namely, prayer and tears, Hosea 12: 5, if we do not wish to make our misery worse. 3) They should use tomorrow to recognize the evils of sin fully and to rid themselves of sin in the order of true conversion, especially since it was true that, in spite of their frequent listening to the Word of God since the last memorial celebration, some of them became better, but their badness had become greater; and for that reason the festival day should also be a day of penance for them, etc. I also reminded them of our earlier memorial and thanksgiving celebrations with a brief application of the texts, Genesis 32: 10 "Lord, I am not worthy etc." and Psalm 50: 14–15, "Offer thanks unto God and pay thy vows unto the most High."

Toward evening the post for Charleston again went through our town after having stayed in Savannah for a long time. If we had expected it, we would have sent our letters and diary to Charleston. The man did not wish to wait, and one of us will therefore go to Savannah for this purpose at the beginning of next week. The pitiful circumstances of the third group also make this trip necessary.

The 13th of March. The people who went to Abercorn last Monday to get their belongings could not attend the sermon and catechization of our thanksgiving and memorial service because they did not return until evening. But they made use of the review lesson and prayer hour. Most of the people of both sexes who were not needed for the care of the sick at Red Bluff came here yesterday and today for the purpose of hearing the Word of God. The morning text was taken from Hebrews 11: 8–10. It was used to speak about the godly conduct which believers show even under the most difficult circumstances of this worldly existence. This afternoon's text was 1 Peter 1: 17–19. From it my dear colleague presented to the listeners two motives for Christian conduct pleasing to God. Instead of the epistle we read Genesis 12, in the morning. In the afternoon, instead of having the children recite the catechism or Biblical verses after the first hymn as we usually do, we had them recite the 118th Psalm.

Monday, the 15th of March. This morning the big boat had to be sent to Savannah for the purpose of getting provisions for the newly arrived people. [Mr. von Reck had promised to ask either Mr. Causton or Mr. Oglethorpe to have the provisions for the people sent here because this hardship with our clumsy boat deprives

them of strength and time for work. But he must not have succeeded with his request and representation, because we waited all
last week in vain. Because of that, the people would have died of
hunger if we had not bought some pigs for them and if the Salzburgers had not advanced them their small reserves of rice, beans,
and corn. I have now also written to Mr. Causton about this latter
distressing point and asked for prompt help. I also informed him
that the distribution of the provisions for the first Salzburgers
comes due on March 29th and asked him to inquire of Mr. Vat,
who has locked everything securely in the store-house, if there are
enough provisions on hand and to advise me how the distribution
of these provisions should be conducted at the designated time.
So that these and other necessary things would not again be postponed too long]. my dear colleague went to Savannah himself in
order to tend to this and to some other matters. He took with him
our diary from the 11th of January to the 13th of March, in addition to some letters to Court Chaplain Ziegenhagen, to Mr. Newman, and to Mr. Vernon. He will put them into safe hands for
delivery in Charleston.

May God continue to hold His hand over our diary and letters
as He has done in the past according to His fatherly goodness.
I see it as a special sign of divine providence that, in our present
circumstances, He has let some Indians come into our region who
are bringing whole deer to our place in order to swap them to the
people for rice, beans, syrup, etc. To our great surprise and upon
their own volition they brought three whole deer to our house,
one almost right after the other. With this deed God undoubtedly
wanted to give us a clear hint that we should share these with the
sick and others who are in need but have nothing. I am told that
some of the listeners, who pay attention to the ways of God, have
been strengthened in their trust in the living God who does not
let anyone perish who waits for Him. Our Heavenly Father receives much praise from the sick for this benefit. May He be pleased
by it, for Christ's sake, and continue to let us experience His
fatherly care.

Hernb. [erger], the tailor, has been bedridden for several days
because of a great physical weakness. It remains to be seen whether
God will give him back his health. Mr. Zwiffler is working diligently. The increase of his knowledge of the great salvation in
Christ is remarkable. All the while he is getting smaller and more
insignificant, poorer and more wretched in his own eyes; and he
praises God for the present benefit of the cross, because he can
distinctly feel its spiritual usefulness. Upon visiting him I took

the opportunity to get information about the divine guidance he
had had in his earlier life; and he related the following point in a
very moving and quite edifying manner: He had experienced many
secret promptings of God in his early childhood so that he fell
upon his knees under the open sky and prayed to Him to let him
know the right religion, and to let him see some of the Lutherans
of whom he had heard such ugly descriptions. God had seen to it
that he learned to read in his ninth year and was sent by his parents
to learn the tailor's trade. After his years of apprenticeship he was
sent into the world as a journeyman. His family gave him a rosary
and a Gertrudebook[119] to take with him, but the verses of the
saints and the prayer directed to them had seemed suspicious [and
idolatrous] to him so that he paid little attention to it. Instead it
had seemed to him that God, who lives in heaven and for whose
holy Majesty he felt a secret respect, must have prescribed a better
way to serve Him, etc.

His first journey had been from Bavaria to Hungary, where he
had been led astray among [the Imperial] soldiers. But through
God's wondrous guidance this school had taught him the better to
see that the Popish religion is full of errors and doctrines of man
and that the Protestant-Lutheran religion shows the right way to
salvation. He had been stationed in Transylvania; and there he had
had the opportunity to hear some good sermons, although his non-
commissioned officers gave him many blows for doing so. But as
long as he could hear good sermons and see only bad examples he
could not be certain. Instead, he had many reservations about the
truth of the Protestant-Lutheran doctrine until God let him become acquainted with a pious farmer who had acquired a Bible
[from Saxony] for a large sum of money. He told him about the
grief of his mind and was led by him to read the Holy Writ. It
penetrated his heart like a thunderclap when he read: "Thus
speaketh the Lord, etc." And then, when he compared the Popish
rules with the divine pronouncements, he found a difference between them as between day and night. [He said that he had had a
remarkable dream before the above-mentioned farmer showed him
the way to better understanding. It seemed that he had been in a
church in which the preacher had stood at the place of the altar
before a table in a bright light, whereas the place where he was
standing was so dark that he could have grasped it. He said that he
could clearly see into the light from this darkness and saw the
preacher holding in his hand a chalice which he held out to him
(the tailor) while reciting the *verba instutionis ex ore Christi*.[120]
At this point such a thunderstorm arose that it caused him to

awaken, but he immediately fell asleep again. After that the chalice was handed to him for a second and third time and always with even greater thunderstorms. When he related this dream to the above-mentioned citizen, he gave him good courage and said he was not far from the Kingdom of God, etc.]

He had much to suffer from [the Jesuits and especially from] his father confessor, to whom he confessed frankly, first at the confessional and later in writing. After getting away from his military service he had much to suffer in Lutheran countries from false Christians. They treated him meanly and said that people who have renounced the religion in which they were baptized are worth nothing, for one must stay with the one in which one was born, etc. Others constantly urged him to go to Holy Communion (without ever looking upon the condition of his heart).[121] And, since he did not want to go along with other journeymen but rebuked their impudence instead, many dark clouds had gathered about him. Subsequently, God had given much blessing to the service rendered him by the late master Schwedler, of which he gave some specific details. His love for his family then drove him back to his fatherland, where he worked on his parents, not without divine blessing. He knew that, although her knowledge was still weak, his mother had died believing in the Son of God. He did not have the same assurance about his father's death, because he had been abroad at the time. But he had heard from his uncle, the brother of his father, that he had not wanted to die as a Catholic. This cousin of his had expressed displeasure with him on account of that.

During his travels as a journeyman he had had an opportunity here and there to do some good; but he had not been very effective, especially among the young journeymen, because most of them had been quite drunk with the lustful spirit of youth. His mother had had some close relatives in Rome and he had gone there twice, partly because she asked him to do so and partly because he was curious to know (how matters stood there) [122] and what sort of people he would find the relatives of the Pope to be. [whether the life of the Pope's relatives was as wicked as described in the Revelation of Saint John and other books.][123] He had found the wickedness and uncommon blindness to be much greater than he had imagined. He had worked in secret on his relative [mother's brother] there, who was a rich baker, without letting him know that he was a Protestant. An opportunity for that came through a Protestant book this baker had in his house. When some truths from it had shone too brightly into his eyes, he had taken the book from him saying that he wanted to read it himself; for he could not believe that this or that was written in it because he had read these gospels many times himself, etc. But this man had been submerged so deeply in avarice and ignorance that no salvation was possible.

From his own experience he has given me such a good description of the numerous clergy with its riches and its life of pleasure [avarice, debauchery, malice, and hypocrisy] and of the extreme poverty of the peasants and other subjects of the Pope, that I was surprised. He said that in Rome no citizen had his own house but everything belonged to the Cardinals and their followers who extracted large sums of money from it. He said that St. Peter's church there was of uncommon size, so large that several pastors could preach in it at the same time without interfering with each other. The pulpits are on wheels and they are rolled to the place where the most people are assembled. He said he had a Popish brother in N, [Hungary, not far from Temeswar] who, for the sake of the truth, had treated him very harshly at the beginning. But toward the end, after he had read and explained to him several times the gospels which he had in the house, his prejudices had nearly disappeared; only his love for money and for a life of ease had kept him back from public confession and emigration.

Because in most places he had [often] found [no upright pastors or true Christians anywhere but had found] the life of the Christians to be contrary to the teachings of Christ and the apostles, he had been tempted to fall in with some erring people whose conduct appeared to be good. But since he had made the Word of God into the guiding star of his faith and his life, neither epicures nor pharisees had been able to do him any particular damage. [Near Nürnberg he had heard Zuchtfeld and read some of his writings. Likewise, he had been in Herrnhut for several days. To be sure, he had not found in either party the evil that was said of them nor had he taken part in their own ways. He was pleased that I could give him a report based on my own experience, both about Zuchtfeld and the disorders he caused here and there and about the Herrnhut Brethren, institutions, and aims of Count Zinzendorf.]

Tuesday, the 16th of March. All day yesterday we had cold and rainy weather, and even a few hailstones started to fall. During the night the wind turned completely to the north, and after that it became nearly as cold as it had been during the coldest nights of this winter. Thus my dear colleague will have a very difficult trip, for so far there is no opportunity for us in Savannah to spend the night with decent people. Between 7 and 8 o'clock yesterday we had such a total eclipse of the moon that I cannot recall ever having seen one like it. Mrs. Brandner brought a young daughter into this world yesterday. She was baptized this afternoon and was named Maria. Earlier the woman had been in a very serious and dangerous condition, but God showed His goodness and faithfulness so wondrously that all of us had to acknowledge to His glory that we have a God and Father who can do infinitely more than we ask or understand. Much praise also was given Him for the Essentiae dulcis which was sent us recently from Halle for our own use.

The wolves about our place are still doing much damage to the Salzburgers' livestock. A few days ago they killed several pigs not far away from the houses, and they have even entered the stalls. In the field they have gone right into the midst of cattle and calves, and only yesterday they devoured a cow which had strayed back from the herd and had remained in the forest for the night. The people have made great efforts to shoot and kill some of them, but so far not much has been accomplished. Besides, they are not in Ebenezer because of the work at the new location for the town. The unmarried men took their pigs and fowl out with them yesterday, because they want to establish their households there. Otherwise, they would have to leave their livestock here without sufficient supervision.

Wednesday, the 17th of March. Yesterday afternoon I visited the sick and the rest of the workers at the new place. At evening prayer I edified myself with them from the Word of God. Mrs. Grimmiger's sickness has progressed so far that she is near death. I prayed over her several times with the people who had assembled and commended her to the eternal mercy of God, who abandons no soul because He loves all of them too much. One woman, who in my absence had read her several accounts from Schaitberger, praises in her that she was very attentive and showed great eagerness for the reading. Some other sick persons from the third transport are demanding Mr. Zwiffler, and he intends to go out to them tomorrow. The people [have become very confused in their house building through an order left behind by Mr. von Reck, for which reason they have had to do this new and completely unnecessary work.] are building their little houses with long shingles (or clapboards). They are building them so solid, nice, and spacious that I would not hesitate to live in them myself. At the end of this week they will start with the building of a solid little house for me so that my family and I can move out to them completely. They have no iron nails or other things usually considered necessary for building houses, yet everything turns out very well. This teaches us that we can do without a number of trades and arts that were developed gradually, more for comfort than out of necessity. Our manner of living up to this time and the many inventions of the people have given me a very impressive picture of the manner of life and work of the Patriarchs.

After evening prayer I distributed to the people the mulberry trees which Governor Oglethorpe had given us.[124] Each family received one, and this small present gave them much joy. Under all these difficult conditions they work with such pleasure, good order, and calmness that one must be very pleased with them. [In my absence Mrs. Rheinländer once again poured out the evil and perverted base of her heart, both yesterday evening and this morning, through scolding and slandering. She has not had the slightest cause for that except that she was denied her worldly claims and selfish petition, which are partly from ambition and partly from avarice. We are now living in the Lenten period, and we want to endure this abuse, which concerns me too, all the more willingly for the sake of our Redeemer's Passion and through His power so that we will not give this highly miserable woman the slightest appearance of self-revenge. She has already been informed long since, as well as recently, that we will have to use real sternness and discipline on her, since she will not let herself be brought into Christian order through God's Word and through the many physical benefits that we have let abundantly flow to her and her family according to 1 Peter 2: 15. We have to put up with the fact that all kinds of people came along in the third transport who do not match the simple Salzburgers and Austrians, because by divine dispensation it may serve either to their or to our best interest. However, I realize in many cases they were accepted without the knowledge or consent of Senior Urlsperger and other worthy patrons in London. A few were picked up here in this country and brought to us with the third transport, and Mr. Oglethorpe still does not know anything about this. We have not failed to make oral presentations to Mr. von Reck.]

For several days the sick Schweighofer has again been singing the words of the 103rd Psalm: "Bless the Lord, O my soul, etc., Who forgiveth all thine iniquities, etc. Who redeemeth thy life from destruction, etc." His heart is again right with God. He has started on Arnd's *True Christianity* and can hardly read enough of it despite the weakness of his body. His wife is now able to get around better than before. Thus God gives strength to one spouse to wait on the other when he is sick. Both of them have noticed this to the praise of divine kindness.

Thursday, the 18th of March. Yesterday evening, after the prayer hour, I learned that Mrs. Grimmiger had died soon after my departure. I will therefore go back out today and make arrangements for her burial. Yesterday we selected a convenient place outside the city for our cemetery. As was done in Ebenezer, the people will surround it with a fence to protect it from pigs and other animals. This morning my dear colleague returned home in good health. Mr. von Reck returned to our new location in the same boat. The big boat with the provisions will follow. [Mr. Vat is there again and, as Mr. Causton said to my dear colleague, is alone to dispose of the provisions because they could not be entrusted to Mr. von Reck.]

Friday, the 19th of March. In answer to my recent letter Mr. Causton has sent me word by my dear colleague that I should encourage the spirits of the last people, for after his return Mr. Oglethorpe will take care of them just as he has the first ones. But he has neither boat nor men to send the provisions for them and for the rest of the Salzburgers. Therefore the last as well as the first members of the congregation will have to take turns in transporting the provisions from Savannah. [In doing so, however, they will lose even more time and strength, because it is uncommonly difficult to travel upstream with the clumsy boat that is blunt and without a cutting edge up front but very broad underneath like a chest. For that reason we have made sufficient complaint and hope that it will be terminated. But the provisions for the next quarter will have to be fetched with it first.

[Mr. von Reck related recently that Mr. Spangenberg traveled to Pennsylvania a few days ago and Mr. Nitchmann (one of their pastors who has just newly arrived) journeyed to the Danish Islands of St. Thomas and St. Crux.[125] The former sent us word many times before his departure that he wanted to visit us once more in Ebenezer. However, he hesitated because he could probably notice that we disapprove *verbis et factis*[126] of his and his Herrnhut Brethren's obvious separation from the Lutheran church and their scorn, yes, downright contempt of the ministerial office, and that we can well do without such people. I cannot help but marvel at the Tübingen response (of which Mr. Spangenberg, as opposed to me, declared Professor Bilfinger and not Dr. Pfaff the author) [127] in favor of the Count and his establishments. After all, it is certain that Mr. Spangenberg and his people in Savannah are genuine Herrnhuters and followers of the Count. By virtue of the general contents of the above-mentioned response, they are to be considered members of the Lutheran church, to which they all confess from their hearts (as Mr. Spangenberg once wanted to convince me contrary to all evidence and personal experience.) [These people openly despise the ministry, the preaching of the Divine Word, the use of the Holy Sacraments and especially of the Holy Communion, which they distribute among themselves; and they have probably been trying to stir up animosity in others against us ministers in Ebenezer and our office. We will leave it to others to judge whether one can believe these people without sinning against his conscience and the truth, or whether he might not rather clearly recognize a crude hypocrisy in such unfounded claims. Meanwhile we let them go their way, since they do not respect our office. We have already told Mr. Spangenberg that which was most urgent.

[The carpenter Volmar, who came over from London with the Herrnhuters and was picked up by Mr. von Reck, now has to earn the five pounds passage-money in the service of these people. He said that otherwise he would gladly be with us for the sake of God's Word. He told me that Court Chaplain Ziegenhagen at the Georgia-Office recommended him and thereafter he was accepted like any other colonist. But now he said he could not reconcile himself to paying the passage-money that was imposed upon him by Mr. Spangenberg and, at the latter's request, by Mr. Causton. Time will clarify which one is right.]

Saturday, the 20th of March. My dear colleague went to the new place today to edify the people there with God's Word today and tomorrow, as well as on Sunday. Most of them will come back here from work tonight, and we will have regular service with them here. We must wait and see whether the twelve people who are working with the big boat will arrive for the Sunday celebration. They have to relieve one another because they do not have much strength.

Sunday, the 21st of March. The Austrian Haberfehner is in a very dangerous and painful physical condition. But he is very well resigned to it and knows how to comfort himself in a fine way from the Word of God. [He has disclosed to me as well as my dear colleague some things that he said happened on the voyage and he did not want to keep on his conscience. They do not concern him but rather another person. God will give us wisdom to see into the matter, of which we can give no particulars, so that all spiritual and physical harm can be prevented.]

This evening between 8 and 9 o'clock, after our prayer hour, I was called to Schweighofer. I found him still fully conscious but in violent pain and engaged in a death struggle. The few people who had assembled fell upon their knees with me and cried to God for an early salvation for this dear man. His constant sigh was: Lord Jesus, please come, etc. Lord Jesus help me, etc. This sigh was soon heard, for he died not long afterwards and thus was saved from the misery of this life of which he had to taste a great deal. This morning he had been strong enough to come to church, but this changed very suddenly during evening prayer. As long as I have known this good man he has been a constant bearer of the cross, and God often visited upon him and his family much sickness, poverty, and other troubles all of which he bore well and still knew how to praise the usefulness of the cross for Christians. He had expected his end for some time, had set his house in order for a Christian death, and had made orderly arrangements for his worldly possessions to be passed on to his children.

He has always set a good example for the congregation with his earnest conduct as a Christian and his regular and devoted use of the means of salvation. He also worked for the betterment of his neighbor to the best of his ability. I learned some particulars of this only yesterday evening. According to his frequent testimony, he had received much benefit and furtherance of his knowledge of the Christian doctrine and the practice of godliness from his consideration of Luther's small *Catechism,* on which we have based our daily evening prayers for several weeks. And, as long as it was possible for him, he had never missed a meeting and had always urged his children to do the same.

He thought the greatest good deed that God did for him in his lifetime was that during his travels as a journeyman abroad He had brought him to the knowledge of truth and finally, after letting him experience many inner and outer temptations, had led him not only from Popery into His kingdom but also into solitude here in America, where he and his children could have constant instruction and comfort from the Word of God, and where he did not have to worry about his children after his departure from this world. He had lost his temper several times, but each time he was almost immediately so sorry that he shed bitter tears and asked the forgiveness of the people who had been scandalized by it. He never was able to keep quiet about anything that his conscience found to be wrong with himself or with others, and he always spoke up freely. His chief consolation at all times, and consequently at the time of his demise, was that the Son of God had suffered for his sins, and he was doubtlessly glad that the good Saviour was freeing him from the passion and suffering of this life during this time of His Passion and sending his soul into the church triumphant.

His wife is very much grieved over his departure, because she lost in him a pious and industrious head of the house and devoted reader (for in times of her physical weakness he read to her regularly from the Bible, Spangenberg's *Postill*,[128] Arnd's *Christianity*, and *Schaitberger*). She would like to follow her husband soon, having had a great desire for her salutary release for some time. But now she has regained so much strength that she was able recently to serve as midwife when Mrs. Brandner was in childbed, although her right side, and consequentally her right arm as well, have been afflicted by a stroke. As said woman in childbed tells us now, she had for some time been praying to God to give back to Mrs. Schweighofer enough strength so that she would not have to have anyone else for her childbirth. Since God has done so, she looks upon it as proof that He has heard her prayer and she uses it for the strengthening of her faith.

Monday, the 22nd of March. R. [Ruprecht] Z. [Zittrauer], who had recently been excluded from the congregation for his offense, came to see me this evening and told me how much he regretted having committed the sin of drunkenness. He said that this sin and his subsequent exclusion from the congregation were resting so heavily on his mind that he could enjoy neither food nor drink and that he returned from the field to Ebenezer every day with fear and trembling. I had meant several times to speak with him in private, but various affairs prevented me from doing so. And a few times, when I was free, he [as herdsman of the congregation] was not. Now it is all the better that he came on his own free will to give evidence of his penance. This week he is to come to me often, whenever I am at home, so that I may pray with him and help him with necessary instruction from the Word of God. On this visit I told him, among other things, that he must show his repentance not only to me but to the entire congregation whom he had scandalized. Indeed, he must prove that he is serious and truthful with his repentance and conversion.

Tuesday, the 23rd of March. Now that the Salzburgers have finished their little houses as well as they could in this haste, they are beginning to fence in the land for the gardens and to clear it of bushes and trees by joint labor. If they were not being slowed up in their work by transporting provisions and of corn, bean, and potato seeds, they would be able to clear a large tract of land by the beginning of May, when it is still early enough to plant. They would like very much to do so. This morning nine men again had to take the small and the large boat to Savannah to get provisions. The congregation had decided to erect a well built little house for me so that we would not need to make the trip out there so frequently. But we prefer to put up with some inconveniences until after the good people get their seeds into the ground, so that the authorities will have no reason to be angry with them.

[We hope that, when Mr. Oglethorpe rightly sees the diligence and patience of the Salzburgers under all afflictions, he will not fulfil Mr. Vat's repeated prognostication that they will have to tear down again the houses they built with bitter effort and draw lots again for their house lots, since at present we cannot anticipate the slightest reason for this troublesome change. Only time will tell whether it is as favorable here in this country for the Salzburgers as alleged by mouth. We see quite clearly that some look upon the new settlement of our people with envious eyes.

[The provisions are being reduced not only for the last transport but also for the other two. From now on they will receive only four pounds of meat weekly but no flour, butter, cheese, vinegar, salt, spice (a kind of pepper), or sugar. In place of these they are supposed to be given only six more pounds of Indian corn and beans for the entire quarter. Thus, much will be taken from them in their hard work. According to mental calculation and rough estimates they probably will not have enough to eat, especially if they have children. So far, even with the provisions they have received, they have had to buy various things. What will happen now? Besides, in Mr. Zwiffler's estimate, the English weight is lighter than the German.]

Praise be to God, who has sent us some money for the poor in the congregation through the dear Court Chaplain Ziegenhagen and other benefactors, so that we are able to assist them in their need. If we had not been able to use this poor-money to purchase flour and butter for the sick of the third transport, they probably would have perished. But as it is, the friendly God who looks upon the lowly has received much praise. Until now the people have labored in uncertainty, not having any good and properly surveyed land. They have torn their clothes and have spent most of their money. Thus it is of particular benefit to them if they are now given some clothing and other necessary things. The almighty Lord who kept His people clothed and fed in the desert and, at the time of the New Testament, also fed several thousands with very small supplies, is aware of our poverty and need. He also recognizes that we have it not on account of laziness and wastefulness but in accord with His wise council and holy purpose. His power and strong force are so great that we cannot lack a single thing. [Meanwhile we shall not fail to report the honest people's poverty and painful circumstances to the proper place and then be quiet.]

Already on our sea voyage we read to our congregation the short hymn: "My soul submerges, etc." P. 11, p. 734.[129] God examines us now and then to see whether it comes from the heart. It is easier to talk and hear about patience before the trials than it is to practice it afterwards, when need has arrived. But our true God also gives plentifully when spiritual need exists. [The curtailment of provisions is supposed to extend to all colonists.]

Wednesday, the 24th of March. Last night Haberfehner thought that his end and hour of death were very near. My dear colleague was called to pray with him: but afterwards he recovered somewhat and continued to stay calm before God in his pain. His talks are very edifying, and they give testimony of the good treasure in his heart. He has a very fine knowledge and knows by heart a great number of verses which he uses very well to comfort himself. Mrs. Schweighofer is in very low spirits. She believes that the state of her soul is not pleasing to God because she can feel little earnestness and power in her prayer, and she sheds many tears because of that. She would like to spend the short time remaining of her life in good preparation for the journey home into the Heavenly Fatherland, but she is encountering many difficulties and obstacles. Her mental powers have been somewhat weakened since her stroke, and in dealing with her one must make many allowances for her weakness and simplicity in order to avoid doing harm. We are observing that this is being done by a number of pious women who are giving some help to her and her children in worldly matters. We are trying to assist her and her children with worldly gifts as much as we can. We wanted to take the smallest child, a little over three years old, into our care. This would have been a service to the mother, but it refused to leave its mother.

Thursday, the 25th of March. So many persons of the third transport, men as well as women, have gotten sick at the new location that we went to see them yesterday in order to assist them with their worldly and spiritual problems. Their need requires one of us to be there at all times to take good care of these poor people [or most of them will die.] Their feet and other limbs are swelling up and many of them have the beginnings of scurvy, weakness in all limbs, etc. On the journey back I received a letter from Governor Oglethorpe which refreshed my grieving spirits. These dear benefactors are sorry that matters have turned out so badly for the poor Salzburgers so far, as he has seen from my last letter, and he will earnestly work for their best interest. He is also very much pleased with our efforts on behalf of their physical and spiritual well being. He is giving permission to use the method of communal labor proposed and is satisfied with our intention to have a shed for the safe-keeping of provisions, but he is displeased with the surveyor's failure to survey our gardens. The people are to get a better boat, and upon my recommendation the last group of people are to get their provisions and tools on credit until the Trustees are able to confirm the arrangements. [He put me in charge of the provisions instead of Mr. Vat until some difficulties between Mr. von Reck and Mr. Vat can be settled. The latter will leave us completely.] Mr. Causton wrote to me at the same time in very friendly fashion. Praise God for His goodness, for not rejecting our prayers, and for not turning His goodness away from us.

Friday, the 26th of March. Today I wrote to Mr. Causton and Mr. Oglethorpe again to report on some matters concerning the congregation. The post came through our place; but, since both letters were not ready, I was able to send only the one to Mr. Causton. The other one will go next week to the Altamaha, via Savannah. Among other things, I reported how much the people have been able to accomplish already at the new location and how they have now started to work together on the part that is to be turned into gardens. [And, because Mr. Vat vehemently complained against the Salzburgers' disobeying the prescribed rules (as reported in Mr. Oglethorpe's letter), I made a brief apology, which was easy to make, because his complaints were refuted by all evidence.] I also asked what we should do with the old clothes [which Mr. Vat still keeps locked up] of two people that died recently and whether he would permit their being given to the poor.

Saturday, the 27th of March. The wolves about our place are increasing greatly in numbers and in the amount of damage they do. They devoured several pigs only recently, and the people would undoubtedly lose many more of their animals if they did not take them to the new location for better supervision. Toward evening they howl in an uncommonly ugly way. Only very few of the people are at home, much large and small livestock is still here, and many houses are standing empty. This is probably the reason why they are becoming increasingly bold. Mr. von Reck came to see me, partly to visit the sick here and partly to confer with me about the letters received. We bound ourselves anew to remain faithful to the Lord and to guide our people in such a way that the honor of God and their salvation will be furthered. [He is truly sincere and honest towards the people, and he is also highly esteemed by them.]

Sunday, the 28th of March. Since many of the people already have their houses at the new location, my dear colleague decided yesterday to go there once again in order to hold services there and also to be of use to the sick. Tomorrow, God willing, I intend to move out there for good, because necessity requires it. Stephan Riedelsperger is letting me have his little house; and I shall live in it until planting time is past, for then a good little house is to be built for me.

Monday, the 29th of March. Mr. Vat has changed his mind and does not want to transfer the matter of the provisions to me before he has express orders from Mr. Causton, even though he got them orally from him before. One single word in the letter from Mr. Oglethorpe, namely "till", is not clear enough for him; therefore, he has misgivings about resigning his office. This is a fresh example of his scrupulous nature. He has, as he says, requested his dismissal himself; and, since Mr. Oglethorpe very obviously consented thereto, he is still not satisfied with it and wants to have an explicit command. That is very likely a sign that he is not serious about his requested dismissal. He is very friendly towards me now, but he does not wish to hear anything at all about Mr. von Reck. He told me (perhaps in overhaste) that Mr. Causton read to him the letter I had received from Mr. Oglethorpe, because it has been sent to him open. Only Mr. Causton himself will know what reason he had for doing that. There is little profitable in it for Mr. Vat. Under a good pretence he still attempts to keep the people from their work at the new place. Hopefully, he will not succeed in that. I find it necessary to excerpt something pertinent here from my letter from Mr. Causton, which Mr. Vat himself brought to me:

> Mr. Oglethorpe having given me order to send, the provisions' for the Saltzburgher under yr. Care & to take your receipt for them, I beg the favour, you would be pleased to adjust with Mr. Vat, how much provisions, or other things have been issued or applied to the use of the last Saltzburghers, & give him your receipt, that I may charge them accordingly.

[In spite of this authority granted, Mr. Vat insists on distributing the provisions outside as he did today. Tomorrow he also wants to go out for the same purpose. I cannot comprehend his reason for giving the second transport some provisions, since their time is not due for two weeks and no one has asked for anything previously. Therefore, I asked him not to distribute anything to them because such premature and incomplete distribution would confuse me in the account and would also deter the people from their work. To miss one day from work now is a great loss, because the planting time is near. He paid no attention to my repeated request but called the people with the little bell. However, he had to put up with the

fact that no one came. The conclusion of the letter from Mr. Causton, in which he reported to me the amount of the present provisions, is a clear testimony in this matter. He wrote thus:

> I beg leave again to acquaint you, that the Allowance for these
> last Saltzburgh. is 200 lb. meat, & 342 bread Kind in Rice, Pease or
> Corn p head per ann. Also 1. qu. Molasses p week, 3 quarts Lamp-Oil
> p. Quarter and 1 lb. Spun-Cotton p year for each man. Also 1 qu. Mo-
> lasses p Week, 3 points Lamp-Oil p Quarter & ½ lb. pound Spun-
> Cotton p year for each woman.

[The expressions in Mr. Oglethorpe's letter which belong here
were:

> Mr. Vat has retired from the Care of the Stores at Ebenezer, having
> first protested against the Disobedience of the people to the Rules
> prescribed & complained of Mr. von Reck etc. I must therefore desire
> you to take Charge of the Stores, as shall be sent up, till the matter
> is Decided, & to give Receipts to Mr. Causton for all, that is delivered
> to you. Item. I have ordered Mr. Causton to give you the extraordinary
> Food to the Value of 10 shillings & tools to the Value of 20 Shill. Sterl.
> to such of the last Transport, as you Shall recommend, upon Credit,
> till the Will of the Trustees is known.

I am reporting these details only so that our friends and benefactors
will see that I am not forcing my way to these and similar material
entanglements but have a legitimate call to them and because Mr.
Vat is still acting hostile. His disposition is also becoming more and
more obvious from this.

Tuesday, the 30th, March. This morning Mr. Vat came out to the
new location and even here demanded to distribute the provisions
as he had done in Ebenezer. I had taken everything that was
brought here the last time into good custody, and this time I could
not consent to his claims. Neither could I behave passively, because
otherwise I would have acted against the orders of Mr. Oglethorpe
and Mr. Causton. Again I told him what I had already said in part
yesterday before my departure from Ebenezer; namely, that I reasonably prefer my written instructions to his alleged oral ones and
to all doubts that he bears because of a few of Mr. Oglethorpe's expressions. Once I had been given orders in this matter, I could not
cede them to him or anyone else without sinning against my superiors. I even read to him the expressions cited under the previous
date. But he protested against my taking over and distributing the
provisions, and he warned me of trouble: he said that Mr. Oglethorpe was wrongly advised and that he could not relinquish the
matter of the provisions to me because he had a lot to report against

me and would first have to settle our dissension. But he went back home again, because he could accomplish nothing with all his protestations and specious arguments.

[I was thus alone with him in my little house, and so he caused no vexation in the congregation with his outcries and protestations. I asked him for some information about how much he had distributed to the people yesterday so that I could be guided by it, but he did not wish to tell me anything. He showed malice towards the first Salzburgers by giving them nothing yesterday but badly salted beef. For lack of butter they need some pork fat. I shall see how I can remedy and improve this matter. He wants to travel today from Ebenezer via Abercorn to Savannah. Our big boat also had to depart for there because of the provisions; and therefore I sent along a letter written last Friday to Mr. Oglethorpe as well as one to Mr. Causton, in which I gave a report about the provisions received and also about Mr. Vat's recent obstinate behavior. The minister in Savannah, Mr. Wesley,[130] had written to Mr. von Reck that he had received orders from Mr. Oglethorpe to confer with him and Mr. Vat on account of their differences. He also asked if I would like to be present for this matter. However, because Mr. von Reck cannot get away now, I wrote to him in connection with the whole affair and gave him a brief outline of Mr. Vat's previous behaviour.]

Wednesday the 31st of March. Tuesday night we had a great thunderstorm with much rain, and last night it turned cold again. But the real cold and the frosts seem to have passed so that seed can now be put into the ground much more safely than before. Consequently, women and others are now occasionally busy putting various garden seeds into the ground. They build fences around it as well as they can because the men are now busy with their communal labor of clearing the land. Everyone is working with particular enthusiasm, and the work is progressing so well that it is a joy to behold. It is a pity that some have had to leave again yesterday on account of the provisions. [If they had only had permission to work here a month ago and had not been hindered by any other business and events, every family would have completed as much as they needed for their bodily sustenance, if God deigned to give a fruitful year. Thus they would soon and gladly relinquish the provisions to others.]

Mr. Zwiffler is sparing no effort with the sick here and in Old Ebenezer. He visits those here frequently and assists with bleeding and with medicines. I would have liked to have all of the sick together at this place so that I could help them more easily with physical care and attendance. The large shelter that was built for

the new arrivals who are now otherwise taken care of could have
served for this purpose. But Mr. Zwiffler did not approve this proposal for a number of reasons, and we will have to take care of their
misery in other ways. So far, they have been supplied with butter,
flour, tea, sugar, etc. But, since many of them must prepare their
own food because of an insufficient number of women folk here
and since the people still have no cooking utensils, our purpose has
not been accomplished. I have therefore decided to have something
cooked for them in a kettle or pot in my little house and to have it
sent out to them three times a day. I intend to give some small pay
to those who carry it to them. As the sick have received nothing so
far except the regular provisions, although their need has been reported to the proper place, I am writing to Mr. Causton again tomorrow. I do not doubt that he will send flour, butter, sugar, wine,
and some spices. [unless he takes recourse to actual new orders from
Mr. Oglethorpe and lets us wait and hope. All such things are already in the store-house at Ebenezer but still in the possession of
Mr. Vat.]

APRIL

Thursday, the 1st of April. [There are many malcontents among
the people Mr. von Reck brought along from Regensburg and to
whom he made too many promises. They speak rather coarsely and
cause me a lot of grief and trouble. Such people do not have the
sense of the upright Salzburgers in our community and, whenever
they think they are in the right, do not let themselves be set right
with remonstrances from the Word of God and other human reasons. Spielbiegler and his old mother, as well as Ernst, are evil-
natured people who, if they remain thus, can scarcely be tolerated
among us for long. There is such a confusion among the people in
the third transport that I am becoming worried and alarmed at the
annoyances that I take care of. As I learned only today, the said
Spielbiegler is supposed to have gotten drunk recently on the trip
to Savannah on rum that he obtained in Purysburg. I shall do with
him whatever conscience and office demand. Rheinländer was on
the same boat and is said not to have acted any better. However, he
is trying so hard to extricate himself from it that he probably will
pass the censure of the people, but not of God. There were two people from Purysburg with them, and I shall better inquire about the
truth from them.
[The causes of the great dissatisfaction among most of them are
partly things that stem from the trip and partly things that are not

yet sufficiently provided for them. They are lacking tools for farming and cooking utensils. Therefore, they must continually resort
to borrowing. I hope these difficulties will subside little by little as
soon as Mr. Causton has sent the aforesaid things to make up their
deficiencies.]

Christ, who was formerly a Jew, has frequent hemorrhages. He
has been advised to guard against all overheating and to refrain
from work until this evil can be checked with medicines and some
good physical care. He has a good disposition. His knowledge is
still weak but he loves the Word of God. He is an industrious worker, although he still lacks strength. All of the sick are happy, and
they thank God that nourishing soup is prepared and sent to them
three times a day. All of the present patients except Christ have the
same disease, namely, scurvy. They are: Bauer, Schmidt and his
wife, Leitner, Peter Reuter, and Cornberger. In Ebenezer Haberfehner and Hernberger are bedridden with the same illness.

Friday, the 2nd of April. I would like very much to start school
for the many children belonging to the third transport, but so far
I have not been able to find the time for it. As yet there are no living quarters available for schoolmaster Ortmann, otherwise he
would move out here. Except for Haberfehner's two girls and Mrs.
Holtzer's one girl, none of the children belong to the Salzburgers
or Austrians. Instead, they belong to the tanner Helffenstein, the
watchmaker Müller, and the shoemaker Ernstdorf.[131] These families were accepted by Mr. von Reck in Frankfurt, in London, and
here in Savannah. Many adults of this group need school and simple
instruction as much as the children, for they are very ignorant and
cannot read: but some of them are sick and others have so much
work to do that we will have to wait for a more opportune time.

Saturday, the 3rd of April. After the recent storm the heat has become rather great during the day. But the people are working very
bravely and in such good spirits that it is a pleasure to watch them.
I am taking the time to visit them often. In the three locations
which they are now preparing for gardens the soil is very beautiful.
A number of plants not known in Ebenezer are to be found here,
and there are many acorns and nuts everywhere so that the peoples'
pigs are very well taken care of here. The chickens are bringing a
better return here with little feed than they did there with much of
it. In the letter we received recently Mr. Oglethorpe had given permission for them to work in groups of six. But, since the letter arrived too late and the gardens had not been surveyed, they had already agreed to work in transport-groups and to clear as much land
as they can prepare by planting time, with the first group starting

on the left side of the town, the second on the right, and the third between them.

In the short time that is left it will probably not be possible to clear all gardens of trees and bushes, especially since they still have to work and fence several acres in Ebenezer. But they are determined to continue working in the present manner throughout the summer until each of the workers has a clear piece of land of two acres for use as a garden. I consider it a sign of divine providence that we requested Governor Oglethorpe to assign us gardens not of five acres, as in Savannah, but of only two acres. Otherwise, with the small strip of land on both sides of the town, only very few would have received good land close by, but now it is hoped that all can be taken care of. According to the content of said letter the first Salzburgers, who had suffered the most, are to get the closest and next-closest gardens.

We are now learning to understand what the Englishmen meant when they said that swamps contained the best land. They do not mean swamps or bogs as we had in Ebenezer, which lie low, are always full of water and cannot be drained. Instead, they mean dry and low cane-covered regions and valleys in which water does not stand except when it is raining and from which it drains off quickly even then. Or they mean those in which nature has provided a small canal in which the water from the two hilly, cane-covered places can drain off. We have such swamps here, and everybody would like to have them. [Here in this country one makes many *Fallacies compositionis* & *divisionis*.][132]

Sunday, the 4th of April. So far at this new location we have had to hold our daily prayer hour under the open sky. But now arrangements have been made to assemble in the boarded-up shed, which is now our storehouse. Many of the people left for Ebenezer yesterday and very early this morning to attend services there and to use the two boats to bring up some of their belongings tomorrow. In the morning we spoke about Jesus, the very best Provider, from the regular gospel, John 6: 1 ff. In the afternoon I continued with our consideration of the Passion story. Instead of a chapter from the Bible, I read to the congregation at the end of the service the 29th chapter of the 2nd. book of Johannes Arnd's *True Christianity*. This fitted in very well with the material discussed in the morning. Upon my suggestion, the congregation had brought said book for the purpose of reading along with me.

Kiefer, the herdsman from Purysburg, arrived last night with his two sons and attended our services all day long. He has exchanged his field and town lot for a piece of land nearly opposite us in Carolina so that he and his family will have the opportunity of receiving edification with us. He also intends to petition Mr. Oglethorpe to give him a building site near us and the fifty acres of land belonging to it so that he can live here and have his farm in Carolina.[133] Through this man a widow from Purysburg[134] asked that she and her three daughters be accepted at our place, but we had to refer them to Governor Oglethorpe. Women in this colony do not get or keep any land, so what could she do here?[135] She is the widow whose oldest daughter married the Salzburger Schweiger and who is conducting herself very well among us.[136]

Monday, the 5th of April. Yesterday afternoon our people returned with the big boat. They brought beef as well as fifty bushels of sweet potatoes for planting. The latter were distributed today, and they pleased the people very much because they were very beautiful. Mr. Causton wrote briefly that, in addition to these, he had sent fifty-eight bushels of sweet potatoes and one hundred bushels of corn to Purysburg for us. Our Salzburgers have gone there to get them. Mr. Causton received the people with great friendliness and told them that in the future only three men should bring the big boat down. He would get the necessary men to bring the provisions up. If this had happened a month earlier, their field work would have been a great deal farther along. He did not have time to answer my last two letters, because Mr. Oglethorpe's warship, that had been given up as lost, had arrived in Savannah and was being loaded with fresh provisions for the Altamaha. However, upon my written request, he did send along the sole-leather in addition to a few shoemaker's knives and awls for shoe repair, which had been sent to the Salzburgers from London. A package of vamp leather is supposed to have been sent also, but we have not received it so far.

My dear colleague visited us today and told me, among other things, that the two sick people in Ebenezer, Haberfehner and Hernberger, are cheerful and full of faith and lively hope in their difficult physical condition. Hernberger thanks God that he is with us and that he has been rescued from the dangerous conditions in which the people of his trade, masters as well as journeymen, find themselves in Germany. He would rather make peasant's clothes of linen here than costly garments there, because there much ungodly business is carried on along with it. The two of us also conferred about celebrating Holy Communion. I had written him I would announce to the congregation here that we would celebrate it in a week, and I had asked him to do the same there if any of the souls desired it. However, some people have let us know that they would prefer to do so at Easter because the hard work of this present planting season gave them too many distractions. We are pleased with this proposition. Meanwhile, we will still have Holy Communion here on next Sunday for those of the third group who made known their desire for it several weeks ago.

Tuesday, the 6th of April. In spite of all the careful attention given the sick here and in Ebenezer, most of them seem to be getting worse instead of better. Some of them appear to be as bad as the late Madereiter and Schoppacher had been, who died in spite of all the medicines that were used and the best possible care that was given. In addition to the patients recently reported, some new ones have begun to complain. Their sickness is starting as it started with the others. They are excessively tired and have pains in their feet. Mr. Zwiffler does not quite know what to do in these cases, although he makes every possible effort in other ways. [Many patients perceive *effectum contrarium* from his medicines.][137] He would be very thankful, he says, if some intelligent and experienced doctor would give him some instructions in this. The main trouble of the people is probably scurvy. Their teeth bleed freely and get very loose. They smell very badly from their throats. Some of them bleed heavily from the nose. Their legs grow stiff, the flesh on them disappears, and various spots appear on them after a while. Their faces usually swell up very badly or they become as pale as death. Some of them also have had bad swellings on their feet, and their sweat smells very bad. With many of them, the heart and upper portion of the body are quite vigorous, etc.

Our big boat will have to be taken to Savannah next Monday. I intend to go with it to get information regarding treatment of this disease from people who have been in this colony longer, and to ask for some things that are necessary for the physical care of those afflicted by it. There are flour, butter, sugar, and wine in the storehouse at Ebenezer, but Mr. Vat still has the key. If we had a sufficient supply of the very much blessed medicines from Halle we could use them to advantage in helping these dear people. They have great trust in them. We have had sufficient testimony of this. Just the day before yesterday, during the absence of Mr. Zwiffler, I had to give some of this medicine to a pious Salzburger who could hardly breathe because he had so much pressure and strain in his chest. During the night he felt its effect so much that he sent me good news in the morning and left his bed toward noon.

Wednesday, the 7th of April. Yesterday and today most of the women from Ebenezer came here to get sweet potatoes, which they wanted to plant there. The Salzburgers and those like them do not need in the least to be driven to work. On the contrary, I have to remind them frequently of the fifth commandment[138] so that they will not do damage or harm to their bodies with too much hard work. As soon as they return from their communal labor, which is about 9 o'clock, each one of them goes to his piece of land near the house to build a good fence around it and to plant something in it afterwards; or they make shingles until they are called back to their communal labor between 2 and 3 o'clock in the afternoon. The first quarter brought us some cool weather and intermittent rain. This is of great advantage in their work.

A few days ago S. [Schweiger] misbehaved again and scandalized a number of people with his conduct. This was reported to me by R. [Christian Riedelsperger] whom he had treated impolitely and through whom I sent S. [Schweiger] word that his rudeness grieved me very much, all the more because he had received frequent warnings and we had worked to improve him for some time. Last night he came to see me without having to be called. He complained and wept about his rashness and gave me an opportunity to give him many admonitions. Another pious man who lives with him told me that the sadness and new grief which he had given me with his present conduct had kept him awake the entire night and that he had made up with the other one on the same evening.

Thursday, the 8th of April. Two Englishmen called on me. They came down from the Cherokee Indians[139] and wanted to speak with Governor Oglethorpe. They expressed a great satisfaction in his wise decision to prohibit the sale of rum in the entire colony and also to the Indians, because it will eliminate many annoyances and provide a good avenue for the conversion of the heathens. They thought that the Creek Indians would probably be displeased with this order at the start, but they would not be able to engage in any hostile acts because said Cherokee Indians were very friendly with the English, particularly with Mr. Oglethorpe, while at the same time living in a state of constant hostility and war with the Creek Indians. The Creek Indians, to which the local Indians belong, are also at peace with the English at present. The two men gave me such a good description of the Cherokee Indians' way of life, their work, and their land, that I was surprised. According to this description their land is full of high cliffs, the soil is very rich and fertile without manure, the weather is cold in the winter and moderately hot in the summer. Their clothes consist only of large woolen blankets or skins which they wrap around themselves, but they live a much more orderly life than the local Indians. They do not tolerate rum or strong drink among themselves. They have their kings and war leaders. This position is usually achieved by one gifted with eloquence who has proved himself to be virtuous and brave. Their language is so different from that of the Creek or local Indians that the two do not agree on a single word. It can be learned easily and well from the Englishmen living among them. They also live from hunting, and they plant corn and raise many pigs and fowl. The Englishmen trade their wares to them for many deer and beaver skins, but the Muscovite beavers are much to be preferred to these. Except for peachtrees there are no fruit trees there, excepting those planted by the Englishmen. They know nothing about wine-growing, but the land is very well suited for it and beautiful grapes grow wild there as they do here. The men thought that wine-growing might be introduced there by arrangement of Mr. Oglethorpe.

Friday, the 9th of April. Our big boat did not return from Purysburg until today, although it had been sent there as early as last Monday to get the sweet potatoes and corn delivered there by Mr. Causton. The Savannah River is higher and swifter than it has been in a long time. The people have not been able to load everything on this trip. For that reason ten persons left again toward evening to get the remaining corn. At present going away comes very hard to the people because they would like to get their sweet potatoes, corn, and beans into the ground and to protect their own pieces of land, as well as the communal fields, with good fences. But they are being patient. A beginning was made today to distribute provisions for one quarter-year to the Salzburgers of the second transport. Mr. Causton himself will send that part which has not been sent so far; we only have to take the boat to Savannah. We hope to get a lighter boat soon, for Mr. Oglethorpe has sent orders to that effect to Mr. Causton. Such a boat does not cost more than twenty pounds sterling, and we hope to purchase it for our congregation. It will have to be paid for in money or corn within two years.

Saturday, the 10th of April. Bauer, an Austrian, is very weak physically and, since he thinks he may be allowed to leave this life unexpectedly, he told me in the presence of two persons what disposition he wants to make of his few belongings. He said he had nothing from his parents who are still sticking with Popery. What he possessed he considered a blessing of God received from good people and his own work. He wanted a piece of his clothing to be given to those who had shown love and kindness to him in spiritual and worldly matters. A widow, Mrs. Holtzer, who had shown him real motherly love in spite of her own physical weakness, was to get the greatest part of his possessions. He also wanted to let me have something, but I would not accept it for my own benefit. Instead, I told him about the poor-box, and he gladly made it over to it, particularly since he himself had received some help and care from it. His spirit seems to be in good condition. He wants to turn away from these earthly things soon so that his heart can feast solely on Jesus and he can prepare himself that much better for heaven. This evening we had preparation for a number of people of the third group who had reported for Holy Communion last week. Earlier two of the men had had trouble between them but they have made up in a Christian spirit, once in the presence of Mr. von Reck and once in mine.

[The watchmaker Müller, who came to the third transport in Frankfurt, intimated very clearly to me that he could not harmonize with the simple Salzburgers and their kind because they had little courtesy and manners in associating with people. He had noticed something about someone that seemed suspicious to him. For that reason he inveighed against the entire community of Salzburgers with a very rude judgment. He is a conceited gossiper and, like the others of his type, thinks that he is better than the plain and honest people in the community. I do not yet see how he will fare. He has a large family; and, since he himself cannot work on the boat and in other communal things, the people are supposed to render service to him and his family by bringing up provisions. This causes many difficulties. Mr. von Reck had ordered him and the tanner Helffenstein to distribute the provisions. Many of the people in the third transport complained about this and did not desist until I was put in charge of the distribution. We shall have our burden and worry with many from this transport, especially with those who were picked up from time to time on the trip.]

Sunday, the 11th of April. After the afternoon service I summoned those people of the third group who [along with Rheinländer] had gone to Savannah recently. I wanted to learn from them whether it was true that two of them [he and Spielbiegler] had got drunk on rum in Purysburg. They all confirmed it; and I shall use my official position against R. [Rheinländer], although he cannot be brought to recognition or confession of the scandal caused by this sin. Instead he tries to extricate himself from it with clever ideas and talk. The shoemaker [Ernstdorff] who had been taken into this group in Savannah is also said to have got drunk in Purysburg this week, to the annoyance of other people. I shall call the congregation together as soon as possible and warn every member against similar excesses. Then, if it happens again, I shall make such annoying matters and persons known to Governor Ogle-thorpe. I do not know whether it will be possible this week, be-cause I have to go to Savannah and also because many of the people want to prepare their fields in Ebenezer this week.

Monday, the 12th. My dear colleague came to see me today and brought me very good news about several people in Ebenezer. We both wish to be together at the same place again soon but we will have to put up with this separation until everyone has moved from Ebenezer to the new place and until a small house has been built for each of us to live in. At present I manage as well as possible in the cottage of a Salzburger. The people who have already planted their corn in Ebenezer are complaining very much about the birds' eating it up, because they cannot guard it as they did last year. For that reason some of them will probably let some of their land lie and plant only as much as possible here. The wolves there are also getting worse and much bolder. Thus, the sooner the better, the Salzburgers want to fence in a large place, to be used instead of a stable, and have a herdsman bring most of the cattle out here.

Tuesday to Thursday, the 13th and 14th of April. On the morn-ing of the 13th I went to Savannah in regard to some matters con-cerning the congregation. Mr. Causton again received me in a most friendly fashion. [Because Mr. Vat refused the request of Mr. Causton himself to give me the key to the store-house in Ebenezer until he received a new order and an answer to his letter from Mr. Oglethorpe], Mr. Causton gave flour, butter, wine, sugar, etc. for the sick from the store-house there. [since, otherwise, one could have fetched it closer to Ebenezer.] He [Mr. Causton] sees very well that good physical care is better for the sick than medicine. Our experience has confirmed this so far. The lying-in women and small children will also get a share of these special provisions. Mr. Causton told me that provisions for the first and second transports of Salzburgers had come to an end. Because they had to face special hardships, the first ones were to be supplied from the store-house for two years and the other for one year; anything they receive after this time they would have to pay for with money or some other way. Meanwhile, the provisions advanced at this time were to be a special benefit to be given only to those whom I recommend.

[To be sure I added little to that, but I shall write all the more about this affair to Mr. Oglethorpe. It is more a burden than a pleasure (as I assured Mr. Causton) for the good people to take their sustenance from the store-house in Savannah. Through divine blessing they would also no longer have to do that, if only they had been given good land initially, and had not had to squander so much time and strength in bringing up provisions and things. The promise given to the people regarding their maintenance they have in their hands, partly printed and partly in letters. The honorable Trustees undoubtedly will not go back on their word, especially since they gave Senior Urlsperger full authority to negotiate with the Salzburgers; and, whatever he promised was supposed to be ratified. I am very glad that I have a copy of this full authority with me. For them it is still unpleasant and a cause of a few distasteful decisions that we do not wish to remain in Old Ebenezer. However, with time everything will change.][140]

Thursday, the 15th of April. I have had it in no uncertain terms from Mr. Causton that he has received reports about the three people who got drunk in Purysburg. I myself expressed my grief to him about the mixed crowd we have now. [These people are: Rheinländer, Joh. Spielbiegler and Ernstdorff.] Mr. Causton thinks we would have been better off to stay in the Old Ebenezer instead of going to the present location on the Savannah river because Purysburg is near there and a lot of strange people will pass by who will infest our place with rum drinking, bad talk, and bad examples. [But it is easy for anyone to give an answer to this if he knows that the regular passage by land goes through Ebenezer from Carolina to Savannah and that Mr. Oglethorpe will see that the way through it is kept in good condition; item: that rum from Purysburg can be brought by dissolute people to old Ebenezer just as easily as to new Ebenezer. There are now more dissolute people among us who indulge in excesses, and hereafter the entire community must pay for it.]

At yesterday's evening prayer I had the whole congregation together, with few exceptions. I publicly expressed my grief at the three drunkards, although only one of them [namely, Spielbiegler] was present, the other two being sick. As the apportionment of provisions and other things will depend upon my recommendation from now on, I have indicated to all of them that disorderly people can expect no assistance, and that instead we shall make complete reports about their [provoking] conduct to Governor Oglethorpe. For the Christian and industrious people we expect to petition here and in Europe for additional provisions; and we expect our kind and worthy benefactors to decide to continue the provisions until the end of the harvest: but such objectionable people who blaspheme the Name of God and the gospel of Christ will have no part in this good deed. Instead, they will be made to pay for their provisions; for otherwise they would invest their money badly anyway, in rum or other disorderly things.

Although it is possible to prevent such excesses through fear of worldly punishment, we expect little change for the better from those who have been picked up now and then [and hastily assembled people of the third transport], for the Word of God can do as little with them as with others like them [Rheinländer and his kind] who have grown old and hard in sin and love of the world. [They are secret enemies of the Salzburgers and will no doubt indicate this clearly in due time. We have been told that many upright people and good workers, some in Augsburg and some in Lindau, wanted to go along but they could not be accepted because they were neither Salzburgers nor Austrians, nor people persecuted for the sake of the Evangelical teachings. We do not know where Mr. von Reck got his full power of authority to pick up people from time to time and bring them to our community.] While in Savannah I had hoped to meet Mr. Wesley, a pastor there, but he had gone to the Altamaha to see Governor Oglethorpe.[141] Meanwhile, he had left a very fine letter for me. In Savannah they now have prayer services in church every day, mornings and evenings; and on Wednesday they have a sermon or catechization. He is said to be most earnest in his pursuit of the duties of his office but also has to suffer his share for it. [The Herrnhuter in Savannah are said to be in good graces with him through Mr. Oglethorpe's recommendation].

Friday, the 16th of April. The physical care of the sick, and even more our poor prayers, have been so blessed by God that some of them have greatly improved. Whenever Mr. Zwiffler has been here he has [also] given splendid service with bleeding and doctoring, although some of them required little or nothing. Now our dear God has taken even better care of the sick because Mr. Causton has sent along wine, flour, butter, sugar, spices, etc., and, if possible, will also get us some fresh meat. [Even contrary to Mr. Causton, Mr. Vat refused to give me the key to the store-house in Ebenezer until he receives an answer to his letter from Mr. Oglethorpe.] The water in Ebenezer Creek is now so high that we can go there in the big boat. [and all the provisions lying there, as well as those Mr. Causton is keeping, could have been brought at one time with the same boat under my supervision and into my custody. On the contrary, the people must drag them a long way when the water is low. The superiors do not like to offend Mr. Vat very much. I wonder how well they know him.]

Saturday, the 17th of April. There are some quite large sassafras trees at our new location which would bring a great deal of money in Europe. At our Old Ebenezer we were able to find only roots and small bushes. This shows the difference in the soil. Some people also have found a long-leafed plant which smells like curled mint. They make this into a tea against scurvy and find it very useful. There are many herbs to be found here which look pretty and have a good smell, but so far we cannot make use of them because we do not know them. Next Monday the people will drive most of their stock up here. For that reason they fenced in a piece of land yesterday in which to keep the animals at night until after planting time when everybody can build stalls for them. Most of the people are already living here now. Only a few women and children will stay in Old Ebenezer to watch out for the seeds planted there and to wait on the sick. Everyone seems pleased with living here, and the air here seems to be healthier than there. May God guide the heart of Governor Oglethorpe so that he will soon have the gardens and the rest of the land surveyed for the people. The surveyor is now with him on the Altamaha.

Sunday, the 18th of April. I announced to the congregation that on Easter day Holy Communion would be served, here as well as in Ebenezer, to those who reported to me for that purpose. [Rheinländer came from Old Ebenezer this evening and called on me. He said he had been very sick again for several days and, since much had taken place in his heart and conscience, God had done a lot of good through this corporal chastisement. My dear colleague would be able to tell me a bit more, etc. I answered him very little about this and ordered him to come to me to speak in detail on another day. My time and circumstances did not allow this tonight. He is a gossiper and has often gone behind my back with his allegations; therefore, I attach little or nothing to his words. Tomorrow he is also moving here with his entire family. He is exceedingly poor and has a wife who still acts arrogantly despite all their wretched circumstances and decks herself with superfluous clothes. Still, one can convince neither him nor her that they are steeped in pride as in other vices, although it shines forth in all their looks, words, and behavior. Since the current provisions depend on my recommendation, I shall ponder very well whether I shall be helpful to this man and his family in this case, because so far little has been accomplished with them through charity.] Once again our faithful and loving God has given us a fine awakening through the magnificent gospel of His Son and the immeasurable grace gained by Him [with dear Mr. von Reck]. This provided me with much edification in a private conversation [with him] after the service.

[He earnestly renewed his resolution to sacrifice the rest of his life to his good Savior alone and to prepare himself truly for blessed eternity by complete denial of himself and the world. He gives a good example to the entire community during public worship. Gradually he is becoming sorry that all kinds of unsuitable people have come to our community and he has promised me to use all caution in accepting other people in the future and also to use all spiritual and physical powers in time to prevent all vexations among us before they become a raging current that is not easily stemmed. May our loving God purify him more and more from all precipitous resolutions and hasty decisions and direct his spirit to the advancement of the best for our community. So far he has acceded and taken our advice concerning matters that we have found more harmful than helpful to the congregation.]

Monday, the 19th of April. Cornberger was very sick with scurvy and had no thought than that he would die soon. But in the past few days God has strengthened him so much that he has been able to work a little in the early morning hours. Today he reported for Holy Communion and told me that once during his sickness he had sincerely sighed to God and prayed to Him for health. From that time on he had been able to feel in his body that his prayer had been heard. His great weakness decreased and he became stronger every day. Now he praises God for having brought him into this wilderness, where trials and various difficult conditions teach him to pay closer attention to the Word. Besides, he has more time and opportunity for it here than he did in his service even under good masters. He has one regret, namely, that he did not bring his sister who is in service in Oettingen. He intends to write a letter on her behalf to Pastor Preu so that she will apply to come over on the next transport.

Two young Salzburgers, Stephan and Christian Riedelsperger, asked my advice about marriage. They do not want to stay single and without a helpmate much longer because it does not help either their health or their household. Stephan Riedelsperger desires Catharina Valentin, who arrived here with the last transport. So far she has conducted herself in a Christian and virtuous fashion and everyone praises her for it. For that reason I could not advise him against it. Instead I told him to continue with earnest prayer and Christian reflection about such an important change. He had hoped earlier that a woman from Augsburg would come with the last transport if he had requested it, but she wrote him a letter to the contrary, which I made him show me.

I have had to advise Christian Riedelsperger against his plans because he had chosen a [German] woman [in Savannah] who [not only has gone over to the Reformed religion but also] is leading a disorderly life. I have had some details of this just recently [in Savannah from the mouth of Mr. Causton]. The information was very welcome to him because he had not known about these circumstances at all, and because his choice would have given him much misfortune.

Tuesday, the 20th of April. This morning I was called to see Bauer because he felt very weak and wanted to see me. As his end seemed to be very near, I fell upon my knees with those present and asked God for a blessed and happy release for this sick man. God heard us and took his soul to His rest after a short death struggle, while we were still praying. He was a good man. Because he expected his end some weeks ago, he brought his worldly affairs in order; and since that time he has paid no more attention to worldly matters. He never prayed to get his health back but only asked God to bring him real rest soon. Carpenter Sanftleben had taken him into his cottage; and Mrs. Holtzer, although very weak physically herself, had cared for him like a mother. The deceased had wanted to make sure to reward this love after his death, and for that reason he left both of them some of his belongings. He wanted to give a special reward to an Austrian, Schmidt by name, who had given him the opportunity to leave Popery.

The two of us are very much grieved at present over the indifference toward Christianity which we find to exist in a number of [many] people of the congregation. We are sighing to God, asking that in His grace He may bless our intercession and presentation of His Word, which surely is given often enough, so that all indifference will be wiped from their eyes and all may be brought to an earnest practice of Christianity. The people are letting themselves be kept from prayer, searching of their hearts, and spiritual vigilance, or at least they are letting themselves get lazy in these things, because of the great amount of work they have to do at the present time. They do not fail to come regularly to the prayer services and to the sermons of the gospel; but, without prayer, testing, and vigilance, they benefit little or not at all from them.

[Towards evening John Spielbiegler asked me whether I would admit him to Holy Communion. I had ordered him several times to come to me and also to present himself before the assembly of those whom he had offended by his drunkenness on the trip to Savannah. But he has excused himself because of the service and routine jobs of Mr. von Reck, whom he assists. Meanwhile, he has already heard publicly last Thursday in the prayer hour that which he would not allow me to say to him privately. Today I held up his disorder and scandal before him earnestly once more with the understanding that he would have to recognize and acknowledge his wickedness penitently beforehand and expirate the vexation he caused by serious atonement before he could be admitted to Holy Communion, which belongs to true Christians alone. He looked for many excuses to justify his behaviour. For example, he said he was not so drunk that he didn't know what he was doing, that he could still row, etc. There was another reason why he fell out of the boat into the water, etc. He could not hold very much, etc. He did not know what kind of rum it was.

[I received his excuses and insolence with frank words and pointed out to him that, according to the understanding of God and His Word, not only excesses and bestial swilling but also all intoxication and clouding of his mind, yea, all misuse of strong drinks, when one takes more than necessity requires, are drunkenness and sin. Since he heard that being drunk was just as bad as being completely intoxicated, he laid the blame on drunkenness: however, because I did not wish to admit him to Holy Communion but admonished him to true repentance, he became defiant in his demeanor. This caused me to warn him seriously about the wrath of God that he attracted through such actions and also about the outward troubles he would invite by his persistent evilness. I also reminded him emphatically not only of the serious sin of disobedience but also of that of defiance and great impudence towards his own old mother, about which she and others have complained to me. Those who knew him in Memmingen can tell a lot about his insolence and evilness.]

Wednesday, the 21st of April. Hans Schmidt, an Austrian, is a righteous man who takes his Christianity seriously and who sets a good example for everyone by his regular use of the means of grace and his Christian conduct. He had been sick but is now almost well again. His wife is still bedridden, but she too is improving. She cannot read, is very ignorant of things divine, and knows only a very few Biblical verses by heart, although her husband reads to her from the Bible and other good books regularly. He complained to me that she could not remember anything. I advised him to read to her the core verses of the Holy Writ, which I would send to him from Ebenezer, and to keep this up until she grasped them. He could tell me from his own experience how good it is in the hours of trial and grief to have a treasure of good verses in one's heart and memory.

[I have been told that Michael Rieser, who came over with the third transport, and wife commenced their marriage in an un-Christian and perverse way and that their child was the fruit of their disorderly life. Since they notified me about going to Holy Communion, I remonstrated with them about what was said to me. But they denied it and swore by their conscience that evil-minded people had only gossiped. I asked for a certificate from their father-confessor in Memmingen; but they said it was ruined in the boat because water had gotten into their trunks. The matter may be true or not. Anyway, both are of little value. His father was a Salzburger who had already emigrated a long time ago, while he (this Rieser) was still a little child.]

My dear colleague often gives me edifying reports on Haber-fehner's attitude on his sickbed. His heart is filled with respect and love for God, and he cannot wonder often enough about how it is possible that He can be gracious and accept a [such an ungodly] man like him as one of His children. All of his talks are full of strength and edification. His physical strength is declining fast, and he seems to be coming closer and closer to his blessed release. He has many good things to say about Mr. Kraft in Regensburg and his [godlike] zeal to add to the honor of his Saviour. The two patients in Ebenezer, Landfelder and Herrnberger, are getting better. Mrs. Landfelder, who is attending and nursing them both, says that fresh garden vegetables such as radishes, cabbage, etc., which she prepared for them, had done so much good that they could feel it distinctly. I have observed the same thing with the patients at our place, and some of them have told me about it themselves. May our good God again refresh those of our benefactors, as in Psalm 41, who with their gifts have enabled us to give good physical care to our patients. Without this our situation would look much more miserable.

Since we now have some good soil, the people soon will have garden vegetables, with God's blessing. They have fenced in the land around their houses and have planted it with sweet potatoes and sowed it with various seeds. The difference between this land and the land we had earlier can be seen very clearly by the way the seeds are coming up. Not only does everything come up faster, but the plants also are stronger and have larger leaves. However, on the little places where the people in Ebenezer have collected a great deal of manure they will also get good lettuce, radishes, cabbage, etc.

Thursday, the 22nd of April. Some time ago R. [Ruprecht] Z. [Zittrauer] was excluded from our Christian community for drunkenness after every other means had been exhausted. He has asked several times to be re-admitted, but we did not wish to hurry with this. Instead we wished to give him time for penance and remorse for his violation. Now he is again begging in earnest to be admitted to Holy Communion in the future. He is now as gentle as a lamb and seems to be serious about his penance and remorse. The congregation, especially a pious Salzburger in whose house he lives, is giving him good testimony. Thus, in accordance with the wish and approbation of every member, he was admitted as a genuine member of our congregation. We hope it will serve to impress and edify him.

The tailor Christ, who used to be a Jew, gives me much pleasure. He thanks God from his heart for having brought him here and for opening his eyes through the preaching of His Word so that he can recognize the main importance of Christianity and prepare himself properly for blessed eternity. He comes with great eagerness to the preaching of the Word of God on Sundays and during prayer hours and returns home awakened and full of praise for God. He also relates simply what the Lord is doing for him in His grace. His physical strength has been rather weakened by frequent hemorrhages, but he is proving to be faithful in his work as much as his strength permits. He cannot work in the fields, but he gives the people good service with mending and sewing. A Salzburger has let him have his own cottage for living quarters, and he is living in it now. However, since he should not be alone because of his unexpected attacks, I am trying to put him in with a pious family.

Friday, the 23rd of April. This day of Christ's death was solemnly celebrated with the congregation, as it was last year. In the morning as well as the afternoon the Passion story was used as a basis for our edification. Our good Lord has given our two hearts much blessing from the study of the suffering of Christ, which we have presented from the story of St. Mark in the evening prayer services of this Lenten period. We have presented it here as well as in Old Ebenezer, and we hope that the congregation has also partaken of this blessing through God's guidance. After the morning sermon Simon Steiner's little boy, who had come into this world yesterday afternoon, was baptized in the presence of the entire congregation. The people report that Mrs. Holtzer has great experience and knowledge as a midwife, and she is said to have rendered excellent service, although she is still weak physically. Mrs. Schweighofer has a lame arm and foot as the result of a stroke, and we are thanking God that a Christian woman is able to take her place.

H. [Helffenstein] and his wife reported for Holy Communion and said [even though they were born and reared in the Reformed Church, nevertheless] they did not have the least scruples about being served by our office, because among us the way to salvation was being taught from the mouth of Christ. They both make a good impression and they quote many practical truths from their experience. All of this will gradually become more evident in time. I told them about a few things which caused misunderstandings and offence to me and others, and they accepted them quite well. [I have heartfelt sympathy with poor Ernstdorff even though he got totally drunk in Purysburg. He and his wife came to me towards evening, and he revealed so much ignorance in spiritual matters that I could not help but wonder. I had not ordered him to come here but had let him know through his wife my opinion concerning his excesses. Today he wanted to excuse his misbehaviour in a very absurd manner, but he succeeded badly. He now promises a lot which concerns restraint from public vexations more than true conversion as a basis on which good behaviour can be built.]

The ignorance of some people [this man and others] in the third transport makes it necessary to start school for the children at this place after the holidays. I shall go through the main truths of the Christian doctrine with them and afterwards repeat and catechize them during evening prayer for the benefit of the adults, as was done some time ago at Old Ebenezer. Until now, various duties have prevented me from taking care of the children here as it is still being done in Ebenezer by my dear colleague and the schoolmaster.

Saturday, the 24th of April. It was reported to me about C. [Christian] R. [Riedelsperger] that he had found some money during the voyage but that he had not returned it even though he knew who had lost it. Upon investigation of the matter I found him not guilty. He was being suspected because of a joke he once had with a very small coin, which he had found and had refused to show when some of them asked him to do so. In punishment of this joke he had then been put under suspicion of theft. Meanwhile I was glad to save this man from suspicion and to help the other people out of their mistrust, which is just as sinful as theft itself. I have admonished the congregation earnestly to report to me whenever they find something objectionable or indecent in one of the members so that they will not have to bear guilt on their account.

The weather has been very fruitful until now. Most of the nights are rather cool, but the days are not too hot and the soil is not suffering from lack of rain. The people have not been able to complete the fencing of the prepared piece of land this week, and they will have to spend several more days on it after the festival. They finished their work early today and some of them have gone to Ebenezer. But most of them remained here, and toward evening they attended a preparation for Holy Easter. It was based on the

last part of the Passion story, Mark 15: 38 ff. May the Lord place
His blessing upon it, and may He turn the outward awakening
which we can feel in some of them into that right and earnest
Christian spirit which is still lacking in some of them.

Sunday, the 25th of April. Yesterday afternoon eight people from
Purysburg arrived here in order to attend the festival service and
to go to Holy Communion. [One of them went to Ebenezer.][142] I
first spoke with each of them seriously; and, after the afternoon
service, I had them all come to me [because of my concern about
the prevailing disorders, discord, hate, envy, and also probably in-
temperance discovered among them, etc. and earnestly admonished
them to conversion and a change in their way of life] in order to
give them sincere admonitions [about converting and changing
their lives, failing which, we shall use our office with and on them
with heavy hearts. There was one among them who had caused scandal and offences through drunkenness. I truly did not want to admit
him to Holy Communion at all; but, because he was already so
inclined and had acknowledged his sins before these people and
promised improvement, he will be let in this time. Meanwhile,
since he has offended some of our congregation, I am informing
them privately about the procedure I used with this man.] Last
night and today our good God has moved the hearts of these
people through His Word and made them more willing so that
the admonitions given them were well received and seemed to have
made an impression. They gladly and happily forgave each other
everything that heretofore had brought enmity and slander, and
they promised to remind each other of this in the future and to
bear with each other in spirit of love.

So far R. [Rupr.] Z. [Zittrauer] has asked several times to be
accepted as a member of the congregation and to be admitted to
Holy Communion. I gave him hope for this but asked that he first
bring four pious men to me to give good testimony regarding his
conduct and to be witnesses to his new promise and pledge which
he wants to give to me for God and the congregation. He came
with four good Salzburgers before our service of penance and confession which was held in the evening between 5 and 6 o'clock. I
reminded him in their presence of his misconduct and told him why
we had excluded him from the congregation after other steps had
failed, namely, that this was done for his and the congregation's
best interest. I then asked him whether he had used this exclusion
to gain knowledge of his sins and his wretched condition, whether
he was truly sorry for the scandal he had caused, as he had been
telling me, and whether he intended to guard himself, with God's

grace, against all disorderly things and ways. He promised every-thing in the presence of these four people, saying that he would be happy if they would remind him of his faults and chastise him for them. I asked the four men what sort of testimony they could give in regard to his conduct. It was good. Before prayer I reminded him [Zittrauer] of the words of Christ: "Watch and pray, etc.",[143] and told him he should know from his own experience how badly good intentions are turned into deeds if they are not accompanied by prayer, wakefulness, and struggle.

During the evening assembly and after the presentation of the Word of God I announced to the congregation that this man [Rupr. Zittrauer] had been excluded some time ago because of his scan-dalous behaviour but that now he was to be accepted again and admitted to Holy Communion; because he had recognized his sins, regretted them sincerely, and had promised a complete change for the better in his conduct not only to me but also to four Christian men who stood for the entire congregation. Therefore they should forgive and forget his offence, pray for him sincerely, and love and treat him as one more member of the Christian community.

[Ernst and his wife are not only so ignorant of the points be-longing to the Christian religion but are wicked too. His wife does not know anything at all from the Catechism; yet, as they both say, she has already gone several times to Holy Communion in Regensburg. They desired to go to the Lord's Table this time. But because they live dissolutely by virtue of their ignorance and are accused of misappropriating other people's property, I had to turn them away this time, to their no little uneasiness, until I can in-struct them better and inquire into the things that they are blamed for. The man has a glib tongue and knows very well how to extricate himself from the charges. But even if this is too hard on him, he will remain under suspicion until the matter is investigated and would scandalize the congregation by going to Holy Communion, particularly since he is known among us as a dissolute man, and his wife likewise.

Monday, the 26th of April. The people from Purysburg went home again after the afternoon service. Time will tell whether the preaching of the gospel has accomplished something real for them. They seem to mean well and they are leaving here with good in-tentions. Schmansgruber,[144] who earlier taught school in Purys-burg, is moving further north again. So far he does not know him-self whether it will be Pennsylvania or New York. His weaver's trade cannot earn him a living in Purysburg. He knows nothing

about agriculture; and, having spent what little money he had in
building his house, he has been suffering grief and want. He is a
good man who works for his salvation in all seriousness. At first
he had wanted to move to us at our new location, but he does not
like some of the conditions under which the colonists have to live
here. These are, among others, that the female sex has no right to
land and soil so that widow without sons cannot keep the land prepared by her dead husband.[145] It reverts to the Trustees instead,
etc. Kieffer had definitely decided to move here because he had
traded his five hundred acres of land in and around Purysburg for
some located opposite us in Carolina. But now his intention has
been brought to naught because he finds that this land is completely
flooded at this time of high water. He has a family with eight
children and would not be able to support it on fifty acres of land,
the amount given to the head of a family in this colony, unless he
also had some land in Carolina.

Tuesday, the 27th of April. My dear colleague visited us and
told me especially about the sick Haberfehner, that his physical
powers are decreasing more each day and that he probably will go
out like a light. Therefore, we agreed that, when news of his death
reached us here, we would send a few men from here to Ebenezer
to make a coffin and grave for him, since there are no men there
except three sick ones. [Mr. Zwiffler asked Mr. von Reck recently
whether or not he could expect anything from the deceased Bauer
for his efforts. Today he put the question to me in the presence of
my dear colleague, and I informed him as follows: It was the will
of the benefactors that the Salzburgers (to whom I also add the
people of the third transport) be spared the payment for medicines
as well as other expenses until they earn their bread themselves by
the work of their hands. For that reason the Society had sent him
not only the requested Simplicia and other things pertaining to
medicine but also had twice sent handsome presents.

[It was expressly pointed out in a printed sheet about the blessed
endeavors of the Society and their expenses that such presents
would reimburse the free medicines for the Salzburgers; therefore,
his claims will likely displease the Society. I am afraid that, if it
were made known that Bauer had to pay for his medicine after his
death, the people would avail themselves of his treatment even
less because they are not able to pay for his medicines and efforts.
I also told him that I had no authority to dispose of Bauer's legacy
because he had made an arrangement himself before his death and
had disclosed his last will to me that certain pious people were to
receive something, the poor-box something, and Mrs. Holtzer what-

ever was left over, which would come to little. The deceased and also Mrs. Holtzer had been of the same opinion that, just because he took so much medicine, he lost his strength completely and died. Those, on the contrary, who took very little or none at all became well through God's blessing.

[Meanwhile I asked him how much he was claiming, since he did not determine anything but said that such illnesses demanded many medicines and much effort and would amount to a great deal. He added that the presents were a slight recompense for his previous efforts, that he could not serve the people if he did not have some conscience. In farming he cannot do anything with his acquired skill; and he does not desire any wealth but an honest livelihood. He says the English doctors in this country are paid quite handsomely for every visit to the patients, for bloodletting, purging, etc. In short, he told us that if he gets the entire provisions as completely as they were given before, likewise all necessary medicines and in addition twenty pounds sterling yearly, then he will serve the people, otherwise not. I told him I would not dare mention this demand to Mr. Oglethorpe, because no English doctor in the country enjoyed anything like that, but that he might make a statement himself to him. However, I wanted to do my best through intercession and recommendation, without presuming upon his kindness. Meanwhile we had to wonder at his contempt of the acquired presents, this new claim, and other things. He is active and industrious, but we are little convinced that he has accomplished as much in the past with his medicines and diligence as he believes and says.]

Wednesday, the 28th of April. We are planning now to use Biblical stories as they follow one another in the Bible as the basis of edification in the evening prayer hours. Through God's blessing we expect profit through this with the old and young and expecially with the naive ones. Stories remain longer in the mind, and we hope that they will [also have a train of thought that will] aid the people to remember all the more easily the teachings and divine truths that lead us to recognize the way to salvation. We then have familiar material for edifying conversation during private visits and for applying to circumstances that arise. We are seriously considering going through such Biblical examples with the children in school and then catechizing them before the congregation in the evening prayer hours. Until my dear colleague can move out here to edify the congregation, I am taking on Saturday the gospel reading for the following Sunday, because on Sunday afternoon I am busy both with repetition and with increased reinforcement and application of the material already presented. May God instruct us in all affairs of our holy office to act only according to His pleasure, for He is our God. May His good spirit guide us and ours on a smooth path.

I had an opportunity to write to Governor Oglethorpe via Savannah. 1) I thanked him for the fatherly concern he has shown anew to the Salzburgers in bringing up their provisions, [2] I asked him to inform us how long and wide the required store-house should be built and whether he would allow the boards in Ebenezer for it-; 3) I said that Mr. Causton told me the provisions now given to the first and second Salzburgers must be paid for in the future. This did not concur with the oral and written promise that the people would enjoy provisions until they are able to support themselves. Rather, I believe this ordinance is more a means of keeping the people hard at work and obedient than the real design of the Trustees; 4)] I reported in addition [that] the Salzburgers work communally with great cheerfulness and would like to continue thus throughout this summer if only they were allotted the land for gardens and the remaining acres, which I once again requested. Furthermore, I stated [5] that three people among us named R. [Rheinländer] S. [Spielbiegler] and E. [Ernstdorff] had caused disorder and annoyance with drunkenness and requested him to pardon their wickedness this time since the church censure must befall them. But he might assist us according to his wisdom and power by sending away even more annoying people and things from our community, since this is his praiseworthy endeavor among Christians and heathens in the entire colony. Finally, [6] I told him that God has blessed our sick to better health through the better care we have received from the store-house and asked him at the same time to allow some flour, butter, and sugar for the little children. I said that fresh meat would be very useful for the weak and sick ones in the congregation. May God lay His blessing upon this and direct the heart of this dear benefactor further to us.

Thursday, the 29th of April. Today I visited my dear colleague and the few people in Ebenezer. At the same time I received the news that Haberfehner was delivered this morning from all evil and, according to his soul, removed to happy eternity. As his wife said, he had a difficult death struggle throughout the entire night until he finally overcame it at the break of day. He belongs to those who come from great afflictions and have their garments made bright in the blood of the Lamb. The Lord Jesus was truly his Jesus who saves poor sinners and thus, as he said, even him. The people who knew him previously and in his illness and can

correctly judge from the truths of Christianity know what a treasure dwelled in him, a treasure which revealed itself richly for the
edification of others. His illness began with a swelling in a [private
and] dangerous spot; and, although it seemed to be getting better,
he was debilitated more and more by a hectic fever and completely
wasted away.

He manifested a great measure of patience during his sufferings
and pains. He never complained; instead, his heart and mouth
were filled with praise and thanks for the many benefits that God
showed him, and still shows, according to the three main Articles.
He also thanked God often for leading him into the desert to tranquility, where he was comforted by God's Word and cared for
physically. He felt completely unworthy of these benefits. He was
very zealous in his Christianity and earnestly reprimanded wickedness in his family and other people wherever he saw it, yet with
love. With ignorant people he had heartfelt compassion, and from
his judgments that were solicited with good reason one person has
profited by his gift of spiritual examination. When I said goodbye
to him at my departure from Ebenezer, he let me know that he was
troubled about a few [evil and] naughty things that went on [are
going on] in our congregation. But he had sincerely sighed to God
about it and received the certain assurance that everything will
become better and that God will show His grace and kindness
richly among us. He received great joy from the saying I left with
him at that time from 2 Timothy 2: 8, etc. "Remember that Jesus
Christ. . ." At my urging he received great profit from the story
of Jacob and his words: "I have enough that my son Joseph still
lives." Not to mention the edifying conversations that he held with
my dear colleague. The dear people tell me from time to time how
our dear God has blessed them very much in the Easter commemo-
ration and its gospel. May He be praised!

Friday, the 30th of April. Some people of the third transport
either have no beds and covers at all or are very incompletely supplied. Therefore, we have to give out a goodly portion of the linen
cloth we bought for pants and shirts for the poor to make beds
from it, since nothing is given from the store-house for that purpose. On the whole, this transport has been very bad off in many
areas and some would have forfeited their health and lives if we
had not come to their aid with care and succour from our poor-box.
Some weeks ago Mr. Causton ceded to me a few exceptional things
such as: one barrel of flour, two dozen bottles of wine, fifty pounds
of brown sugar, one keg of butter, and six pounds of spice called
allspice. I consider this a great benefit. Still, in former times we

supplied the sick and weak ones from the poor-box with these exceptional things because they would have been unable to live from the ordinary provisions. Besides these supplies for the sick, more is being spent than in the past for the poor in the congregation on poor clothing, shoes, and shirts because they have had to spend their little money in these two years for indispensable and necessary things that they require besides the provisions. Only when the good people can make ends meet in the new country will we be able to apply the money that flows to us from charitable hearts for setting up a few useful institutions. Now we have to be governed by present needs.

The still sick Grimmiger, whose wife recently died here, has a sickly six-month-old child that would have weakened and died like its mother if we had not provided for nursing care. A pious woman took it, neglecting her own affairs, especially the work in the fields; and, because of it, she has many inconveniences with it day and night because the child has always been sickly and ailing from birth. She receives compensation from the poor-box for her troubles, since the father of the child is very poor and needs our assistance in his weak physical condition. Jesus lives and is Lord over the entire world. He will let us and ours suffer as little need as Joseph did his family after his elevation. May He only strengthen this belief in us!

According to all appearances, the people who planted a few pieces of land in old Ebenezer with corn will probably have to expect a poor harvest, because they cannot guard it. It cannot grow there because the crows and other large birds scratch up and devour the corn as soon as it sprouts. For that reason some have had to plant more corn two to three times. Last year they had to keep an eye on it a long time until it developed a strong stalk and anchored itself with deep roots. Terriculamenta[146] and scarecrows do not help here.

Saturday, the 1st of May. Yesterday evening I received a letter from Savannah written to us both by Mr. Vernon, one of the Trustees. We find in it nothing but proofs of a sincere love and care for us and our congregation from dear Mr. Vernon and other benefactors. We cannot extol the name of the Lord our God enough for that. He hopes that Governor Oglethorpe will place the Salzburgers on very good land. Besides the handsome present he is giving our wives, he is also sending the congregation a large German Bible printed in Frankfurt on the Oder, a gift to our church from the Count of Egmont.[147] At present we have received only the letter. The ship that brought it and the specified articles probably arrived at Charleston. I suppose we shall receive more letters from England and Germany on the same ship, because I gather from this letter that our letters of September 1st have arrived. The contents of this letter gave the congregation occasion during the evening prayer to praise and trust in God.

[Yesterday I had an opportunity to talk with Rheinländer and to reproach him earnestly about his latest drunkenness. Up to now he has tried rather to avoid this admonition. Because he was also quite as arrogant as previously and made all kinds of foolish and rude excuses and did not give the slightest appearance of recognizing and repenting his sins, I immediately pointed out to him that my conscience would not let me give him any more provisions because of his obstinate behaviour, since I recently heard from Mr. Causton that the current assistance (as he calls the present provisions) should be given to none other than the upright people whom I recommend. He remained defiant and departed stomping and snorting. Previously we have shown all degrees of warnings, patience, and indulgence toward him and his wife. But since nothing has been accomplished up to now through the way of love, except that they have played the hypocrite a long time for the sake of their own interest, we can not do otherwise with their continuing disorders than to be serious and strict, no matter if it is said afterwards that we preach much about love but demonstrate little, etc.

[Once, without my knowledge, this man charged two pairs of stockings and two summer caps to me in Charleston. Recently the merchant named Smalwood dunned me through a captain from Purysburg. I immediately turned upon Rheinländer, because no one in our congregation except him and his family admitted to being in Charleston. I told him about this unpleasant affair, that I had been a debtor for almost two years in Charleston without my knowledge or fault. But together with his wife he knew how to extricate himself masterfully and to set himself up in such a manner that I almost began to be ashamed because of my fixed suspicion against him.

[However, not long after that, God touched his conscience through His Word and therewith affected him severely physically. Afterwards he came to me and confessed not only this embezzlement but also other deceits. I admonished him then to pay off the debt to the man who is commissioned by Mr. Smalwood, and I would keep the matter quiet. But since he has not made any restitution up to now for the promises he made then, I indicated to him earnestly that he would have to send the money to Purysburg at the first opportunity or I could not do otherwise than make his frauds known to the proper place. His wife, according to her custom, had so evilly and harshly upbraided the upright Mrs. Holtzer, who recently performed a Christian act for Mrs. Steiner just as she did for Mrs. Schweighoffer some time ago, that I also gave her a piece of my mind regarding her arrogance and self-conceit and warned her against further disorder.]

Sunday, the 2nd of May. Bans have been proclaimed to the congregation for Johann Cornberger and Gertraud Einecker, Ruprecht Zittrauer and Anna Leihoffer, in addition to Stephen Riedelsperger, who wants to marry Catherine Valentin. May God grant our wish and prayer also for these newly-weds and may they commence and continue such a holy state to His glory, their salvation, and the edification of the congregation!

[Rheinländer came to me and told an entirely different story. He admitted that he was sorry for both the drunkenness and the rudeness he demonstrated towards me and put all the blame on Satan. He wanted very much to submit himself to church discipline and wished to have the matter settled, the sooner the better. I gave him my opinion about the evil foundation of his perverted heart. I pointed out to him clearly his serious entanglement in the toils of sin and how much it would cost him to become free from them as well as from many other obstacles to conversion. That demands a great earnestness, or else he and his wife will be stuck even if not in public annoyances, at least in hypocrisy and thus in a damned condition. I reminded him of all his customary evasions and coarse expressions, but he did not excuse them this time at all but rather wanted to profess his love and high esteem towards our office, etc.

[I also showed him that it was an evil characteristic in him that, although he recognized and confessed in qualms of conscience the sin of the fraud committed in Charleston, he nevertheless had not yet made any restitution. Whoever has other people's goods in his house is not yet penitent but still has a curse upon himself despite all his pretensions. I could tell him, without mentioning any names, of a few examples from the congregation who, although very poor, had restored misappropriated objects when I gave them time to do so. Of these I had one example just before the celebration. As far as the settling of the scandal caused by his drunkenness is concerned, he should not act rashly but make it his object seriously to seek grace and forgiveness in the blood of the Saviour through a sincere humility before God. Only then would I designate a time for him and say to whom and how he should make amends for his scandals before the congregation. The recent disciplinary action against Zittrauer shut his mouth so that he did not again accuse me of partiality: otherwise, he had customarily said that I am very strict with him and other High Germans[148] whereas I let the Salzburgers get by, etc. This much he said: he has never in his life been so often called to the minister and examined as in Ebenezer. But then I gave him the necessary answer for that. He departed from me with many good resolutions.]

Monday, the 3rd of May. [Because I have an opportunity to send letters to Pennsylvania through Schomansgruber from Purysburg, I am writing a few to Messrs. Siron and Weisiger, who have not written to me for a long time or answered two letters. Whether one of us shall travel there some time and inquire about church matters and whether they are sincere about Evangelical teachers and schoolmasters rests with our Father in Heaven, who directs everything well. We cannot and shall not do it without permission of the benefactors in London which, for good reasons, we do not wish to request. Nor do our current move to a new location and the various preoccupations in official and external matters yet permit such a long trip. Our future and our resolution are in God's hands.][149]

For some time we have been having dry, arid weather. Because of this the seeds we have sown and the green shoots that have come up are suffering. Already the heat is great by day. However, the nights are still cool.

Tuesday, the 4th of May. This forenoon I married three couples here at our new location, and God did not let it take place without edification. The couples were Stephan Riedelsperger with Catherine Valentin, Johann Cornberger with Gertraud Einecker, and Ruprecht Zittrauer with Anna Leihoffer. Since God has blessed Riedelsperger with cattle and in other ways, he had a meal set up for his relatives and friends and also invited the two other betrothed couples who are very poor. Then, to my delight, they spent their time partaking of the material blessings bestowed by God with good conversation and in much sincere love and intimacy. The manner of living and the circumstances of the people make it well nigh necessary that they be supplied with helpmates. But there is no opportunity for that around here, and the honest souls have neither inclination to nor our consent for just any kind of people.

Wednesday, the 5th of May. This morning Mr. von Reck traveled to Savannah together with his brother and servant. For this he needed our two little boats and five men because of the many things he took along.[150] [He has information that Governor Oglethorpe is expected soon in Savannah and therefore he does not wish to make the trip to Altamaha. Even if he resolves to travel there, he will not, because of my arguments, take along any people from the congregation except Spielbiegler, his servant, and Grüning, a young Reformed person from Switzerland, whom he picked up in London for the transport. No one else except these two are inclined to be so long without the Word of God and to venture into unnecessary spiritual and physical danger.]

Mr. von Reck has many kinds of necessary and important matters to report to Mr. Oglethorpe, especially concerning the badly organized provisions of the third transport, their great lack of cooking utensils, farm implements, and building tools, etc., and cattle that had been promised them in Germany. He intends to bring the surveyor here so that the people will, for once, have assurance about their land. I still do not know what kind of a cause lies hidden under such a long uncertainty: but God will turn everything for the best. Up to now there has been no lack of presentations and petitions. Our wise and wonderful God has always previously heard our prayer in grace and has bestowed upon us His blessing gradually and, as it were, piecemeal. We, like David, thank Him for each benefit with a beautiful hymn and are incited with each particular assistance to new praise of His majesty. This He will also do well by us in our future life.

At this opportunity I wrote to Mr. Causton that I have nothing in the store-house for the people except salted beef and corn. Therefore, I am asking for the remaining things belonging to the provisions and likewise a barrel of flour for the sick. [I am also informing him that I cannot possibly settle the provisions of the third transport fairly until Mr. Vat gives me the accounts as Mr. Oglethorpe commanded. He is in Savannah and has the key to the storehouse in Ebenezer still on him, so that we cannot even take a saddle or bridle, not to mention anything else. I cannot comprehend why they tolerate such an obstinate man so long and let him have his own way to our detriment. Recently, when Mr. Causton demanded the account and the key from him in my presence, I noticed distinctly during his refusal that he has accused me more than ever before Mr. Oglethorpe, whose answer he is awaiting first.

[I understand from the words he said to Mr. Causton about me and my dear colleague what the content of his complaint may be: namely, Mr. Gronau dared to distribute nails and I had dared to distribute rice and gunpowder among the people in his absence. As usual, he is now again making a great crime out of that, as if this were an intrusion into his sphere of duty and a confusion in his accounts, etc. However, I told Mr. Causton that, in view of the fact that Mr. Vat had to send the key back to Ebenezer at his command, we had never imagined he would make a big fuss about the very few nails used for coffins for the dead, for the bushel,[151] and for my fireplace, concerning which we submitted to him (Mr. Vat) an accurate statement immediately after his return. And it is the same way with the rice and gunpowder we distributed. The people were in obvious need and suffering from hunger as the entire congregation will tell him this to his face, so Mr. Zwiffler then distributed the aforesaid things in good order with my consent and has conveyed to him in writing the quantity to each and every family. At that time I would have considered him our friend and thought I was doing him a favor by removing the people's complaints about want and hunger, and in the beginning I would not have expected the hostile attitude toward us that he revealed afterwards. The people are also supposed to stand watch without gunpowder, which is burdensome and against the intention of the Trustees.

[And if he wished to say that none of us should have interfered in the things in the store-house because they were entrusted to him alone, then I did not know 1) that he had received complete authority and disposition over it, since we had been doing that before his arrival. Therefore, our superiors should have let us know about the change in their intent. While Mr. Vat was still friendly toward us, whenever I desired something from the store-house for the congregation from Mr. Causton, he gave and sent it at my request. If the matter concerned Mr. Vat alone, Mr. Causton would probably have told me. 2) Thus others may ponder whether it is fair that Mr. Vat took along the key from the store-house and allowed the people to suffer in the meanwhile. Whenever Mr. Causton journeys from Savannah, he hands over the things in the store-house there for the time to conscientious persons, so that no one will suffer deprivation or harm in his absence, to say nothing of other arguments that belong here.]

The English boy Robinson, who was sent to my dear colleague a short time ago from England, is being taken to Savannah at the present opportunity because, at our request, he has been summoned to Altamaha by Governor Oglethorpe. [Nothing could be accomplished with him here unless there was always an overseer and driver near him. It looks the same with the other boy, Nicolas Carpenter. I cannot use him for the kind of work for which he was sent to me; therefore, I am handing him over to Mr. von Reck until I have spoken to Mr. Oglethorpe on his account. Bishop would have become naughty in the company of these two boys if I had not separated them in time. Now he is doing a lot of service for me again in external things pertaining to housekeeping, for which he also has far more inclination than for writing and other sedentary occupations.]

Thursday, the 6th of May. Yesterday evening shortly before the prayer hour Mrs. Helffenstein told me that she and her family would soon get a spacious hut, for which our dear God had made a few people of the third transport, with whom she had come across the sea, volunteer. She had thought the people hated her and her husband, but now she saw it was only a misunderstanding. This news pleased me all the better, because before the celebration I sought to dissuade her and her husband from the delusion that the Salzburgers and Austrians loved none other than their own countrymen and to show them what would fall to their share if the people who feared God should live in harmony with them. Experience teaches sufficiently that even those who are not Salzburgers assimilate and fuse with them very simply and sincerely, if only they prove honest and Christian. But there are others among us who always demand love from the people as proof of Christianity but demonstrate none themselves and demand all kinds of things from them as peasant people and claim to be better than they.

[Whenever one makes a few objections to them about such pious and honest souls and tells the truth about their own ill-breeding, annoying talk, and neglect of their duties in communal things, then this is called hate, animosity, rudeness, etc. For them Christianity consists only in external good appearances, etc. They are feigning something, etc. I am often astonished how ill-bred people among us can invent obvious malice and annoying things about the honest members of our congregation and misrepresent the circumstances in such a way that, before I can investigate the matter, I believe the accusations to be true, if not completely, at least in good part. After the investigation I have often found nothing but malicious slander, wicked reversal of innocent words and actions or an unfounded suspicion instead of the truth. For some time, experience has taught me in the case of the evil ones and their charges always to press for details of what they say about the Salzburgers and to write them down so that they cannot reverse themselves afterwards or deny them. Sometimes I take the trouble to inquire exactly and with real seriousness into the things themselves, even if, as often, they do not wish it. And thus I get at the truth and make them shut up.]

Friday, the 7th of May. Having completely finished planting corn yesterday, the Salzburgers are now continuing in the communal work of fencing in a house plot, planting corn in it, and building a hut for the two herdsmen who cannot work for themselves. After this is finished, they have volunteered to construct for me and my dear colleague a spacious and well secured hut of clapboards or long split shingles like everyone builds here. The people are poor and have worked up to now long enough without pay; therefore, we would gladly pay them for this work if we were now able to. However, their sincere love for us will allow no payment for this work. Meanwhile, we will not allow them to build anything except the huts and perhaps a kitchen without pay: we shall pay those who have time for such building for the fence around the house lots and other necessary things pertaining to housekeeping.

It is now very hot and, if they do not want to ruin their health, they must not work on such arduous things the entire day under the open sky, as in fall, winter, and spring, but only in the morning and towards evening. Their work with their houses is still manifold. A few still lack huts, most lack animal stalls and also well secured fences to keep garden vegetables safe from chickens and so forth. Thus they do not have much time left over, especially since unusual things that have to be done occur now and then. It will not be long before they will have to build a store-house, and who knows what else, at the command of Governor Oglethorpe. Thus they will not have much time left over for clearing out the remaining gardens that they started in the spring and had resolved to continue. Haymaking will also be a chief occupation for the people this summer, since the cattle have less feed in the winter here than in Old Ebenezer on the other side of the river, where a lot of cane grows in the swampy and watery regions. But the bogs are fewer around here, although the cattle use the grass very well that grows on the high and dry land in spring and summer, and the milk from that is said to be better and richer.

[Perhaps God will govern the hearts of the honorable Trustees so that the Salzburgers will still get the good land across the Ebenezer River in our present neighborhood, which Governor Oglethorpe completely denied us when we moved. Not only the most splendid land for farming is there, but also the most beautiful pasture. I and others who know this stretch of land only slightly cannot understand where good land at forty eight acres per family will be found around here without going on the above mentioned place. The people cannot manage with the limited good land for their house and garden plots. If the Salzburgers had had to stay in Old Ebenezer they would not have gotten along well either in farming or in cattle-breeding, if, as is now the case, they had not had permission to retain the little prepared land and to drive the cattle there on the pasture, because on this side of the Ebenezer River there is little, but on the other side the most magnificent and beautiful pasture up to the Savannah River. I perceive very clearly the difference of the two regions in the cattle.]

[Saturday, the 8th of May. Yesterday evening I received a letter from Charleston which reported that our letters we addressed to Mr. Eveleigh in the month of March were delivered to a good captain. Mr. von Reck also wrote a few lines to me from Savannah by way of our own people who brought our boat back that he could neither come to terms with Mr. Causton nor move Mr. Vat to surrender the accounts and the key to the store-house. He is only waiting for an opportunity to go to Altamaha, where he is taking along his brother, his lackey, his servant, and Grüning. May God accompany him and give him a great measure of wisdom and caution in all his conversations and presentations. Mr. Causton sent me nothing but a little barrel of flour for the sick, although I have nothing in the way of provisions for the third transport, whose new quarter begins the 12th of this month, except salted beef and three barrels of corn. I have also been unable to give any beans to the second transport but must distribute corn in their place today. Such being the case, I wish a new opportunity to go to Savannah to report the need and miserable circumstances of the people in a moving way to Mr. Causton as well as to Mr. Oglethorpe. They have to live very pitifully on salted meat and on Indian corn, which they cannot grind properly because of the wretched iron mills that easily break. And what are four pounds of meat and a little corn weekly for a hard worker?

I hear from Ebenezer that Grimminger's little child, whom I entrusted to a sensible and Christian married woman after the death of its mother, has again become very dangerously ill. It absorbed a lot of poison from its mother both on the trip and here and it has reacted to it up to now even though I have made all possible arrangements and spared no expense for its care and support, since the father himself is very poor.]

Sunday, the 9th of May. This past Monday I began to hold school at our new place with the children, of whom there are now fourteen here. I again hold it as earlier reported; namely, I begin and end the school with song and prayer. Before I begin to catechize them with a story, I let them repeat an article of faith from the Catechism a few times and retain both the hymn and the article of faith throughout the week so that the new children may learn it while the old ones are repeating it. In the evening prayer hours last week the Bible stories that I had previously gone through with the children were repeated in question and answer before the congregation with suitable application. I have learned that the congregation finds great favor and edification in this method. Since I have become somewhat used to the new school children, I began again this morning before the hymn: "Dear Jesus, we are, etc."[152] to repeat, through questions to the children before the congregation, the sermon given eight days ago; and this afternoon I went through today's sermon in the same way. This method, which was previously used at Ebenezer, is highly necessary and useful with simple and ignorant listeners. Otherwise, they hear one sermon after the other, and at the end of the year they are just as foolish and inexperienced in spiritual things as they were in the beginning. Not to mention that the attention of the listeners is retained more in this way and the children's answers suggest to the teacher himself many teachings and admonitions that are necessary to know and to practice.

Our dear God has also wrought a few blessings today in the children who came into my little hut towards evening to pray with me and to be edified from the Word of God. Their encouragement, the first in this place, was very dear to me. I wrote their names down and told each child the meaning of its name and how it would have to make use of the meaning for the edification of its heart.[153] I told them simply how much good the dear Son of God, our Saviour, had won for us and them and how good pious Christians and children had it with Him. After a short narration, I also made use of a story of a youth who had finally been persuaded by a patriarch to seek to love Christ and to savour His grace for only three days. If he did not like it, he might turn back again. But afterwards he did not desire to leave Christ but said with Peter (John 6) : "Lord, to whom shall we go," etc. Lastly, I went through the edifying little hymn, "Good Shepherd, wilt Thou not have pity on Thy little sheep"[154] simply with them, and let them go home again with several admonitions after a prayer was offered and after they promised me much good regarding the truths I had presented.

I still live in a very small hut. If some day the people build something better for me and my dear colleague, we hope to have many a pleasurable and edifying meeting with the children and also other members of the congregation. If I can get as many copies of the little book called Cooing Dove[155] as there are children in the congregation, I plan to go through this in the future with them for edification. Otherwise, I would like either to tell them something applicable to the previous Sunday material or to seek to impress on their minds, with God's help, the content and edifying expressions of the hymn: "O Jesus Christ, My Loveliest Light, etc."¹⁵⁶ May the Lord give wisdom and simplicity. I am afraid that the evening prayer hour, when most of the members of the congregation came to my room after the evening meal in Ebenezer, will have to cease for lack of space facilities. Perhaps our dear God will show an opportunity for it; for we prefer to be guided to it by the hand of God rather than to drive ourselves and others to it. Meanwhile, there is no lack of opportunity for edification either here or in Old Ebenezer.

Monday, the 10th of May. A short time ago we procured out of necessity a small and light boat that is also proving useful to the whole community. Now the people are lacking not only the very large boat but also the old boat that Mr. von Reck took along to Savannah for repair. Therefore, they would now be in a bad way if they did not have ours, because they still have to bring some of their things here from Ebenezer. Governor Oglethorpe has sent orders to Mr. Causton to procure another large and suitable boat for us in place of the former one; [but it is proceeding very slowly because we are asking for other things.] Once the people come to more order in farming and to some growth in crops, they themselves will build such boats as suit their needs. Today our dear God has revived our land with a fruitful rain according to our desire and prayer. If He continues with this favor for several days, the planted corn and other plants that have stopped growing because of the persistent drought will soon gain a pleasing appearance again.

Tuesday, the 11th of May. It has become very cool again at night after yesterday's rain, which did not last long. At our new place there are many gnats that pester us during the day, and especially in the mornings and evenings; but they are subdued whenever cold weather sets in. There are many snakes here just as in Old Ebenezer, of which a few are of great length and girth. The people are very seriously engaged in exterminating them as far as it is possible. There are a great many squirrels here of which the soups have a very good taste. Also there are many wild Turkish¹⁵⁷ or Welsh chickens in this region which the people do not shoot now, both because they are too busy and because they have misgivings about shooting them up in this breeding season.

Today I distributed some provisions to the people of the third transport, because their new quarter commences tomorrow morning. I have been unable to give them anything other than beef and corn. There is no rice, beans, syrup, or molasses for cooking beer, nor any more corn there, although I have already asked for these necessary items time and again [from Mr. Causton]. Because I cannot let the people's dearth become too extreme, I am sending three men to Savannah with our little boat along with a letter to Mr. Causton. In this I am informing him once more about the great lack of provisions and asking him to send up the necessary food-stuffs soon. If they have no people to bring up the provisions with the big boat, then our people must fetch them themselves rather than suffer want. He should write me his opinion about that. It is also time to plant Indian beans, and he should send us seeds for that as he promised. Besides provisions, the new people lack iron mills; and those that belong to the other Salzburgers are all broken. I sent them down to him with a request to have them repaired and to send a couple of new ones. We should also like a few little mill-stones in place of them. Lastly, I am requesting him to send our old boat down soon again that Mr. von Reck recently took to Savannah for repair, because we have the direst need of it to fetch the things from Ebenezer.

Likewise, I am taking the same opportunity to write to the merchant Eveleigh at Charleston to ask him to report whether he received the pack of letters for London that we wrote on the 9th of January and dispatched to him on the 19th of the same month, in connection with which there was another pack containing the book translated into English: *Christ the Core of the Holy Scriptures*.[158] He sent no word about them in his last letter but was concerned only with our letters addressed to him on the 13th of March. At the same time I asked him for seeds for our people next fall. He has often sent us seeds unasked, and just recently some large English beans. This time I sent along to him a letter to Court Chaplain Ziegenhagen in which, among other things, I reported the reason why we previously delayed and are still delaying in our letter writing. As soon as we are able to write something definite about the Salzburgers' land that is still not yet assigned to them, we shall not put it off. The above mentioned merchant offered to have all letters written to us from England forwarded to us safely if they are addressed to him. He is very well known everywhere in Charleston and has many connections with ship captains because of his far reaching trade. Our letters and packages can very safely be addressed to this man even if no ships at all depart from London for Savannah, but only for Charleston. His complete name is Samuel Eveleigh, Senior.

Wednesday, the 12th of May. Mrs. Helffenstein has a very sincere attitude, although she is no doubt in miserable circumstances with her weak old husband and many children. Even though she is undergoing many vexations and great uncharitableness, she still shows herself to be so Christian, resigned, and consoled in all these trials that I can reasonably perceive a clear sign of an honest heart. [She and her husband were blamed from the outset of their arrival for various rude things that have been disproved. In the beginning I also suspected her because of her polylogis[159] of spiritual matters: but I am getting used to this too. The misunderstanding that has continued since the sea journey between them and a few people of the third transport will be settled through the grace of God, if they continue to behave as they have done so far.] Meanwhile, these people are to be pitied. They cannot pursue their trade here in this colony, and they are too weak and inexperienced to work in the fields and at the same time are very poor. Still, they are assured that our living God who led them here will provide for them and make everything heavy light and the bitter sweet. What we can do, we do gladly.

Today the first and second transports started to build a little house for the first herdsman and to fence in his house plot securely with long shingles or clapboards, just as they did last week for the other one. As soon as it can be done, they will build some kind of a dwelling for the widowed Mrs. Schweighoffer and her children. Meanwhile, Adam Riedelsperger is taking her into his house, which is now completely finished. His wife will give her and her children a helping hand with the washing and bodily care now as previously and also in the future, because she is unable to do it herself. The Salzburgers would have already begun to build a hut for the two of us if we had wished it. But, since we well know the circumstances of the poor people, we preferred to see them do the necessary things first, especially since I can surely still make do in Stephan Riedelsperger's little dwelling and my dear colleague in his house in Ebenezer. The Salzburgers are finding many bees on high trees in this region, especially along and in the water. They have already obtained a lot of honey from them, but it tastes like pine trees and is not as good as that in Germany. They are waiting until fall for the remainder that they know of in hope of finding all the more honey. They cannot obtain the honey and wax in any other way except by chopping the trees into the water or burning up the bees. They have tried to put the bees in regular beehives and tame them, but they have flown away again and again.

[Thursday, the 13th of May. Mr. Zwiffler once more asked me to help him with the payment for the efforts and medicines that he used on the dead Bauer. In doing so he explained that he was, to be sure, bound to serve the first and second transports with medicines, but the third could have no part in it. Mr. von Reck had also told him recently that he should write down whatever he gives in the way of medicines to the people he brought along, for he wants to help him with the payment. That is just how he talked with me about Bauer. But, after he conferred with me about it, he changed his tune entirely in respect to the payment concerning Bauer. If he were supposed to serve the people further, then I would have to ask Mr. Oglethorpe for provisions, salary, and supplies as he recently told me, or else he would have to seek his bread elsewhere. I informed him unmistakeably that his new claims, together with his underestimation of the presents he received, seemed very strange to me; and, I believe, they would also be very surprised about it in England. I shall not dictate to Mr. Oglethorpe. I had to be content that he exclude the new people from the benefits of free medicines and seek a payment for this through Mr. von Reck. He might be able to turn to Mr. von Reck for Bauer's debt, but he will not be able to demand anything from the people themselves because of their poverty. I cannot make a claim against the widow Holtzer, to whom the deceased Bauer bequeathed his little legacy because of the mother-loyalty she showed him. The benefactors in England might also think suspiciously of me.

[I am very amazed that the good Mr. Zwiffler is making such a big to-do about his service and selfishly emphasizes his skill and applied diligence but does not want the presents he received and the benefits and provisions he enjoys to be compared to them. In so doing he forgets the hard labor the Salzburgers had over two years ago on account of him and his wife when they brought him his provisions, partly on their backs. He also forgets that he has had the upper floor in the store-house as his dwelling for the entire time and that now again a well secured hut and a good fence of long thin boards is to be built for him around his house lot. The people will even clear his two acres of trees and undergrowth for a garden, if he does not look too much to his own interests and to their detriment. This time he wanted to dictate to me that I should have his hut built at least as long as the store-house in Ebenezer. But I could not accede to this, because he recently described the length and breadth to me quite differently after we had agreed upon it. We cannot let too much burden be placed upon us. Meanwhile, I worry that we will earn little thanks during this construction and not attain the goal we seek, because he is valuing his services too high.

[Today a man by the name of Ernst from the third transport unleashed his malice in such a manner that we had not a little fright over it. Mr. von Reck had given the watchmaker Müller a large wood-saw belonging to the congregation. This Ernst demanded it from the watchmaker with mild words first and then with great crudeness. Since it was refused him, he went with force into the hut, shoved the watchmaker's wife aside, took the saw forcibly; and, since the wife was holding one end of the saw, ripped it from her hands and hit her with it in such a way on one side of her head that her ear was almost cut in pieces and a few parts of her head were wounded. I immediately inquired from three Salzburgers who were just working in this region about all the circumstances. Otherwise, he would have denied everything and extricated himself by his cunning and empty talk. I had him fetched from his hut and then locked in the store-house, which is now empty except for a few nailed up meat barrels, as in a prison. He is guarded in the day by one man but at night by two; and I have a mind to send this evil man, who already made a lot of trouble and threatened with shooting and beating (just like the wicked Rott),[160] to Savannah as soon as our little boat comes back. But I have changed my mind again and think I shall first report this miserable affair to Mr. Causton and ask him for his verdict. Still, I must send down the three witnesses and the watchmaker; but the people have uncommonly much to do. We cannot do without our boat for lack of another to fetch my things and those of my dear colleague as long as there is still enough water in Ebenezer Creek during this drought. Besides, we would gladly be rid of the man from our congregation, because he and his wife are acting just like the two Rott people. If I sent him to Savannah now to be punished, we would have to keep him after he endured the punishment; so I hope that Mr. Oglethorpe will remove him from our congregation rather than punish him.

[In today's evening prayer hour we just had the history of Cain, Genesis 2, and we said the most necessary things both to this man, who had to be present, and also to the congregation concerning his un-Christian action. Even before the prayer hour I took up his case in the presence of the three witnesses since he, like Cain, was impudent during his wickedness and relied on lying, distortion of the circumstances, and all kinds of excuses. I shall let him stay in jail tonight and will hear him again tomorrow in the presence of several people. Then I shall let him go about his business, but with suitable restrictions, until I get an answer from Savannah or until Mr. von Reck has returned to Ebenezer. I am afraid that, if this deplorable affair comes to Savannah, the community of Salzburgers will again be maligned and that the move to this place will be blamed, as I have already heard people do. We have had a lot of grief over it, but it nevertheless comforts us that even in the Apostolic congregations there were also annoying people and miscreants with whom the servants and other true members of Christ had great sorrow. May God give us wisdom and not let our courage sink!

[Friday, the 14th of May. Late yesterday evening our little boat arrived again from Savannah and brought the news that eight days ago Mr. Causton had already dispatched seven people in our big boat with provisions for us, but they cannot come any farther than to Purysburg; they are therefore requesting more people either from Savannah or from us. But I cannot send anyone down; because I cannot possibly do without our little boat, since Mr. von Reck took along our old boat to Savannah for repair. Also, Mr. Causton has not sent me any order on this account, although I wrote to him that our people would rather fetch their provisions themselves than be in want of them. He was supposed to write me his opinion about this, but he has not done so. He has not answered my last letter at all, as well as some previous letters.

[Meanwhile, the man who is in Purysburg with our provisions sent me a letter from Mr. Causton that was composed in the following terminology:

As several idle stories are (I believe) designedly spread, I advise, that Mr. Zwiffler be very strict in the Guard, and the peopel take great Care, that their Cattle don't go on the other side of Ebenezer River. I have now sent Provisions etc. Your advice of the Receipt (s), as also what you think will be necessary for me to know, because I would acquaint Mr. Oglethorpe of such Credit, before I go to far. I mean as to the 1 &2^d Saltzburgh, who have received already, that, I have order, to deliver.

May 5th.1736. Th. Causton.

[I do not wish to write my reflections now about the main points of this letter. I am waiting until Mr. Oglethorpe answers my last letter, in which I asked for the continuation of free provisions until the Salzburgers can maintain themselves. This I shall write to Mr. Causton with the answer to his inquiry. If the people should have to pay for the provisions from now on despite all the promises made for them in the name of the Trustees, then they will have to be slaves for many years and live very miserably, even though they are not to blame for being unable to support themselves, because their little money is spent for necessary things and at the same time they cannot earn anything. The move to a better place was granted too late and many other tasks have been placed on the people;

therefore, they can not possibly prepare as much land as necessary for their maintenance. Indeed, neither the gardens nor the remaining fields in Old Ebenezer and now here have been surveyed and allotted as their own. How can people always demand of them that they support themselves or pay for the provisions that they get from the store-house? In this manner the poor people will lose courage more and more during the misery that they have encountered up to now. Our conjecture can almost be confirmed that they would rather see the Salzburgers remain continual slaves than come to their own support and quiet life. But the Lord hears and sees it and has sufficient means to help the miserable one when his hour comes.

[Today I read Isaiah 25: 4 to strengthen my belief: "Thou art a strength to the poor, a strength to the needy in his distress, a refuge from the storm, a shadow from the heat, when the blast of the terrible ones is as a storm against the wall." Thy Words, oh God, must be the truth. Thou shalt again be able to reveal to us a new source of Thy blessing, even if one and the other has been stopped. Because we and other people still have many things in Ebenezer, and since there is no other boat except our small one, we intended to borrow one in Purysburg and to pay something for it daily. But we hoped in vain because all suitable boats were either bought by Mr. Oglethorpe or lent out. If we had not bought our own little boat, then we and the congregation would have been in a bad way for some time. But since it must be used so often in the Ebenezer River where there are many trees and bends, it will all the sooner be beaten to pieces because it is so thin. The old boat that Mr. von Reck took to Savannah for refitting is still there, and Mr. Causton informed me that he gave orders to have it repaired. The new iron mills, or millstones in place of them, are not in the store-house; but Mr. Causton took the old ones for repair.]

Saturday, the 15th of May. The entire congregation is now very intently occupied with building two spacious cottages and a good kitchen for me and my dear colleague. They even intend to have them finished in the following week, because they are all working joyfully and in good order on them. We both shall be sincerely happy when we can work together again in the community in the same place and one can help the other through advice, support, and consolation to ease the burden and all kinds of troublesome circumstances. May God be praised, Who not only brought us to *one* congregation but also gave us *one* mind in Christ, to promote only the honor of His glorious Name and the spiritual and physical salvation of our dear listeners.

The great drought is still persisting and has thus lasted a long time. And, although there was promise of rain a few days ago, the clouds were soon pushed asunder again by the wind. During the day it is very hot and at night very cool. The health of the people in the community is now so good that we now have no patients except Pichler's wife, Ossenecker, and Michael Rieser. There is indeed no lack of weaknesses, but still they do not let them hinder their work. We cannot wonder enough at the untiring diligence of each and every one at our place, and now it is only to be wished that the poor people could eat sufficiently with the current provisions. They have lived very poorly for some time and have had to buy a few things for themselves and their cattle: how much more they need to buy if only the money were there! What they do not have to buy in provisions has been spent for livestock and hand tools as well as for other things they could not get from the store-house.

As soon as I receive an answer to my last letter to Governor Oglethorpe, I shall lodge a few humble complaints with him on account of the inadequate provisions. Or, if he postpones an answer too long, I intend to write again in the coming week. The people have been accustomed, from their youth up, to foods made with flour; and, since they cannot get any at all now, it goes very hard with them, especially when they have children. [If the hearts of the benefactors here in this country are too harsh against the people, then I shall seek to present their want in Europe at the speediest opportunity.] It consoles us that many upright souls help to pray for us: "Give us this day our daily bread;" which our Father granted before and will grant still further in the manner that is laudable to Him and useful to us.

Sunday, the 16th of May. An Englishman with two servants arrived here yesterday toward evening and requested me to have the Salzburgers fetch the provisions that he could bring no farther than Purysburg on our big boat. He had orders from Mr. Causton to unload them there, but I told him that Mr. Causton wrote to me that he was sending the provisions up and that I was supposed to give a receipt for them. I read nothing about our people having to pick them up in Purysburg, which I cannot do anyway because we have no boat, so he must go back with his people in the big boat. If he does it now and unloads the provisions there, then our people will have to suffer want in the meantime. Therefore, I said I would go this coming Monday to Savannah to lodge a complaint about it. After that he was, to be sure, willing to deliver the provisions up here; yet, since his people, as he said, had rowed themselves half dead and powerless, I should send along a few Salzburgers with him or otherwise he could not possibly come up in the strong current with the unsuitable boat. Under such circumstances I had to give in, and after sundown I sent along our little boat with four people who probably would have preferred to stay home on account of Sunday. We are glad that now others [the Englishmen] can experience it [the slavery] themselves on our boat and can testify about it in the proper place. They have already been underway eleven days; and, since they get provisions for twelve days, they have to, as the man said, lay their hands on those that are on the boat. [Yet they have only given our poor people provisions for one week, namely, one pound salted meat and one pound of rice for each day.]

Because the current Sunday epistle, 1 Peter 2: 11–20, again lends itself very nicely to our circumstances, I attempted through God's grace to make use of it for the listeners in this way in yesterday's evening prayer hour, since we endeavor to use it as the basis of Saturday's edification, as their own previous and current conditions warrant. After I presented to them the questionable titles of believers (pilgrims and strangers) in their emphasis and understanding, I then pointed out why true Christians like to involve themselves in all kinds of non-sinful things and let various burdens be placed upon them, many of which they should not rightfully bear, namely, all that, as it is called in the text, "for the sake of the Lord," that the Name of the Lord be not defamed but glorified. For the actions of the pious are seen and judged by the world entirely differently than as if a worldly human being did them. I also told them clearly that this ("for the sake of the Lord") was the very reason why my dear colleague and I allow so many unfamiliar things [that they did not place upon us at our vocation] to be placed upon us here, and how much it costs here and there, both to prevent scandals, and to dispose of them after they have occurred. In so doing we must of course overcome many hardships [the details of which I could not report.] I admonished the congregation, who were all present except those who had gone to Ebenezer, to put up gladly with all human regulation and the burdens imposed by it for the sake of the Lord; the Lord is indeed with us and still gives His help as we have previously experienced. He will continue to do it. I knew in advance that many burdens would be placed upon us this summer. I shudder to think of it, because I worry that some members of the congregation might show their bitterness about it and cause harm; but I asked them to do it thus-and-so for the sake of the Lord.

I reminded them of God's way with all His children, especially with the Jewish people who came out of Babel in troubled times under many burdens and hindrances but nevertheless arrived at their goal through God's blessing and help. Today I had almost the same material concerning the regular gospel for Jubilate Sunday.[161] Of course, I pointed out that the children of God had only anguish in the world but an eternal consolation in Christ. We find it very necessary [whenever we foresee to some extent the new burdens that are to be inflicted on the poor people with all the hardship of their life] to prepare the spirits of our listeners [in time] from God's Word for that which God has always blessed up to now according to His eternal grace.

[It now looks as if, although they are denied free provisions, the Salzburgers will not only have to build a store and guard house, but will also be burdened with guarding the store-house in Old Ebenezer, despite the fact that Mr. Vat, who does not want to give out the key for fetching the provisions that are lying there, is to blame for everything. The water is getting lower and lower and the people now want to move everything here, since Mr. Causton does not want the aforementioned provisions to be left alone. Not to mention other burdensome circumstances which, I hope, the good people will accept as they have before, whenever an official request is there.]

The postman from Savannah came to our place after the afternoon service and brought along a letter to me from Mr. Causton in which he requested a few Salzburgers to mark out the way to Charleston with the postman. He is willing to pay for this effort. In the future the mail is supposed to go through our place to Charleston, which will be a great advantage for us. But it just happens that we have no boat on hand, because I had to send four people with our little boat to Purysburg to help on the big boat. Therefore, the above mentioned postman will take along two of our people in the morning to mark out the way from here to Abercorn.

Monday, the 17th of May. This morning the Englishman returned from Purysburg with three people and asked me to have the provisions fetched by our people alone, because his people were unable to bring them to our place with the clumsy boat. The Salzburgers whom I had sent down on Saturday had remained in Purysburg and had sent word requesting help. Although the good people here have their hands full of work, we could not do otherwise than send six men to work with the boat; for otherwise the two barrels of sweet potatoes that are with the provisions would spoil and other things might be damaged. Since the seven English-men returned to Savannah in their little canoe, I gave them a letter for Mr. Causton in which I reported: 1) that I had had to send people to Purysburg twice to bring up the provisions. 2) that I was again asking for molasses and also Indian beans as food and seed, likewise for the iron mills that we recently sent down and for our old boat, otherwise the one we two had acquired for our own use would be stove in. And since he sent iron pots for the third transport this time but no rings by which to hang them over the fire, I requested some. 3) Coming to the contents of his letter, I reported that the people are heartily ready to obey his commands regarding their cattle and the careful watch; but I complained that they had not received powder or bullets for a long time [which objects, along with other necessities belonging to the community, were still being kept locked up by Mr. Vat]. Also, the last transport had not yet received any muskets, but meanwhile they would mount the guard with good staves in their hands. 4) I asked whether it were not possible to bring the things and food-stuffs that are still in the store-house in Ebenezer here and put them under my super-vision. Ebenezer Creek is getting lower and lower and therefore harder to travel in the boat. Also, because many frightening re-ports are arriving, the few people who are still there wish to come here too. I let them know that I could not be responsible if any damage occurred to the provisions remaining there. I also hoped that no new burden would be laid upon the Salzburgers with guarding the store-house in Old Ebenezer, which might increase the people's suffering and miserable condition.

I do not doubt that Mr. Oglethorpe and other worthy bene-factors in London would be very displeased with Mr. Vat's audac-ity and obstinacy if they heard about it. 5) I could not determine anything about the quantity and quality of the provisions that he wished to credit to the first and second transport until I had re-ceived an answer to the letter I sent Mr. Oglethorpe. The chief content of this letter was to beg Mr. Oglethorpe humbly to kindly continue the free provisions for the people until they could sup-port themselves, as was promised orally and in writing in the name of the Lord Trustees. He (Mr. Causton) would well know that it was not the people's fault that they still had to eat other people's bread. Neither in Old Ebenezer nor here has their land been sur-veyed for them and transferred to them as theirs; and, moreover, they had had almost unspeakable fatigues and obstacles in their field work on the barren soil. Therefore I did not doubt that Mr. Oglethorpe and others of their benefactors would let them have not only the free provisions but also the former complete provisions until they could support themselves. Otherwise they would have to suffer want during their hard work, especially since they are no longer able to buy anything.] 6) Finally, I reported to him that the postman would get people for blazing the trail to Charleston and that he had begun to mark the trail to Abercorn with two of them. However, I did not know how he expected to get across the Savannah River to the Carolina side, because I had to send our little boat down to Purysburg today with six Salzburgers on account of the provisions. 7) Lastly, I asked him very humbly not to take amiss my frank manner of writing in trying to present the people's want.

Tuesday, the 18th of May. Today, after school, I was called to Michael Rieser, who belongs to the third transport, to pray with him and also to give him some advice. I found him in a severe fantasy because of a fever he has had for several days; and, although I could hardly speak with him, I prayed for him with those present. Not long afterwards he jumped up out of bed and ran around almost naked in the front part of the town singing, shouting, and striking. Therefore I was compelled to have him seized and guarded by strong men, which cost the people not a little effort, since he is a strong man. When I visited him yesterday he told me that he had caught the sickness on his last trip from Savannah. He had wanted to scoop up some drinking water from the river with his hat when, to his great fright, a large snake had bitten at his hat, since which time he had noticed a great change in his body. [He is a very poor Christian, even if he does not neglect external practices. I would like to have spoken with him sufficiently, according to his understanding, if it had been possible with the people who still live in the big hut. I sent word to him through his wife, who requested some medicine for him a few days ago, that I had just heard how evilly he had treated his wife in his anger, much to the offense of other people. This sin, along with others, he should confess penitently on his sick bed. Today I asked his wife whether she had told him what she had heard from me. She affirmed this and assured me that he had received it well and had regretted his misbehavior. Although his words and actions today came from his paroxysm, they nevertheless attest the wicked foundation of his heart in that he not only made indecent and vexing gestures and words but also beat his wife severely and jumped on other people against whom he had previously had a grievance.]

Toward evening Mr. Zwiffler came to bleed him, to which he finally let himself be persuaded. Today it was excessively hot and

the workmen who are jointly building our huts with much zeal
lost a lot of sweat. The soil is becoming very dry and all the plants
are suffering much damage, in Ebenezer more than here, unless
one waters the gardens there every day.

Wednesday, the 19th of May. Because the land has not yet been
surveyed and some of the Salzburgers want to prepare some pieces
of land for Indian beans and sweet potato vines in their off-time
before and after the communal work, I assigned some of those who
wanted it a part of the market place, which runs right through the
whole city and has very good soil. They will plant it this year, and
in this way the city will be cleared of the many trees. [This cannot
displease Mr. Oglethorpe because, according to the surveyor's suggestion, the entire city square should be cut down and planted.
Michael Rieser is faring a bit better, since his great fever and
fantasies abated somewhat after he was bled. In his fantasies he
spoke a lot about strong enemies through whom he would have to
fight his way, and he said that it would be much harder to win than
he had ever believed but that now he had almost succeeded. From
this, one should conclude that before his paroxysm a hard spiritual
battle had taken place in him, to which one should relate his previous serious prayer and consideration of certain Biblical passages.
However, because I knew the man's bad condition and had already
heard such words in his fantasies, I took it as a sign of his recupera-
tion and recovery from his sickness rather than to consider such
expressions a work of the Holy Ghost in his soul. Meanwhile, I
prayed to God with sighs that He might prolong his life and give
him time for penitence. In time I shall have occasion to speak more
about this with him. Things look quite miserable among some of
our now increased community. May the Lord give us strength and
wisdom to conduct our office with profit.]

Thursday, the 20th of May. Last night there was a thunder
storm, after which it began to rain somewhat but soon stopped.
Today the heat was again very intense, because of which the little
rain and moisture were soon dried up. Our people arrived this
morning with the provisions and complained that the two barrels
of sweet potatoes were almost entirely spoiled through the negligence of the Englishmen, who let them get hot in the barrels. To
be sure, they soon dumped them out and spread them out but
found the greatest part already heated through and rotten and
stinking. Today, when I had them select and measure the good
ones, only five pecks out of the nineteen bushels were usable. If,
according to Governor Oglethorpe's order, we were given a good
big boat such as are used on the Savannah River and if our people

were given more provisions than one pound of salt meat and one pound of rice for the journey, they would gladly fetch the provisions themselves. Otherwise much is damaged, and the Lord Trustees are caused much unnecessary expense.

Friday, the 21st of May. Today we unexpectedly received two slaughtered oxen as fresh meat, which was immediately distributed to each and every member of the community by weight. In my last letter I had reported to Governor Oglethorpe that God had greatly blessed the supplementary victuals that I had received from the store-house for the sick; and at the same time I asked him to send them some fresh meat to preserve and strengthen their health. May God be praised for this too, and may He continue to guide the heart of our dear Mr. Oglethorpe to that which redounds to His divine glory and to our salvation.

Saturday, the 22nd of May. Today, for the first time at our new place, we saw an Indian, who had a wife and a little boy with him. We did as much for him as we could. He was very reasonable and orderly. It is said that some have passed through Old Ebenezer and have received gifts from Governor Oglethorpe, with which they are said to have been very pleased. I wrote Mr. Causton a letter that is to be sent to Savannah early next Monday with the large boat, which our people have to take down again. In it I give him 1) news of the provisions received, which were inadequate as far as the pork and rice are concerned. I am again requesting beans for eating and planting, also molasses for brewing beer, iron hooks for the iron pots of the last transport, wedges, chisels, and large and small drills. 2) I show him that of nineteen bushels of sweet potatoes fourteen and three-quarter bushels were ruined through the fault of the English boatmen who brought the boat to Purysburg and let the potatoes get heated one against the other. 3) I ask whether he will permit us to give some flour to the pregnant women among us, because some of them cannot eat the regular provisions, in which there is neither flour nor butter. 4) I ask him to send two barrels of flour for three families, for which I am sending money. I hope very much for Governor Oglethorpe to return soon from Altamaha, because the change in our situation depends upon his arrival.

Sunday, the 23rd of May. Because I still have to preach God's Word alone in the community this Sunday, I was prevented from visiting the sick partly through faintness and partly because of the children who came to me to pray. Late in the evening Michael Rieser had me called twice because his sickness had become more critical. The first time he spoke quite clearly and edifyingly and prayed with me devoutly; but the second time the fever had again seized his head so that he was again fantasying. When I visited him Friday he spoke with much emotion of God's great mercy that was granted him and of His great patience and long-suffering. And he firmly promised his Creator and Redeemer, through the mercy of the Holy Ghost, to apply his time better in the future and to devote himself entirely to the Lord. In this fantasy he remembered that, when he presented himself for Holy Communion, I had reproached him for having begun his marriage with his wife in a disorderly and un-Christian way; and he asked me whether I had not been told about it by the two Floerls. He said God had revealed to him that He would judge it on Judgement Day, etc. He spoke much about revealed things and prophesied both for me and for my dear colleague much good that we would someday find in heaven. Instead of answering, I prayed a second time with some people who wanted to stay up with him all night. On Friday I visited him; and he spoke with great emotion about the great mercy of God that swayed over him and of His great patience and forbearance, and he promised his Creator and Redeemer firmly to apply his time better in the future through the grace of the Holy Ghost and to give himself entirely to the Lord.

Monday, the 24th of May. Last night God granted us such a fruitful rain, but without the thunder storm that is customary here at this time, that we could not have wished for or asked the Donor for a better one. It lasted all this morning and thus thoroughly revived the parched soil. The many squirrels that are found in this new place have dug up and eaten so many of the corn seeds so that they had to be replanted today. [Already more than a year ago powder and shot were entrusted to Mr. Vat for our people from the store-house in Savannah, but it is all still lying locked up in the store-house in Ebenezer. They greatly need powder and shot to shoot away the harmful animals and birds, but in this too they must be patient. We cannot comprehend why people are so indulgent with this man's obstinacy and austere manner and let us suffer in so many ways and be deprived of the many things lying in the store-house.]

Today I again had to change the location of my dwelling, as another strong reminder that we are merely pilgrims here and have no permanent abode. My hut was completed last week and I have moved into it and have vacated the small hut I have lived in so far to its owner, Stephan Riedelsperger. My dear colleague's is also almost ready; and, God willing, he will probably move here tomorrow. We are arranging our domestic affairs here just as we did in

Old Ebenezer so that each, to be sure, has his own place as a dwelling, whereas the yard, stalls, kitchen, garden etc. are in common. We plan to live in these huts as long as it pleases God, since the dear people have built them well and spaciously. We ourselves are not able to have houses built, and we would not agree if our superiors expected the Salzburgers to do it for nothing, since they have had enough difficulty with all sorts of matters.

Tuesday, the 25th of May. Today my dear colleague moved from Ebenezer into his new hut. May our heavenly Father let us continue to live together for His glory and for our and our congregation's good. It stands in our Lord's hands whether we will spend our short lives in these huts or whether we will journey further according to God's will. We are satisfied as long as we go to heaven and remain with Jesus.

Wednesday, the 26th of May. The few people who have been in Ebenezer until now are moving here, some of them today and some of them tomorrow. They have had their cows driven here today; but the calves that cannot go to the cows shall be kept there a short time longer, even though there is not much to win from the cow pastures now since Mr. Causton has again denied them the region across the Ebenezer River, where the most splendid pastures are. The four Salzburgers who had to take the big boat to Savannah came back again today and brought nothing except the two little barrels of flour for some of the Salzburger families, [although I had requested some wine for the sick and women in childbirth, some beans for seed, some farm tools for the last transport, etc. This time again he writes me no answer, although I need it in regard to the flour I requested for the pregnant women.] In God's name I shall continue to give some supplementary flour, butter, wine, etc. to those who cannot eat the regular provisions because of their special circumstances, even if it has to be paid from the poor-box, as has already happened several times. Praise be to God, who has previously provided for the wants of the poor people. [Otherwise they would have fared very badly.]

Thursday, the 27th of May. The wife of Schmidt, an Austrian of the third transport, brought a young son into the world yesterday evening. Since the child is strong and healthy, it will be baptized at its parents' request next Sunday before the congregation. To be sure, it was said a few days ago that Governor Oglethorpe would arrive in Savannah again shortly, but now we hear that he is so occupied with establishing a fortress [and so many apparently dangerous things], that his return will probably be delayed a while longer. The store-house in Savannah is not supplied with enough foodstuffs, and therefore our people must be patient in many things and get along with the generally poor provisions. [If I were not afraid of offending Mr. Causton, I would clearly report our hardships to Mr. Oglethorpe; and I do not doubt then help would be given.] With regard to the Spaniards and our neighbors, the Carolinians, things now look pretty bad, [details about which I hesitate to give. I requested some carpenter's tools from Mr. Causton for the last transport, such as large and small drills, chisels, wedges, etc.; but he answered the people who were to bring them that they had already received a great many from Mr. von Reck and also that the last iron pots were so heavy that they could not expect many of them. Thus the poor people are in a bad way in this regard too. In the beginning, when Mr. von Reck could not get anything from Mr. Oglethorpe, he overhastily obtained all sorts of things from a merchant and then distributed them among his people. This is a questionable matter and hardly adequate, and it will surely be reckoned very expensively.]

Friday, the 28th of May. Shortly before evening we heard here the cannons being fired loudly and often in Savannah, and from this we concluded that Governor Oglethorpe had arrived. We are most anxious for his arrival, because we hope many things will be improved afterwards. I would gladly go down, if Sunday were not so near and if we were sure of it. Just as soon as the dear Salzburgers are somewhat sure about their land, we will at once write to our friends and benefactors in England and send our diary, as we have long wished to do.

Saturday, the 29th of May. Throughout almost the whole night we have had intermittent rains, the value of which can be easily seen in the gardens and fields. If our people had received their own gardens and fields, they would have had more gain than they will have from the plots of ground they have cleared collectively. Less diligence, supervision, and care are applied in communal work than each householder expends on what belongs to him. If the people should have to continue to perform their work communally, there would be many evil consequences that are not to be avoided.[162]

Sunday, the 30th of May. Already last Sunday and again today I announced to the congregation that Holy Communion would be held next Sunday for those who reported to me. Again I reminded people that those who secretly live in a disorderly way and cause scandal should be reported in time so that, as is right, they can be excluded until they have shown improvement. [A short time ago the shoemaker Ernstdorff received Holy Communion from us, although a few days previously he had sinned against God by excessive drinking in Purysburg; and this was reported to us only after he had partaken of Holy Communion. Since that time, when Communion has been announced, we are accustomed to ask the members of the congregation to inform us in time about disorderly people and their behavior.] We no longer have the congregation so close together as in Old Ebenezer, rather each family lives on the house lot assigned to it, with few exceptions. The streets are still full of trees, and the squares that belong to the public are covered with such high grass that frequent visits are tiring for us.

Monday, the 31st of May. I had intended to go to Savannah this morning and had already engaged three people for it; but obstacles presented themselves so that it must be cancelled this time. We implore our loyal God to incline the heart of our worthy Mr. Oglethorpe to that which will redound to His glory and to the welfare of our congregation. Perhaps it will soon please our dear Lord to have our dear Salzburgers assigned their own land, for which they have long sighed. [Communal work, in the way we have practiced it so far, is no good and brings little profit. If the people were given their own land and were allowed some freedom in their work and their arrangements, one would soon detect excellent gains.] Even though the Salzburgers of the second transport have secured their cleared land with a firm fence, some pigs (no one knows how) got into the corn that they had planted and which was already growing and almost ruined the largest and best part. Therefore they must replant it tomorrow. The same thing happened to the first transport a few weeks ago, when the cattle found a way into the field that no one had expected.

Tuesday, the 1st of June. E. [Ernst], together with his wife, reported to me already the day before yesterday for Holy Communion. Today he came again for this purpose. I showed them both very clearly that they were not yet ready to partake of it worthily and what they would have to do to prepare themselves for it correctly. Also, his case [deed of Cain], which was known in the entire community, would have to be settled before the authorities, and his wife would have to apply more diligence to come to a right literal recognition. [The man was again very angry about this, boasted of the diligence he had shown elsewhere and here, complained of maligners who always denigrated him, and said he wished to leave us because people here do not like him. I spoke to him with great love and very cordially and showed him the reason why I had to proceed thus. I told him something about Rott and God's judgement over him and his family because he did not wish to live an orderly life here.[163] I promised him this time to speak a good word for him to Mr. Oglethorpe and said I would investigate whether people really caused him so much vexation and did him so much wrong as he claimed. I also admonished him to a diligent use of the means of salvation so that he and his wife might be converted in their hearts and become children of God, in which case we would be happy for them and help them to, rather than keep them from, Holy Communion. His wife had to promise me to come to me for a half hour each day so that I might teach her the basic truths of the Christian Evangelical religion. So far she has used both her own and her child's physical weakness as a pretext for their not being able to attend the evening services diligently. When people are ignorant and at the same time wicked, yet bring a good recommendation from their father-confessor or someone else, not much can be done with them.]

Several of those who reported to me for Holy Communion can hardly complain enough about their worldly hearts that are revealing themselves in their present circumstances. Probably many a Salzburger is harmed in his Christianity and often kept from serious and diligent practice of prayer by the excessive work and distraction as well as by great poverty, which they would like to escape through hard work, and thereby get into all sorts of worries. Yet in the case of some good souls I find that they consider the well ordered and serious application of their minds and bodies in their work and practicing their profession to be a carnal concern and worldly desire, a worry about food, etc. Therefore I shall give them some necessary instruction. Our dear Lord has caused to be written in His Word not only the internal but also the external life of believers, as to what their worldly work and way of life was. This is most useful in the case of simple people who, in seriously preparing their salvation, consider much to be a sin that is not.

[Wednesday, the 2nd of June. Mrs. Ernst has begun today to come to me privately so that she can be instructed in the basic truths of the Christian religion. She was brought up as a Catholic and still has a very poor knowledge of our Evangelical religion. She cannot read and has little understanding or memory. Therefore much time will pass before she learns anything. Although it is difficult to make her learn anything by heart, I must nevertheless read her the words of Luther's *Catechism* without explanation until she learns to grasp them. Moreover, I also say for her short Biblical passages, e.g. "Blessed are they who hunger and thirst," etc. and "Sin is the people's ruin"; and I try to teach her, through question and answer, the basic strength-bringing truths of the catechism and Christian dogma in the simplest way. Also, she should bring her husband's Bible, in which I underline certain passages for repetition. Now at the beginning she is showing some pleasure at this private practice. In addition to her, Zettler must also come to me and let himself be better instructed before I can admit him to the Lord's Table. He can read somewhat, and therefore he has to learn the principle articles of the catechism himself in an hour set apart for it. When he has learnd his assignment he recites it to me and is catechized about one of the other divine truths. When he has grasped the catechism, then he is to learn some Biblical verses.]

Thursday, the 3rd of June, was Ascension Day. Our dear Lord has laid a blessing on the repetition hour in Old Ebenezer; and therefore I wished to make a start in it in this place too, but I was hindered in this partly by the great heat that lasted until evening and partly by the demands of some people. Meanwhile our listeners have been told so much both in the morning and afternoon about the gospel and epistle for the day that they cannot complain of any lack, even if the repetition was dropped this time. Our school children greatly encourage my dear colleague on Sundays when he tells them something useful from God's Word and prays with them. Some of the new children are starting well in school, may the Lord Jesus anoint them with His spirit so that they will grow like grass, like the willows on the water courses. Now that there are more of them, we have an even better opportunity to teach the congregation the unknown melodies through them. We sing the songs with them in the school until they have learned them, and then from time to time we make a trial in the prayer hour or in the public divine service. The people find great pleasure in the edifying songs in the first part of the Halle songbook,[164] and it were a shame if they could not be used.

Friday, the 4th of June. I am very troubled because the uncertainty among some of the people, especially among those of the third transport, is so great that you can hardly imagine it. I have learned a lot about this matter. However much we would like to apply all our time and energy to help remove this evil, there are now many obstacles in our way. In particular, all of our people are involved in so much necessary work that they have no time during the day to come to us for private instruction. And, even if we wished to visit them diligently, that can hardly be done; because they are scattered around in field and forest, and also such encouragement and conversation is not adequate. May God teach us in this too to act according to His pleasure, and may His spirit lead us upon the path we must follow for the best of these unknowing sheep. To be sure, they do not fail to visit the prayer hours, public divine service, and the catechization; and, as they often say, they feel the power of the Word in their hearts. But since some of them are of poor understanding and limited ability and have learned nothing in their youth, it takes a long time to bring them to a right understanding and recognition of the basic strength-giving truths of the Christian religion.

Saturday, the 5th of June. The Salzburgers have considered it necessary for the time being to distribute among themselves the land that they have cleared communally so that each can care properly for the piece that has fallen to him and plant whatever he wishes between the corn. In communal work the one depends upon the other; and many, particularly the lazy people, stay away with all kinds of excuses. But some of them who have a lot of work in Old Ebenezer and here cannot always be present when it pleases the community, or they must neglect other necessary things. There are so many difficulties when an entire community should work together that not half as much can be accomplished as would be accomplished if the people had their freedom and could work in small groups on their own land that has been allotted to them. Now some of them are working on the squares belonging to the city to prepare them for planting sweet-potatoes, because their own gardens have not yet been surveyed. These pieces of land, which they are clearing with the sweat of their brow, they can use only this summer; and after that their fence and all their work is in vain. And thus it has always been with their work. Who knows who will receive the large pieces of land that they cleared in these areas around the city in the spring. Certainly they will not be allotted to them alone, for many who did not work on them will want a share.

Sunday, the 6th of June. I received definite news from Ebenezer that Governor Oglethorpe is in Savannah, so toward evening I got ready with some Salzburgers for the trip to Savannah. God give me much wisdom to present our congregation's want and circumstances to our [worthy] Mr. Oglethorpe in such a way that we will receive much joy and reason to praise God.

Monday, the 7th of June. This morning I had an opportunity to speak with Governor Oglethorpe about our congregation. He showed me much affection, clarified many things I had not been able to accept, and promised to remedy so far as possible the things that have been burdening us. He permitted me to write down some points concerning the welfare of our congregation and to give them to him as a reminder. This mainly concerned the Salzburgers' present inadequate provisions, which, I hope, will be improved. He promises to have the land surveyed for the people as soon as the surveyor returns home, he now being among the Indians to lay out a town for the merchants.[165] However, he would have preferred to see the people continue to work communally without knowing their own land. He promises much advantage from this, but I was able to assure him of the contrary from experience. He is allowing houses and gardens for the three widows among us without sons because they will remain unmarried on account of their age. [Mr. von Reck is still in Altamaha with his brother and the people they took with them and is helping to build the fort there. I was told that he sent me a letter, which I have not received, requesting a large number of people from our community. Nor would I have agreed to this request, because it would be to the harm of the community and I have no order from Mr. Oglethorpe to do so.]

Tuesday, the 8th of June. Toward midday I arrived again in the community safely. God be praised for all His fatherly care. E. [Ernst], who recently committed an evil deed in the community, was sent to prison in Savannah at the command of Mr. Oglethorpe, to whom I had to report the sad story. After the witnesses have been heard, he will receive his due. I have asked Mr. Oglethorpe rather to take him away from us, because he and his wife do not fit in our community; and he promised me with fatherly concern to remove from us all those disorderly people whom I reported. [Also he was not pleased with Mr. von Reck because he had picked up, on his own authority, all sorts of people whom the Rev. Urlsperger had not recommended.] In the store-house in Savannah I unexpectedly found a letter that Secretary Newman had written to us two in the name of the Society. It was dated Dec. 9, 1735, and contained the answer to our letter of Sept. 1 of last year to the praiseworthy Society. Mr. Newman's words were so kind and affectionate that we thank God cordially for them. We do not know whether the worthy Mr. Ziegenhagen or other friends and benefactors also wrote with this ship, which came only as far as Charleston.

Wednesday, the 9th of June. I received a letter from the merchant Grurg, who has his business in Pennsylvania. He was surprised that the letters written to me by the Evangelical congregation in Philadelphia had not, as he had heard, arrived. He also complained that the seeds that were sent to us from there long ago have been detained until now in Charleston, from where he is now sending them. [He has a very bad opinion of Mr. Siron and his sympathy with all sorts of sects, and he also reports that Mr. Spangenberg is lodging in his house and stands in high credit with the Schwankfelders.]

Thursday, the 10th of June. Michael Rieser is not yet restored from his sickness, but he gets better every day. When I visited him I found him reading a song book to edify himself, after having read some edifying chapters from Arnd, which he showed me. The judgments he passed about his previous sickness were most edifying for me. He thanked God sincerely for letting him get sick and letting him recognize his miserable condition, especially during the violent paroxysms, and for not yet taking him away. God had worked wonders in him; through the grace of God, and he would not forget it as long as he lived but seriously seek to win salvation. God give him faith and constancy! [Rauner and his wife not only live in great poverty but are now even more defiant than formerly and believe that the benefactions that are sent to the poor Salzburgers belong almost to them alone. Therefore they can hardly be satisfied and yet can not be led to any recognition or gratitude toward God. There are other such people among those who are not Salzburgers;[166] and we must hold back from them because they are shameless and at the same time arrogant and defiant. But no distinction would be made if they conducted themselves well.] The poor Salzburgers, who are righteous, must be urged and admonished despite their want before they will come to us and accept our help in matters of clothes, shoes, and other necessities. To be sure, poverty is great among the people in the community and provisions are measured so scantily that they cannot subsist on them. I presented this with great emotion to Governor Oglethorpe and have great hope he will remedy this want. He said nothing about payment for the provisions.

Friday, the 11th of June. Governor Oglethorpe gave me permission to present the great poverty of the congregation in writing, as I had already done orally; and this I have done in detail today. The request was made 1) because of our land, that it should be allotted to the people as quickly as possible, for which I gave sufficient grounds, 2) because of the inadequate provisions, which was not enough for them to eat, 3) because of the third transport, which had received neither cattle nor tools like the other transports, 4) because of the dead or strayed cows of the first and second transports. I said the people were very poor and could therefore buy no cows and would remain without any unless the governor helped. 5) He recently demanded to know whether there were any people among the Salzburgers who wished to guard the cows that he was going to send in great numbers to Old Ebenezer. To this I wrote the answer that there were some cattle experts and loyal people there who wished to serve the Lord Trustees out of gratitude for the many benefactions they had received, but here in our neighborhood rather than in the distance so that they might have their preachers and the Word of God. I also asked him not to send any more workers to the Salzburgers, because it might cause harm. 6) I also requested some payment, which they greatly needed because of their poverty, for the four carpenters who built Mr. Gronau's house in Old Ebenezer at Mr. Causton's command, and also did a lot of work in the store-house there at Mr. Vat's command. I also wrote a letter to Mr. Wesley, Jr.,[167] now filling the office of his brother in Savannah, who is now providing the people in Altamaha with God's Word. I asked this Mr. Wesley to report to me Governor Oglethorpe's resolution from his own mouth, because Mr. Oglethorpe himself cannot write because of excessive work; and I also asked this of the governor himself. This Mr. Wesley proved very friendly toward me in Savannah and is ready to show all possible service to me and the community. He actually came only as secretary to Mr. Oglethorpe; but, since there is a great shortage of preachers, he has let himself be persuaded to accept a position as preacher.

Saturday, the 12th of June. This morning at Governor Oglethorpe's command, we received a slaughtered ox from Purysburg that weighed 513 pounds and was distributed by weight to the entire community. The Savannah River is very high, and therefore live cattle cannot be brought into this province now from South Carolina. [At the same time I received a letter from Mr. von Reck from Fort St. George in Altamaha in which he 1) expected me to have four acres of land on both sides of the city surveyed as fields for him and his brother, by which the poor Salzburgers will have to lose a large part of the land they have cleared up. As I conclude from Mr. Oglethorpe's letter, Mr. Zwiffler and the schoolmaster Ortmann will also receive their gardens near the city; and the preachers should have the first choice, which they may not refuse because of their successors in office. What will finally become of all this? Those are but a few of the consequences of communal work. Who knows what the real reason is that they do not wish to distribute the land to the people?

[Yesterday I wrote very humbly but with great emotion to Mr. Oglethorpe regarding this matter. However, since the surveyor, who is both a lazy and hostile man,[168] was sent to Savannah Town only a few days ago, we shall probably have to wait all this summer. But I shall write to Mr. Oglethorpe again and request his opinion about Mr. von Reck's claims and other worries. 2) He demanded at least twenty men from the community to work on the Altamaha

River, for which he says Mr. Oglethorpe commissioned him. It was already said in Savannah that he had assured Mr. Oglethorpe that forty men were ready to report to Mr. Oglethorpe's service at the first wind, yet I know of not a one. I believe that if Mr. Oglethorpe had wanted it that way he would have told me so. I shall not agree, even if I have to stop being preacher in Ebenezer.[169] I am fed up with all the heavy burdens that people continue to load on the congregation, along with all the flattery and kind words; and, if the promises that were given to the people both orally and in writing continue to be unkept, and if the Salzburgers are not treated like other Englishmen but like slaves, then I don't see how I should or could perform my office here. God have mercy on this misery.]

Sunday, the 13th of June. This evening some of the listeners came to the evening prayer for the first time in this new place. And since God crowned these gatherings and our communal prayers with His blessing in Old Ebenezer, we hope for it here too through His kindness. Such private worship gives us both much edification, now that we are both present. If we had been free to choose a place for ourselves in the city to build our huts, we would have chosen a place in the midst of the Salzburgers rather than in the first row where we now live, for then it would not have been so difficult for them to go the long way to our huts in the evening. To be sure, two lots are being reserved about thirty paces behind our present dwellings for the preachers' houses; but, because they have not yet been properly surveyed and because we preferred to live on land given to us as our own rather than on someone else's, we will leave the lots unoccupied and unused until someday the Lord Trustees themselves undertake to build houses. We ourselves neither will nor can build a house from our salaries but rather make do with huts as best we can. The members of the congregation have built us the two huts; but, so far as the stalls and the fences around the garden are concerned, we have had them built as we did in Old Ebenezer. We had intended to make it possible to pay for such things from our salary. However, because it is insufficient in that we see to all our provisions ourselves and have to pay dearly for all necessities, we paid for it with the hundred Reichsthaler[170] [that Professor Francke] sent to us some time ago for our use and disposition, especially since [in his letter] he gave us complete liberty for the second time to use this money for our needs and to apply the rest to the poor in the congregation. May God richly repay this and all other benefactions.

[Monday, the 14th of June. This morning Mr. von Reck arrived here again unexpectedly with his brother and was well pleased that none of our people had yet gone to Altamaha. He could not describe how dangerous and difficult the circumstances were in which he and the two people he had taken with him had been; and he has had his fill of such journeys and work.[171] God grant that he has learned wisdom and caution from this one example of his over-hastiness, which has served him no good and that he will better consider his decision in advance with our dear Lord and with good Christian people. The reason he came back is probably because Mr. Oglethorpe did not wish to use him in the way he wished to be used, namely in the position of a commander. He is now very mal-content and dissatisfied with Mr. Oglethorpe and his treatment of him, but even more so with Mr. Causton. I was told in Savannah that the young Mr. von Reck had already accepted a town lot in Frederica, but now he is resolved to settle here in Ebenezer, all of which Mr. Oglethorpe will doubtlessly take very badly.

[Tuesday, the 15th of June. This morning I had to send our Salzburgers to Savannah for provisions and Indian beans for seeds because Mr. Causton cannot get any people to bring our clumsy boat up here with provisions. On this occasion Mr. von Reck wrote a copious and rather serious letter to Mr. Oglethorpe in which he complained of the treatment he had received here in this country and asked what kind of authority and business he would have among the people at Ebenezer. He also presented anew the plight of the people he brought with him, since he had been unable to get a verbal hearing with him. He told me that Mr. Oglethorpe had frankly told him that the third transport was not to expect any cattle. What the first Salzburgers received he had paid for out of his own purse. With this opportunity I also sent the English boy Nicolas Carpenter, who had been sent up here for my service, back to Savannah, because he refuses to live an orderly life here since, on account of my office, I cannot keep after him and cannot give him the kind of work that suits him. Oglethorpe is taking him on and will know how to use him.] Yesterday and today we have had strong rain and thunder storms. The soil was very parched, but it is now thoroughly softened. The people should have planted Indian beans long ago, but they had no seeds.

Wednesday, the 16th of June. Bacher and his wife have [both] become violently sick most unexpectedly; but they let themselves be driven all the more through their pains and attacks to Jesus, their Physician and Savior. May the other young married people learn from their example what Christian married love is. Their conduct and sickness is edifying, and we never visit them without receiving much edification and spiritual profit. As they said, our dear Lord let them gather in much blessing at the Pentacost service and the preparatory lessons before it, which they have been able to use well. The wife finds nothing but sin and fraility in herself, but in the wounds of Jesus she finds forgiveness, life, and bliss; and therefore she too is concerned with the words found in Psalm 132: 13–18, which were applied to the good of the congregation in the preparation for the Pentacost service.

Thursday, the 17th of June. For several days we have had heavy cloudbursts with thunder showers, as a result of which the Savannah River is rising again; and this will make a very difficult passage for our Salzburgers who are fetching the provisions. Hossenecker,[172] a Salzburger of the last transport, has long been bedridden; and now his sickness has become so severe that he seems to be almost at his end. In his life he has had a secret hate toward some people [many animosities and a secret and bitter hate against Mr. von Reck], which he now recognizes and regrets; and he promises to forgive and forget whatever injustice and evil he has experienced. He now prays diligently, sighs for mercy like a broken sinner, which he shall surely receive from the Father for the sake of the blood of Jesus. Yet, if it were agreeable to the Lord concerning life and death, I would gladly wish and request for this man a longer life so that he and we might become a bit more certain about his state of grace.

Friday, the 18th of June. G. [Grüning], who has been with Mr. von Reck in Frederica, wishes to move there because there is an opportunity to earn money there. [He is not much concerned with God's Word because he thinks himself intelligent enough. But Mr. von Reck will not allow him to go away from here because he cost the Society much money. If it were up to us, we would not prevent him if he could improve his lot there; for people like him who have Herrnhut principles do not fit well into the community anyway. He enjoys much love and kindness among us and comes to the prayer hour and sermons, at least he used to do so previously.] Late yesterday evening two Englishmen came to me and brought me a letter from Governor Oglethorpe in which he requested that those houses in Old Ebenezer that we are no longer using be vacated for the captain of the fort at Palachocolas and that after the harvest he be given possession of everything that was abandoned in Old Ebenezer. He also demanded three people from the community for guarding Governor Oglethorpe's cattle there, for which he promised them provisions and a modest pay. Many have applied to take on this work, even though much difficulty is connected to it. They are forced into it by the great poverty in which they find themselves and by the inadequate provisions.

Saturday, the 19th of June. I received a letter from the preacher in Savannah, Charles Wesley, in which he gave me answers from Mr. Oglethorpe's mouth to only a few of the points I had written him. [To be sure, Mr. Oglethorpe speaks kind words, but his heart is not to be moved to pity or sympathy towards our poor people. As Mr. Zwiffler, who delivered my letter to him, says, he must have taken it badly that I reminded him in writing of the things that I had already told him orally. I am now writing to England and Germany, since I cannot refrain from presenting the plight of our poor Salzburgers as it really is, even though I cannot report any specific details to the Trustees and the Society because it might appear that I wished to complain of Mr. Oglethorpe. It seems to us that it is intended, with all good appearances, to let the Salzburgers become so impoverished that they will scatter themselves throughout the entire colony and be servants of the Englishmen. A multitude of lies are fabricated about us; and, even though we disprove them immediately to our superiors and present matters in their true nature and in their real circumstances, people still believe our enemies and calumniators more than our explanations and apologies.

[The surveyor Jones[173] is a lazy, selfish, and hostile man who frankly refused in my presence to survey the people's gardens and placed the blame on the Salzburgers before Mr. Oglethorpe because they did not wish to go and accept land where he had wished.[174] Now he has orders to survey, but he is gone to Savannah Town to lay out a city. And, if he does finally come at our oft repeated request, he will, as Mr. Vat says, measure it out as it comes, even if it is as miserable as in Old Ebenezer, for which he claims to have orders from Mr. Oglethorpe. How would that improve the lot of the poor people who have remained all this time in such anxiety and misery? If we make any remonstrances, it will be called insubordination, disobedience to orders, and who knows what. It will be said that preachers should not concern themselves with secular matters like that, etc. How this would concur with the thoughts and intentions of the benefactors can be seen from a passage from Mr. Vernon's letter, which is dated the 25th of December 1735. His words read thus: "It has given me great trouble to learn from your Letters and the reports from others, that the place, you are settled in, is not well chosen, nor any ways answer the end proposed by the Trustees, who meant, that your people should be

placed, where the Goodness of the Soil might make returns suitable
to their Industry etc. but as Mr. Oglethorpe sailed from England
on the 10th of this month I hope, he will be with you long before
this Letter. And being fully instructed by the Trustees to redress
all grievances, he will particularly apply himself to sett out lands
for the Saltzburghers, as may incourage their industry."

[There are all sorts of apparent excuses for the difficulties the
people are caused, and the chief blame for everything must be put
on Mr. von Reck, who brought the third transport to our community against the will of Mr. Oglethorpe and the stipulations of
the Lord Trustees. It is said that the provisions, tools, cattle, etc.
were planned and sent only for Frederica, the newly established
town on the Altamaha River, and that our people would have participated in them if they had gone there. Letters have been written
to England for better maintenance, and now we must wait for the
answer and resolution from them. Even though I have incorporated
the contents of my letter to Mr. Oglethorpe into this diary under
the date of 11 June, I still find it necessary to quote it word for
word, as well as Mr. Oglethorpe's resolution as written by Mr.
Wesley, because of the answer I received to it.

["Being assured that your Honourable had the Goodness to receive the letters, which I took the liberty to write to you formerly,
& since you gave me leave lately to lay mine & our people's humble
petitions before you in writing, I make now bold to use this granted
leave with much joy & satisfaction, hoping with all strongly, you
will accept these humble lines with the same Generosity & Benevolence, as you was pleased to accept myself, as I had lately the
Honnour to wait upon you at yr. town, for which benefit as well
as many others I return most humble thanks. God Almighty has
Riches of Mercies & Blessings to reward yr. real favour to us more
than thousand times, to whom we put up our daily prayers for yr.
Welfare & the happy success of yr. prizeworthy Undertakings.

["1. The Saltzburghers humbly beg yr. Honorable's favour for
granting to them a fuller allowance of Provisions, since the present
victuals, which are allowed to them, are no ways sufficient to satisfy
them, which I know by experience to my great sorrows. They had
from their youth & forward bread & flower, which gave them the
best nourishment & strength of body to an happy fartherance of
their works, which now is a very hard thing to them, to be quite
destitute of this kind of victuals & of money too to buy for themselves. There are in my Congregation several young women in their
peculiar circumstance & little children too, who suffer much being
disabled of having any flower for their refreshment. Indeed, Sir,

they suffer hardships in their present Condition, & hope to be rid of this unhappy & unexpected accidence by yr. fatherly Care, for which I intreat yr. Honourable in the name of all our dearest Benefactors in England & Germany. 2. yr. Honourable was so generous as to resolve the people's laying out of their Garden-Lots, which to be accelerated. I beg humbly yr. favour, being sufficiently informed of the many difficulties & hinderances, the people are exposed to as long as they are forced to work in such uncertainty of Grounds. Our favourers in Europe wish not only this benefit for the Saltzburghers with all their hearts, & will be mightily pleased with the long expected account of it, but I make also bold to assure yr. Honourable, that the work in the Grounds will be ten times more profitable to them for gaining their own victuals, as it can be, if they must continue to work joyntly in uncertain grounds. Old, weak & sick people are not forgotten, but the better considered & cared for, which to explain would be too troublesome & too tedious to you, being clogged with many weighty businesses for the Welfare of the Colony.

["3. The people, that came under the conduct of Mr. von Reck, are not yet furnished with such tools, as were granted to the first & second Saltzburghers, they humbly crave therefore yr. Honourable's Goodness & generosity to let them have chisels, gimlets, Augars, Iron Hooks to their pots, Iron tools for making shingles, wedges, Cross Cut Saws, more frying pans (they received only 17 in all) wooden dishes, Cans, Door-Locks, Hinges, Steel-mills, grind Stones etc. They believe with me, the things, which Mr. von Reck bought upon his own accord for a great prize & for a little use won't be laid to their charge, or else they must suffer for an other man's fault. And since it is very adventageous for new Settlers to have cattle, Sows & Poultry in the beginning of their settlement, they intreat yr Honourable very earnestly to let them have such great benefit, as is granted to their brethern to a very great profit for themselves, & Satisfaction to their Friends & Favourers in Europe. 4. The first & Second Saltzburghers had the misfortune, that Several Cows & Calves partly ran away, partly died & were killed by the Wolves, & being extreamly poor & quite disabled to buy them again for money, they allways would be in a want of cattel for breeding, if not prevented by your generous care, which they long for with an earnest humble Desire.

["5. There are some people in my Congregation well experienced in keeping et breeding cattle, & are very ready in regard of so manny spiritual & temporal benefits, bestow'd upon them hitherto to be serviceable in some measure to their Dear Benefactors rather here et in our neighbourhood, than in other far far places, too removed from the Overseeing et Exhortations of their Ministers, wherefore they are very willing to feed et keep the Cows, you Honourable please to send to old EbenEzer. They know the Contrey well & very good Pasturadges, & if you are pleased to let me know, how many people you want, & about which time the Cattle shal be brought hither, they would built a month's time sooner some Cowpens for keeping them at night in those places, where they fed by day. However for their Welfare I beg humbly leave, your Honourable would order the Saltzburghers for keeping the Cattle rather alone than in Company of other Servants.[175] 6. Our Carpenters, who have built by Order of Mr. Causton my Fellow labourer's House at old EbenEzer, desire your Honourable very humbly to let them have some payiment for this work as well as for that, they have done in the Store at old EbenEzer by order of Mr. Vat. They are poor, et want a little money very necessary.

["7. Some people have built by my advice for Mr. Zwiffler et the School Master Ortmann Hutts, et seing that Clapbords are not fit for flooring it, they intreat your Honourable to grant them as many planks, saw'd at one side, as are necessary for the laid floors.[176] Be pleased to let me know, whether all the saw'd stuff at old EbenEzer must be fetched from thence to our place, for having them under my Care. The EbenEzer River is now high, et so the fetching of the Said Bords & Planks will be easily done with our great boat, which the people now carry up with provisions from your to our Town. Be pleased to tell the Revd. Mr. Wesley yr. generous Resolution about my humble Petitions, since yr. weighty Affairs won't give you leisure to trouble your self to write. Lest I wear your Honourable with my Scribble, & for fear I steal from you that time, which you do wholly imploy for the care & Prosperity of the Publick I conclude, and commending you heartily to the blessings of the Almighty & me & the Saltzburghers with all their Needs et Difficulties to your generous & fatherly Love & favour I remain"

[The answer to this was given by Mr. Wesley on 16 June 1736 and was as follows: "Mr. Oglethorpe, whom I waited upon immediately after the Receit of yours, is the same true Friend he has ever been to your People. They have used a Quarters Provision in Six Weeks, yet does he allow them Provision for another Quarter, till your answer comes from Europe. Flower, he says, is no part of the Allowance, notwith Standing they may have it in proportion according to the Value of Rice. It was a Mistake to let Mr. Jonas[177] come away before he had finished his Work, but he has Orders now to run out your Lands, as soon as he returns from laying out a new Town."]

Continuation of the Diary
Sunday, the 20th of June, 1736.

Our dear people arrived here today before the repetition hour with the provisions and still had an opportunity to edify themselves out of God's Word. We had sent two men down to Purysburg in the little boat to meet them because the water was high and the current running strong. The dear Lord granted us two many blessings from His Word for the edification of our own hearts, and we believe He will also grant just such blessings to others in the congregation who hunger for the Word of Life. It is a great cross for some of the sick to be unable to come with the others to hear the sermons. But since they are hungry and thirsty, poor and miserable, the Lord knows how to refresh them even on their sickbed. There are large and small bears in our region that usually eat only grass, black berries, chestnuts, etc.; but today a large one killed one of the Salzburger's pigs and badly mauled it, yet the meat was saved from its mouth by a Salzburger who happened by.

Monday, the 21st of June. This morning Mrs. Ossenecker called me to come again to her husband, who is struggling with death. We knelt together and prayed for us and for him, but he himself probably heard nothing of our prayer. Soon thereafter I heard that he was dead. [He had felt many animosities in his life, especially a bitter and secret vexation and hatred against Mr. von Reck, which however he deeply regretted upon his sickbed.] While he still had some strength he read diligently in edifying books, especially in Arnd's *True Christianity*, and had his wife read to him and gladly prayed with us. Therefore we hope that he is among those who save their souls and come to peace. Toward evening my dear colleague journeyed to Savannah to give the letters we wrote last week to London and Germany to a safe man for forwarding to Charleston. We have written to the Society, Mr. Vernon, Senior Urlsperger, Prof. Francke, and Court Preacher Ziegenhagen; and we also sent him an extensive diary together with the account of our heavy expenditures so far. [This time they are partly letters of complaint in which we tell our friends and benefactors of our bad conditions, because the misery of our congregation drives us to it.

[Tuesday, the 22nd of June. Mr. Vat came to Ebenezer already last week and has orders to deliver to me the things in the store-house there. But now again he is causing me trouble, namely he wishes to take the salt meat there out of the barrels and weigh it and then compel me to distribute it immediately, because it would not last when the brine has run off. And for this he wished us to send him our large scale and weights. I cannot consent to this for the following reasons: 1) The time is not due to distribute provisions to the people; and, even though it comes on the 29th of this month for the first Salzburgers, they will receive only a little meat this time because every head has been advanced sixteen pounds of pork and nineteen pounds of fresh beef, and each grown person receives only fifty pounds per quarter. Consequently I would have to give the extra meat to the second transport (whose provision day is 12 July). 2) With the present scanty allowance I cannot weigh out just this meat, which is very bad, but must mix it with the good English beef that I have here so that everyone will have some good and some bad. Also, I give them provisions for only a half of a quarter year because they must be very economical now and they would also prefer to take the meat out of the barrels every half quarter rather than hang it in the smoke for an entire quarter. 3) Thirty men who are willing to go from us to work at Altamaha will receive provisions there; and therefore I shall hold back the provisions here because they would otherwise receive doubles. What will I do with so much meat that has been taken out of the barrels and out of the brine? Mr. Vat should deliver it to me as he received it from the store-house, namely in barrels. But he thinks that, in order to keep his accounts correctly, he must weigh not only the barrels but also the meat. 4) It appears that some of the barrels of meat here have begun to smell through lack of brine. Therefore I must hurry to distribute it first, wherein I would be hindered if I had to accept the meat from Mr. Vat outside of the barrels.]

Wednesday, the 23rd of June. This morning Mr. Zwiffler and Mr. von Reck came from Ebenezer and [gave me hope that Mr. Vat would give up his intention of taking the meat out of the brine, and they said he was very friendly again. Last week I had gone to see him in Ebenezer but could accomplish nothing through my representations, so it pleased me that they would give me some hope. Therefore, although it was very hot, I journeyed to Old Ebenezer; but I found the man there just as immovable and obstinate as before, even though I presented the above-mentioned arguments clearly and begged him urgently not to seek the people's harm that way. Now, because I cannot send him the scale and weights, he threatens to take his complaints to Savannah. He has a great aversion against our new place, and therefore he does not wish to weigh or distribute here any of the things he has held back and must still distribute to the second transport, rather the people must go back to Old Ebenezer. Last Monday they took the trouble to go there, but in vain. I have written a letter to Mr. Causton about Mr. Vat's plan, which I will send down at the first opportunity.]

Because nothing has been done yet about surveying the land and our people are in great poverty and have already cultivated the field and garden they cleared, thirty men are willing to go to Altamaha to work for two or three months. We see in several ways that Governor Oglethorpe would like to have them there, even if he has not ordered it expressly. If it is the will of the Lord, whom we try more and more to test in our prayers, then one of us, perhaps the one who can get away first, will go with them so that they will have an opportunity to hear God's Word and to receive advice from time to time. [Want drives the people to this resolution, otherwise they prefer to remain here. Therefore I recently wrote through my dear colleague the following letter to Mr. Causton (for Mr. Oglethorpe has gone to Frederica again): "As for the fresh meat, you was pleased, to send us Several times, I beg leave, to acquaint you, that the most part of our sick people recovered, wherefore they are satisfyed to have their ordinary salt meat, which is by the present Short allowance of better use to them, than fresh meat, since they don't receive salt for keeping the fresh meat a little longer in this hot season. You will remember, that our allowd not above ½ pound meat, et about 3 quarters of a pound breadkind, wherefore they must live very Sparingly, since their money, gained by their work in Germany is gone: Being fully acquainted with the great wants of the people in regard to the victuals, clothes, money et own land too, I endeavoured myself to persuade them to leave for some months rather our Ebenezer, et to go to Frederica for gaining there some money et victuals, than suffer here hardships.[178] They are ready to do so, if you are pleased to speake about it to Mr. Oglethorpe et to send me word, when et by what opportunity they shall be sent toward the Southward. For my Fellow laborer shall go thither in their Company, et stay there for having care of their Spiritual Welfare etc."

In answer to this Mr. Causton reported to me that it would, to be sure, please Mr. Oglethorpe if Salzburgers wished to be used but that it was a delicate matter if they did so only out of misery. He had no orders about this but would speak to Mr. Oglethorpe as soon as he returned to Savannah. Oh, how gladly the people would remain here if only such dire misery did not compel them to work there. With the exception of Grüning and Rauner they would not do it unless one of us went with them.]

The uncertainty about the land and the communal work is a great harm to the people. A few weeks ago they distributed among themselves, just for this summer, the land that they had cleared communally so that each of them can work when opportune and pleasing to him. Whereas it used to look so poor and miserable while it was held in common that I was afraid of all sorts of slander [calumny, and reproach], the corn and beans, which they planted even before they received the seeds, are now so beautiful that the people are overjoyed and praise God. [We should give reasonable people their share of this field and grant them freedom to work, and then you would soon see the advantage.[179] But now people who have never learned agriculture and fieldwork wish to give orders; and, if we say something about it or make objections, then that is called disobedience.] Three Salzburgers have hired themselves out [also through distress] to guard cattle for some time in Old Ebenezer, where Governor Oglethorpe is having three hundred head of cattle brought to pasture. Two of them are well grounded in grace and can perhaps be a blessing for the Englishmen with whom they will have to deal there. [They will also watch out somewhat for the Salzburgers' gardens there so that nothing will be carried away, as the English laborers began to do in our gardens right after their arrival, even though the English captain under whom they are serving promised to make the loss good. My dear colleague and I have had to vacate our houses for them, and therefore our garden is the nearest.]

Thursday, the 24th of June. Some time ago our people received as a gift from England a considerable supply of square pieces of shoe leather, which we are distributing among them. A man and woman receive four pieces, out of which eight soles can be cut. The people received this benefaction with much joy and gratitude. I have delayed so long with the distribution because Mr. von Reck had told me that leather for the uppers had also been sent to the people too, for which I have been waiting for so long, but in vain. We still lack a convenient dwelling for holding school. After Mr. von Reck went away, we used for this purpose the hut that had first served in place of the store-house and in which we still hold the prayer hours and Sunday service. [Since the return of Mr. von Reck this can no longer be done, because he and his brother and servants will occupy it until his hut is finished.] Meanwhile we instruct the children in our huts. However, they can not yet be introduced to writing because we lack a large table. Everything will gradually get better.

Friday, the 25th of June. For a few days we have had great heat, which is very uncomfortable for working people. It starts already at eight o'clock in the morning and lasts almost till evening. In spite of it the water is so high that it has almost entirely flooded our gardens in Old Ebenezer. In this heat that began after the lasting rainy weather some weaknesses are appearing among the people that may have been caused by drinking so much water during the heat. For the past half year we have received no molasses or syrup, which is generally used for brewing beer. In my intercourse with our people I am often much cheered when I find in them a comforted spirit despite all their poverty [and difficult circumstances,] and they assure me that they would not exchange places with their countrymen in Germany even if they had good times with their employers. They, and we too with them, regret only that without their fault they still have to eat other people's bread, since this may cause surprise and questioning among our benefactors and friends, who perhaps do not know the state of affairs [and might cause calumny amongst our enemies and enviers.]

Saturday, the 26th of June. Since our listeners live in poverty and other difficult [hard] conditions and well need instruction and comfort from God's Word, I had looked forward to tomorrow's Sunday gospel in the hope of having our listeners together and telling them, as the occasion arises, the story of Lazarus and his miserable physical condition so that they can learn to resign themselves all the better, with patience and contentment, to God's leadership, which he too followed. However, the good people will be compelled [both by a man of authority and also by Mr. von Reck] to journey to Purysburg in the large boat [and take a fine horse belonging to Mr. Oglethorpe from there to Savannah; and therefore, on account of a horse, they will have to miss the beautiful Sunday, which means so much to them. I have expressed my opinion about it often enough to Mr. von Reck; but his rational arguments seem to him more solid and more urgent than God's command or the congregation's edification.

[I did not wish to resist with force, especially since we now have our spies, enemies, accusers, and calumniators on all sides. God will surely save His honor and grant His people help and rest; for He is merciful and hears the cries of the miserable. If they were without preachers, they would be treated miserably, but now people are somewhat afraid and lay this or that burden on them with a good excuse because they know that we report everything to England and Germany. To be sure, we make ourselves no friends either here or in Savannah by standing up for the common people, as it is called. But who asks for that? We have already prepared ourselves to lose our favor in London too, because people will not delay in sending all sorts of accusations from our opponents' side. But our own listeners are so dear to us that we can do nothing else but support them even if it costs our health, the favor of our patrons, and even life itself. God will surely uphold the just cause, as He has always done, and assist it with His cross and finally show that He is the Lord of the earth and the Refuge of the righteous poor.]

Sunday, the 27th of June. Today I announced for the second time that Holy Communion will be held again next Sunday. However, if the trip to Altamaha should occur in this week, it can be held some convenient day this week for those who report to me for it tomorrow. Because a [serious] theft was committed among us a few weeks ago, the perpetrator of which we have not been able to discover despite much effort, I used this opportunity to inform the congregation publicly about what had happened and earnestly admonished the perpetrator not to keep such a curse on himself or to approach the Lord's Table with it, for surely spiritual [and secular] judgments would follow. [With the congregation in Old Ebenezer it was not the way it is now that the third transport has come to us and with it all sorts of people.]

I visited in a Salzburger's house where a woman told me with many tears how God let the sins of her youth appear in her heart this morning in such a way that she thought she would surely die in her pangs of conscience. She was all alone in the house with her little child, and she had wished nothing more than a pious and righteous fellow-prayer and fellow-struggler. Yet in her spiritual terror and hard struggle, when she was despairing of comfort, some Biblical verses occurred to her, such as: "Behold, that is the Lamb of God," and "Come unto me all ye who are laden," etc. and this strengthened her heart like balm. She said that, because her husband must be in Ebenezer with [Mr. Oglethorpe's] cattle, she is always alone but that much occurs in her soul during such solitude and she hopes that God will add her to the little flock who save their souls. I gave her the necessary instruction and comfort and spoke with her a while, both of the great seriousness that is required for being saved and of the great loyalty and love of God that He shows by clearly laying out the path to salvation and by working so much on our hearts.

Monday, the 28th of June. Mr. von Reck has heard that Governor Oglethorpe has reached Savannah again; and, because he had recently requested by letter to speak with him after his return and because he wished certainty about the Salzburgers' trip to Altamaha, he had three Salzburgers take him down there this morning in the little boat. For several reasons it was necessary for one of us to go down with him, and this would have occurred except that I have to distribute provisions tomorrow to the first Salzburgers and my dear colleague was held back by an injury to his hand.

Tuesday, the 29th of June. The two Bachers are still bearing with great patience the cross that God has laid upon them through a violent fever; and they are making good spiritual use of the alternation of heat and cold, of good and bad days. Pious neighbors give them much pleasure through their Christian encouragement, assistance, and conversation, and by reading to them. Things go very simply and honestly among them, since they are simple and honest souls. The wife told me that yesterday, while it was so dark and she felt miserable in body and soul, God had shown her great mercy when a young Salzburger had read her something from the late Francke's *Preparation for the Pentacost Service*[180] about the Acts of the Apostles 22: 17, which my dear colleague had lent her a few weeks ago. Her joy was great at the grace God had shown her.

[Mr. Zwiffler, his wife,[181] and Mrs. Ortmann do not seem to like our new location even though people immediately built them huts and also a good garden fence for Mr. Zwiffler. They dislike it because they had already arranged everything in Old Ebenezer but have to suffer new inconveniences here, as cannot be avoided at first because of the move. But if they had had the least love for the poor and heavily enough burdened Salzburgers they would, along with us, heartily thank our dear Lord for the removal.] Today, when I visited the people after finishing my work at home, I was greatly refreshed and awakened to the praise of God at seeing everything in the people's garden, which they must tend hastily and only in their off-hours, so green and jolly, that one can hope for a joyful harvest of some produce. [I wish Mr. Oglethorpe would come here now. Perhaps he would recognize the truth rather than what our opponents tell him; and, since he means well with the people, perhaps he would be moved to give them their own bread, because the advantage is entirely obvious.] We well perceive that the Lord and His blessing are with us in our need [tribulation and opposition]. Halleluiah! Glory to Him alone!

Wednesday, the 30th of June. This afternoon M. [Müller, Mr. von Reck's servant,] reported and regretted from his heart that he had been kept away from Holy Communion for so long. He is surely an honest and true soul and is grateful for the good that God grants him from His Word among us. He has revealed many things to me that assure me even more of the sincerity of his disposition. His present service [and the things demanded of him] hinder him in his Christianity, but he hopes through the grace of God to tear himself away.

[This morning I again took a quick trip to Old Ebenezer on horseback to learn what orders Mr. Vat had received from Savannah, because someone from Savannah had passed through there; but he had not yet received an answer to his letter. Meanwhile he stands by his previous intention and will not let himself be dissuaded from it, as he told me, even if Mr. Causton and Mr. Oglethorpe should command him. In this he could not obey, etc. Outwardly he acted rather friendly toward me, yet behind my back he utters the most terrible and horrible words. I should not mind if Mr. Causton or Mr. Oglethorpe should order me to accept the meat unpacked. If afterwards a stench[182] developed in this meat, then it could not be distributed to me or to our people.

Thursday, the 1st of July. Mr. von Reck arrived here again about noon and brought me a written answer from Mr. Causton to my last letter, in which he reported:) 1 that the wine he sent for our sick people is French red wine, which greatly helps people suffering from dysentery, 2) that he is now sending a barrel of salt and several barrels of rice in the large boat and will send corn and molasses or sirup when the boat goes down again. 3) I should write down the names of the Salzburgers who fetch the provisions from Savannah because they can expect some payment for their efforts. 4) Governor Oglethorpe is leaving it up to the Salzburgers whether or not they wish to go to Altamaha to work, he no longer needs so many people as previously. The Salzburgers would have a priority, but they must submit to the strict orders that are maintained there. [5) He was sorry that I was again inconvenienced by Mr. Vat. He is in favor of Mr. Vat's weighing the things he is to give me in New Ebenezer, because both the scale and the center of business are here. He should leave a few barrels of meat there for Captain Mackintache's[183] people and give the rest to me. Should there still be any difficulties, I would find means to remedy them so that we would attain the goal we are seeking, namely that Mr. Vat finally leave us. Mr. Oglethorpe did not wish Mr. von Reck to intervene in the least way in matters of provisions, as he is said to have done according to a report by Mr. Vat. If I could not take on the trouble of the provisions, then Mr. Oglethorpe would have to look for a person of consideration and skill. He finally closed as follows: "I beg leave to assure you, that I am Sincerely concerned for the Welfare of the Salzburghers et am with great Respect, etc."

[Even though, according to the contents of this letter, Mr. Vat is obliged to use the scale here and to leave some meat in barrels in Old Ebenezer for the use of Captain Machentache and to deliver all the things to me as quickly as possible, I can see his insubordination in advance. In order to get rid of him quickly and to give our superiors an example of how we concede in order to advance the enemy and accept the harm for ourselves, I am planning to send him the scale at his request on the large boat. If he should unpack the old meat and mix good with bad, he would not be able to give it indiscriminately to the people in view of the restricted provisions, now that I have written to Mr. Causton about my anxiety. Had I not been too weak physically today, I myself would have taken him the letter Mr. Causton wrote to him and heard his resolutions, but instead I sent it to him by a Salzburger with the request to report his decision to me and to make everything as easy as possible for me and our people.]

Friday, the 2nd of July. This week several Salzburgers were willing to build a hut for the widow left by Ossenecker, since this is required by the peculiar circumstances she is in and will continue to be in. Mr. Oglethorpe allows a house lot and garden for the widows; and, since there are still some widows in the community, they will soon be cared for in the same way. Mr. Oglethorpe told Mr. von Reck that the surveyor Jones had been dismissed and that he did not yet know who would survey our land, but he would see to it or, in the absence of a surveyor, he would measure out the gardens himself. If the people received their own land in the fall, many of them would plant all sorts of trees, especially peach trees, which they already have in large numbers in [Old] Ebenezer and can get elsewhere too. Most of them have cows and are very careful in collecting the manure; and they would therefore fertilize the field, which does not have rich soil. [Those are bad off who have wives and children but count only as one man in the communal work, because in the harvest they will receive only one portion just like the single young men. Yet their wives and children will receive nothing and have had no land to plant on.

Some of the people in the community have a profession: they are carpenters, tailors, shoemakers, glazers, coopers, etc. and find an opportunity to earn something in their poverty either here or elsewhere; but they cannot undertake anything else because of the communal work, because they would be acting against love and causing anger. Thus they lose their earnings; and others who need workers and cannot get any for this reason must suffer too, even if they would gladly pay. I am not mentioning many other inconveniences that are connected with the communal work and are noted here and there in the diary. But if God does not help, no representation will succeed. The case is entirely different with the communal work of some servants in Savannah (for the masters and gentlemen there do not work) and also with the work of the Herrnhuters, because there is a great difference between our Salzburgers and those servants (under which title the Herrnhuters also are included, having for two masters only two town lots, two gardens, and two plantations).][184]

Saturday, the 3rd of July. Today there were rain and thunder storms, which are very good for the soil, since it has been very dry for some time. Yesterday our Salzburgers returned here with our large boat. If the heavy rain had hit them on the trip the rice would have been ruined, [since it was in very badly secured barrels.] A pious Salzburger told me that he and others had prayed diligently to God to prolong the good weather so their victuals would not spoil, since rain has been threatening for several days. They were both edified and happy that God had heard their prayer. Because R. [Rheinländer] wished to go to Holy Communion tomorrow and could not be accepted until he had expiated the annoyance he caused by his drunkenness, I had him come to me with those people who knew of his excess to settle the annoyance. He was ready for this and recognized it as necessary and useful.

I recently remembered that he [Rheinländer] had scandalized some of the people of the third transport a while ago on the boat by drinking too much. This he sincerely recognizes and regrets, and he himself has asked for a chance to acknowledge his sin before those whom he vexed and to ask their pardon. Thereupon I asked him whether he still recognized the sin as a sin and regretted it. He not only assured me of this but also, with outstretched hand, asked each of them to pardon his deed; and he warned them against the deceptive rum. Hereupon we fell upon our knees and prayed, and we parted with the word of the last Biblical passage we had contemplated: "Hasten, save thy soul, stand not still and look not behind you."[185] R. [Rheinländer] is again giving good indications of a change for the better; and among these I rightfully include his behaviour today [which was so contrary to his natural temperament]. His wife, who so far has been almost constantly sickly and miserable, is also making a good showing. I could not let her son attend Holy Communion this time, because he needs still more time for preparation and must come to us more diligently for that reason. The parents were satisfied with that. Nor could I admit the Austrian Grimmiger, because he is still much too uninformed [and because he is under suspicion of taking someone else's property.] He promises to come to us at noon to make use of our private instruction and to postpone Holy Communion for the sake of better preparation.

Sunday, the 4th of July. Today twenty-six persons came to Holy Communion. Our dear Lord again accompanied the preaching of His Word with a noticeable blessing, of which examples have been revealed to us. During the evening hour two married people came to us and earnestly deplored and lamented the ingratitude they had shown toward the mercy that had been granted them so abundantly until now. They are honest people; and, since God has granted them to recognize such deep corruption, we hope they will dig even deeper and become the firstborn and chosen ones of His creatures in eternity and at the Marriage of the Lamb through the word of Truth. We gave them both instruction and comfort from the Word of God and finally prayed with them. Oh, if only all the listeners would consider their salvation rightly and come to a proper zeal in achieving their blessedness, for which purpose we cordially invite them both on Sundays and in the prayer hours on the occasion of the Bible stories, which are very dear to us.

Monday, the 5th of July. Various people are getting all sorts of fever; and even the strong natures, who can usually bear it well, are suffering right violently. Mr. Zwiffler is showing his industry [but speaks a lot of a rich compensation and of an extremely good salary. Because we told him that his requests have already been sent to London several times, he is waiting to see what decisions will come. Because Mr. Oglethorpe, to whom he recently disclosed his request, will not declare himself ready to give him something definite, he is planning, as he says, to seek his bread elsewhere so he will not have to live on other people's charity, should no good resolution come for him from England. If the people would pay him for his medicines and service or pay it off with work, then they could not endure it long in their present poverty and great want.

Today he reported to Mr. von Reck to be paid for the late Bauer, and he had me come too. In the case of this man and later ones, Mr. von Reck considered it just, if they had no heirs, that the medicine should be paid. Because many people were present and I feared a violent contradiction if I objected, I did not say much at the time but went to Mr. von Reck afterwards and showed him the injustice of this claim. My argument was as follows: Mrs. Holtzer, to whom the deceased had promised and left his small legacy in an orderly

manner and in my presence, had shown him true mother-love in
her own physical weakness, waited on him day and night, gave him
her own bed, because Mr. von Reck had not given him one, and
almost ruined it, and she also spent some of her own money for
eggs and other care. The compensation that she received for it
through his legacy and last testament is very little, as is attested by
the people who live with her. Through a mistake of Mr. von
Reck's[186] he lost most of his little money in exchanging his German
money in Rotterdam; and therefore his legacy consists of only a
few clothes, of which he gave some to his friends, and a flintlock,
which he left to the poor-box and for which we were given only
fifteen shillings. Moreover, she is a widow with a child, and it
would be a grave sin to demand from her the little that belongs
to her. If Mr. Zwiffler demanded something from the deceased, it
could cause harm in the community and arouse suspicions that he
was just waiting for the death of people in the hope of payment.
Before we would trouble this widow, who is also so useful to the
women in matrimonial circumstances, we would rather satisfy his
demands with the fifteen shillings that were donated to the
poor-box.]

Tuesday, the 6th of July. God has placed a great domestic burden
on the Austrian Schmidt. His wife has been sick during almost all
her six-week childbed with cold fever, of which the child has also
had to suffer many attacks. Now he has caught a hot fever and is
seized by it very violently. In all these circumstances he is very
much strengthened and finds much comfort in his Savior and in
his gospel. When I visited him it was very edifying for me to see
from his words how the conditions of the entire community lies
upon his heart. [It troubles him that there are still so many evil
things there and that so few people praise God for the many benefactions that He always shows us.] In my conversation with him he
found the last verse of the 13th Psalm edifying: "I have hope, that
Thou wilt be so merciful."[187] Yesterday morning Mrs. Ossenecker
brought into the world a young daughter, who was baptized today.

[Wednesday, the 7th of July. A magistrate in Savannah informed
me by letter that court would be held today and that Ernst, who
has been detained there in the guard house until now, would be
tried, for which reason the witnesses were to appear. They went
away yesterday afternoon in a small boat, and at the same time I
gave them a letter to Mr. Causton that contained an answer to his
last letter. Mr. von Reck sent a letter, the content of which is, to
be sure, known to me but was not approved by me or by my dear
colleague. He means it well, but good intentions do not make

things good. Privately we invoked our God, who is merciful, to hold His merciful hand over us so that no one among us will cause himself or others any tribulation, for we already have enough to suffer from that which He Himself has laid upon us.]

[Thursday, the 8th of July. Mr. Vat has had everything that was in the store-house in Old Ebenezer, including his own things, brought here in the large boat; and he arrived here himself today. The good souls in the community are afraid that he wishes to cause harm, confusion, and discord through an unfair distribution of some things that he has held back from London to the present and now wishes to distribute (perhaps at the command of the authorities). Some of them have asked me to prevent the matter if possible; But I shall not intervene, because I have no orders from Savannah and would also like to try everything possible to keep him from leaving us with an unreconcilable and hostile heart. Some to whom he has already given some things have offered to bring back everything after his departure and to have the distribution made fairly and according to the intentions of the benefactors. Some of them did not wish to accept anything at all, but I advised against this because he might not only get angry but also take with him what was given back and use it elsewhere and have a good excuse for doing so. On this occasion many in the community reveal the evil foundation of their hearts through envy, suspicion, and evil opinions; and this causes us no little concern. God is revealing this for our great humiliation and so that we will come all the closer to the poor souls in accordance with their circumstances and be able to help them properly.]

[Friday, the 9th of July. Our people returned from Savannah this morning in the little boat, and they had made the trip in vain because the trial was postponed for fourteen days. Mr. Oglethorpe told them to submit their evidence concerning Ernst and not to come back, or Mr. von Reck or I could write it down from their mouths and send it down.]

Saturday, the 10th of July. For some days our dear Lord has visited the wife of my dear colleague, Mr. Boltzius, with a violent fever; and today he has been taken sick too. To be sure, he has not been very well for a couple of days, but it has especially afflicted him today. It appears that he has the fever too. All week he has looked forward keenly to tomorrow's glorious gospel. Therefore, while he was well yesterday, he prepared himself for it; but it will be quite impossible for him to give the sermon, since his physical strength is so weakened. This is a great cross for us; but our dear Father does not treat us according to our sins and does not repay us according to our misdeeds but merely chastises us and, to be sure, in a right fatherly way; and He seeks to tear us away from everything and wishes to reveal His Son in us so that we will seek our salvation and bliss in Him and nowhere else.

Sunday, the 11th of July. Our dear God has sent us a great blessing through our contemplation of today's Sunday gospel and epistle. May He be thanked for it! [Mr. Vat was in church too, as has probably not occurred for over a year, and was very much moved during the singing of the song: "Away, my heart, with all thy thoughts, as if thou, etc."[188] May God grant that it not be an emotion that soon subsides but that he come to a true knowledge of himself, of his great and profound corruption, and of the great grace of God in Jesus Christ! Oh, what a different man he will become!]

Monday, the 12th of July. Because my dear colleague is still unwell, the Bible story has been dropped from the prayer hour and a short and edifying passage of the Bible has been put in its place. Our dear Father has placed a great blessing on this in my soul and in other people's too.

Tuesday, the 13th of July. In visiting the sick people I noticed that our dear God has caused much good through the sickness. In particular I notice that they are brought by it more and more to a recognition of their great corruption. They see how often they have rejected God's grace, but this they heartily regret and they seek forgiveness from their dear Savior. It is their earnest resolution, if God prolongs their life, to spend it better for His glory. One of them pressed my hand and confessed how much he had sinned until now, and he asked me to visit him often and give him instruction to fit his circumstances.

[Wednesday, the 14th of July. Today Mr. Vat delivered the things from the store-house and is now ready, God willing, to leave us tomorrow. As I was taking leave of him I asked him sincerely to drop any enmity he might have in his mind. I assured him that I loved him cordially and had remembered him in my prayers to God and would continue to do so in the future even though he had left us. Even though the dear man has done much against us previously, I cannot say that it has caused us any harm, but rather good, and that it has driven us all the more to sincere prayer.]

Thursday, the 15th of July. [When Mr. Vat left us this morning, Mr. von Reck made it very clear how vain his heart still is and how much he loves the world and what is in it.] Not only my dear colleague and his wife, but many people in the congregation are lying sick and weak; and there are many other conditions into which our Father in heaven has led us in His wonderful dispensation. [Nevertheless, in spite of that he had some people make a great racket by firing their guns not only once but very often, while he and a couple of servants blew a bugle, which made great unrest and greatly annoyed my dear colleague and other sick people.[189] In the evening he (Mr. von Reck) came to my dear colleague and visited him; but when Boltzius spoke to him about it on this occasion, Mr. von Reck excused this matter and his other doings as permissible and not contrary to Christianity. My dear colleague recited to him particularly the passage Romans 12: 2, "And be not conformed to this world, etc."; James 1: 27, "To keep himself unspotted from the world"; Colossians 3: 17, "And whatsoever ye do in word and deed, do all in the name of Jesus, etc." He should reflect whether such behavior concurs with Christianity and whether he could have done it in the Name of the Lord Jesus.

[Friday, the 16th of July. Today I and several others learned how much vexation was caused by Mr. von Reck's behavior yesterday. One of the sick people himself began to speak of it and said that he was just then lying in the hottest fever and was disturbed even more by it and caused a great fright. Still another was greatly amazed and could not excuse Mr. von Reck for doing such a thing. And even yesterday someone said that nothing is more annoying than someone who wants to appear pious and yet conforms to the world. God have mercy on him and awaken him to a true seriousness in his Christianity, otherwise I fear he will come to no good end. If one is not satisfied with him, then he takes it very badly.

[Saturday, the 17th of July. It has been mentioned that Mr. Vat has not distributed but has held back the things belonging to the Salzburgers; but now he has distributed them before his departure. It would have been better however, if he had distributed them earlier; for then the ginger would not have been devoured by the worms and the candles would not have become so spoiled by the great heat. The people have often needed candles in their peculiar circumstances. Therefore, if Mr. Vat had given them to them earlier, they would have been able to use them better. As it was, they had to suffer want or else try to acquire some elsewhere. Yet our heavenly Father be praised that he has finally left us in rest and peace. May God have mercy on him!] Some of the sick are beginning to recover. For some time Mr. Zwiffler has been showing especial industry. He visits them mornings and evenings, with occasional exceptions, and tends them as best he can. [Today he had a soup prepared for some of the sick, especially for those who cannot prepare anything for themselves.]

Sunday, the 18th of July. Today's Sunday epistle gave us a splendid opportunity to think of future splendor and to arouse us to pursue the same with great earnestness. May the dear Lord place His blessing on such contemplation! One of the sick people said, "Oh, if only all men would run after heaven as they chase after worldly things!" Many of our listeners complain of their worldly hearts and are much troubled because of it; and they wish for our dear Lord to free them from it and incline their hearts to heaven. [Mr. von Reck journeyed to Palachocolas last Friday to attend the festival that the heathens are to have there.[190] But nothing came of it, and the poor people who took him up in the boat troubled themselves in vain and spent this beautiful Sunday with them so uselessly. We were much amazed about Mr. von Reck. He is no longer like he was at first and as we then imagined. Before he returned to this country we told our Salzburgers much good about him; and we hoped he would come soon, because we certainly thought things would go much better than they did in Mr. Vat's time. But we find it quite different, and the Salzburgers themselves are getting to know him very well. It is regrettable that he has such a good opinion of himself and thinks all is well with him. When he was first with us he would let us admonish him and would accept our good admonitions well; but now, say what we will, he is not averse to things that are really sins but considers them bagatelles. God have mercy on him and give us wisdom to get along with him.]

Monday, the 19th of July. This morning Mrs. Ruprecht Steiner brought two little children into the world, who were baptized immediately after their birth because they were premature and therefore weak. One is a girl and has been named Margaret, and the other is a boy who has received the name Matthias. Our dear Lord has so strengthened my dear colleague that he could take some exercise on horseback this morning. To be sure, we thought the fever would stay away, but two hours after his return it began again. However, it is not so strong as it was at first. Thus our dear Father helps again and lets all such things redound to the soul's salvation. May He be heartily praised for it!

Tuesday, the 20th of July. This afternoon the people returned from Savannah with the big boat and brought with them some corn, which was immediately distributed among the congregation. Mr. Causton has not sent any molasses, since there is none in the store-house. No molasses has been distributed for a long time; the people of the third transport have not received any as long as they have been here. Now that there are so many sick people it would do the people a lot of good; because they could brew beer with it, whereas now they always have to drink water that cannot be good for them in the great heat. Both of Steiner's little children have died, one yesterday and the other today. God be praised for letting them participate in His glory so soon.

Wednesday, the 21st of July. The Salzburger Herzog is very pleased that our dear Lord has let him become sick again. "For," he says, "that is best for me. When I am healthy, so much evil is in my heart that I am often anxious and afraid." In his healthy days he is especially sorry that he cannot practice his miller's trade and therefore often longs to be back in Germany. Now that he sees that his wish cannot be fulfilled, it troubles him so much that he thinks all sorts of strange thoughts, which he would like to get rid of if he could. Whenever he is in such a condition, we cannot get anywhere with him because he is simple by nature. But, when our dear Lord comes and humbles him, all that disappears and God's Word tastes so sweet to him that he can find no better pasture for his soul anywhere else.

Thursday, the 22nd of July. It has been mentioned elsewhere in the diary that we sent the late Prof. Francke's tractate, *Christ, the Sun and Substance of the Holy Scriptures*,[191] which has been translated into English with a preface about the life of the late author, to a merchant in Charleston who is accustomed to forward our mail.[192] The said merchant has read through quite a bit of it and gives a good opinion of it in his letter. Governor Oglethorpe sent word by the Salzburgers who were recently in Savannah that he would soon send a surveyor, not the old one but a new one, who would survey our land. The people should therefore look around to see where there is good land. May the dear Lord let him come soon so that the Salzburgers can get get started and prepare some ground for turnips and other seeds, which people here are accustomed to plant already in August and September.

Friday, the 23rd of July. For some time there has been a thunder storm with rain almost every day, which has helped our land and the crops on it very much in this heat. Therefore it looks so pretty and green on the common field and the gardens that it is a joy to see. Watermelons are to be counted among the best of all the fruits that refresh people during the excessive heat here in this country. One cannot describe what a benefaction of our dear Lord this is: when nothing else will quench thirst, the melons will. They also give great refreshment to those sick with fever and are, as we have noted, not in the least harmful. There are many of them, and our people also bring many from Old Ebenezer. There is another type

of melon, which is the kind people have in Germany; but they are
much healthier here than there, because here the sun can distill
them better. They are called sugar or muskmelons.

Saturday, the 24th of July. There are still a great number of
sick people at our place. They all have fever; and many of them are
very debilitated, especially during the great heat. Yet so far no
one has died of it, rather several have recovered again and others
seem to be getting better.

Sunday, the 25th of July. The Lord be praised for the blessing
He granted us through contemplating His Word today. May He
give us grace so that the preachers will cast their nets properly at
the Word of the Lord Jesus and also that the listeners, at His Word,
will dare to lead their Christian lives with great earnestness. For
it is He who guides our wills and our accomplishments according
to His pleasure.

Monday, the 26th to 28th July. Before his departure, Mr. Vat
delivered many kinds of things that he had in the store-house in
Old Ebenezer, for which I had to give him a receipt. Because some
things cannot lie around any longer unused yet we cannot dispose
of them without an order from the superiors in Savannah, my dear
colleague Mr. Gronau had to undertake a trip there. I have given
him two letters, one for Mr. Oglethorpe and the other from Mr.
Causton. As a response to our poor prayer God has let this trip be
of advantage too. Governor Oglethorpe received my dear colleague
with great affection and declared himself to be concerned most
paternally about better provisions for us in the future. He has
been given a present, of which the third transport should also enjoy some. He will apply it towards buying ten cows and as many
calves, which will be given first to the neediest among them until
the rest have gradually been supplied. He has also provided for our
sick and let them have as much of the butter and sugar that Mr.
Vat transferred to me as I find necessary. God be praised for this
benefaction too. In my letter to Mr. Causton I had asked what I
should do with the things left behind by the deceased Schweikert
and Glantz,[193] an inventory of which Mr. Vat had wished to submit
to the magistrates in Savannah. But now these things too have been
turned over for my disposition to distribute among the poor and
to write down in a book to whom it was all given.

Thursday, the 29th of July. Our heavenly Father has graciously
heard the prayer I made in Christ's name and has freed me from
the apparently dangerous attacks of my fever so much that I can
again do some tasks at home, although I cannot yet undertake
holding school or performing other official functions, as gladly as

I would like to, because of the very severe and in part very serious rash over my whole body. Praise be to God who has apparently strengthened my worthy and dearly loved colleague in body and mind that neither the healthy nor the sick have any lack of spiritual care, attention, and supervision. The Lord will soon reveal what He has decided about my dear wife and her physical weakness. We lack some medicines from Halle, which were sent over either not at all or in very small quantities last time. What has been applied so far has been blessed.

What a fatherly concern of God it was that He prevented the Salzburgers from going to work on the Altamaha River. If He had ordained such a general sickness for the people there, how miserable they would have been with regard to their dwellings, physical care, and medication! Oh, how the Lord looks out for us! If He will only let us overcome our own will more and more and just test and follow His will, then it will go well even in time of tribulations. Our community is in [great] need of a rod of chastisement, which those who have eyes can well recognize. How God does everything in due time! This is the best time for the people to be sick, because they have no surveyed field and the heat would not allow them to work; and, because the fields and gardens which were cleared in the spring are completely prepared, they can rest all the better in their work. For God lets everything grow well in this good weather without their care and attention.

Friday, the 30th of July. [Mr. von Reck has told me that he as well as his brother have resolved to leave this province and return to Europe. But I cannot reconcile this resolution with the work he has undertaken with a large hut and three house lots that he is having fenced in. His conduct among us is very imprudent, selfish, and offensive. Consequently, his credit has fallen in the community, as he himself has noticed. He complains a great deal about the two of us because we cannot approve of his deeds or let him run over the people. The name of God is not seldom blasphemed because, although with the appearance of piety, he caused much evil on the trip and is causing much here, yet he considers it permissible and of no importance. We cannot possibly approve his deeds, because they are diametrically opposed to the teachings and life of Christ. Therefore it will always be hard to put up with him.]

Most of the clothes of the deceased Glantz and Schweikert have been divided among the neediest in the congregation, whereby the name of God, the Giver of all good, is praised. From Purysburg we have received the certain news that the German man T. [Tullius], who has been mentioned a few times in our diary, has been lost in the forest. This is a manifest judgment of God over him, against which we have warned him for a long time. This is the poor man who came to Holy Communion in our community on Easter with several other Lutheran people from Purysburg, against whom, however, we had to act because of his previous repeated drunkenness and offensive conduct, as was written down. Before he got lost in the forest he had drunk too much rum, so that the previous taking of Holy Communion was his last. At that time we told him that, if he continued to fall into this or other such sins, he would no longer receive Holy Communion from us. God has often worked very powerfully on his soul through His Word so that I once had good hope that he would be entirely converted to Him. But what a terrible thing disloyalty is! What responsibility it brings when a person so often receives God's grace in vain and rejects it!

Saturday, the 31st of July. [A few days ago two of the people whom Mr. von Reck misled into making noise came to me and expressed regret for their thoughtless behavior. Yesterday another one, whose conscience was troubled by this vexation during his sickness, came and tearfully asked forgiveness. He said that he too had been with Mr. von Reck and had expressed to him the displeasure he felt at what had happened. But Mr. von Reck asked him where it was written that shooting is a sin. We cannot be blamed if we seriously inquire right away into such things in the community that pave the way to impudence, ungodly behavior, and conformity to the world. And our dear Lord has let us succeed so far, even if we are called scrupulous and superstitious by those who consider themselves very intelligent and the Salzburgers very stupid.]

A sick and at the same time very pious man has so far been visited by our dear Lord with many kinds of domestic tribulations. He called on me today after his fever paroxysm had passed and praised God for his bodily weakness, with which God had visited him not only now but also previously after his departure from Salzburg. In his fatherland he was constantly strong and healthy, but at the same time frivolous, selfish, and worldly. However, after God had begun to show his soul much mercy, He has always held him under His rod of chastisement with physical weakness, which now as always greatly humbles him beneath the powerful hand of God. A few days ago it was very dark in his soul, and his sins caused him much concern; but the Lord has accepted him again in a fatherly manner, and he is now entirely content. I discussed with him briefly what the dear Saviour had let me experience in my school of tribulation on my sickbed; and I finally gave him, with explanation, the verses: "Have I not told thee, if thou wouldest believe, thou shouldest see the glory of God?"[194]

Sunday, the 1st of August. Today my dear colleague had to preach and catechize alone both morning and afternoon [because the many sores with which my whole body is covered prevent me from public work.] Our meeting is still small, most people are lying sick with fever and even more of them are getting sick, and Mr. Zwiffler himself caught fever a few days ago. Mr. Causton paid some Salzburgers to go to Palachocolas with the large boat, and they too had to miss the divine service. The sick are visited very industriously by my dear colleague, who, according to their condition, tells them something useful for the edification of their souls and prays with them. Now that God is strengthening me again, I too shall undertake such necessary and useful house visits again. May God let everything be agreeable and pleasant for the sake of Christ.

Monday, the 2nd of August. Schmid's wife has contracted a severe and dangerous swelling over her entire body, which is getting nearer and nearer her heart and could easily cause her demise. Yesterday her husband called me to give her a comforting word from the holy gospel, which she received most eagerly, since it treated of Jesus the Friend of poor sinners. She is simple and at the same time right uninformed, and therefore I spoke with her this time, as usual, with questions and recited her the easiest and shortest strength-giving verses in the Holy Scripture. If God should grant health and life to her again, we would try to remedy her ignorance through private instruction with God's grace; and for this we would have as a helper her husband, who is an experienced Christian and well versed in Holy Writ. This has not been possible so far, because she has been sick and mostly bedridden as long as she has been here and was in child-bed a few weeks ago. She is honest and seeks purification of her sins only in Jesus and His blood of reconciliation and strives to come through Him to the Father, even if it means dying. Her husband, who is not yet freed from his violent sickness, has a great domestic cross to bear with his wife and very small child as well as great poverty and other difficult circumstances; but he knows how to resign himself to it and be comforted by God's Word so that we can see that Truth and the spirit of God are in him. Whatever we can do to alleviate his situation, we do with all our hearts, even though he is bashful about asking or receiving and would rather suffer.

We have thunder and rain storms almost every day, through which the soil is made fruitful and the heat of the day is made bearable. The latter is a great help to our people with fever, most of whom are weakened by the violent heat for several hours every day. What the people have planted here and in Old Ebenezer is growing exceptionally well with God's blessing. In our watermelons we have a true refreshment in this heat, and they do no harm to the people with fever when they are eaten ripe and with moderation. They are so full of sun-distilled sweet water that they completely quench the thirst, and afterwards one cannot drink very much. [It is a great blessing that the Englishmen cannot come to Old Ebenezer with their cattle because of the high water, otherwise we would lose most of the crops.] The game is doing some harm to the beans and corn in the gardens, because the people cannot guard there because of their fever. Here in New Ebenezer the pigs had dug up and ruined almost all the corn in the second transport's communal field in twenty-four hours, because the fence was not made strong enough on one side. But the people immediately planted more corn; and, because we have had much rain up to now yet also much sunshine, that is to say right fertile weather, everything has grown back again so beautifully that we are all very happy about it. This soil is rich, and everything grows much faster than in Old Ebenezer.

Tuesday, the 3rd of August. The large boat could not be used for transporting the cattle at Palachocolas, where seven Salzburgers took it last week at the command of Governor Oglethorpe, but instead several Salzburgers must take it to Savannah again. It will probably remain there, because Mr. Oglethorpe has provided for another and better one for bringing up the provisions. At this opportunity I wrote again to Mr. Causton and gave him, at his request, a report of the trips the Salzburgers had made so far in fetching the provisions; and I also wrote him the names of those who had worked on the boat each time. He has orders from Mr. Oglethorpe to pay our people for this work. I also advised him that the twelfth of this month is the provision day for the third transport, for which reason I asked him to send corn and, if possible, also molasses or syrup for brewing beer. Because the people have been due molasses for several quarters past, Mr. Causton asked whether the people wished to accept butter in its place. They are inclined to do so; and therefore I asked him to send both butter and molasses and to inform me how much butter he would give for a gallon of molasses.

During my walk in the garden a young Salzburger who had been sick visited me and told me very simply how much good the Lord had done on his soul during his sickness, and he said that he was thanking Him for the blessing of this sickness. He could tell me of others who had received similar blessing. Another one was there who often experiences suffering, but also help, from the Lord and is therefore very comforted. Some time ago I told him that during my physical weakness I had tried to practice the words of the blessing we said at meals and found much splendor in it for strengthening my faith: "The Lord does not joy in the strength of the steed, nor"[195] . . . . *but He takes pleasure in those who fear Him and wait for His goodness.* These words now give him much encouragement, comfort, and edification too.

Wednesday, the 4th of August. Toward evening I received a letter from Governor Oglethorpe via Purysburg in which he reported in very friendly and affectionate terms that he is sending us a surveyor, who is to survey the Salzburgers' gardens at once and their plantations afterwards. In doing this [as Mr. Oglethorpe writes] he is not to burden the Salzburgers in any way; rather, if he needs anyone for his work, he must pay them. Our present Salzburgers are to have their land entirely free and without charge. Mr. Oglethorpe also sent me a copy of the contract he had made with the surveyor and advised me how the surveyor's instructions read with regard to surveying the land. Mr. Oglethorpe wants much of this to be under my supervision; and the surveyor has received from Governor Oglethorpe many points that he is to communicate to me upon his arrival. Finally, the Governor wrote that he will send ten cows and as many calves for the last transport; and he requests me and my dear colleague to give them to the neediest among this transport. He has recently promised to take care of the others too gradually. The Lord be praised for these and all other blessings!

Thursday, the 5th of August. This afternoon I had the people of the third transport come to me and told them what proof God was giving them of His fatherly care by inclining Mr. Oglethorpe's heart to give them ten cows and as many calves, which has not been possible before this. But, since it was only ten cows, it was Mr. Oglethorpe's wish to give them to the neediest. However, since all of them were needy and poor, we were trying to think of a way to distribute the cows and avoid any appearance of partiality, suspicion, or envy, through which this newly shown blessing of God could be spoiled. God surely wished to put them to the test and reveal the foundation of their hearts by giving them such an inadequate number. They should therefore be on their guard and not sin in receiving them, because they could not all have a share of them since they are too few. I then read them something out of the letter of Court Preacher Butjenter,[196] which we received along with the third transport. In it he reports that there are some very honest people in this transport, but also some who have betrayed the foundation of their hearts through suspicion and envy when others have received more than they. Hereupon I told them that we had decided to distribute the cows in this way: I and my dear colleague would privately cast lots for them and privately tell those to whom the cows would go. For we had no orders from Governor Oglethorpe to cast lots publicly, and several considerations made it impossible. Therefore it would be best if we cast lots privately; and all that mattered was that they would have confidence in us, we would be as impartial as before the countenance of God. Nor would be over-hasty in this but pray earnestly to God about it. They should do the same and afterwards consider it as having come from God, however it comes out. The dear people were all most heartily satisfied with this suggestion.

[After the prayer hour Mr. von Reck came to me and expressed his displeasure both at our intention to distribute the cows and also because Mr. Oglethorpe had committed the various matters pertaining to surveying the land to me and not to him. He will insist forcefully (as he adds) until Mr. Oglethorpe tells him expressly that he has nothing to do with it. Mr. Oglethorpe is freeing the Salzburgers from all work and burdens that the surveyor could cause them; but, in order to hasten the surveying to his own advantage, he wishes to involve our people in such work even though he has not the least orders for it. He is revealing himself more and more, and we shall surely have our trouble with him. He wanted to make a copy of my letter and of the contract between the Lord Trustees and the surveyor. However, because some instructions are appended to the surveyor's contract that include some points not suitable for him, I had to refuse to let him make it; and thereby I experienced his anger even more.

[Friday, the 6th of August. Yesterday toward evening, in anger, Mr. von Reck caused a great scandal in the community because of a trifling mater and thereby caused us great distress. An Indian had brought some honey to our place. He took the Indian into his hut. A woman of the congregation also wished to buy some of the honey, but Mr. von Reck soon sent her away very sternly. However, because she thought she had as much right as Mr. von Reck to buy some of the honey from the Indian, she turned to him and grasped the skin on the floor in which the honey was. Thereupon she was thrust out of the door by Mr. von Reck with force; and her other hand, which was already injured, was so jammed in the door that she screamed as loudly as she could. He drove her further and shoved her to the ground and struck her in the back with his fist on the public street. Her husband came running up; and, hearing what had happened from his wife's words, he told Mr. von Reck that he would suffer according to English law for treating his wife publicly that way on the king's highway. Mr. von Reck then called for his pistol and ran into his hut himself and fetched his sword to shut the man's mouth and chase him away. He did all this with so much shouting that I could hear it all the way from my hut. The husband saw his excessive anger and that he was entirely beside himself. Therefore, before Mr. von Reck could get to him with his sword, he and his wife took off hastily; but I shall report this matter to Mr. Oglethorpe because the wife, who has a suckling child, has received a new injury on her breast while the old one has not yet healed. Mr. von Reck committed this excess not only in the presence of his servant and several other people but also before the eyes of the Indian and his boy, who then came into the woman's house and expressed his sympathy with gestures and indicated that, if such a thing had happened among them, their king Tomochichi would have such a man bound. Instead of having later contemplated his scandal in quiet and regretted it, he, along with his servant, blew on a bugle, perhaps to signify that he had performed a heroic action and had triumphed over a woman. In the case of this offense he is not to be brought to recognition and remorse, as in earlier times, but feels himself to have been entirely in the right.]

Saturday, the 7th of August. My dear colleague observed much matter for edification while visiting a sick Salzburger and a girl. Both of them were occupied in gaining certainty of the inestimable grace of the forgiveness of sins and thus being prepared for eternity. Hereupon they received the necessary instructions, which they received eagerly and willingly. In the case of the three-day fevers, which all the sick people except Bishop and the girl have, the temperature is very high. A few, especially at first, have no chills. Some of them lack the chills a few days or weeks, but then it seizes them again. Hardly anyone among us has been spared, even the smallest children have to suffer this tertian-fever. In some huts everyone is sick, in which cases their neighbors and friends help them as best they can even though they have patients in their own huts. In the evening prayer hour I made good use of the Bible story about the expulsion of Hagar and Ishmael by applying it to our situation; and in the application I showed the congregation what was most necessary in order to understand the incomprehensible ways and judgments of God, which He has already ordained for many among us.

[We have already been reproached several times for having made a spiritual and secular mistake in the case of Ernst, whose wickedness and Cain's nature we reported to Mr. Oglethorpe. If he were in Ebenezer, then he would have an opportunity to hear God's Word often and might still be converted. In addition, he is missing his work here and is in danger of being removed from here entirely; and his wife and child are suffering want here. And, it is also said, evil gossip and calumnies are arising about us, even among the English who hear about it. We had to endure such judgments at Rott's dismissal and his subsequent miserable and impenitent death.[197] In Rott's case not only did our happy conscience attest that we had always treated him most gently and that his wickedness had reached a peak and that he was ripe for the judgment of God, against which we had always warned him, so that things had to happen as they did, but also we were comforted by the fact that Mr. Oglethorpe entirely approved our procedure with Rott and his wife in my room in Old Ebenezer.

[As far as Ernst is concerned, it might also appear that we had made a spiritual and secular mistake (as especially Mr. von Reck and Mr. Zwiffler reproach us) . However, this is not his first wickedness, rather he has already committed many excesses both on the trip and here and has been admonished, both publicly and privately, to penitence, but in vain; and therefore we must again rely not on men but on the justice of God and His holy judgments. And it is the duty of a righteous minister to practice not only the mercy but also the justice of God. Ishmael and Hagar were for a long time with God's Word in the house of the Lord's dear servant and prophet Abraham; but, because they would not be converted, God sent them away so that they would no longer cause vexation or hinder others from conversion. At first Sarah's suggestion did not please Abraham; because he without doubt thought that both of them, especially his son Ishmael, would be deprived of the opportunity of being converted. He also feared the great calumnies that could not be avoided if he expelled these people. However, since he recognized the will of the Lord, he let nothing deter him, but simply did what he had to.] At this opportunity our listeners were earnestly enjoined to occupy themselves with the dear treasure of the gospel, or otherwise the Lord will demand it of them. Thereupon I also gave them the two passages Amos 8: 11–12 and Sirach 32: 19 to take home for further contemplation.

Sunday, the 8th of August. Since the dear Lord has again strengthened me in body and spirit, I took the occasion of today's regular gospel for the Seventh Sunday after Trinity to present a matter which the Lord let my heart too experience in my sickness. I spoke of the recognition of the splendor of the Lord Jesus with and under the cross. In the first part I told something about the cross and the difficult spiritual and physical conditions of the pious, using as an example the people in the gospel, among which multitude there were without doubt many good and salvation-hungry souls; and I particularly had to remember their spiritual misery, since they were as the Lord describes them in Matthew 9: 36. I could not help but show the congregation in suitable terms what an especial mercy the dear Lord had shown them above this people and above so many thousands of people in America through His Word and His holy sacraments. I said further that I could not help being amazed that there were still a few among us who always spoke of going away whenever they did not have their way in matters of the flesh and thus valued this spiritual benefit less than bodily sustenance and convenience. Perhaps they think that they have Bibles, postils, and other good books with which they can edify themselves. But I asked them to reflect whether they had not learned from experience that there is no small difference between hearing and reading, and whether their conscience had not been touched through the latter more often than through the former.

While I am writing this, a fresh example occurs to me of a man in Purysburg who left there only a short time ago and wished to seek his fortune and sustenance for himself and his family in Charleston or in the northern provinces of America. [This is Schoemansgruber, who has already been mentioned several times in this diary.] He had come from Pennsylvania to Charleston a year ago with the intention of settling among the Salzburgers in Ebenezer and being with the Lutheran religion; but people diverted him from this resolution with all sorts of arguments about earning a living and persuaded him to accept a lot in Purysburg. He did this, and he and his wife availed themselves of our office as often as they could, and not without blessing. After Mr. Oglethorpe's arrival and our removal to better land, he again felt a strong desire to move to us and therefore wrote me a letter asking me to intercede for him; and finally he came himself to our place to find out about the conditions the Salzburgers had to enter into. But because this and that did not please him and because he could not subsist in Purysburg, he set out a couple of months ago with his wife and two children on the trip to Charleston with the intention of earning some money there with his wife and then to seek his fortune further on. But he wrote a strange plaintive letter back from Charleston telling not only how he got into obvious mortal danger on the water before coming to Charleston and how he had to lose most of his things in order to save himself and his family, but also how he was now living in the greatest poverty and had no opportunity to earn anything so that he saw nothing but even greater misery and suffering ahead for himself and his family. Had the man moved to us in simplicity and had not thought so much about providing for himself better physically, our dear Lord would not have let him lack necessary support in either well days or sick any more than the others in the community. And because we love our listeners and do not want them to plunge into misfortune by moving away and at the same time cause calumny, we warn them against it at every opportunity. Among the Salzburgers I do not know of a one with such an intention, even if even more trials were inflicted upon us according to God's will; but it is mostly those who are not Salzburgers and find no pleasure in their disposition and simple conduct.

[Mr. von Reck wrote to Mr. Oglethorpe a few weeks ago that he was told, especially by the first Salzburgers, that they would move away after three years had passed because people in this country were not keeping the promises made them orally and in writing and especially because they would not survey their land. However, it would be very difficult for Mr. von Reck if he had to prove this and report the names of the Salzburgers who had spoken this way. I told him this even before he sent his letters, yet he hardly listened. But even in my last letter to Mr. Oglethorpe I asked him in his kindness not to hold against me and the Salzburgers what Mr. von Reck might incautiously say and undertake. He has already told not only his transport but also others in the community several times something that seems incredible to me, namely he was told in London that, should there not be enough good land in Georgia for the Salzburgers (as it was feared), they would be transported to South Carolina. But he finds as little credibility in this as in other things. He has already made himself very suspect in the community.]

Monday, the 9th of August. Last week we heard the cannons being fired loudly in Savannah, and today we heard the reason for it via Old Ebenezer. Several deputies from the council in Charleston have arrived there to talk with Governor Oglethorpe about the differences that have occurred between the two provinces, particularly concerning commerce.[198] We always hope for a ship from

London and at the same time for some answers to the diaries and letters we have submitted so far. We also lack the medicines from Halle, which we hope to receive at the same time. R. [Rheinländer] was with me and admitted that he was one of those who often spoke of moving away and did not wish to submit to God's repeated trials. In this he had sinned and acted foolishly, he said; and through God's grace it would not happen again, especially since God was letting his and his wife's eyes open more and more to recognize what a treasure and opportunity they have here to prepare themselves for blessed eternity. His wife and son had asked him not to make room for such thoughts any more, etc. This evening I had another attack of fever, which was, however, not violent. May the Lord do as He wishes, and may He just strengthen my worthy colleague, then the congregation will suffer no loss of spiritual care.

Tuesday, the 10th of August. Yesterday evening God safely delivered Adam Riedelsperger's wife of a young son and gave the parents and us new material for His praise by saving the mother and child from very dangerous circumstances. When the husband was with me this morning I reminded him of his duty and recited for him the song: "Praise and glory be to the highest Good, etc.",[199] which he should not forget to sing and to read to the glory of God. With respect to godparents, the Salzburgers have some customs that do not please me and which will be dropped gradually after I have given them instructions. E. g., that the child must always receive the name of the godfather, whether it means anything or not, otherwise it would be taken badly. Likewise, he who is chosen as a godfather by another must afterwards be asked by him again in the same circumstances. And this continues on both sides as often as a child is brought to Holy Baptism, so that one may have been godfather three or four or even more times for a single family.[200]

The first custom has already been abolished among us, and we ask ahead of time what name the child will receive. If it is a mere sound without a meaning, like Veit, Ruprecht, Charlotte, etc., we admonish them against it.[201] Recently I told the congregation the most important things about this on the occasion of the story of Isaac, who, like other children of the Old Testament, received a name with a beautiful meaning.[202] In regard to godparents among the Salzburgers, we are pleased that they choose husband and wife and not just any two people, as is done in Germany often with evil intent and vexation, and also that no godparent-money is given at or after the baptism but that they do all the good they can for the convalescing mother and the child. Our Salzburgers know nothing about baptisms at which the godparents, neighbors, and friends gather as soon as the baptism is finished, or else after the six-week period, for eating, drinking, and worldly merriment. God should and will preserve us from that. Recently when we came to the point in the Bible story when Abraham gave a great feast at the weaning of Isaac, we showed that, since Abraham loved the pious, poor and strangers, he doubtlessly invited only such people and, while they were enjoying the physical blessings, spoke edifyingly with them about the great benefaction of the redemption, of which he had received such a powerful assurance at the birth of Isaac, and praised the Lord for it. Therefore, I told them, there is a great difference between Abraham's banquet and the banquets at baptisms, weddings, and so forth as they are usually given today among Christians.

Wednesday, the 11th of August. This morning I began to distribute provisions to the third transport. Beforehand I assembled all the people who could come; and before the distribution we prayed together to God, thanked Him for the provisions that we enjoy here in the wilderness through His loving care, and implored Him to look further for Christ's sake upon our wants with mercy. With the manifold want, poverty, and sickness of our listeners, the money from our poor-box has been almost entirely expended, but we hope that our kind Father, who has long known of our needs, will have already taken care of us and that perhaps at the arrival of the first ship a blessing from Europe will be sent across the sea to alleviate our needs. This afternoon I was again attacked by fever, and therefore my dear colleague continued with the distribution.

Thursday, the 12th of August. Because the provisions were not adequate for the last transport and some of them would have to suffer some lack if something were not done at once, I wrote a letter to Mr. Causton very early this morning and described our wants in it. My dear colleague went along to Savannah in my place in order to request all the sooner the things for which I had written and to hear from the mouth of Mr. Causton or of Governor Oglethorpe the answer to several points in the letter. Here in this country, when something must be deliberated, people often tend to answer orally rather than in writing. Schoolmaster Ortmann has also contracted fever; and we often have to close the school, because Mr. Gronau has more to do because of my physical weakness. It is also necessary for the sick people whose children must help them in their huts and in the neighborhood. Last Sunday I had indicated that I was intending to accept the older children into the preparation for Holy Communion, for which purpose the parents of the same should come to me. But my physical weakness prevented me from carrying out my intentions, so I shall have to wait for this until I and the children who have gotten sick recover our health again.

Friday, the 13th of August. [Mr. von Reck has also caught tertiary fever. When his paroxysm was passed, he had me called to him and announced to me that, if God gave him back some strength, he would gladly hold a conference with me and my dear colleague and confer with us concerning the congregation and several things which we could not accept. The people would not obey him, in most matters they appealed to me as if he could not command them, his authority had been greatly weakened, he was entirely useless here, and therefore he would resolve to go completely out of the country and to spend his life somewhere in tranquility. He could not permit the things that happen here to reach the magistrates in Savannah to be remedied there. His physical weakness did not allow me to answer much to his lecture here, but I assured him that we would be pleased to have a conference hour with him.]

We hear many complaints that various things, especially melons and gourds, are being taken from the gardens in Old Ebenezer and sometimes plucked unripe and thrown away. Also a Salzburger announced that during the night his and his comrade's meat was stolen from the kitchen that stands on a public road and is open on all sides. [We never heard of any disorders like that before the arrival of the third transport. There are people among them who have planted nothing themselves and cannot get along with their provisions. Because they are poor and in part incapable of working, they cannot buy anything; and perhaps for this reason they fall into temptation.] I am admonishing the people privately to watch out for everything from now on more diligently so we can catch someone and make an example of him. [Also some children are sent to Ebenezer, who are not without suspicion.] Those among us who do not like me or my dear colleague or the Salzburgers use these sad affairs to calumniate the entire congregation; and, when we have to work on them or cannot let them have their way, they tell us a lot about how things are going in the community, how godless the people are, etc. But from their stories we recognize their purpose. Such people can easily notice from our sermons on Sunday and in the prayer hours that we do not consider everyone in the congregation to be pious and that we therefore earnestly admonish to repentence and that we do not let the vices of which we hear go without chastisement. Therefore I have recently had to speak a bit about this point in the evening prayer hour when we hear in the Bible story that a wicked Ishmael and Hagar (Genesis 13: 7), likewise wicked herdsmen, were in the family of the pious Abraham and in his tabernacle.[203]

Saturday, the 14th of August. My dear colleague returned again last night from Savannah and brought back from Mr. Causton a good answer to my letters. One point he wishes to forward to Governor Oglethorpe, who has again journeyed to the South for fourteen days, and report his answer to me. The large boat that the Governor had repaired for us is ready, to be sure; but it is not now in Savannah. However, it is to be sent up here in the near future with provisions. [Ernst came back to us this time after having received his sentence from the magistrate, which consists of the following: 1) He was advised of his wickedness and told that it would have cost him his life if he had killed the woman. 2) He had to promise in writing and orally to submit to our correction, and he also pledged himself with his signature to pay a penalty of twenty pounds sterling if he should commit another excess. 3) He was required to ask forgiveness publicly of us two and of the clock-maker's wife whom he struck and finally of the entire congregation for the annoyance he had caused. And it was already a punishment that he had had to remain in Savannah so long as a prisoner. To be sure, he promised the magistrate in Savannah, but he will not wish to carry out his promise here and is again making himself very innocent. But that will not help. Today toward evening I shall call the congregation together, because I wish to take up his case along with some other things.

Müller had sinned through a hard, unChristian, and unfounded charge against his neighbor; and therefore I summoned him to come to me with the Salzburger who had heard it from his mouth. He had to hear his incautious and imprudent charges and could not deny them fully even though he tried as best he could to expound them very gently. The occasion for this was given by the ten cows we hoped for, of which this Müller preferred one to all the others. He had supposed that he had the greatest right because he has a lot of children and because he had heard that the lords of the land wanted to give these cows to those families who have a lot of children. Otherwise this man behaves himself in an orderly way; and his two little girls, who are sent regularly to school, are beginning very well. Nevertheless the father and mother will not come to any righteousness; because, in their opinion, they were already good Christians for a long time in Germany. The man often boasts of what good credit he stands in with the Court Preacher in London.

Shortly before evening many people assembled in the church at a given signal, as many as were well or did not have their fever-day. I then poured out before them the sorrow of my heart at the condition of the congregation and attempted to reach their consciences with requests, pleading, remonstrances, and admonitions. Next I took up Ernst's case, informed the congregation of the sentence he had received, and called upon him to comply with the apology for his offense and the vexation he had caused. This Ernst and the clockmaker's wife wanted to get into a conversation, perhaps to defend themselves; but they were separated by me and the admonition I found it necessary to give them.

After this had been done, I had to take up a matter that had occurred between three Salzburgers and the indiscreet and gossipy Mrs. Ortmann and had become public in the congregation. She had lost some melons and beans from her garden in Old Ebenezer. Now, because three Salzburgers were working there in the service of an Englishman at the time she heard about it, she accused these honest and conscientious people throughout almost the entire town as thieves, and charged one of them in the presence of other people on the public street of stealing her garden produce. This morning I had Mrs. Ortmann and the three accused Salzburgers come to me, along with some others who had heard her calumnies, in order to examine her complaint and accusations and to ask for proof. But there was not the least trace of evidence there, rather the suspicion for pilfering her garden fell partly on some children, whom she had formerly allowed to take some greens out of it, and partly on the transient Englishmen who have often taken shelter in her house and were so bold in her and her husband's absence to open the door that had been nailed shut and to go into the garden.

Because she was lacking evidence, she tried to deny and twist her words and declared these three people to be entirely innocent. However, because she had started an evil rumor about these men, it was necessary for her too to take back her overhastiness in front of the entire congregation and declare these Salzburgers to be the kind about whom she could not rightfully say anything evil. She resisted somewhat and wanted to say something in the meeting in her own defense, but I did not give her an opportunity. Finally I recommended to her the words in Sirach 22: 23, "Oh, if only I could put a lock on my mouth, etc."[204] and applied them also, just *per transitum*, to another gossiper, Schweiger, whose mouth has already caused him much trouble. He accused Mrs. Kalcher and her husband *directe* of a grave theft; and, even though he immediately regretted this matter (as has always happened) and apologized to them for his rudeness and for the harsh words he had spoken all too hastily and had reported his regret and apology to me too, I had to take up his case publicly here because of his repeated excesses in this point and to chastise, admonish, and make him show his remorse. Kalcher and his wife have fallen under much suspicion and calumny because of Mr. Vat, who showed them more affection and benefactions than he did the others. This may well be without grounds, and therefore I said something about it on this occasion and warned everyone against suspicion, envy, calumny, and judgments as grievous sins.]

Sunday, the 15th of August. On this Sunday fever has prevented me from preaching the Word of God to the congregation. Today it was weaker than usual; perhaps it will please the Lord to free me of it soon entirely. On good days I have enough strength to perform my duties. Toward evening the schoolmaster Ortmann called on me to edify himself with a good conversation and a prayer. For some time the condition of his heart has appeared very good to me; and he has derived much good for his soul from his physical weakness, of which he is now freed again. It appears that the days of his life might soon pass away, and therefore the Lord wishes to prepare him all the more for his departure from the world and for his entrance into joyful eternity. [His wife hinders him in this, yet it appears that she can now do less harm than previously.] A certain person told me that during her paroxysms it had appeared to her more than once that she was walking down a long road that she believed to be the road to heaven. She walked for a long time yet could not reach the end. Often she imagined that she was at the gates of heaven, but she was not, etc. I explained this to her out of today's gospel, Matthew 7: 15 ff., where we hear from the mouth of the future Judge that many Lord-Lord-sayers, who do many external good works and appear as if they should come to heaven before all others, will be cast out with disgrace, even though they had never imagined it possible. I applied this to her with the request not to go so blindly, uncertainly, and with empty and imaginary hope of eternity, since it is a road on which there is no turning back, etc.

[After his arrival, Mr. von Reck's brother gave us more hope for earnest and true Christianity than he is now doing. He clearly reveals his earthly mind, which is aimed at worldly matters, even though, because of his timid temperament, he has not yet committed any excesses. If the purpose of his coming to our community were to act as a commander, then the Salzburgers would be just as badly provided with him as with the older Mr. von Reck. As they themselves relate, God showed them great mercy on their last ocean voyage and they made many promises, which they have not yet kept; and they are still sinning against our dear and good God.]

Monday, the 16th of August. The Salzburger Felser has become so weak and miserable since the fever left him that there is hardly any life left in him. If the Lord lets him die, then he will die with faith in the Son of God. He can still well understand everything that is spoken or prayed with him, even if he is not able to speak himself. I was told by a pious Salzburger woman who was tending him that for some days he has constantly had the words of the symbolum Apostolicum[205] in his mouth: "I believe in the forgiveness of sins, the resurrection of the body", which words he often repeated. Today I asked him whether he knew and could believe with certainty that our heavenly Father had forgiven him all his sins for Christ's sake? To this he answered "yes"; and he would gladly have spoken more if only he had been able. I tried briefly to strengthen his heart with the words from yesterday's Sunday epistle: "If we are children, then we are heirs too, namely heirs of God and co-heirs of Christ, etc." Because he can eat nothing at all, he has requested some coffee from us several times, which strengthens him and does him good. At Mr. Zwiffler's orders and at their own request, tea has been administered regularly to the people when they have had fever; and this has previously helped very much against scurvy, diarrhea, and dysentery. They are not yet used to the water here, and they lack molasses for brewing beer.

Before his sickness, R. [Rothenberger] was an externally honest man and industrious and skillfull worker, who was very useful to the congregation; but now through God's grace he is progressing further. Last night our dear Lord placed him, so to speak, before the gates of eternity. Just as previously in his sickness, he was able to recognize that, as he has often been told, more is necessary for Christianity and being saved than frivolous people imagine. Therefore, he has begun to pray to God for true conversion; and he is now even more concerned about his salvation. It seems to me that he feels sin as sin in his conscience and knows that he cannot get rid of it but that he can attain merciful forgiveness for it through the blood of Jesus. In the presence of his wife I spoke of the horror and abomination of sin and told how much God hated it and how seriously He chastised it on His own Son, etc.; and I also told him what is necessary if one wishes to get rid of this abomination and thus attain forgiveness and become a child and glorious heir of God and Jesus Christ. The man accepted all this and then prayed with me with such eagerness that it caused me a great joy.

Tuesday, the 17th of August. For a short time the heat of day has been greater than we could have expected; but at night it is already getting cooler and there is a heavy dew. Right after the full moon some of our people planted turnips, as is customary in this country; and we will have to wait and see whether or not the hot and scorching sunshine will hinder them in their sprouting and growing. Yesterday evening we heard a thunder storm, and the sky was covered with clouds; but everything gradually cleared up again. The few people who have remained well so far are now catching the fever too, one after the other, so that now almost everyone is either sick or at least weak in body and without strength. The strongest natures are seized most violently by the heat of the fever. Some of them now have it every day, but most of them on every third day. Mr. Zwiffler is well again and visits the sick people again as much as his strength allows. [Whenever he knows the *statum morbi*,[206] he applies effective medicines; but at first he diagnosed my and my wife's sickness in such a way that, if we had accepted his suggestions and cure, much harm would doubtlessly have been caused. Incidentally, he is very active and ready to serve, and he does not shirk at any effort.]

Wednesday, the 18th of August. Mrs. Schmid, whose whole body was swollen, has recovered so much to our great amazement that she now knows of no more swelling. She used nothing but some warm wine, which she rubbed on herself at the suggestion of a clever woman; and we also gave her some *essentia amara*. The serious prayer of her husband and other pious Christians surely contributed most to her recovery. In this same hut Mrs. Haber-fehner is lying sick with fever and severely swollen feet, and her *symtomata* do not appear good to me. [She does not have the best testimony from her host, the honest Schmidt; and, therefore, we are working on her in accordance with the condition of her soul.]

Pichler and his wife came to me and complained of the location of their house and asked that it be changed, since their bodily health and happiness depends to a large part on it. To the right side and into the city runs a deep and usually dry ditch, into which the back part of Pichler's house-lot extends. The surveyor put the house lots of several people in this ditch, but he also gave them others in their stead because they did not please them. This Pichler let himself, however, be persuaded to take his lot here. But now it is bad for both him and his cattle here, because every rain inconveniences him, and the vapors that linger in this ditch and on the other side in the high reeds and mud obviously damage his and his family's health; and therefore he is compelled to change this house-lot even though he has already expended much work on the hut and the garden fence. We will refer the matter to Savannah.

Thursday, the 19th of August. Yesterday, late in the evening, Felser died after a difficult death struggle and doubtlessly went into the rest of his Lord. His patience and resignation in his sickness, as in all trials and troublesome circumstances, was most edifying. He loved God's Word with all his heart and was no mere listener. In Salzburg he had the reputation of being a very strong and industrious worker; but he had expended most of his strength there, as he himself complained to me, and could therefore not do such heavy work here, especially since the food is so bad. He was entirely disinterested in his work and gladly served his neighbor. He loyally helped the pious old Bacher, who is incapable of building huts and cultivating the soil because of his age and bodily weakness, in his work; and therefore he enjoyed the loyalty and help of this man and his wife in a right edifying manner during his sickness and death. [In Salzburg he sinned against the sixth commandment and brought his illegitimate son to Germany. It seems to me that this sin has caused him no little worry in his last hours.] Otherwise he was never sick. His last sickness began with a fever, which left him after eight days; and immediately afterwards he became so weak and helpless that he could neither eat nor stand up.

He bequeathed his legacy of money and things to the Bachers, who had been very good to him. But I have already been commanded by Mr. Oglethorpe and Mr. Causton to have the constable write down everything that a single person leaves behind him at his death and to send the inventory to Savannah; and this I had Mr. Zwiffler and three Salzburgers do today before the burial. I shall report his will to Savannah and await the magistry's decision. The Bachers are content with little and will gladly relinquish the rest to other poor people. Mrs. Schweighofer has long requested me to have a hut built for her and her three children, but it was impossible to do anything about this because of so much work and because of the people's sickness. Now she is asking for the hut of the late Felser, but it is not within my power to give it. Meanwhile I have promised to compose a supplication to the magistry in Savannah for her and to accompany it with my intercession and signature. If God has intended the hut for her as a poor and heartily pious widow, it will surely go to her.

Friday, the 20th of August. The healthy men of the congregation and those who have regained some of their strength since their sickness have been occupied today in remodelling the large hut

built for the third transport as a church and school. For a long
time no one has occupied this hut except for Mr. von Reck, his
brother, and his servant; and so far we have had only a small part
where the provisions were stored at first, and even there we were
bad off because we lacked benches and sufficient space. Because
Mr. von Reck has now moved into his well built hut and our listeners now have a little time, they have undertaken this necessary work
and have not only secured it all around but have also arranged
pews for men, women, and children, our pulpit, and facilities for
holding Holy Communion; and they have done this so well that
we can be very satisfied.

Two of them set out on the road to Abercorn to blaze it correctly, because this was done recently by the postman only super-
ficially and through big bogs that one cannot cross on foot. When
God has healed those who are now sick, they will secure our cemetery with a good fence so that our dead will be protected from the
pigs and other animals and also from people who might walk
through it. Thus one thing after the other is done by the people
with joyful hearts, if they are given time and freedom. We have
received news from Abercorn that almost everyone there is lying
sick with fever and that they are suffering much want at the same
time. We receive similar reports from Purysburg, and from this
we can see that the removal to a new location is not the true cause
of this sickness.[207] We do not yet know how things look in this
regard in Savannah and other places in the colony.

Sunday, the 21st of August. As far as time and strength allowed,
I tidied up my accounts of the provisions received and distributed;
because I must journey to Savannah for the sake of the congregation in the first days of next week. The fever has left me, and may
the name of the Lord be praised because of it! In the evening the
surveyor arrived; and he will begin his work surveying the gardens
on Monday. He appears to be a good man, with whom we will get
along all right. He was sick in Purysburg and he also surveyed a
tract of ground, and this prevented him from coming to us sooner.

Sunday, the 22nd of August. At their request Mr. von Reck and
his brother and his servant Müller received private Holy Communion, because the first two will be prevented by fever and the
last by a trip from receiving it next Sunday when we hold it with
the congregation. They manifested a great desire for it, because
they do not know how the fever will end. [Yesterday I visited Mr.
von Reck and reminded him again of the things that we cannot
at all reconcile with his Christianity and good pretences. Much
occurred on the ocean voyage and much here that has scandalized

the congregation. Especially the third transport has so much against him that (as I told him) he would scandalize the congregation by going to Holy Communion, for which reason I would prefer to see it take place privately; yet I intruded into his conscience all the things I had seen or known so far, and I said he himself should decide whether he was in a condition to go to Holy Communion worthily. He attested that he had a clear conscience in all the things the people accused him of from the trip; and of the things that have scandalized people here he gave good explanations for some, and some he recognized as sinful and expressed his remorse. He intends, as I gather from his words, to return to Germany, even though he has spent so much on his construction. After his departure he intends to consign his house and gardens so that honest strangers can lodge in it and get some victuals from the gardens. But we will not allow any inn to be established here.]

Monday, the 23rd of August. [Mr. von Reck is losing his servant Müller, who will go to Savannah and do some work in his trade and then hopes to go by ship to England. He has many reasons for this resolution, as he disclosed to me today. He is a skilful and also Godfearing man, who has given a good example to all of us.] Mr. Zwiffler and his wife are greatly weakened by the fever and have lost all their strength. He is rather annoyed that we moved here from Old Ebenezer [as we have already detected in him many times whenever things are inconvenient for him]. There he had already established himself, and here he must arrange everything again; and this does not please him. He and his kind will not consider the nature of the soil and other things that serve for the welfare and alleviation of the Salzburgers, because he does not want to hear anything about agriculture [but always talks about the practice of his well learned profession.]

Tuesday, the 24th of August. Last night we had a thunder storm and heavy rain. So far the weather has been very hot and dry, but very good for the corn that is now ripening. If it rains too much at this time, water gets in the ears and causes them to rot and be wormy. The nights are quite cool and very comfortable for sleeping, both for the well and the sick. This morning I journeyed to Savannah on our light boat partly in order to bring Mr. Causton my accounts for the provisions that have been received and distributed and partly to discuss with him other necessary matters concerning the congregation and to see about new provisions for the Salzburgers. He again received me with much love and friendliness. It happened that Captain Thomson arrived in Savannah from London and brought me letters from England and Germany, from which we have again received much matter for the praise of God.

Wednesday, the 25th of August. This morning I had myself taken to Abercorn, from where I rode on my horse to New Ebenezer and arrived here about noon. Praise be to God, who again let me find everything in good order. It troubles me to hear that my dear colleague was seized yesterday by a violent fever that has taken much of his strength. His dear wife had been attacked by the fever several days previously, and thus God is going the same way with him as He did with me and my family. The Lord who hears prayers will not scorn our prayer but receive it graciously for him and others in the congregation. This time Mr. Zwiffler received the medicines that he requested from the Society. [However, he informed me with very rude and unfriendly words that he had gained little thereby because he had not been sent any money for the service he had given to the sick so far. And thus he shows little gratitude for the benefaction of twenty pounds sterling that he received from the Society a half a year ago via Mr. von Reck, Now he wishes to write his opinion clearly to the Trustees and the Society and then move from us to some other place where he can practice his Christianity and his profession better than here.]

Thursday, the 26th of August. This evening the captain from Fort Palachocolas[208] stopped in and brought the news that ten oxen for fresh meat and ten cows and a like number of calves for the third transport were underway and would come to Old Ebenezer about next Tuesday, for which reason I should send some people to drive them here. We have been waiting for both of them but have had little hope, because the water is still very high in the river and swamps through which the cattle must be driven. The [Trustees'] cattle that are to be brought to Old Ebenezer for breeding and to Frederica for the colonists there have been driven back again and are not expected until next spring. On my trip I heard the reliable report in Purysburg that the old Mr. Pury, who brought so many people from Switzerland to our neighborhood in Carolina, has died. In Purysburg almost everyone is sick with fever, and it appears the same in Savannah.

Friday, the 27th of August. This morning ten Salzburgers went to Savannah to fetch molasses and a few other provisions with the new boat that Mr. Oglethorpe gave us. If possible, they should also bring our things that are in Captain Thomson's ship; and for this reason I have written to the captain and to Mr. Causton and sent the bill of lading along. It was difficult to find so many people in the face of the universal sickness. Some of these people would have gladly gone to the Lord's Table next Sunday; but at their request it will be served to them a week from Sunday on the eleventh Sunday after Trinity, expecially since some sick people also have a great desire for it and hope at that time to be entirely freed of fever or at least to have a better day.

Today I had only seven children in school, because the rest had to stay at home because of sickness. People who are used to this country give us hope that there will be a change in the sicknesses of our people if the heat of the day subsides a bit more. It is now hotter than at any time this year.

Today I distributed a few pounds of flour to those who needed it most, and because of it some syrup will be deducted at the command of Mr. Causton. Despite that, they consider this a benefit; because without flour they would be very bad off in their sickness. So far, Mr. Causton has given out butter and flour. Some of them have produced some butter from their cows in the spring and summer, and they have gladly relinquished this benefaction to others.

Saturday, the 28th of August. Rothenberger had me called to him yesterday evening shortly before the prayer hour, and I found him very miserable in body but in a very fine spiritual condition. His sickness has lasted for a long time, in which time he was able to review his prior life carefully and test his Christianity according to the teachings and life of Christ; and this he did. The misery of his sins lies on his heart so heavily that trouble and sorrow will hardly let him rest and he prays constantly and movingly for mercy and forgiveness. His heart is like a barren soil, which thirstily drinks up a fruitful rain. He grasps the comfort of the gospel with unusual yearning, even though he considers himself, as the greatest of sinners, unworthy of any mercy. In his healthy days his Christianity consisted mostly of external practices and bourgeois respectability, which now strike him almost as stinking filth.[209] [His wife is worthless. Perhaps God will bless her husband's example in her and bring her to greater reflection.]

Sunday, the 29th of August. Yesterday toward evening my fever announced itself again, and today I felt great lassitude all day long. Yet our dear Lord granted me enough strength to edify the congregation in the morning with God's Word and to read the story of the destruction of the city of Jerusalem this afternoon with some application. My dear colleague seems to be freed of his fever (perhaps also only for a while, but according to God's will); but he must hold back for a few more days in order to gather strength.

Toward evening I was called to Mrs. Spielbiegler; but, because she was lying again with a high temperature and fantasying, I could not speak with her but prayed with her son. Because Stephan Riedelsperger lives in her neighborhod and is also much weakened by fever, I called on him to ask about his physical and spiritual condition. His confession about his previous [frivolous and miserable] Christianity and the tears he shed because of it made a great impression on me. He confessed that only now had God powerfully awakened him through His Word and brought him to many good resolutions. He had also begun to pray; and, whenever he had found an edifying prayer or beautiful meditation in Schaitberger or some other good book,[210] he had immediately found comfort in it, but his heart had always remained without any feeling of his great inner corruption and without remorse and conversion.

Until now his prayer had been a great abomination before our holy and living God; and therefore it was no wonder that, despite all good emotions and resolutions, he had not yet attained anything genuine in his Christianity. He was lacking only in true prayer and sincerity. But now God was revealing. . . , [the dreadful sins he had committed in Salzburg and also what had happened to him in Germany and here,] and he could not marvel enough at the divine patience and kindness that had led him out of Germany; and he hoped that, with God's grace, he might now see the Truth. He asked me to intercede for him diligently and to observe his life carefully and, should I notice any laxness in him, to admonish him. As much as my strength allowed, I spoke with him in accordance with his understanding; and, because he spoke a great deal about earnest and sincere prayer and said it is impossible to become or remain a Christian without practicing it truly, I looked up Part II, Chapter 20, of Arnd's *True Christianity* for him so that he might read it after regaining his strength.

Monday, the 30th of August. Last Friday, for want of people, I let my servant go along with the boat so that he could take the place of a helmsman. Today he returned again via Abercorn with a Salzburger who had caught fever and brought me the sad news that our poor weak people were having to drag our provisions up here with our former [disgraceful] boat, because the one that Mr. Oglethorpe had had repaired had filled with water and was therefore useless. With haste I had to send a couple of people, who are now very few, to meet them with the little boat as an advanced team[211] (for they have to tie the thin rope to the bow of the big boat and then, holding the rope in their hands, they row the small boat to a bush to which one of them hangs on tightly while the others pull the big boat up to them). The provisions they are bringing with them will not go far; the present rowers will become sick and miserable again from drinking so much water in the great heat, and I know of almost no one else in the congregation whom I can send on the boat in the future. Mr. Causton has no people and will not get any for this boat, even if he wished to pay a half crown in addition to provisions. God have mercy on us in our need. If the dear Lord frees me again from fever, I shall have to go to Savannah again and see that better arrangements are made, otherwise our dear people will be annihilated. [Mr. Oglethorpe is not there; and, as long as he is not[212] absent, little can be done.]

This afternoon my dear colleague assembled the people of the third transport who had received a cow through divine providence in order to announce it to them and to admonish them to gratitude toward God and the benefactors and to pray with them. The cows will arrive in Old Ebenezer tomorrow along with ten oxen for fresh meat for the community. For this the Englishmen are asking for some of our people to drive them, and these will be hard to find. Nearly all who have received a cow are sick, otherwise they would see to bringing the cattle here. The surveyor also needs three men every day for his work, whom he pays for their effort; but it is hard to find them for him and it causes us much trouble.

Tuesday, the 31st of August. The little boat that I sent down to meet the large one returned this afternoon, having taken aboard Michael Rieser, who had caught fever. Last night and this morning we have had a very strong wind, after which we received a fruitful rain. At the same time it has become very cool, and this is very helpful for many of those sick with fever. This is the period in which people worry about the great and destructive winds that often arise entirely unexpectedly. On the water the boatmen are very careful with their boats, especially if they are not far from the sea.

I informed Mrs. Schweighofer that ninety-six florins had arrived for her and her children and would soon be paid to her. At my short admonition she was very ashamed and wept for having often been so weak in her faith and having almost despaired when she thought of her widowhood, her physical weakness, and her three still small children. But God is the Father of orphans and the Judge of widows. In addition to having suffered a stroke on the right side, this woman has also had the fever along with her three children.

Wednesday, the 1st of September. This evening the ten cows promised to the third transport, along with fifteen oxen for fresh meat, were brought to us via Old Ebenezer. We find contentment and tranquility in those who did not receive any cows this time; because they are assured that there was no partiality in the distribution. Perhaps Mr. Oglethorpe can be persuaded to send the remaining people their cattle, which they need greatly. There has been no lack of requests and representations on our part, nor will there be any lack in the future.

Thursday, the 2nd of September. Toward noon today our dear people arrived here weak and tired with the large boat and provisions and complained not a little about this difficult trip. This time we received several things that had been donated to us and the Salzburgers from London and Germany. The large supply of books for us and especially for the congregation and school is surely an unusual blessing, at which everyone who sees it or hears of it is amazed and overjoyed. May God grant temporal and eternal blessings to the benefactor in London who donated twenty pounds sterling for it. We also received medicine from Halle that is very necessary in our present circumstances. May God Himself be the rewarder [since the worthy Professor Francke accepts no reimbursement from us but rather donates it all and promises to do even more in the future.] Today we had a thunder storm and an unusual downpour. This morning we had an ox slaughtered for the good of the sick, and it was distributed toward evening. We would rather have live oxen than have the meat brought to us. Now we can slaughter when we need to.

Friday, the 3rd of September. Already last week Mr. von Reck told me that, because he could not regain his health here, he wished to go to Savannah and take his brother and all his things, for which purpose he needed the large boat. He would gladly have departed today because there were people to be had, but now he must be patient until next week. Lies and calumnies had been made about a pious married couple claiming that they, although wishing to appear pious, had committed an obvious injustice against their neighbor and were therefore hypocrites [of which there are some in our place.] The matter seemed wrong to us right away; and, when my dear colleague questioned both of them and I questioned the man, who has an honest heart, we found it all untrue. With their good will and all possible caution they have used they bought themselves enemies and calumniators. Such stories often take place between those who fear the Lord and those who do not; but they make us careful (as must be the case of our friends and benefactors too) not to believe immediately everything that is reported even with a good appearance.

Sunday, the 4th of September. The Salzburgers who have so far lacked either songbooks or Bibles (or perhaps only the husband had one) are heartily pleased that they can now be fully supplied.

Our wonderful God has arranged, as if from afar, for setting up our school, not only for ourselves but also for other people's children. Not only has He sent us many New Testaments, catechisms, and ABC books through the charity of a benefactor in London who paid for the other books, but He has also sent a considerable sum of money through the hands of Senior Urlsperger and Court Preacher Ziegenhagen, of which even the heathens are to partake for the salvation of their souls. Oh, how we yearn to work on the children in the school! ! But now there is so little time because we are involved in so many worldly matters for the congregation, and physical weakness is still there. We may not and cannot yet refuse to look out for the worldly affairs of the congregation, not only because there is no one else to whom it can be entrusted without harm to the congregation, but also because we know the desires of our benefactors and especially those of Governor Oglethorpe. [As it is, there is enough hardship in Ebenezer, but it would be even worse if an unconscientious and severe justiciary were there.][213] The Lord who hears our prayers will surely know how to free us in due time from this burden which we gladly bear through our love for our congregation, even though it hinders us from some salutory matters that pertain to the purpose of our office.

Sunday, the 5th of September. Because I still have fever, my dear colleague took care of divine services in both the morning and the afternoon. May God strengthen him further, and also do with me according to His will.

Monday, the 6th of September. Mr. Zwiffler advised me that he had resolved to return to Germany. [Mr. Zwiffler showed very clearly his animosity towards me because neither the Society nor the Trustees sent him any money this time for the effort he had applied in the community but only as much medicine as he requested. Because they did not value his art but wished to make him into a peasant who had to depend on farming, he had resolved to return to Germany. But before this he wished to earn some money in our community for the trip, and therefore he would not give medicine to anyone for nothing or do anything else for them from now on. He would give medicine to anyone or bleed anyone who paid him or to anyone who brought him a certificate from me that I would be responsible for the payment. No persuasion could make him change his mind, rather he has already begun to carry out his resolution by rejecting some people who could not pay him. He speaks very contemptuously of the thirty pounds sterling, the many kinds of medicines, the flasks, etc. he previously received. Once he gets emotional, little can be accomplished with him through persuasion; therefore I shall find an occasion to speak with him again in a few days.]

Tuesday, the 7th of September. Because some things are still in Savannah, particularly the money that was sent for the community with the last ship, and because we should receive our salaries from Governor Oglethorpe, my dear colleague went there this morning in the company of Mr. von Reck and his brother. The large boat had to be sent down so that new provisions could be sent to us. If Mr. Causton cannot find any people for rowing, then we shall suffer want, because I could scarcely find five healthy men in the congregation for bringing the boat down. I have written to Mr. Causton about this and other things concerning the congregation. The surveyor has now gone away again after having finished with the surveying of the gardens on one side of the town. On Saturday afternoon, in my presence, he assigned the first Salzburgers their land, which is next to the city and very beautiful. Monday morning the gardens of the second transport were drawn by lots in my hut and those of the third transport were drawn in the afternoon; and these were later distributed partly in my presence and partly in that of my dear colleague. Some from these two transports have received very bad land; and, even though I tried here and there to exchange it, there is not enough good land to please everyone. There is still very good land just behind the gardens that have been surveyed, which I hope Governor Oglethorpe will have surveyed at my request for those who are now badly supplied.

Wednesday, the 8th of September. Since yesterday evening there has been very cool weather with rain, which is now very convenient for sowing and planting. Anyone who is not careful contracts the fever again, as I experienced this morning myself while I was busy distributing some things to the first transport. However, it was only *motus febriles,* and I tried to prevent it with warm drinks and continuous exercise in the garden. In our houses everyone is sick with fever, or else still very weak. But the Lord will help us through everything. It is a fine benefit for the sick that we have recently received fifteen live oxen for fresh meat. Today another one of them was slaughtered and distributed. The fever so weakens some people, both male and female, that they cannot even stand up; and at the same time they have a burning in the chest and sometimes almost lose all breath. Some of them can take nothing but a bit of tea, which we serve them with sugar.

Thursday, the 9th of September. Kieffer [the only pious man], whom we know in Purysburg, called on us with his two sons and still has a great desire to be near us because of divine services and because of his children. He has now again inspected his piece of land that lies almost opposite us in Carolina and is beginning to wish to do so more than recently when it was flooded by the high Savannah River. Because it seems to him that the recent innundation was something extraordinary, he is ready to accept the said piece of land and to let go of his present one, which lies in another region. There is a family of Indians with us again who supply the sick with fresh meat, for which they are given some rice, gourds, etc. The wife and child have also contracted fever, and therefore it does not attack only us new colonists. Kieffer in Purysburg has been in the country for several years but has had to endure the fever this time with his whole family, in fact very seriously.

Friday, the 10th of September. Today at noon my dear colleague returned from Savannah and brought two sick people, whom he had received on board the boat as healthy rowers. He himself was violently attacked by fever in Savannah, and he had scarcely crossed his threshhold before he had to go to bed again. But it was a great blessing of God, who hears prayers, that he first reached our place. Mr. Causton promised to have Englishmen bring the provisions up here, because in my letter I informed him of the general sickness of the people. The money that was fetched this time is so heavy that it could not be brought up here in our light and weak boat.[214] And because the congregation now has none at all, my dear colleague had to borrow a stronger one in Purysburg, for which, however, we must pay somewhat more than two shillings sterling per day.

Captain Thomson plans to return to London in four weeks and has offered to take letters for us. I shall begin to write as soon as I have collected some strength and have finished up some business. We received a letter from Secretary Newman via Charleston, in which he advised us that we would receive our present salary from Mr. Oglethorpe. The letter had been written the 11th of May, old style, and was therefore older than the one we received through Captain Thomson. Governor Oglethorpe is still in Frederica and will probably remain a good deal longer in that region; and therefore we must be patient a while longer about receiving our promised salaries, even though we need them very much. The worthy Lord Trustees have given us and our wives some fine material for clothing and some beautiful linen. May the Giver of all good gifts mercifully repay this in both a physical and a spiritual way. We are entirely unworthy of all the benefactions that flow to us wretches from England and Germany; and our recognition of our unworthiness gives us sufficient material to humble ourselves before God. The benefactions themselves, however, compel us to hearty thanksgiving to our dear Father and to intercession for our worthy benefactors; and they encourage us to appeal all the more to God for His grace and for strength to fulfil carefully the intention of our benefactors by a loyal performance of our office.

Saturday, the 11th of September. This morning I had the fever more violently than in previous days. So far our loyal God has always so dealt with us that, after the fever has left us and we have taken some warm drinks, we regain enough strength to take care of some of the duties pertaining to our office and to speak with the people who call on us. And He will continue to do everything right. Oh, how we fear that we will not be able to hold school, partly because of our own weakness and partly because of the children. The schoolmaster Ortmann is also very miserable. The prayer hours are held occasionally, but we have very few listeners, because those who are still well must wait on the sick. Because of the shortage of children we cannot catechize now in the prayer hour; but the Bible stories are told simply and applied for their edification. Now both the old and young should, so to say, recite to our dear Lord what they have learned in their healthy days in school and in church. The people have a great desire for us to visit them often, they are quite hungry and thirsty for comfort from the Divine Word. Yet, since our dear God keeps us at home through physical weakness, and mostly in bed, both they and we must be patient.

Sunday, the 12th of September. Today I had no fever, so through the grace of God I was able to hold the morning and afternoon divine service. My dear colleague contracted fever this afternoon. I was not yet in a condition to visit the sick or otherwise to speak privately with anyone for his edification; rather my weakness compelled me to remain warm in my hut. For the same reasons we cannot hold the repetition hour, which God has previously crowned with many blessings of edification. May God meanwhile teach us through His spirit to pray at home all the more ardently for our listeners' spiritual and physical well being and to gather in tranquility a rich treasure for the future. Finally it will again please our merciful God to restore our health completely, since we have again promised Him to devote ourselves entirely to His service and to the service of our so loved congregation.

Monday, the 13th of September. Already yesterday one of our sick listeners asked me to come to him, but I could not visit him in his house until today before my fever began. I found him sitting at the table and holding a book full of Biblical verses in his hand. My arrival pleased him greatly. Instead of saying something at first, he began to weep very loudly and to lament his pitiable condition. Finally he composed himself and told me what was lying on his conscience as an unusual burden. [He disclosed to me sins in which he had been entangled in Salzburg already in his sixth year and subsequently, at which I was appalled and of which I can mention nothing further here.] I read him several pertinent verses from the Old and New Testaments and spoke according to the content of his confession. He needs someone to pray for him earnestly, and I cordially invited him to come to me after regaining his strength so that I might cry to God with him for the sake of his soul and its salvation and impart to him some instruction out of God's Word, and this he promised very gladly to do.

Both in Germany and here the man has often suffered great pangs of conscience despite zealous use of the means of grace, and only now do I know the main reason for this. When I merely told him that grace was there for the sake of Christ and His perfect merit but that it would cost him much to achieve comfort through applying and experiencing it, this was such a comfort to him that he began to weep about it. [Driven by his conscience he told his wife the details of his sins, and this did not please me.] From this example too I have learned to understand better the expression of the song: "Through Adam's fall man's nature and being have been entirely corrupted, etc."[215] For a couple of days we have had cold and raw air both day and night; but last night a gentle and fruitful rain began, which continued almost all day. The thunder storm that began with it soon passed away. Our dear Lord has granted some people in Old Ebenezer a fine blessing in corn and beans on the well fertilized pieces of good land, but they are prevented by the continuing sickness from harvesting such a blessing properly. But they are doing it all together as best they can. Some of them have been exhausting themselves in going there and carrying the stuff back.

Tuesday, the 14th of September. [Despite all the effort we have made, we have not yet been able to persuade Mr. Zwiffler to give up his already started practice of selling his medicines and bloodletting to our sick for money. Because he received no money this time from England and because Mr. Oglethorpe would not listen to his petition, he will certainly follow his intention and make the Salzburgers pay for his medicines and his service, or else I must give him assurance for twenty or at least ten pounds sterling that the Society or the Lord Trustees will compensate him for his efforts. I explained to him that I had no calling to fulfil these claims of his and that this was not the Christian way to choose such paths but to trust in the living God and to be content with that which He has granted. He had had evidence enough of the care He took of him, and he should risk it another time.

[In addition, I assured him that he was causing himself more harm than good by his present procedure, because 1) This was wrong and it would displease the benefactors that he was selling our poor people the medicines that had been sent him free at his request from England on several occasions. 2) If he continued to serve the people as previously until his departure (which is to take place in five months) and we reported this to London, then I hope he would receive a compensation from the Society. On the other hand, he would win their disfavor by his present methods. I advised him to write to the Lord Trustees and the Society and properly request permission to return to Germany and give as his reason that he cannot live from farming and cannot subsist without a salary. But he does not think such evasive methods necessary because he is not obligated. It was not certain that he would receive a compensation in London, the medicines that had been sent over had not been nearly adequate, he had to add his own to them. And, because they were only *simplicia* and mostly crude and bad, he had a lot of work in preparing them and making them usable; and therefore he could rightfully demand payment. He had to earn something for his voyage.

[In order to give my arguments a special emphasis, I read him the passage from Court Preacher Ziegenhagen, in which it is reported that Mr. Zwiffler is obligated to take good care of the medicines he has received and to administer them to the people in Ebenezer without payment. In case he were to move away he would have to leave behind him the flasks, instruments, and *simplicia* he had received from the Society, because they had been obtained with charitable funds for the benefit of the Salzburgers. He had me read this to him twice and was very displeased with it. The hut and the fences around his lot that we had built for him are not good enough for him, so he has exchanged it for Mr. von Reck's with the latter's permission. One can hardly please him in any way, since his mind is set on money, provisions, and convenience.]

Kalcher and his wife and child are still sick and miserable with the fever, but he resigns himself to it in a Christian way and makes good use of his sickbed. Whenever he has some strength, he visits me and is very edifying for me. Helfenstein's family, which is very large, are also all sick and also in the direst poverty, and therefore they receive most of what we have in hand for the poor and sick. She is an honest woman, whose heart is turned to God; and I never find her depressed by her and her family's misery, but rather her mouth is always full of the praise of God or else quiet and content with the ways of the Lord. God has previously led her into many external and internal trials; and therefore her present need, poverty, and sickness are no strangers to her. Her husband appears to have a comsumptive sickness and may not live much longer. [Meanwhile it has seemed to me that Mr. von Reck did not do well in London to persuade such a feeble old man with such a large family to support to come into this wilderness. He is a tanner, and he was told how well he would be able to practice his profession here; and, now that he is here, farming should be his best profession, but he is not suited to either because of his age and physical weakness. His children are still un-reared, except for the daughter, who is already sixteen.]

Wednesday, the 15th of September. Dr. Gerdes in London took up quite a large collection in his congregation for the third Salzburger transport. The total amounts to twenty pounds sterling, of which Mr. Ortmann, who was formerly schoolmaster at that church, has received one pound sterling at his (Dr. Gerdes') order. In his letter he gave us complete authority to draw a bill on him to the amount of twenty pounds sterling and to receive the money here in this country in that way; and I shall do this just as soon as I go to Savannah. Meanwhile, because the people are in need of the money because of their poverty and sickness, they have been advanced some of the money that Court Preacher Ziegenhagen transmitted to us in copper. This afternoon I assembled the people of the third transport, both young and old, as many of them as the fever allowed to go out. Before the distribution I led them in singing the familiar and beautiful song: "If thou but suffer God to guide thee, etc."[216] After it was finished I told them how the hearts of the benefactors in England and Germany, and especially of the worthy Dr. Gerdes, was disposed toward their need and poverty, which had been reported to them, and how the latter had transmitted to us a considerable blessing that he had collected for them in his congregation.

At this time I tried to encourage them briefly to continued trust in the living God through these words from the song they had just sung: "Whoever trusts the Lord on high, he has not built on sand."[217] Afterwards I concluded with a prayer in which we humbly beseeched the Father of all mercies for spiritual and physical reward for these and all other benefactions we have enjoyed so far. At the distribution (with the exception of the schoolmaster's one pound sterling) there was eight shillings sixpence for each adult, four shillings threepence for each grown child, and two shillings one pence halfpenny for each very small child.

A shoemaker named Ernstdorf was accepted into the third transport by Mr. von Reck here in Savannah; and because of his and his family's great poverty he was given what was left, this being twenty-three shillings sterling for him, his wife, and his children. The dear people received this blessing with great humility and gratitude, and they will not forget to pray for the worthy benefactor and for everyone who has contributed something. It is better for them that this money was sent after them than if they had received it in London, otherwise they would have spent it for pewter, platters, dishes, etc. and other bagatelles, as many did who had thought they could derive a great profit from them here.[218]

Thursday, the 16th of September. Last night the little Ossenecker child died of a choking catarrh, by which it has been attacked several times. Nearly all the little children have had the fever or still have it, but no medicine is used on them. Even most of the grown people take nothing for their fever except warm drinks, for which they receive either tea or, at the suggestion of Mr. Causton and with the approval of Mr. Zwiffler, cardo-benedicten herbs together with sugar.

Friday, the 17th of September. [Mr. Zwiffler has pondered at home over my recent remonstrances and has now changed his mind. He is therefore requesting me, when the occasion presents itself, to tell the people that things will remain as they were and that they will continue to have the medicine and bloodletting for nothing. I notice that he wishes to exclude from the benefit of free medicine those who are not Salzburgers; but this will not do either and runs counter to the intentions of the benefactors.

[I have great need of two well dried boards and therefore asked Mr. Causton to let me have two from Old Ebenezer, with the assurance that I would soon pay him for them or replace them when our people's health again permits them to cut boards. However, he refused to give them to me, just as Mr. Oglethorpe refused my dear colleague, Mr. Zwiffler, and Mr. Ortmann the half-sawed slabs for floors in their huts.[219] Not even a nail will be given to us for nothing at our new location, perhaps out of anger because of our almost forceful removal from Old Ebenezer. I shall take the liberty of presenting Mr. Oglethorpe the expenditures we have had to make for some little buildings in Old Ebenezer and here and humbly request him to reimburse them; because otherwise, if we had to pay it all from our salaries, we would have to suffer want or else be a burden to the poor-box, from which we have meanwhile had to borrow such money.]

Saturday, the 18th of September. We had planned, God willing, to hold Holy Communion tomorrow for those who reported for it; but there were not more than six people who came to me for that reason; and three of those have become even weaker and more miserable, so that we have had to postpone it for a week or until more report for it. One of these confessors told me that, since the entire congregation and also the people in other places in this colony have been so attacked and chastised by this fever, he was often reminded of the 28th chapter of Deuteronomy, namely, that God will chastise still seven times more if we do not improve, and therefore we might well apply the present general chastisement to our conversion.

Sunday, the 19th of September. Mrs. Adam Riedelsperger was churched today. She, her husband, and her child have had to put up a great deal with the fever; and they have a double cross because they are very poor, yet they resign themselves to it with great patience and contentment. They are our neighbors, and therefore their behavior is all the better known to us and all the more edifying. So far Mrs. Schweighoffer has lived in her hut with her three children; and, because they all have the fever, they have been a considerable burden to these good people because of their own physical weakness. Nevertheless, we have heard no complaint on Riedelsperger's part. We have now arranged for Mrs. Schweighofer to move into the deceased Felser's hut, in which neighborhood more women live who know her and are fond of her and who will take turns in helping her. Because of the paralysis on her entire right side, the woman is almost childish; and we must look out for all sorts of little matters for her, for she asks us for advice and help in all cases and gives us much to do. The ninety-six florins that came to her [out of Salzburg][220] from the hands of Senior Urlsperger she accepts as a gift from the hand of God, who knew her poverty and that she had no money. Because of her infirmity and her small children she cannot get along with the usual provisions and therefore needs money for buying additional flour, butter, etc.

Monday, the 20th of September. [I was most amazed that Mr. Causton is not sending us any provisions according to his promise. I reported to him clearly enough what limited supplies are on hand and stated that I owe the third transport corn and also that the time for the first Salzburgers' provisions occurs at the end of this month. We have likewise received far too little syrup. Instead of it most of the people wish to take flour and butter, which they need very greatly in their sickness.] In our congregation I could not find four really well men whom I could send to Savannah for the provisions. I have no opportunity to write to Mr. Causton to remind him about our lack and his promises. [He must be reminded, because he has many preoccupations and can easily forget us because of them.] If the dear Lord would completely free me from fever, the first thing I would do would be to go to Savannah. Perhaps Governor Oglethorpe has now returned and I can present to him the plight of the third transport, which remains in its previous condition and lacks many necessary things, and also receive our salary. I would so gladly write letters to England and Germany, but I lack strength and time, because on the good days when the fever remains away there are all kinds of necessary tasks to do in the community.

Tuesday, the 21st of September. This morning we began to distribute the money that Senior Urlsperger sent to the third transport from the Regensburg emigrant fund.[221] The adult Austrians[222] had already received four florins each in Germany and were therefore not to receive any now. But, because they had lost almost half their money in exchanging it [which was partly Mr. von Reck's error], I gave each family of the Austrians three shillings, and the others heartily approved of this. In addition to this each of those who had received no viaticum received ten shillings sterling [but this did not include the people whom Mr. von Reck picked up without Senior Urlsperger's knowledge or volition and who were not expelled for the sake of the gospel]. Before we distributed the money we sang together the song: "My hope stands firm, etc.";[223] and after its completion I took the opportunity to say something of the ways God is accustomed to take with those whom He is leading to heaven. He does not lead them according to reason and the five senses but, as a hidden God, through all sorts of dark and hidden ways, as one can recognize from so many divine proofs from Scripture and in the example of all children of God. And, even though such ways do not befit reason and the flesh, they are nevertheless blessed ways that eventually take an unforgettably glorious end. And, according to Psalm 73: 24, "Thou shalt guide me, etc.," they teach one to recognize our dear Lord as a merciful, loving, loyal, and mighty Lord. In the application I showed what God's purpose had been in the previous trials and also in the recent and present ones; and I also showed what they must prepare themselves to face if they wish to be led in accordance with God's counsel and finally be received to glory, namely just that which all children of God had to take upon themselves. Last of all we prayed for ourselves, our congregation and their particular circumstances, and especially for our dear benefactors; and we praised God for all the physical and spiritual benefits He had shown us so far.

Wednesday, the 22nd of September. We have a right beautiful treasure in the books that were sent to us as a gift for our own use; and for them we rightfully praise God and beseech Him to reward this benefaction graciously. The sermons of the worthy Pastor Freylinghausen and the matter that is found in the *Contribution to the Building of God's Kingdom*,[224] have served me much spiritual good since we received these books, even though time and sickness have not often allowed me to read them. God be praised, and may He reward such benefactions richly in our place.

A certain kind of chestnut[225] grows in our place on low bushes, but today someone showed us some high trees too on which we found them in rather large numbers. Both types have an agreeable flavor like chestnuts, yet people prefer those that grow on trees. When they are ripe the prickly shell, which looks like a hedgehog, bursts open and the coffee-brown kernel is seen hanging in the shell.

Thursday, the 23rd of September. Yesterday late in the evening our dear Lord mercifully helped Eischberger's wife through her birth-pains and blessed her with a healthy young daughter. Like other women she was sick up to now with fever, but this did not harm her in her present circumstances. When the second transport received their cows they also received a fat ox as a gift. It was found necessary to let it graze all summer; but, because it was injured by another ox, we had to get ready to slaughter it this morning.

Friday, the 24th of September. This morning Mr. Zwiffler and his wife requested private communion, because they are both unable to commune publicly. She in particular is lying very miserably; and in all respect things look bad with regard to her recovery. During this holy act they both appeared very devout and in a good spiritual condition. The shoemaker from Purysburg,[226] who has already worked for us several times, is in our place again in order to earn something by his profession. The Salzburgers often come to us and request shoes, which request cannot easily be refused them not only because they need shoes for the winter but also because they are poor and unable to buy them. The amount in our poor box is, to be sure, little; yet, since the Lord knows our need and has promised not to desert or abandon us, we neither will nor can withdraw our hand from the poor. This time Senior Urlsperger remembered the poor and sick with ten florins.

Saturday, the 25th of September. We are again having very hot summer days, but we lack the rain that is so necessary for the seeds that have been planted in the gardens. Nor are the nights so cold as we noted last week. Because I am planning to go to Savannah if my fever stays away, as it has begun to do, several Salzburgers of the second and third transports have reported to me and asked me to mention them to Mr. Oglethorpe so that better gardens will be surveyed for them, since some of them have sandy soil like those in Old Ebenezer. There is still enough land for good gardens in the vicinity, and therefore I hope Mr. Oglethorpe will consent to this petition. I shall do my best in this. May the Lord bless my weak efforts.

Sunday, the 26th of September. Today our dear Lord gave us both so much strength that we could preach the Word of God. The repetition hour has been cancelled again. Few people had reported to me last week to go to Holy Communion, and allowance was made for them this morning. The period of penitence and confession was held an hour before the morning sermon for the sake of those who had been unable to be present yesterday afternoon because of fever.

Monday, the 27th of September. Schweiger's wife brought a healthy child into the world this morning that was to be baptized this afternoon, but it died unexpectedly and the husband and wife claim not to know how it happened. They are very much dismayed about it; but they think their consciences are clear of having made any mistake. [We count this case among the divine judgments over these people. They are both worthless and do not get any better from their plentiful and rich hearing of the Word of God. All circumstances show that the man married the woman for worldly reasons rather than in the fear of the Lord (about which he was admonished greatly at the time) .[227] He already has a second wife, is still right young; and, because he still has an unconverted heart, he can govern neither himself nor his wife in a Christian manner. The wife, whose mother is in Purysburg, gave us good hope at first with regard to her Christianity and good housekeeping; but our hope has greatly lessened recently since she has fallen into the company of a certain woman, who does her much harm through her example and advice. When she is again able to go out, I shall try to speak to her and to him more intimately and, through God's grace, to bring him to better paths. They can grasp with their hands that the Lord is not with them and their work, for they have received the least increase this year in their field and garden and are much poorer and more miserable than others of the first transport (to which they belong).]

Mrs. Rothenberger brought a dead child into the world. She has been greatly afflicted by fever for a long time; and, because her husband has also been constantly bedridden with fever, she must have lacked necessary physical care. During this fever season (which will never end) it is hard on even the smallest children, and it is only through the goodness of God that they are preserved, otherwise even more of them would die. Because my fever remained away again today and because the greatest necessity required it, I journeyed to Savannah about noon and arrived there at seven o'clock in the evening. I expected to find Governor Oglethorpe here and to speak with him about the still needy condition of the congregation according to the content of the letter that we recently received, and also to receive our salaries from him. But he had not yet arrived; and, therefore, I must take this trip again in two weeks, and all the more so because he is going to return to London with Captain Thomson soon after his arrival from Frederica. Meanwhile, I have written to him from Savannah and briefly recommended that he remedy the plight of the congregation and particularly that of the third transport; and I asked him to give Mr. Causton orders to pay us our salaries in his name, because we are much in need of them.

I wished to write out a draft in order to obtain the money that Dr. Gerdes sent to the third transport and which was recently distributed to them with borrowed money. However, I had to fulfil the following conditions for the young Mr. Pury, who manages Mr. Montagut's store-house: namely, he will pay me the money in two installments, which he will begin in three months; and he will pay half only after he has received news that the bill has arrived and has been paid to Mr. Simon by Dr. Gerdes. Because there is no one else here who will accept the bill of exchange, I have had to agree to these conditions. Meanwhile I have written to Dr. Gerdes from Savannah that we would prefer for money to be sent to us instead of a bill. Spanish silver is not highly esteemed, because enough such money comes into the country from Spanish colonies that are very near us. Therefore English copper money is more useful to us (if gold or silver may not be sent).

The purpose of this trip was also to notify Mr. Causton of our lack of provisions again so that he can make arrangements for sending them up, especially since scarcely three or four men in the congregation are free of the fever and have some strength. So far he has been unable to find a boat or people here in Savannah, but now he has promised to find some remedy. Incidentally, Mr. Causton was very friendly toward me and assured me of all concern for our people. Yet he still had no orders to give the third transport adequate tools, kitchen utensils, etc. [for which Mr. von Reck is entirely to blame]. I submitted to him a catalogue of all the things that were given to each family of the third transport, from which he can recognize [at a glance] how badly these poor people have been supplied. [Mr. Vat was so friendly and helpful toward me and the Salzburgers that I was amazed. He is going to London with the same Captain Thomson. Mr. von Reck arrived here still sick and miserable; and, because he is lacking sufficient care and healthy food, he resolved to go to Charleston with his brother on Thursday and, having collected some strength, to go from there to London and Germany. As his brother has already done, he will doubtlessly make a lot of calumnies about us and our congregation; but he will more and more reveal his nakedness and his false intentions to those who can distinguish between light and dark.]

I became acquainted with a captain named Williams, who had sent two ships to the West Indies and has a house here in Savannah. He gave me some rare seeds such as coffee, indigo and cotton, the latter being better than the local variety, which dies every year and has to be replanted, because it grows into trees.[228] He wishes our Salzburgers to plant it, because it produces a great deal; and for that reason he gave me a large quantity of such seeds. In addition he gave me a coconut, of which I had heard and read but which I had never seen. He brought them for planting too, but they became too hard. Thursday afternoon I arrived again with divine protection in our dear Ebenezer. God had mercifully preserved me and my companions from the fever, which up to now had always caught up with some of them on the voyage.

Friday, the 1st of October. This afternoon I distributed the limited supply of meat and rice to the people of the first transport, and I am now awaiting more from Savannah. In their sickness the people need flour and butter most of all; and, because such things have not been given this time from the store-house with the provisions, I have requested them from Mr. Causton, partly in lieu of the syrup that is still owed and partly for the work they had in bringing up the provisions; and he has promised to send them.

[Mr. Causton keeps saying that the first transport must now receive its provisions on credit and will have to pay for them in the future. Mr. Oglethorpe has never told me a word about it; and I have represented to him often enough, just as I did to Mr.

Causton, that it is not the fault of these people that they must still eat other people's bread. One should have settled them on a good piece of land right away and not have placed so many burdens on them, because of which they have either become sick or been detained from farming, or one should have allowed their removal to their present better land sooner and surveyed their fields. I hope that our worthy friends who have some influence on the Trustees and who read this will take especial care of this point.]

Saturday, the 2nd of October. Hans Maurer and the widowed Mrs. Ossenecker wish to enter matrimony; and they already called on me about it last week, and their bans were declared last week for the first time. He is a carpenter and good worker, [has few external manners],[229] keeps God's Word diligently, and takes Holy Communion. However, if he wishes to be saved, he will have to fight his way through the narrow gate and leave the Old Adam with his trappings behind. Mrs. Ossenecker too has behaved herself in a very orderly way so far but must show even more seriousness in her Christianity.

Sunday, the 3rd of October. In the repetition hour today I made a beginning of acquainting the congregation, for their edification, with some of the written reports that we have received from England and Germany, from which we have been prevented until now by our own ailments and by the sicknesses of the people. Perhaps all were present who did not have fever this evening. I read to them, with application, those parts of the written report of the year 1735, which Professor Francke[230] sent us, and which record the external and internal conditions of the Salzburgers in Prussia[231] and also in their old fatherland of Salzburg. Because some time still remained, I also read them the little letter that was sent to us from London by an unknown and unnamed hand and consists of strength-giving Bible verses. I do not doubt that God has laid some blessing on this double reading (not only for me but also for the others). Yesterday a double family of Indians arrived here by water, who observed our divine service for a short time. These people are very crude and daring, and we are as careful as possible not to come too near them. One can offend some of these heathens through a very slight oversight.

Monday, the 4th of October. Simon Steiner's little baby died this afternoon. To all appearance it suffered from the now general sickness, against which both parents have been struggling. I asked about this man's spiritual condition; and he assured me not only that our dear Lord is giving him much grace for his prayers in his great physical weakness, but also that he notices that his sighs and

prayers are being heard and that he can well feel the work of the
Lord in his soul. Because I must travel to Savannah at the beginning
of next week to speak with Mr. Oglethorpe, I began today answering the letters we recently received from England and Germany.
May God give His blessing to all this.

Tuesday, the 5th of October. A certain captain,[232] who needs
some Salzburgers for a month for some of his business, spoke to me
today along with some other Englishmen and advised me that an
English family would now move to Old Ebenezer with Mr. Oglethorpe's permission. [This caused me to suggest to the listeners at
the evening prayer hour that they should bring to our place the
corn and beans they had stored in our houses so far until they should
be well or else guard them better, because these people are going
to move into our houses. Their skimpy crops will be less safe than
previously. The water is very low and the boat is difficult to use.
The horses have run off, and therefore they will have to carry the
crop on their backs, but for this they lack strength. I advised them
to pile it together in the store-house and to take turns watching it.]
The Englishmen were travelling to Savannah to speak with Mr.
Oglethorpe, and they presume that his arrival from Altamaha is
imminent. Through them I again beseeched Mr. Causton in a
friendly way to remedy our lack of provisions by sending up a boat
full of foodstuffs, which they should do all the more willingly because the said family is to receive its provisions from here.

Wednesday, the 6th of October. Mr. Zwiffler's wife has been sick
with fever for some time and had lost so much strength that she
died this evening, even though Mr. Zwiffler had done his utmost to
save her, if God had wished to give His blessing to it.[233] Because I
am very occupied in letter writing, my dear colleague has been
with her several times lately in my place to speak with her from
God's Word and to pray with her. He, Mr. Zwiffler, says much good
about her; and she answered affirmatively when she was asked
whether she was humbly approaching Jesus, who receives sinners,
as a poor and great sinner who wished to be saved by Him alone.
We hope with love for her salvation; the last time I was with her
I found that she was having her husband read her many beautiful
prayers and edifying songs and that she was reading them too. At
that time she thanked very appreciatively for the song book with
large print, which served her very well in her sickness.

Thursday, the 7th of October. Our dear people are now suffering
some loss in their cattle. Several head of cattle, among them several
oxen, have run away, because the regular herdsman cannot be with
the cattle because of fever. Among them are several that have been

giving milk, and therefore the loss is all the more regrettable. They will be found again if only we can send out some men who are familiar with the forest and the good pastureland in it.

At night, as well as in the morning and evening, it is now so cold that you can hardly imagine it, if you consider the heat of the day. In order for us two not to lose our mornings and evenings or suffer harm to our health, we must have a fireplace of wood and clay built into our huts so that a fire may be kept in it when necessary. So far we have had to spend a lot of money in our great need for building, and we shall soon ask Mr. Oglethorpe to reimburse it. *With the approach of winter, our poor need winter clothing. There are not few of these, both adults and children, who got along in summer with clothes made of linen. God has already looked out for that; for we not only have some money from Senior Urlsperger in our poor-box but have also received fifteen guineas from Saalfeld[234] [from Privy Counselor Walbaum.]* To be sure, this last sum should be applied for the good of the heathens; but we were given permission, if there were no opportunity for that, to use it for our poor and miserable. I have written to our benefactors in detail on this point. In the evening prayer hour I told the listeners how God was still awakening benefactors in England and Germany who were looking out for them and contributing many beautiful blessings for the need of the poor, which they should repay by praising God and interceding for such benefactors.

Friday, the 8th of October. [Since her sicknesses, by which she was severely afflicted, Mrs. Rheinländer is conducting herself externally much better than formerly; and she says that God has made her believe in Jesus Christ and that she is now sure of salvation. Yet, when we are with her for a while, we can well see that the Old Adam is still unkilled and still sovereign, even if not in any way that is crude or punishable in this world. Her self-love, arrogance, and worldly desires still possess her heart; and she can tolerate such bad qualities in her children, in fact she even furthers them by word and example as virtues under another name. Meanwhile she and her husband know how to speak very well, they know better how to accomodate themselves and perform now and then many kind deeds. A few years ago she did a kindness for a married woman in her peculiar circumstances, which one could almost have considered more as the work of the grace of God dwelling in her than as a work of human nature; yet it is not more than that if one judges it in the light of Holy Scripture. Oh, nature and clever reason can go a long way in imitating grace! How sad it is that so deeply corrupted people are so convinced by their extremely corrupted condition and leprosy of sin that they hurry right to their Helper as miserable sinners.]

I am amazed that Mr. Causton does not send up the promised provisions, since he well knows our great need. He must be unable to find a boat or any people for it. The Englishmen who know the way are shunning the work. Next week I should distribute the foodstuffs to the second transport; and the Salzburgers of the first transport have not yet received adequate rice, and no corn or beans at all. In addition, our sick people need flour and butter, which they wish to accept in place of syrup. When I was in Savannah the German carpenter[235] came to me again, having received permission from Mr. Causton to move back to us in Ebenezer, now that he has earned and paid back the money he owed the gentlemen [Herrnhuters] for his passage. I asked him to look around in the town for people who would bring up a boat full of provisions; and he promised to do this sincerely, because at this opportunity he could come up himself with his things.

Saturday, the 9th of October. I found Nicolas Riedelsperger in great physical weakness; and it seems to him that, if his fever continues in its present violence, he will lose all his strength and will die; and for that reason he wishes to partake of Holy Communion tomorrow morning. He recognizes himself as a miserable sinner, whom (as he acknowledges with humility and gratitude) God has suffered so far with great patience; otherwise he would long ago have been in hell. I spoke with him a bit about the verse (without my asking him he could tell me in which chapter it is to be found) : "Behold, that is the Lamb of God, which taketh away the sin of the world," also "Come unto me all ye who are laden, etc."[236] God gave much edification to him, me, and all those present. Oh how much good it would do my heart if, after recovering my health and finishing my letter writing, I could again visit the members of our congregation often, for which they themselves so sincerely yearn. Their yearning and longing paves our way to even greater edification. Private visits also have an external value, not only do the people keep a better trust in us and remain free from all formality and untimely veneration; but we also discover on such occasions what the people are lacking for their physical care, and we try to find a solution when possible.

Today, God be praised, we finished answering the letters we recently received from Europe and also other letter writing, so that, God willing, I can take them with me to Savannah on Monday. The following letters have been written: to the secretary of the Lord Trustees, Mr. Martyn, to their comptroller, Mr. Verelst, to Mr.

Vernon, to Mr. Newman, to Court Preacher Ziegenhagen, to Court Preacher Butjenter, to Dr. Gerdes, to Senior Urlsperger, to Prof. Francke, to [Privy] Counselor Walbaum, to Landeshauptmann[237] von Burgsdorff, to Inspector Bötticher, and to my mother .

[I must mention something of the contents of the letter to Mr. Martyn, Mr. Oglethorpe had sent the letter I wrote to him from here on March 16th of this year to the Lord Trustees, who then, in their answer written by their secretary, let me know that they were annoyed by some points which were, however, not to be found in my letter.: e.g. that our people did not wish to stand watch at all, or not on Sundays and holy days; also, that I was displeased that they had their officers give their commands to our people at the place church was being held, which authority they did have; also, that I had reported in said letter that some of the Salzburgers had let themselves be persuaded to leave their former good conditions, in which they were because of the charity and kindness of many benefactors in Germany, because one had delayed so long in the promise to let them enjoy free exercise of religion and all English rights and liberties just like other born Englishmen and also to give every family fifty acres of land as their own property *soon after their arrival.*

[In my answer I clarified the last point and reported in what connection and for what purpose (as the letter itself proves) I wrote such a thing to Mr. Oglethorpe. I answered what was essential concerning the first two points, that it nowhere appeared in my letter, which had been laid before the Lord Trustees in that connection, that our people had refused guard duty. They had merely requested such a method as Mr. Oglethorpe approved of in my presence before the publication of the rules for which Mr. Vat was to blame. Also, I for my part would never presume to feel the least displeasure if the Lord Trustees wished to have their commands to the Salzburgers announced in the church or elsewhere. I only meant another day would be more suitable for it than Sunday (since such confusion was caused by Mr. Vat) ; and that an undisturbed Sunday celebration was more welcome than repugnant to the Lord Trustees.

[He reports last of all that the Lord Trustees are, to be sure, sorry that the Salzburgers have fallen into some hardship; but they are amazed that in bearing their physical sufferings they do not recall the spiritual suffering they had to bear in their fatherland. To this too I answered enough for the Lord Trustees to recognize that we fear no suffering through the grace of God, but that we had believed that the benefactors would not hold it against us if we complained against unjustly inflicted hardship and difficulties, as happened in the case of Mr. Vat.]

This afternoon we again buried a child, which belonged to the shoemaker Ernstdorf. The poor little children are discomfitted by the fever just as their parents are; and since all of them, with one or two exceptions, are suffering it with their mothers and are very miserable, many more will probably die. May the Lord, who is merciful, have mercy on our misery.

Sunday, the 10th of October 1736. Old Balthasar Rieser and his wife and three children still have the fever, but the children not as severely as the parents. They both requested Holy Communion some day this week, for which they will be ready. They have always preferred to take it with the congregation, but they have been prevented from it partly by all sorts of work and distraction (which they greatly regretted) and partly by the long-lasting sickness. I told them what I found necessary according to their spiritual condition. [They are both of the kind that have always been converted, but never rightly, and have been like a false bow. The man has a beautiful insight into an active Christianity and would also like to be saved, if only he could take the world along and did not have to deny the flesh. He well recognizes his spiritual condition and natural inclinations and disapproves of them too; but it remains to be seen whether he will now really become serious. His wife has had Grimmiger's little child in her care and done much good for it, but we had to take it away from her and entrust it to another woman because of her lasting sickness.]

For a long time I have not been able to visit Pichler and his wife, who are still sick together with their child. I found him today just as he was lying with a high fever and quite beside himself and speaking unintelligibly. His wife is not quite so bad off and can help her husband somewhat; but she was so depressed that she needed comfort and encouragement from God's Word, which I gave her from today's gospel for the sixteenth Sunday after Trinity. May God let it take, and may He strengthen her in patience through His spirit. Today we had a penetrating rain, during which it was also quite cold. The repetition hour was cancelled, because it gets even colder towards evening and the poor people still have their attacks of fever, even though they sometimes appear to be well. That is the reason that the evening prayer hour is held only now and then and not as regularly as in the days when the people were well.

[Monday, the 11th of October. When I asked an honest husband how his house was faring, he disclosed to me the troubles of his heart because of his wife, who is not only unknowing but also wicked and restless and impatient in all the many trials. When he holds up to her the holy teachings and the example of the Lord Jesus, she speaks sarcastically of certain saints and excuses herself because of human weakness, etc.[238] He had worked on her for a long time and had taken great pains during her so-far continuous sickness to preserve her by performing all the tasks that fall upon women and to win her through admonitions and by reciting verses of the Bible; but she always remained the same, even if she sometimes gave some hope of improvement. May God strengthen him in his patience through all that and let him learn that she can be won less by zeal and force than by love and gentleness. In the last case I reminded him of 1 Kings 19: 11 ff. and talked with him about some other things pertaining to the matter. I was pleased to hear this unpleasant account because I have considered the woman better and have therefore not arranged my conversation and work with and on her according to her condition.

[The widowed Mrs. Haberfehner is not treading in the Christian steps of her late husband but is causing us and others much distress. She helps the above-mentioned righteous man in his house but causes him as much vexation and trouble as his wife does. Recently she scandalized almost the entire congregation both by drinking rum with an Indian woman who stopped here for a short time with her husband and children and by taking some honey from her without her knowledge or consent, about which the Indian woman, who knows some English, complained to other people. To be sure, Mrs. Haberfehner replaced the honey with rice, but that still did not make amends for the bad deed. God is chastising her body severely through sickness; He wishes thereby to cause her to recognize her miserable condition. Her late husband was not content with her and worked on her with all his strength in his sickness.]

Tuesday, the 12th of October. Hans Maurer was married today by my dear colleague with the widowed Mrs. Ossenecker.

Wednesday, the 13th of October. Last Monday I had gone to Savannah in hope of finding Mr. Oglethorpe there and turning our letters over to Captain Thomson. However, Mr. Oglethorpe was not yet there, but he is expected soon according to the content of his letter. Nor did I find the captain of the ship; and therefore I gave the letters to Mr. Müller, whom Mr. von Reck brought with him as a servant [and left behind him in very bad circumstances and without any money. He is well disposed toward us; and] because he is going back to London with said Captain Thomson with the permission and help of Mr. Oglethorpe, which he hopes to attain by presenting his beautifully elaborated portrait. He will deliver our letters well.

Mr. Causton still had no orders to pay our salaries but told me to await Mr. Oglethorpe's arrival. The minister in Savannah, Mr. Wesley, journeyed toward Frederica this morning to meet Mr. Oglethorpe; and I gave him a letter in which I humbly beseeched him for some things that we and our congregation need. This petition is all the more necessary, not only because we will have very little opportunity to speak with him on account of his accumulated business but also because I was told that he would not remain there more than three days and therefore could have departed for London before we learned of his arrival in Savannah. [The letter I wrote him read from word to word thus: "Being informed of yr. Honourables intended Departure for England, I beg humbly pardon to trouble you once again with some humble Petitions, which I am forced to by the several Wants & difficulties, the Saltzburghers laboured under till now, & which will & can be removed by yr. Generosity et Power.

["1. I delivered lately to Mr. Causton's hands an account of tools & utensils, which are delivered to the last comers by Mr. von Reck & out of yr. store. And since they did receive not the half part of the necessary utensils & tools which the Honourable Trustees have generously resolved to give to new Settlers in this Colony, I crave yr. fatherly Goodness for these necessary things as well as for granting them a full Quantity of Cows, Sows et Poultrey, seeing that they are quite disabled by this poverty to buy them for themselves.

["2. The Surveyor has laid out 92 Gardens,[239] & went afterwards again to Purrisburgh to do there some work for a long time. Wherefore humbly beg yr. favour to order him again to EbenEzer for finishing the Gardens as well as the Farms. Some Gardens happined to be run out upon barren pine Land, which, we confidently believe will be exchanged for better Grounds by yr. good Order. There lies very fine tract of Land behind the peoples Gardens towards Ebenezer River Besides this the spots in the middle of the town, which are reserved for publick Building are not yet exactly laid out, therefore nither a Store nor any publick Building else can be built before a Surveyor does here his work, which you would be pleased to order.

["3. I humbly beseech yr. Honourable, to allow me & my fellow labourer some Money for building a Dwelling House, since our

Salary is hardly sufficient for our Substance & can't be applied to any great Building. We lived hitherto in Huts, which are not profitable for our Health & the Performing of our ministerial office. I cannot forget to mention that we were constrained to spend some Money for some little Buildings at old EbenEzer & in this new settlement. Likewise we found it very necessary to buy a little Boat for doing our & our peoples Affairs at yr. Town, which, we are in confidence yr. Honourable will have the Goodness & favour to repay. The School Master and Doctor Zwiffler were likewise disabled to pay the building of Hutts & Garden fence, to which we advanced the Money from that which is sent to our care for the poor in our congregation.

["4. Four Carpenters have built, at old EbenEzer Mr. Gronau's House, which desire yr. Honourable very humbly for letting them have their promised payment.

["5. I make bold once again to remember yr. Honourable, that the people's Provisions are very Short, by which they are constrained either to buy more for Money or if they are too poor, to suffer hardships & hunger. What we have bestowed upon the poor people's Clothes & other Wants, is more than 60£ Sterling, which great benefit is sent to their behalf from Benefactors from Europe, which money is now almost gone & what we have still in hands, must rather be applied for clothing & maintaining some poor children of our congregation & of other poor people for bringing them up in the fear of God. Wherefore I most humbly crave, yr. fatherly Goodness to let the poor people have for a little time the same Provisions, we had in the first time. I have told Mr. Causton several times, that the people must go rather to the Southerd[240] than to suffer so great Hardships, if their settling at Ebenezer is the only reason of the Shortening & Denying their ful provisions. At least, I hope, you will grant us this favour, to let the people have flower & Butter, as long as they are affected with this present sickness. Hitherto they did receive the said things instead of their allowed Molasses, which they want likewise necessary. Without flower & Butter they can't Subsist in their Sicknesses.

["6. We are extreamly desirous of bringing up in our School not only our people's but also other children, which would give, as we hope, a happy Opportunity by the blessings of God for preventing Impiety & Profaneness, & for gaining grown people, & perhaps some of the Native Savages too to the living knowledge of Jesus Christ. But being disabled in the first time to spend a great deal of Money for the Clothes & victuals of the children & for exstructing a great House for keeping & teaching them therein we humbly desire yr. Honourable to allow us some Provisions for their Maintainance, or what else yr. Generosity & Goodness thinks proper for that purpose."

[Finally I mentioned that our people still had no boat of their own and that, if they were further compelled to fetch their provisions with the clumsy large boat, their health and lives would suffer even greater harm. May God bless this too to His glory and our good.]

This morning God brought me back again safely to Ebenezer. One of the three people who took me down and back up on the boat contracted fever underway.

Thursday, the 14th of October. During my absence Mr. Causton sent up a boat full of provisions, which were distributed yesterday, and today as far as they went. He promised me in his letter, and also orally, to send more with the same boat and to see to it that the boat intended for us would be finished very soon. Balthasar Rieser and his wife received Holy Communion privately from my dear colleague. Already yesterday we spoke a great deal with him and revealed to him, according to God's Word, his heart, which is inclined to the world and the cares of this life. We told him he must free himself from these through the grace of Jesus Christ through a true conversion, or else he would not be able to receive Holy Communion worthily for the salvation of his soul. [However, he considers himself penitent, and he has no lack of excuses and fig-leaves to hide the Old Adam behind. His wife seems to be in a better condition and accepts what is told her with more application.]

Friday, the 15th of October. [We two have had a necessary little fireplace of wood and clay built in our hut; and we must wait and see whether Mr. Oglethorpe will give us anything for it. Except for our huts, we have so far had to build everything in Old Ebenezer and here with our own money, whereas in other places preachers are taken care of in this regard. Because we have to buy all our own food and have to be very careful and cautious in our physical care in order to maintain our health in this unaccustomed country, we should be spared such expenses. We cannot presume upon our sick and poor people to work for us for nothing, since they have enough difficult and at times fruitless work to do to earn their bread.] Because most of us are entirely without money, yet lack clothes for winter, we brought back some stockings and also some coarse cloth and linen from Savannah to fill their needs. They also lack woolen blankets to keep themselves warm at night; but they are unable to buy these because they cost nine shillings sterling each. May God bless what we have written to Court Preacher Budjenter about this.

Saturday, the 16th of October. In their long-lasting sickness some people are somewhat ill at ease and troubled that they are being kept from visiting the public divine service and the prayer hour. A woman disclosed her sorrow about it with tears, but she also said various things about the great grace that God had laid upon her and her husband; and she told how He had revealed to them on their sickbed that their hearts were worldly-minded and tended to be distracted by worldly matters and how He was drawing them better and better to heaven.

I was told that, because of their continued tribulations with respect to the land and their food supplies, some people of the congregation had hit upon the plan of leaving this colony again after a few years and looking around for a better, orderly, and productive work and way of life. We do not know whether they were brought to this indiscreet resolution merely by the talk of the Englishmen, who often speak of leaving the colony after three years,[241] or by someone else, or whether this thing that was told me, and which we have never heard from any Salzburger despite all suffering, had a basis in truth, or in what connection any words had been spoken by anyone in this regard.

In the meantime, while reading one of Professor Francke's last letters during yesterday's and today's prayer hour, I could not help but pour out the sorrow of my heart before the people, who were assembled there in a considerable number, and speak a bit about the pitiable results of such [wicked] resolutions with respect to their physical and spiritual condition, even with respect to the Kingdom and Glory of Christ Himself. Among other things I showed that the path of tribulation on which God is still leading us is the very path that Christ the Lord, His Apostles, and all believers of the Old and New Testament have gone. They would, I added, someday praise our dear Lord on their deathbed more for affliction than for good days, etc. God wished to test them to see whether they had really emigrated for the sake of the gospel, etc. I likewise told them that those who wished to run away from God's school of the cross and try to better themselves by choosing their own paths did not actually believe in divine providence and did not consider God's promises true: e.g. "But seek ye first the kingdom of God, etc." and "I will never leave thee, nor forsake thee."[242] Both of these were dreadful things. After all, none of us had come here without God's special direction, especially since this matter was conducted through much prayer by many servants and children of God and everything had been well proved and there was no lack of evidence of God's providence, etc.

Sunday, the 17th of October. During the morning divine service another boat full of provisions arrived here for us; and a man brought word that Mr. Causton will send more. He himself did not write to me. The Englishmen do not load up much at a time; and, because they have to make so many trips and demand good pay for each trip, it comes much higher for the Lord Trustees to send the provisions up than to buy us a regular boat, with which the Salzburgers would bring the provisions up here a lot at a time and for little pay. I wrote to Mr. Causton that Mr. Kieffer in Purysburg was building a boat with his sons, which is to be twenty-six feet long and four or five feet in inner breadth. [Mr. Oglethorpe has not yet arrived in Savannah.]

Monday, the 18th of October. Both today and last week I distributed flour and butter to our people, which they had asked Mr. Causton to send them instead of syrup. They were due syrup for three quarters of a year, which they then, to be sure needed for brewing beer; but the butter and flour given them in place of it stands them in good stead in their present sickness, that has lasted so long. They cordially thank God, who has in this way saved until now what is useful for them now. To be sure, some extra things are being given to the sick from the store-house in Savannah. However, since it is being given so frugally for a few sick and, as it is said, is being given on credit, how could we expect to be given as much as would be necessary for the entire congregation?

Tuesday the 19th to Friday the 22nd of October. This afternoon I was afflicted with cold fever again. The chill lasted for about an hour, and then I started vomiting so terribly that a good deal of blood was torn from my stomach. The fever that then began lasted for only about two hours; yet afterward my lassitude was so great that I had to sleep in anxiety both day and night and could hardly use any limb of my body. My nature must have been greatly irritated by the violent, and for me unusual, vomiting; and I had great internal heat but no sweat with it, frightening dreams, etc. Therefore, in addition to warm tea and coffee, I used *pulv. antisps.* several times and alternately, against the sharpness and to strengthen my nature, *essentia dulci*,[243] which our dear Lord in His great mercy so blessed that my strength increased again noticeably this morning, the 21st, when a gentle perspiration, which I have been waiting for, appeared. Our dear people make a mistake in not waiting for the sweat; but they are compelled to this partly by many domestic chores, partly because one spouse cannot help the other because they are all sick, or unmarried people must see to their own cooking and other things.

The fever in this country has a peculiar characteristic. Some people have already caught it again for the third and fourth time; some of them have been lying sick with it for more than a quarter of a year and have it daily with violent shaking, fever, and headaches so that they lose all their strength and can eat and drink nothing. Some have the chills for a few hours and are so shaken that they moan and groan; and they can bear the high fever better than such chills. Some with the fever feel pressure on their chests and can hardly breathe; and their pain is so great that they cannot relax. Most people swell when they have the fever, or when they do not have it, some of them only in their feet, others in the face, and sometimes on several parts of the body. They swell especially around the middle part of the body, right under the heart cavity; and this they must bear for a long time. Some of them constantly have a good appetite but are satiated at once and complain that they have eaten too much. The headaches are severe for some of them, bearable for others. In the beginning most of them get large and small sores all over their bodies and also break out at the mouth; yet they have no, or else only brief, alleviation of their fever. In the case of many it is associated with great pains in the small of their backs; but others have no pains at all except for the painful fever and lassitude.[244]

Saturday, the 23rd of October. Helffenstein, the tanner whom Mr. von Reck brought here with the third transport, died this afternoon. He has been sick as long as he has been here because of his age and the troubles on the ship and since then. At the end it was probably a consumptive fever. He leaves a widow and six small children in the direst poverty. He appeared to have a foundation and experience in Christianity and proved himself patient in suffering; and without doubt he has gone into the peace of his Lord. So far the widow has known how to resign herself to her difficult cross and bear herself erect under it.[245]

Sunday, the 24th of October. I had prepared myself, to be sure, to preach the Word of God to the congregation; but I was compelled by a new physical weakness to keep myself warm at home all day long. It was a catarrhal fever, which I had already noticed yesterday. Our dear Lord so strengthened my dear colleague that he was able to hold both divine services and also accompany the late Helffenstein to his rest and to give an admonition at the same time. To be sure, he too is not lacking in physical weaknesses and

other difficult circumstances; yet the Lord strengthens and helps,
when strength and help is needed, so that the congregation never
remains unattended.

Monday, the 25th of October. For some time the weather has
been rather warm at night too; but quite raw and frosty nights
are beginning now that the wind has shifted towards the northwest
with the new moon. We are now harvesting the Indian beans and
peas completely so that the frost will not spoil them, since they cannot bear any cold at all. We are also digging up the sweet potatoes,
which must be well protected against the cold. Otherwise they
spoil at once, becoming rotten immediately through and through
or getting hard as wood so that no livestock can eat them. This time
some of our people have also gathered a fine blessing of this kind
of crop, but they do not know just what to do with regard to pre-
serving it. One person tells them this, the other tells them that, yet
last year they were spoiled for those who had them. It is especially
important for these sweet potatoes to lie dry and warm and not to
get overheated by lying against each other. Digging up this crop
is rather tiring and requires diligence and care. To be sure, in the
spring the seed-roots are planted only a hand-breadth deep in the
piled up soil; but afterward the vines run to the right and left
from there and deep underground so that the potatoes from a single
vine must be sought for one of them here and the other one there.

Tuesday, the 26th of October. Today I finished another letter
to Mr. Oglethorpe, which my dear colleague will take with him in
case I cannot travel. We would not wish to miss the opportunity
during the last period of his sojourn here, but rather do our utmost
with request and presentations to get help for the dear people. In
it I remind him of the content of my last letters that I sent him to
Frederica, and I also request the payment of our salaries. I likewise remind him that he should give our people the deer skins for
clothes, which he promised before our removal but which we have
not yet received.[246] I also asked him for an iron for branding our
cattle so that they can be recognized and brought back again when
they run away. Finally I am asking him not to refuse the things we
recently requested. I commend ourselves and our congregation to
his continued affection and wish him God's blessing for his intended voyage.

Three robust young Indians called on me, who gave the appearance of being true marksmen and warriors. They said they had
come down from Savannah Town and were journeying to Mr.
Oglethorpe at Savannah. If they come into our hut, it is not in
vain; for they are hungry and thirsty and are well pleased if we

take care of them as we do to the best of our ability. In Savannah Mr. Causton is much burdened by these guests, as I myself have recently seen. One flatters these savage people greatly to keep them well disposed and friendly; but because of it they become more and more daring and think that we must treat them as they wish and give them what they demand. Nor do we like to look displeased. A while ago some Indians came to Savannah from the French region[247] and wish to settle among the local Indians because they were persecuted there. These are also being supplied from the store-house; and, when I was there, several of them had their lodgings in Mr. Causton's house. They speak a language that none of the Indians here understand; yet they are entirely similar to our Indians in clothing and way of life.

Thursday, the 28th of October, 1736. Yesterday morning we heard the cannons firing many times; and every one considered this a sign that Mr. Oglethorpe has arrived in Savannah. Therefore we packed up the last part of our diary together with several letters; and my dear colleague took them along today to Savannah, to which he journeyed this morning in my place (since I cannot risk going on the water because of my night fever), in order to receive our salaries from Mr. Oglethorpe and to receive an answer to the letters sent to him. [What I wrote to Mr. Oglethorpe this time is recorded under October 26.] At this time I also sent a little letter to Court Preacher Ziegenhagen and forwarded the diary to him, whereas the previous thick diary and the many letters that are going to England with Captain Thomson are addressed to Secretary Newman. At midday Mrs. Haberfehner, an Austrian widow, died. I wished to visit her this morning but found her without understanding. Last night things changed rapidly, for even yesterday she was talking about getting better. [For her salvation we have little well-founded hope. She was a greedy and wicked woman during her entire sickness and would not let herself be brought to any contemplation or betterment by us or by her heartily pious host (Schmidt), who put up with a lot from her. In her life she has had opportunity enough to turn herself to God, both in Regensburg and through the example and daily admonitions of her late husband, who found an edifying end about a year ago in Old Ebenezer. But because she did not have any regard for grace, such judgments followed that at her end she became unreceptive toward the means of salvation and unconcerned about her eternal bliss. This example humbles me greatly, and it grieves me that sickness and business have detained me from visiting her more often in her sickness.]

Friday, the 29th of October. Some of the young people who do

not like to bear the cross long have had for some time a repugnance
and indignation at the tribulations that have lasted so long, especially since they are perhaps more often afflicted by the hardships
and difficulties than the married people are. Therefore several of
them [four have revealed themselves clearly] have complained to
me of the [laziness and the] shirking of the married men from the
communal work; and they demanded that the extra work they had
done should be repaid and deducted for them through a matter
that they proposed. However, because this complaint smacks of
both self-love and self-will, they received a negative answer. Subsequently they wished to be angry at this judgment [and to defy it];
but I reproved them emphatically for this through other people.
When they came to me to justify themselves, they had to hear even
more clearly from God's Word just what the basic nature of their
hearts is. I hope God will bless this for the healing of this harm.
[Kogler is the chief instigator. He is a very skilled carpenter, who
can do any kind of cabinet work he sees; and, because Mr. Vat
preferred him and set him, so to say, as a master above the others,
the Old Adam in him has become stronger.]

Saturday, the 30th of October. Last night a very heavy frost fell,
and it killed everything in the gardens that cannot stand the cold,
so that this morning we found everything lying as if scalded.

Sunday, the 31st of October. My dear colleague came back from
Savannah this afternoon, without having met Mr. Oglethorpe. The
recent heavy firing that we heard here occurred because of a small
ship that had arrived bringing all sorts of provisions to Savannah.
Because we are both weak and have so many tasks in our community, the constant journeying to Savannah is very grievous to us
[especially since it has always been in vain so far. Mr. Oglethorpe
could have given Mr. Causton orders long ago concerning our
salaries, as he was requested long ago.] It is now very difficult to
find healthy people to take us down there. Whoever has any strength
must build a kitchen for himself or others against the cold or finds
enough else to do. Mr. Zwiffler went along to Savannah with the
intention of asking Mr. Oglethorpe for permission to go with him
in Captain Thomson's ship to England and then on to Germany.
[If the man had any conscience, he would not resolve upon such a
departure until the benefactors in England have sufficient and
certain news of such a plan, in fact he should ask the permission of
the Society for this, since he has cost them much both on the voyage
and here. Perhaps Mr. Oglethorpe will think of this and not give
him permission. I do not wish to write to Mr. Oglethorpe about it,
because this would only embitter the poor Mr. Zwiffler against me

all the more, he being, even without it, already full of bitterness and calumny. A man is not suitable for us if, in unbridled anger, he can call the Salzburgers oxen, asses, rascals, etc., as he does, and treat them as a scorned rabble.]

Monday, the 1st of November. Yesterday it was again announced that Holy Communion would be held next Sunday, and today various people signed up for it. It is very edifying for me that there are some among them who cordially thank our dear God for the sicknesses they have borne and assure me that the spiritual gain is much greater than the bodily harm caused when the long-lasting sickness kept them from their professional activities so that they had suffered some loss in harvesting their crops.[248] Yet there is no lack of those who look upon such trials as a hard yoke and probably grumble under it; but by this they reveal the foundation of their hearts. Some of them complain that they do not take enough care of themselves after regaining their health and therefore return to work with too much zeal, which is harmful to their health and their Christianity. This suggests to me the temptation that students at the universities have in this regard, especially when they are poor and cannot remain long at the university and therefore fall upon their studies with such impetus that they suffer harm to body and soul. It is a grace of God when they, like the honest souls in our congregation, recognize this snare of the devil, under a good appearance, which makes them invalid for God's service, and let themselves be instructed.

Tuesday, the 2nd of November. Toward evening Veit Lemmenhoffer's little child died after having suffered for a long time, like both parents, from fever and finally from diarrhea. The shoemaker from Purysburg (Reck) has worked here for several weeks and has also registered for Holy Communion. [In Purysburg I was told this and that about the company he kept and of his disorderly life. I held this up to him very seriously and showed him that he could not possibly come to Holy Communion worthily in such a bad condition. But he denied everything and claimed that he had fallen under such suspicion in his position as constable, which he had to hold for a year. To be sure, he sometimes had to be in company that brought him no profit, but no one had ever seen him drunk.] It is his present resolution to prepare himself for Holy Communion through the grace of God; for he says that God has again wrought much good in his heart and that I shall discover in the future that he did not go to Holy Communion without profit.

Wednesday, the 3rd of November. For several days we have again had warm weather both day and night. We are only lacking warm rain, otherwise the garden crops that are planted in fall and winter flourish well in such weather. We are amazed that, so far, we have not been able to get any root-crops like white turnips, parsnips, carrots, etc., even though we have tried them both in the spring and the fall with good seeds. Radishes and cabbages grow very well; and we have no lack of them, except that the cabbages do not grow any head (perhaps because of the heat) and we have to use the leaves. They do, however, have a good flavor. Of trees, the peach trees grow best and fastest; the other kinds are unsuccessful.

Thursday, the 4th of November. All our widows are now provided with dwellings. Mrs. Resch has had her hut and fenced-in garden for a long time. She helps Geschwandel in his housekeeping and in raising his little child, and he has felt obligated to build her a hut. Today Hans Maurer called on me and announced that, if I were satisfied, he would sell his hut and his very well fenced-in garden and other appurtenances to Mrs. Holtzer for a small sum of money, since he was building a hut on the house-lot of his wife, the widow Ossenecker. This widow has already expressed to me her desire for this hut. The third widow is Mrs. Schweighoffer, who has moved into the hut of the late Felser, where she has found everything already well arranged. [To be sure, I still have no permission for this from Savannah (even though I submitted a supplication in her name to the magistracy there several weeks ago, since that's the way they want it to be). However, because the hut was standing empty and because this woman's request will probably not be refused, I had her things taken there a couple of weeks ago and let her move in.] The two little girls of the recently deceased Mrs. Haberfehner must be provided for and put under someone's supervision and care, and we are now concerning ourselves with this.

Friday, the 5th of November. Some of those who had the intention of going to Holy Communion but are not Salzburgers were examined to see whether they are properly familiar with the words of the catechism. For, among both old and young who had already attended Holy Communion in other places, I hardly found any who could recite the five chief articles without explication. I indicated to these what their future duty was. I also read some of them the pertinent words of the late Luther from the preface of his catechism. In the future I shall treat in this way all of them who seem suspicious to me because of their ignorance. May God strengthen us in our bodies for the sake of His goodness and truth. I am now dragging myself around with a kind of tertian fever, with which I have no real chill or fever but lie all night with restless and depressing dreams and which makes my body so tired that I have to lie in bed almost all the next day because of exhaustion and headaches. Nevertheless, my appetite for eating is regular all the while, except that things taste a bit bad on my fever days. On good days I sometimes have complete, sometimes less, strength so that I can still accomplish something.

Saturday, the 6th of November. In our present sad circumstances it gave me no little encouragement when a Salzburger, upon my inquiry as to how he utilized his time at home with his family, told me that from time to time neighbors gathered at his house and recollected their former miserable life in Salzburg and also talked together about those things that had been said and made known to them from the sweet gospel of Jesus. One of them would help guide the other in their simple discourse so that the time passed in great enjoyment. In this they sometimes made use of Schaitberger, which they understood better than other books because he used their dialect. Others have told me about such useful gatherings, when several young people and a family of married persons gather together for the sake of singing, praying, and reading. However, they thereby incur the anger of several rough single people, who do not follow suit and are reprimanded in their lax Christianity through this good Christian conduct and serious use of the means of grace. Such unity [*pia animorum conjunctio*][249] is a very blessed thing in the congregation. Not only does the Lord lay His blessing upon it in accordance with the promise of His dear Son, but also the hypocrites and sanctimonious Christians reveal themselves through the resentment they feel at it and through their secret envy and evil calumny of those who do things better than they.

It is a great loss that we do not have a house and heated room here as we had in Old Ebenezer, in which these and those honest souls might gather together for private edification, as occurred in Old Ebenezer with much communal revival. Because of our household belongings and some things belonging to the congregation, our hut is so small that it is filled by just a few, and there is no room for sitting or kneeling. In addition, we live in the first row of the city, and thus right far from most of the listeners (which arose through an error [of Mr. von Reck], since we would have preferred to choose a dwelling place among the listeners if all the lots had not been allotted before we could report that). In time everything can be arranged better. If only we had a spacious place, the hungry souls would object just as little to the inconvenient path to our house as they object to that of the church, which is held in a spacious hut right on the river.

Some time ago [the shoemaker] E[Ernstdorf] got drunk to the scandal of other people and was not only chastised for it publicly in the congregation at that time and reminded of the horror of this sin but also kept from Holy Communion until he acknowledged this sin and the vexation caused by it and showed remorse for it. His wife fears God and has always helped work on him as on a very unknowing man so that he has recently begun to turn over a new leaf. I examined this man today in the presence of those whom he had vexed by his drunkenness and reminded him again of his sin and had him confess whether he recognized this sin as a sin and whether he heartily regretted it and made him tell what his present resolutions were. He answered these questions in such a way that we could well be satisfied. Finally he promised me with mouth and hand never, with God's grace, to walk such paths again; and he said he was grateful for the love and benevolence shown to him. One has cause to have patience and sympathy with this [poor] man. He was a soldier for many years [with the Danish troops], never learned to read, and heard little of God's Word. He grew up wild and remained wild until God led him and his family to us, where he not only has no opportunity for his disorderly life but also hears often from God's Word that such conduct is inconsistent with Christianity and cannot be tolerated among us.

Sunday, the 7th of November. Yesterday evening seven people from Purysburg arrived here to take Holy Communion with us today; and immediately after their arrival, when they informed me of their intention, I held a small preparation for them concerning the importance and blessedness of true Christianity and prayed with them. Among them was Müller, whom Mr. von Reck brought to this country as his servant and then abandoned. After having completed and presented a beautiful work for Mr. Oglethorpe,[250] this man instructed children for a few weeks in Purysburg, for which people gave him his food. In that he showed much loyalty and diligence. In the morning there were forty-two communicants; and, since three pious women could not attend in the morning because of fever, they took Communion in my hut after the afternoon divine service, which holy performance was very edifying for both me and them.

Monday, the 8th of November. This morning my dear colleague journeyed to Savannah with the people from Purysburg, some of whom have some business with Mr. Oglethorpe, who certainly must have arrived last Friday. Next Wednesday I shall send our little boat to Purysburg, at about which time my dear colleague expects to arrive there. May God give his divine prosperity to everything (that has been written to Mr. Oglethorpe and that is to be discussed with him for the good of the congregation). Now that the fever is ceasing for some people, they are catching severe diarrhea and dysentery, which come from the cold in the present fluctuating and mostly cold weather. We help them to the best of our ability in whatever seems to serve them in such circumstances. In the congregation there is now no lack of want and misery; and our dear Lord wishes to teach us right sharply that this world is a vale of tears, through which we must journey as pilgrims. Yet this valley will soon come to an end; and then those who remain constant followers of Christ will come to Mount Zion, where all our sighs are to be changed into an everlasting jubilation.

Tuesday, the 9th of November. Contrary to my expectation my dear colleague returned yesterday evening from his trip to Savannah. He learned in Purysburg that Mr. Oglethorpe had not yet arrived, even though it had been reported last week as a fact. Kieffer and his sons brought him to us again. [Again there has been a lot of difficulty connected with the reception of our salaries. The trips that we both have made so often in vain are very difficult and hinder our office. It will therefore be better if we receive copper money from London rather than receive it through bills of exchange. Since we were asked about that by Secretary Newman and Dr. Gerdes, I wrote something about our opinion in my last letters.]

An Englishman who trades with the Indians in this country arrived here and brought an Indian woman and child with him and asked me to baptize the child, which he had sired with the Indian woman in dishonor. The child was already rather large, almost a year old. As soon as I had well considered the conditions of the case, I could do nothing but refuse to baptize this child. For (1) no one except this man, the father of the child, could assure me that it was not yet baptized. [The country is full of scoffers and worthless people]. There are some outside people who amuse themselves with their preachers and their holy office and think nothing of the means of grace. I could not put the least faith in this man, who was committing his disgrace with this woman and is still doing so and does not conceal but says publicly that this is his illegitimate child. (2) It amazes me that he has delayed so long if, as he calls it, he wished to make a Christian of the child. (3) He must have his secret reasons for not wishing to go to the preachers in Savannah, since one of them has been sent here from London for the sake of the heathens and heathen children.[251] The latter would surely suspect me if I encroached on his office and baptized a child that does not belong to our congregation, especially since the

way to Savannah is not long and since necessity, such as the child's
weakness, does not demand it. [He sent the schoolmaster Ortmann,
with whom he was lodging, and Mr. Zwiffler, and also Volmar, the
German carpenter who has come from London, to me several times
and let them both request and also threaten (with Mr. Oglethorpe). But this could not move me to do his will. In anger at
this he went to Purysburg in order to accomplish his purpose
there.]

Wednesday, the 10th of November. Mr. Causton hired six Englishmen to bring some provisions up for us with our old large
boat; but they could not come more than a short piece of the way
above Purysburg, even though the water is now very low. Two of
them arrived here in a little boat and demanded at least two of our
people for help; otherwise they would be compelled either to unload the provisions or to take them back again, because it was impossible for them to bring them up. I gave them two people and
some provisions and told them of the method used by the Salzburgers to control the boat, and for this they also received a thin
rope for the forward team.[252] [The Englishmen had to load this
(clumsy) boat with provisions once more before they could bring
it up to us, (and from this one can judge about its characteristics
and about what hardships and what obvious harm to their health
our poor people must have had from it.)]

Thursday, the 11th of November. Although it is now right cold
evenings and mornings and most people are not yet entirely free
of fever, they nevertheless attend to God's Word zealously in the
prayer hour. In my sermon I adjust myself to their circumstances
and do not detain them long. For a good time I have omitted the
story of the Old Testament, which has otherwise been treated in
the prayer hours, and have read something for their edification out
of the letters we received; and I have also repeated and further
discussed and applied that which was preached on Sunday about the
gospel. Whenever I have not been able to hold the prayer hour,
my dear colleague has laid several selected Bible verses as his basis.
Next week we plan to open the school with the children who have
no fever, and then we will continue with the Bible stories in the
prayer hour with questions and answers. In these present (right
miserable) circumstances, may God let His Holy Word be our
hearts' joy and delight, by which we can be comforted and made
right joyful to cling quietly to the Lord in all things and perform
His will even with suffering.

Friday, the 12th of November. The schoolmaster Ortmann has,
to be sure, recently recovered from the fever; but now he has con-

tracted another ailment (which is not unusual among old people),[253] so that the situation now looks very dangerous. Even when he appears healthy, he is so weak that we can see that he has already lived most of his life in this world and needs nothing more than to put his house in order and to prepare himself to die. All this he has observed. [It is an especial blessing for him that he now has no opportunity to consort with Englishmen and other profane people, for otherwise they would do great harm to him in his soul; because he is much too weak and naturally simple to resist their enticements. We can perceive this easily as soon as any worldly-minded person comes here and lodges with him. *She is still dangerous for him.*][254]

Saturday, the 13th of November. N. B. Nicolas Riedelsperger has been bedridden with fever for some sixteen weeks; and, although he has conscientiously taken all the drugs that Mr. Zwiffler has administered to him, he has become weaker and weaker and yesterday he died. A short time ago he caught diarrhea. To be sure, this quieted down, but in its place he became greatly swollen in his entire body. In his long-lasting sickbed he was always patient and had a great desire for God's Word and for the comfort of the gospel and the sufferings of Christ, and he had long yearned for a blessed end. He could not read himself; and therefore in his well days he attended church all the more, and in his sickness both his son and his brother-in-law Eischberger read aloud to him. Just yesterday evening my dear colleague was with him and brought me the news that he was rapidly losing strength, yet we did not imagine that his hour of death was so near. He had a great honesty and was ready to serve everyone with what he had. He had had much experience with cattle and curing them and giving good advice. Shortly before his end he made an arrangement concerning the few things and cattle he was leaving behind him, by which he divided everything between his son and his sister, Mrs. Eischberger, so that no misunderstanding might arise afterwards. This afternoon the large boat finally arrived here and brought chiefly sirup and rice, also some corn. God be praised for this benefaction!

Sunday, the 14th of November. Through the goodness of God our school children are beginning to get healthier and healthier and attend divine service in greater numbers. Therefore a small beginning has been made in the afternoon catechism class, because for some time the congregation has been instructed only through a regular sermon. We cannot now hold the repetition hour as regularly as usual, partly because the evening hours are too cold for the people who have just been freed of fever and partly because we must spare our strength because of our often occurring weaknesses. The school will not be able to be begun again in the first days of the week, not only because the schoolmaster is sick again but also because my dear colleague must travel to Savannah again, God willing, now that a passing boat has brought us news that Mr. Oglethorpe arrived in Savannah last Friday.

Monday, the 15th of November. Haberfehner's oldest girl, approximately sixteen years old, will be put in the care of Pichler, an honest Salzburger, for her Christian nurture and support. She is exceptionally simple, and the people will have much trouble with her; but we shall try to compensate them for this every year from the poor-box. Together with her youngest sister, who is with the Austrian Hans Schmidt and is well cared for there, she must still go to school. She has already fairly well comprehended reading, the catechism, and a few Bible verses, so that we have not lost all hope; and we will probably be able to make her more useful for domestic chores. The other girl is very spirited, awake, and clever, but not well reared in many respects by her deceased mother. Toward evening Rheinländer came to me with his son, sixteen years old, and announced that he was to take leave of me, because he wished to have him learn the shoemaker trade [from the Herrnhuters]. I prayed with both and gave the boy some necessary admonitions. [He is a naughty person out of whom, despite all admonitions and representations so far, we have made at best nothing more than a respectable being for a while].[255]

Tuesday, the 16th of November. The six Englishmen who brought our provisions up here last Saturday could not go back down until this morning, because the very large sirup barrels could not be unloaded, rather I spent all day yesterday in distributing the sirup in the boat. Such quiet and orderly Englishmen we have not seen for a long time at our place, especially among those who travel on the water. The dear Lord arranges things well by visiting my fever upon me after my work. Today I hardly noticed it and could therefore distribute unhindered. My dear colleague could not have assisted me, because he has gone to Savannah.

Wednesday, the 17th of November. Yesterday and today we have had rainy weather and very raw air with it. Despite the nocturnal freeze and frequent cold by day some things that were sowed and planted at the right time in a good soil are growing almost as well as in spring, but they must be root plants or plants of a kind that do not grow up high and can endure the raw air. In the fall and winter here there are often warm nights and pleasant days; and, if a warm rain comes too, then the said things grow right rapidly. For us, nothing good will come of the root crops like carrots, beets, parsnips, etc., even though people are supposed to have a lot of them in Carolina, where they are also sowed in the fall.

Adam Riedelsperger has had a violent fever for a long time and has now lost so much strength that we are worrying about his life. He is a heartily honest man, full of love and uprightness toward his neighbor, and in his healthy days we could well use him here and there in various tasks. Since Schweighoffer died, he has been the only man among us who can make wooden shoes, and therefore all the people in the congregation are waiting for his recovery, because almost nobody is in a position to pay for a pair of leather shoes. Nor can they always wear wooden shoes, especially not on Sundays and holy days. Also, some of them, especially women, cannot wear them. Consequently, because the people have no money at all, we are constantly asked to have shoes made for them now that the German shoemaker from Purysburg is here; and for this much money is demanded. To be sure, the shoemaker does his work well, but he demands five shillings eight-pence sterling for every pair of men's shoes.

Thursday, the 18th of November. This afternoon my dear colleague returned again healthy, God be praised, through considerable rain storms. Mr. Oglethorpe showed him much affection and sent us two some wine and sugar. He could not find, or remember the content of, my detailed letter that I sent to him at Altamaha and to which I referred in my last letter. In the meantime he said what the Lord Trustees had written him about the Salzburgers. The first and second transport will receive the present provisions until the month of March next year, after which time they will have to pay for what they receive from the store-house. But annexed to this is the fact that from now on the Salzburgers will have to fetch the provisions themselves. They will be docked for the amounts of course linen and flour they were paid by Mr. Causton for their trips at the orders of Mr. Oglethorpe. The third transport should have the provisions as complete as at first, but with the above condition that they either fetch the provisions themselves or let the costs of transportation be deducted from the provisions. Because of their sickness the poor people have so far not been able to work on the boat, which is so miserably constructed for that purpose; and they probably will not be able to very soon.

Mr. Oglethorpe is having a board mill built in Old Ebenezer, at which our people who understand such work can also get employment. In the future, parsonages will be built for us two from these cut boards; but this will take a long time, because the construction of the mill alone requires nine months. And, because the workers there need provisions, Mr. Oglethorpe wishes to buy up our people's crop of corn and sweet potatoes there and to give them one shilling sterling more than the customary price. Similarly, all the others are to receive as many shillings recompense as the number of bushels of corn they have harvested. [Nor did he answer anything to the letter which my dear colleague himself delivered to him, in which I requested some things necessary for the congregation; and from his behavior we can make easy conclusions about the previous letter.]

We are to have a new boat; and, since Kieffer and his sons in Purysburg have just completed a large new boat, it will be bought for us if we are satisfied with the price. [He demands twenty pounds sterling, which is very unreasonable according to everyone's judgement. The decision as to whether it is to be accepted at such a price has been delegated to us because (as Mr. Oglethorpe long ago wrote to me) the Salzburgers are going to have to pay for it after some time.] Mr. Zwiffler also presented his case to Mr. Oglethorpe and requested permission to return to Europe. Mr. Oglethorpe [claims to think as little of him as other people do, yet he] suggested that he might tend the patients in Frederica as doctor, for which he would pay him a salary and adequate provisions. But he refused this too, because his mind is still on Germany, where, in his opinion, there is healthier air and way of life.

[He would not give us any hope that those Salzburgers who have received poor land for their gardens might expect any better in its place, rather he said that all the land is good and that the people just do not understand it; it would not be proper if the gardens lay here and there and the trees remained in other places.[256] Therefore the poor people concerned are bad off with their land.]

Friday, the 19th of November. After I was finished this morning with the distribution of the provisions, with which I have been occupied this week, I assembled the congregation this afternoon in order to announce what orders Mr. Oglethorpe had left behind regarding the provisions so that they could all arrange accordingly. According to the order of the Trustees, the provisions of the first and second transports will cease about the end of next March; and from that time on until September 1737 they will have an advance payment from the store-house, but not more than two pounds of meat each week and a half bushel of corn each month. Mr. Causton will not be able to advance any more. Now, because this provision is not [at all] adequate, I warned them to put their house lots in such a condition this fall and winter that they could raise all sorts of garden crops this spring, both to sell some of it in Savannah and to supply their own needs. Also, people in Savannah were expecting chickens, ducks, geese, pigs, etc. to be brought there for sale. I also advised them that Mr. Oglethorpe was not inclined to have better land surveyed for gardens. Therefore they should help each other all this winter and cultivate the good gardens and prepare them for planting; perhaps God will dispose the hearts of the Lord Trustees to give them the good land that now lies idle behind the present gardens, and then those who enjoyed others' help this winter would in turn help their helpers when the latter received their good land.

Above all I sincerely asked the listeners not to use what I had told them to become discouraged or dismayed or to grumble, for this would be but the fruit of a blamable lack of faith. The truth of Christianity must be legitimated in trials and tribulations; and everyone who paid attention to the movements of his heart would learn to recognize whether he believed the divine promises to be true. I at once called their attention to several Bible verses such as 1 Peter 5: "Casting all your care upon Him; for, etc.", "Cast thy requests, etc.," "Commend thy ways unto the Lord, and, etc.",[257] and finally I told them something about the extremely many and difficult trials and miseries of the first Christians and how comforted and joyful they were in them because they had no resting place here but sought for a future one.

We nevertheless hope and trust the goodness of our dear benefactors that they will take to heart the many obstacles to the Salzburgers' work and the many burdens heaped them and will not let them suffer want of food because of them, since through no fault of their own they are unable to sustain themselves. [For it would be too hard: (1) if the provisions were cut off next spring before they had had a real harvest here and then were allowed such a limited advance.] They received such late permission to move from Old Ebenezer and then had so many obstacles in their field work, were sick all summer long (and still are to a large extent), and had no land of their own for so long; and therefore they are still in bad circumstances and it is not their fault that they are still unable to sustain themselves. [If the people were not so poor and entirely devoid of money, they could buy food to still their hunger. But in this way they will have to suffer even greater want than they have previously.] Even if some of them have raised some corn and sweet potatoes in Old Ebenezer and here, it is little. Because of sickness they could not care for these crops rightly, but most of them got nothing in Old Ebenezer because they could not find any more good land and nothing would grow for them on the sand. [(2) if

they were refused good land for their gardens, while it is to be had
very near the city. It is surely a poor excuse that it would not look
good if the gardens lay here and there and that they should all lie
together, etc. Should the people perish for that reason and continue
to work in vain? Through lack of horses, wagons, cattle, etc. they
are not now in a condition to fertilize such sandy regions abundantly, especially since it must be done every year if they are to
bear anything. Therefore it is Christian fairness that good land
be given to each and every one after so many hardships and so much
misery, at least for their gardens, since it is there. After all, the remaining forty-eight acres will surely turn out very badly in any
case, because Mr. Oglethorpe cannot be moved to give the Salzburgers even a foot of land across Ebenezer Creek. As long as we
must observe the plan that all the land in a given district must lie
together and all must be surveyed as it comes, we cannot hope for
much good land and the poor people will not be able to promise
themselves much profit from their hard labor. (3) if the third transport still has to pay for the mistakes that Mr. von Reck made. These
poor people do not yet have all their tools and no kitchen utensils
except for a pan and an iron pot without a handle. Only ten families
have received cattle; and the others have no hope of receiving cows
or pigs or poultry as the first and second transports have received
and as one gives to all colonists in Carolina; and all this occurs only
because they did not go to the new city.][258]

Saturday, the 20th of November. About five weeks ago the German shoemaker who came from London sought and received permission from Mr. Causton to move back here to us; and he claimed
to us that his advanced age, since he is already seventy-three years
old, was compelling him to prepare himself properly for a blessed
death and for eternity through God's Word, for which he had a
good opportunity in our place. But before we knew it, he had
packed up his things and gone away secretly, no doubt with the
Englishman whose illegitimate half-Indian child we hesitated to
baptize here and who later accomplished his purpose with the
preacher in Purysburg. [For this irregular departure the Ortmann
people, with whom he stayed, advanced him some things and con-
cealed the matter from us as long as they could.] He is said to have
gone to Charleston via Purysburg, which Mr. Causton will take
very badly. [Therefore he is the way Court Preacher Ziegenhagen
characterized him in his last letter. Otherwise he acted very well
and could listen to the truth without embitterment or contradiction
and went to Holy Communion two weeks ago with considerable
devotion.]

This afternoon we had a severe thunder storm with much rain, which was followed by a wind that seemed to tear everything down. If Mr. Oglethorpe has already gone aboard ship as he intended, he will have a very hard time of it. Mr. Oglethorpe has given many people permission to go with him, and they will have the passage free. Yet, because the ship is small and is loaded full with rice and deer skins, they will have to be satisfied with a half quart of water and a half pound of bread, along with adequate rice, as food; and, because there is little space for sleeping, the young people will have to stay awake one night after the other. [Mr. von Hernersdorff, who came here along with the last Herrnhuters and has been used so far as a captain against the Spaniards on the Altamaha River, would have gone along if he had not been detained by sickness.]259

Sunday, the 21st of November. I visited three members of our congregation, whose resignation to the divine will and whose patience in their long and hard sickbed was most edifying for me. They were able to tell me that even these incidents had come upon them from the hand of their so merciful Father in heaven, who lays a burden on them but also, N. B., helps again *in His time.* In this He has the very salutary purpose of purifying their souls; and, when He attains it, everything will be all right. As the best medicine for their body and their souls they need a childish and constant prayer, for which purpose God has already given them some quiet hours too. Adam Riedelsperger and Brandner have had the fever from the very first until now; yet we have not noticed that they are very uneasy even though their bodily care was so bad that their domestic tasks, in which they were otherwise so loyal, had to be omitted to the harm of their households. They now try to practice the little verse: "Commend thy ways to the Lord, and etc."260

Monday, the 22nd of November. Mr. Causton asked me to come down to Savannah as soon as possible to calculate all the provisions that have been received so far for the Salzburgers, so that he and we might know how much can still be expected. I shall not delay in this as soon as my health permits it. Whatever foodstuffs we need we must borrow from the store-house or elsewhere, because Mr. Oglethorpe has not yet been able to pay our salary. The Lord Trustees are said to have sent us bills like those introduced here some time ago in place of others coins. As soon as they arrive, we too shall have our money.

Our school was started today, God be praised, with some children who have recovered. We are letting it stand at a four-hour school-day so that we can spare the children, especially in the present cold weather. Our huts are too small for holding school, so we assemble in the church, where we can maintain a fire, for which the parents of the children take turns splitting the wood and bringing it here. May God crown this beginning with His divine blessing! This is a very pleasant work for us, which is also influential in edifying the entire congregation.

Tuesday, the 23rd of November. B[Barbara Maurer], who is still unmarried, has so far lived in such circumstances that she has, so to speak, never really been at home and has had no regular work. Rather she has helped the sick people here and there for a short time; and, because she is very simple, has many improper habits and very little skill, and can only do household chores, she has become scorned. But now God has so disposed that she has willingly been brought into better order and into circumstances which will, with divine blessing, be best for her physical and spiritual welfare.

Christ, the baptized Jew, is conducting himself very well among us, he uses the means of grace seriously and we can note in his behavior that he is not just a hearer of the Word. He has become acquainted with the honest Austrian Schmidt, who is very helpful to him not only in agriculture but also in Christianity. Christ is not only inexperienced in farming, but also of very weak physical constitution; and therefore the said Schmidt, who is his neighbor, cares for him as for a son through right Christian love. He has secured his hut against cold, fenced in his house lot, and works along with him, since he works as much as he can and will in time come by a piece of cleared up land.

Wednesday, the 24th of November. A woman who is conducting her Christianity with poverty of spirit and all kinds of temptation called me from the street into her hut and said these, as her first words: She wished me to pray with her; she had two kinds of trouble, namely poverty and physical weakness, yet these were slight in comparison with her spiritual concern. She lacked certainty of God's mercy, she did not know how she stood with the dear Lord, and everything was going badly. Before the prayer I reminded her of what I had presented last Sunday in the regular gospel for the twenty-second Sunday after Trinity about the loving father-heart of God which is inclined to reconciliation with us, and which was clarified with the story of the prodigal son. Upon that she said no more but merely waited eagerly for the prayer. Those of us who are serious in our Christianity are very pleased when there is an occasion for us to pray with them and them with us. In a discussion, another woman remembered the many physical and spiritual benefactions and the hearty intercession of her deceased mother; and, since her ungrateful behavior often comes to her mind, she has much unrest and would not know what to do about this or that youthful sin if the gospel had not taught her to know Jesus Christ and, in Him, the free open spring against sin and impurity. She shed many tears in saying this.

Thursday, the 25th of November. *Some Salzburgers have found so much honey in some trees in Ebenezer Creek* that they could fill three wash tubs or barrels. It was so white, pure, and pleasant that we have not yet seen its likes here in this country. Some of them lack health, others lack time, otherwise they would be able to gather much honey this winter from the beehives they know. After our dear Lord granted them their health again, some of them, as many as have even tolerably good land, are seriously occupied in clearing it and fencing it, as they did with their recently surveyed gardens, and also to build the necessary things on their house lots. The deceased Mrs. Haberfehner has left various men's and women's clothes, which, *because they are of wool and not capable of being preserved in this warm climate,* have been changed into money for her two children. There are various poor people in the congregation who can be served by this; but the payment for some pieces will fall upon the poor-box, for the poverty is great and we cannot let them remain unprovided for. The praise of God which arises because of it among our poor, and for which our dear benefactors gave the occasion, is truly a fine fruit of this seed that has been sown. He Himself, our loving God, will repay it.

Friday, the 26th of November. N.B. N.B. This week we had several nights with a heavy freeze, after which we had much cold rainy weather. Ebenezer Creek, which has been almost dried up until now, is rising again. The Salzburgers who still have their crops of corn and sweet potatoes in Old Ebenezer have been hoping for this for a long time, because they can fetch the said things with the boat at high water. It remains to be seen whether a board mill can be built for the use of the colony in this river, whose flow in summer is exceedingly slight and whose water rises and falls very irregularly. The mill was already manufactured in England and brought to Savannah in Captain Thomson's ship.

A Salzburger woman, who has been lying sick of fever for a long time together with her family, told me that in her sickness she had simply asked our dear Lord to make her well toward Advent in order that she might prepare herself properly for the holy Christmas celebration by hearing the divine Word since she, like her husband, cannot read. And now, to the strengthening of her faith, she noticed that she had not asked God in vain, for He had already begun to show her body some help. She also told me how, despite all her worry and concern that she was not yet converted and therefore without forgiveness of her sins, our dear Lord was raising her up; it had occurred to her, namely, that man himself cannot think or wish anything good that would pass as good before God. But she could not deny the work of God in her soul, even though it was still weak through her fault. The hate she felt for all her sins and her struggle against them were not a work of her nature, but rather a gift and effect of God; yet she nevertheless believed that He would eventually complete the work He had begun in her. With tears she praised the wealth of divine patience and forbearance, and she severely lamented her ingratitude toward the manifold mercy she had received from God.

She had applied to herself the many serious presentations and admonitions that we had found it necessary to give in our sermons, for which reason I imparted to her the necessary explanations, some comfort, and a brief instruction on how she should conduct her Christianity. I told her at this time that she should guard herself against her own heart, and pay all the more attention to the promises of God that are preached to the poor. She should also guard herself against seeking comfort and rest in her struggle against sin in piety and good works;[261] that was some of the leaven that was still lying in our hearts from Popery; rather she should cling as a miserably poor sinner to Jesus and the redemption He won for us sinners and seek rest only in His wounds. The more her sins frightened her, and the more her heart wished to damn her, the more she should penetrate to Jesus through prayer and struggle. He wished to have right poor sinners and to show His splendor in them. She knew the verse: "Come unto me all ye (not who are pious and holy, but rather) that labour and are heavy laden, and I will give you rest."[262] But along with this there is also a yoke of Christ, which God's children must bear all their lives; and to it belong the painful feeling of sin and the constant struggle as a disciple of this loyal Savior. She might recognize how He was disposed toward weak and fragile Christians from the lives of the Apostles and their association with this, their and our, Savior.

Saturday, the 27th of November. I have received news that Mr. Causton is sending a lot of provisions up here on our large boat and a periagua,[263] a large part of which is going to Old Ebenezer for the workers on the mill there. But, because Ebenezer Creek is still low, I shall have to guard such provisions here for a time. And, because I have no space in the present provisions hut, some of the people in the congregation are ready next Monday, at my request, to remodel Mr. Zwiffler's hut, which we exchanged for that of Mr. von Reck, as a little store-house.

In our prayer hour we were able to give many salutary lessons to the congregation, particularly to the young people, also with regard to their public conduct; and this we did through the twenty-fourth chapter of Genesis, which followed in order yesterday and today. It is significant that, when Abraham sent Eliezer to find a bride for his son, he bound him by an oath not to take any Canaan-ite, among whom he lived, as a wife for his son under any pretext, and that he would by no means allow him to lead him back into his previous fatherland, out of which God had led Abraham. From the example of the God-fearing, wise, and cautious Eliezer[264] all righteous pastors and spiritual *Brautwerber*[265] can learn very important points for the right performance of their office. God make us loyal!

Sunday, the 28th of November. A Salzburger was greatly awak-ened by the Word of God today and came to me toward evening so that we might kneel together before Jesus Christ, our kindhearted King of Mercies. He has been sick of fever for a long while; and, because he has been looking forward to Advent and Christmastide for a long time, he has wished to be well again in order to visit public divine service at that time. Therefore he presented this his request many times to our dear Lord and promised Him, after recovering his health, to apply his time and energies entirely to the service of his Lord, his great Benefactor. Deep in his mind lay the example of the nine[266] lepers who, after recovering their health, were ungrateful like the Samaritan; and he needed much prayer and admonition if he were not to fall into their sin but should keep his oath. He could not trust his heart at all.

In this church year the regular Sunday gospels are again to be laid as a basis for the morning sermon. Instead of the introduction there is a prayer, after which the content of the gospel is presented to the congregation with necessary application; and finally a few important lessons are deduced from it, which can lead us to a better recognition of the road to salvation and to the practice of a true Christianity. In the afternoon catechism hour Luther's little cate-chism is being resumed; and, between the first and the second song the little children must recite publicly and in turn both the chief articles of the catechism and also some major Bible verses. The repetition hour will be omitted for a while longer; because it is now quite cold toward evening, and the people, especially the children, are still weak.

Monday, the 29th of November. Mr. Causton wishes to go through the accounts with me in order to discover how much provisions the Salzburgers are still to receive according to the Lord Trustees. Because some rowers have been found, and because the dear Lord has freed me of the fever (which so far has only been weak and not much hinderance to my activities), I set out this morning in Jesus' name for Savannah. God give me grace and wisdom to arrange everything for the best of the congregation.

DECEMBER

Thursday, the 2nd of December. This afternoon I arrived again under divine protection in our dear Ebenezer. Mr. Causton was exceptionally occupied, and therefore I had to delay in Savannah longer if I wished to consider and arrange something with him for the sake of the congregation. His affection and friendliness toward me was very great; and he showed great willingness to advance the Salzburgers' interests in every way. This time I could not get my accounts back again; and, therefore, I do not know whether the people have received too much or too little provisions. He gave me a whole keg of English or German peas to distribute to our people for planting, whereby he gave me some instruction in the proper way to sow and plant in this country. On Monday I must send down four men with the new boat that is to be bought for us in Purysburg, because Mr. Causton wants to see it and buy it himself. The man will let us have it for eighteen pounds sterling.[267]

Friday, the 3rd of December. Since Tuesday[268] we have had unusual cold at night, which is almost more painful for us here than in Germany. In the daytime the sunshine is very pleasant. Up to now Rauner has done all sorts of services for the sick people in the congregation and has neglected his own affairs because of it. Therefore we wished to help him fence in the garden at his house instead of any payment so that he will continue with his service in the community and yet not be hindered in his planting.

[Saturday, the 4th of December. Schoolmaster Ortmann's wife cannot resign herself to our miserable conditions because of her worldly disposition; and therefore she has been planning for some time to make the long journey to Charleston to visit a certain friend and to take her some presents. But, because her husband is sick and miserable and we know what calumnies and gossip have arisen whenever she went even a few miles amidst the English, I advised strongly against this trip and reminded Ortmann what had happened and been rumored among the people during his wife's other absences. Thereupon he attested that this planned trip was occurring against his will but that she could not be held back, etc. The woman became so angry at my dissuasion, however, that she again entirely revealed her wicked nature through her rude, defiant, and awkward words. Next Monday she wishes to travel with the boat that I am sending to Savannah for provisions. However, I had to refuse her this so as not to give her any occasion for disorderliness on her part, which, because of her great frivolity would certainly arise on so long a journey among such wild boatmen. Presumably she will go to Savannah overland through many swampy places. I doubt very much whether Mr. Causton will let her pass on without a permit from here, but she does not think that she can be restrained by Mr. Causton. May God convert her and purify her from her insubordination against His mercy and against human ordinances.

[It was reported to me that a certain husband, who is otherwise very serious in his religious practices, has shown little patience with his young wife in her sickness and is very severe and rough with her. I had the man come to me and contrasted his behavior with the rules of Christianity, and thereupon he assured me that he felt remorse immediately after such overhastiness; but he also told me what a great domestic burden he had in this wife, who had caused much damage in his household because of her youth and carelessness. However, when I reminded him of his previous extramarital behavior, which he once revealed to me in a pang of conscience, and showed him that what was now troubling him did not come by chance but that God was intending something salutary by it, he was very much ashamed and said that he surely deserved it and even something much worse. He was probably lacking prayer. I added that, because of his fiery temperament, he was probably lacking vigil too; for praying without vigil does no good., etc.

[Sunday, the 5th of December. In defiance of us Mrs. Ortmann went to Old Ebenezer yesterday about evening and wishes to go from there by land to Musgrove's Cowpen and be taken from there to Savannah. I cannot do otherwise than write to Mr. Causton tomorrow to inform him about the trip she is planning, which we cannot possibly condone. Otherwise she might have herself taken to Charleston without Mr. Causton's knowledge by unscrupulous boatmen. We consider this trip she is undertaking very serious because of the following circumstances: (1) Her husband, who had had a dangerous attack, is remaining without help or bodily care. No other woman, except a wife, can help him in these symptomate.[269] It appears very clearly that she is tired of the old man. (2) This trip is taking place against her husband's wish, as he expressly attested yesterday. Just as, to the scandal of all people, she rules at home in all things, she did not let herself be dissuaded from her purpose even by her husband. (3) The carpenter Volmar lodged in her house, and she advanced him something secretly for his secret journey; and, together with her husband, who, because of his simplicity, lets himself be persuaded and used for anything by her cunning and rhetoric, kept it secret from us as long as it was possible. Volmar has travelled via Purysburg cross-country to Charleston; and, now that she is chasing after him, such circumstances make her journey suspicious.[270] Because of her frivolous and voluptuous temperament she is inclined to everything.]

CONTINUATION OF THE DIARY

Monday, the 6th of December 1736. My dear colleague went to Savannah with the boat that was sent there today, partly in order to hear from Mr. Causton whether he wishes to buy us the new boat, which Kieffer of Purysburg is letting our people take down with them, and partly to forward by a dependable hand via Charleston our diary that we have addressed to Mr. Newman and also a little letter that we have enclosed addressed to him and Court Preacher Ziegenhagen. May Gold hold His fatherly hand over it, as He has done so far, for which His great Name is to be praised. We have wished to send the present diary immediately after the previous one that went with Mr. Oglethorpe's ship because, hopefully, our benefactors will wish to know our present status after the departure of this benefactor. The Lord, who does all things well, will know what to do about the Salzburgers' physical needs, which still continue. We are waiting for His goodness, may He teach us better and better.

I have beseeched Mr. Causton to buy the said boat and have given the following reason: that it is now hard for me to find three or four men who can risk going on the water after their recovery. Now that they must fetch their provisions themselves or have the transportation of the same deducted from the provisions, we would more easily find four men for a boat like the just mentioned one than ten men for our old one, because they would not only have easier work on the former but would also have to remain underway only a few days and probably not have to sleep a single night in the open in this cold and unhealthy weather. To be sure, eighteen pounds sterling is a lot of money; but we think it better to spend a few pounds for it than the health and lives of the poor and almost emaciated people. And, since Mr. Oglethorpe has laid the payment for the boat upon the congregation but Mr. Causton is to advance the money for some time, we are relying upon our heart-guiding and almighty Father in heaven to awaken the hearts of the dear Lord Trustees or of other benefactors in England and Germany, who will pay instead of these poor people and expect for it a merciful reward from the Lord. 2 Corinthians 9: 6.

Tuesday, the 7th of December. Last night we had such a destructive storm wind that we have never heard anything like it in our lives. This was without a doubt a hurricane,[271] of which the boatmen here tend to be in great fear at the end of August and the beginning of September, and because of which they do not like to risk going far out on the water at this time in large boats or in pirogues.[272] Since this storm arose so unexpectedly and at night, we may well hear of many accidents, especially from Charleston, where the ships have no good harbor.

I had hoped with some certainty that, at my written request and at my dear colleague's oral intercession, the worthy Mr. Oglethorpe would leave orders for better land to be surveyed for those who had received a bad piece of land for their garden, which good hope I had also acknowledged some time ago in the letters to Mr. Vernon and Mr. Newman. Since nothing has come of it and the good people would like to start their farming in order to earn their bread with divine blessing, I have done all that was possible to satisfy them. Mr. Zwiffler is leaving and letting Rauner have his garden lot. The surveyor considered the first garden worthless because of a large swamp in it; but Christian Riedelsperger has accepted it, because half of it is good and because he has gotten his dear friend Leimberger as a neighbor. Some have died; and their gardens, if good, were exchanged for poor and sandy ones. I hope the worthy benefactors will not hold it against us that we are trying to help the people through such exchanges. But, since some are still very poorly provided for, we hope with them that, after receipt of our diary and our letter to Court Preacher Ziegenhagen that were sent yesterday, a good resolution will be made in London concerning them. Since, at the recommendation of the Society, the Lord Trustees have agreed that Mr. Oglethorpe should procure and give the Salzburgers the land across Ebenezer Creek [of which, however, there is absolutely no hope], how much more should they agree that they should receive the good land on this side of Ebenezer Creek not far from the city in exchange for their infertile soil.

Many gardens are only moderately good, which they do not refuse to keep and in which they are making the greatest efforts possible. Those who have gardens nearby have resolved to carry the manure out to them as they did in Old Ebenezer.

During my visit I found Adam Riedelsperger, who is still lying with some fever and diarrhea, in a fine frame of mind on his long-lasting sickbed. He attested that he has had much time to weigh his past life and that, with divine blessing, so many of the sins he committed in his youth have been revealed to him that he has fallen into great fear and anxiety. Yet our loyal Jesus has drawn him like a miserable little worm into His wounds and hidden him there, so he is very happy in his Redeemer. He has, he said, always yearned for a blessed release in order to be with his Savior; but now it seems that his bodily health is getting better, and he is satisfied with this too, because God, who does everything right, wishes it so. Since, in his eyes, he is a great sinner and miserable creature, who would belong in eternal damnation if God had not invented and revealed any means of grace. Therefore he knew how to magnify Christ and His holy merit so high and to speak of it with tears so reverently and full of faith that it gave me no little edification. I noticed that he was lacking a few things for his physical care, and these were taken care of as far as possible.

Wednesday, the 8th of December. Zettler, a boy of the third transport, is (very) badly provided for physically and spiritually in the home of his brother-in-law Michael Rieser; and therefore we must contemplate making a change, if this young person is not to be ruined. Kalcher is taking him into his house, where we hope he will be well provided for. This man is an honest Christian and an untiring and skillful worker. [Things will not turn out well with the said Rieser. He and his wife live in a disorderly way, he does not understand field work, and he cannot resign himself to our miserable conditions. Therefore he has already sold many of his things for the better care of his body. He grumbles much and calumniates Mr. von Reck most often and most rudely for leading him into this misfortune. He and his wife show little pleasure in the work of God.]

Thursday, the 9th of December. My dear colleague returned from Savannah today with the Salzburgers and brought with him the new boat, which Mr. Causton had bought for eighteen pounds, laden with corn. In previous times the people have received a certain amount of provisions, as much as pleased the Lord Trustees; but now each person is allotted a certain sum of money, to the amount of which he receives his provisions. Until next March the people of the first and second transports will have three pounds, three shillings, six pence; but those of the third transport seven pounds, fifteen shillings sterling. May the Lord look upon our wants with mercy. Such a cold has begun at night that we have had nothing like it this year.

Friday, the 10th of December. I spoke to a pious husband and his wife while they were grinding corn; but, because he could not expectorate[273] there, he came to my hut and disclosed the great domestic cross caused him during his still-lasting sickness by his wife, who cannot resign herself to the hardships and lack of healthy and customary food. He felt bound by his conscience to look out for his wife's spiritual and eternal salvation, because he must account for her and would not wish an eternal separation between two people who are joined in wedlock here and have been familiar with each other so long. I asked him to tell me how he acted with her, how he made his admonitions, how he reacted [to her scoldings, ridicule of what is good, impatience, wicked judgements about others, etc.] All this was so well arranged that I could easily see that he was acting as the Lord's anointed and being led by the spirit of God. He could also tell me that God had already heard his prayer several times in such circumstances and that, at my urging, he would continue to do so for himself and his wife. I told him this and that from Holy Scripture for his instruction and comfort and then let him go home in God's name, since he had just then contracted fever.

This afternoon a boat full of sweet potatoes was brought to us from Carolina, which were sold for one shilling sterling per bushel and therefore very cheaply; and for this reason many were bought by our people. Because there are buyers here, the man will bring more next week. To be sure, our people have had sweet potatoes by their huts and also in the communal field; but these were only a few bushels and, now that there are other arrangements with regard to provisions, they must buy their foodstuffs if they are not to hunger. The lack of money and other things necessary for life is now so great in the community that I often return from my house calls with a heavy and depressed spirit, as occurred again today. But may the Lord make all among us righteous, [so that the Name of God will not be blasphemed through the bad behavior and actions of this person or that, if the hardship should become greater. One thing is very much in the people's minds, that they were promised good and adequate land and also support until they should be capable of maintaining themselves. Because the people in Purysburg are not receiving enough assistance either, the common people there cannot get ahead; it looks wretched there now, almost everyone is moving away and leaving his house and gardens behind. And many of them are just dying away.]

Saturday, the 11th of December. At my urging, Rauner is again relinquishing the garden that Mr. Zwiffler gave him and is taking back the one that fell to him by lot. Of this one he can at least say that it is his own; but from the other he could be driven away after Mr. Zwiffler's departure, and then all the work he had done on it would have been in vain. It could also be preserved for the doctor or surgeon whom we are expecting.[274] Its convenience is that it lies near the city; otherwise, because of the swamp that lies in it, it is not the best. This afternoon I have been occupied with distributing the recently received corn and beans.

Sunday, the 12th of December. I had Michael Rieser come to me and first discussed with him the condition of his brother-in-law Zettler, whom I shall take from him this week and place under Kalcher's supervision. At this opportunity I warned him against ingratitude toward God, who saved him from a long-lasting and severe sickness; and I reminded him of Christ: "Behold, thou art made whole."[275] [Since his recovery, he and his wife have been very irregular in visiting divine services and the prayer hours, for which, however, he has no lack of excuses. He has a great anger, which would have broken out against his neighbors (who are not the best either), if we and our dwelling were not so near him. His hut is almost opposite ours, and we can understand almost every word that is spoken there.]

It strengthened my faith when I heard during a house visit that God had powerfully blessed last week's sermon in a married man; because, after giving the sermon, I had been troubled and almost depressed on account of the barrenness I then detected and my lack of awakening. Oh, how gladly we would like, during this Advent and approaching holy Christmastide, to impress God's great salvation and the inestimable grace that the Father showed mankind in sending His Son into the flesh so firmly in the minds of our listeners that they might experience all this salvation themselves and become true New Testament Christians. May He Himself in His mercy give us wisdom and strength and so fill us with His spirit that our witness of Jesus and His salvation will flow from our anointing and not be presented in a human way. Many of our listeners are still held back by this or that good thing, e.g. by their own righteousness, piety, regular home and church services, etc., and they do not come to Christ rightly as miserable sinners; and this troubles us.

Monday, the 13th of December. After the very cold weather we have had, we have again received lovely warm weather, which is lasting. With the changing weather certain people, children too, get their fever again; and some of them have the paroxysms more violently, against which we know of no other means than a trusting and patient waiting for God's help. The dear people are lacking physical care, especially flour and butter or fat, to which they have been accustomed since childhood and neither of which they now receive. The small children are very bad off in this. The small amount of fat that I had gradually melted and collected from the slaughtered oxen is very quickly expended among so many needy people.

Tuesday, the 14th of December. Christian Riedelsperger intends to marry; and he wishes, if it is God's will, to choose the oldest daughter of Kieffer in Purysburg as his helpmate. He is an industrious worker, good housekeeper, and more helpful than most in the community, and he is also concerned with saving his soul; so the parents would be providing their daughter well with him. There is much good in the Kieffer family, especially in the two parents: they love God's Word, Holy Communion, etc. and do many kindnesses for the Salzburgers, who often lodge with them on their trips to or from Savannah. [Yet we well notice that the cares about sustenance and their love for temporal goods and getting ahead economically is still a burden for their hearts and that they know little about the denial of temporal things just for the sake of the Word of God and salvation. If they should still wish to take up their plantation opposite us in Carolina and entrust their many children to our care for the salvation of their souls, we should have no little effort with them, because they are not only ignorant but also very badly reared and badly mannered because of their parents' permissiveness.]

Wednesday, the 15th of December. Yesterday and today I have been occupied in distributing some necessary foodstuffs, and I also sent the new boat back this morning for corn so that I can satisfy all three transports. It was a great benefaction for us that the said boat was procured for us; otherwise the people would surely suffer want, because in our present circumstances four or five men can bring it up better than the nine or ten who were required for the old boat. Because, at Mr. Oglethorpe's command, Mr. Causton wishes to pay our people as many English shillings as the number of bushels of corn they have harvested this year, I shall measure their corn when the occasion presents itself so that I can submit a reliable specification to Savannah. I also intend in the future, when I am able to do it, to incorporate into this diary the names of the people and the quantity of the crop they have harvested[276] and to mention several necessary conditions so that our friends will not only know how great the total quantity of the harvested crops is, but also how much each individual harvested himself, from which the conclusion can be easily and quickly drawn that they can not yet subsist from this production.[277]

Thursday, the 16th of December. Because we now have most of the larger children together in the school and some of them are to be prepared for Holy Communion, I have resolved to use Pastor Freylinghausen's *Compendium Theol.*[278] a few hours each week in order to present the children the divine truths from it, to impress upon their memories the scriptural verses that are cited there for proof or for explication, and, with divine blessing, to apply everything so that their tender hearts may be filled with the living recognition of God and Christ and that they may be gradually prepared for Holy Communion. Several young people in the congregation need to be led further in such recognition; and, because the public instruction is not adequate, I intend to reserve an hour every day for it in which to repeat the catechism briefly. Public instruction is inadequate for this because, in our sermons and catechizing, we have aimed at awakening hearts for a foundation and practice of true Christianity more than at adequate drilling of Christian dogma (even if this is not forgotten).[279]

[Friday, the 17th of December. With our boat, that arrived with corn this afternoon, I received a letter from Purysburg in which a dealer in rum and tea asked me to help him get his money that the schoolmaster owes him for things he borrowed. Not long ago I received a similar note, in which the debt was also very great. His running up debts has been known to me for some time, and therefore I recently spoke to the schoolmaster about it and admonished them both to frugality and good economy. But, as long as she has the dominion over the money and is free to borrow at will, there will be no economy; and, since they are now making so many debts by receiving provisions from the store-house yet still cannot get along, how will they fare in the future when no more provisions are given? We fear much evil and bad resolutions on the part of his wife, because she simply will not resign herself to lack, trials, and frugal housekeeping. In her absence he himself complains of this, whereas in her presence he praises her good housekeeping and cannot stand it if we speak earnestly with her.] This morning small hailstones fell, and already since the day before yesterday there has been a more cutting and painful cold than we have had so far this year by day.

Saturday, the 18th of December. N. [Rheinländer] is causing me much trouble and distress by shirking his public duties through all sorts of pretexts. We are using all possible patience, admonition, and indulgence with him in order not to embitter him, nor do we neglect to show material benefactions; yet so far we have not achieved what we have sought from him and his wife. [I fear that the judgments of God will strike and pursue these miserable people as we could see in the case of Rott and his wife.] God have mercy on them both! [It will come to pass with him and her as it is written in Genesis 27: "The voice is Jacob's voice, but the hands are the hands of Esau." They speak fine words about Christianity and believe themselves to be assured of God's grace and their own salvation; but their deeds and works show something quite different. Yet they are not to be convinced. They are ruled by selfishness.]

Sunday, the 19th of December. We have had very cold rain from morning until evening, and the raw air at the public divine worship has greatly inconvenienced those among us who still feel the weaknesses caused by the fever; yet we have tried to adjust ourselves to the cold and to their weakness. The raw air brings the fever back to some of us, as I too have noticed in my body, but in such a way that I am not hindered in my work, because it comes in the evening and lasts all night mixed equally with cold and heat. Because we are getting closer and closer to the holy Christmas celebration, our sermons in the prayer hour and on Sunday are always arranged so that the listeners may give attention to these days of salvation and collect a true Christmas blessing with heartily continued prayer and devoted contemplation of the holy gospel. Last week the story in Genesis 27 was catechized in the evening prayer hour; and Jacob's remarkable dream on his pilgrimage, Chapter 28, will follow this week. Both of these give occasion to aim the sermon at the joyful Advent and Christmas period. It has been announced that we wish to go to Holy Communion on the second Christmas holiday, and then we will have more opportunity to work on their souls privately, too.

Monday, the 20th of December. Last Saturday I found it necessary to call the entire community together for a special meeting and to tell them a few necessary points pertaining to the keeping of good public order. On some of them we have so far detected some [much] self-interest, because of which they have gladly shirked, with all sorts of pretexts, from the communal work whenever it was their turn. These we reminded of their duty from God's Word and according to the laws of fair play. Our dear Lord so blessed this meeting and the sermon given in it which was both earnest and straight from the gospel, that after it ended I not only saw clear traces of it but also found such a willingness and unity in today's communal work that I was made glad in my heart. Today the entire congregation made a way for going and for carrying heavy barrels and other things from the bluff to the river, and they also secured the church yard with a fence; and tomorrow some will build a bridge for the herdsman over a little stream that flows in the forest in order to be able to drive the cattle to the pasture on the other side.

Tuesday, the 21st of December. Our dear Lord showed great mercy to Rothenberger's soul during his violent fever, as he asserts humbly and with words of praise and gratitude; and he has promised to become and to remain truer and truer to the Lord. His wife has become mellowed by her sickness and more attentive to the good. [God has not yet been able to achieve His purpose so well in the case of his wife through the sickness and another very hard dispensation, even though she appears to have become more mellow and more attentive to what is good than in previous times.] They both registered for Holy Communion, since they remember their oaths; and I spoke with them according to their understanding. [She is quarrelsome and has previously made her husband's life sour with indecent speech and reproaches and has also caused scandal with such quarreling. Therefore I warned her against this heartily and told her what I had had to hear from the children in school.

[On the occasion of the story of Esau and Jacob I had admonished the children to a God-pleasing harmony and had warned them heartily against discord and contention as the works of Satan; and I also told them that, if they should hear or see any discord, quarreling, or fighting among grown people, they should run to the nearest corner and pray to God for such poor people, whom Satan was ruling from hell. I said further that I did not believe that they had seen any un-matrimonial behavior like that in our community, etc. Thereupon a child answered, yes, Ernst (which name, however, I did not then give) quarrels and fights with his wife. I made good use of this story, which seemed so dreadful to me, in the case of these two miserable people by not only speaking of this sin as a work of the flesh and an obstacle to the kingdom of God but also by showing what a scandal arose from it even for children and that the woe of Christ would surely come over them (whoso shall offend one of these little ones which believe in me).[280]

[In addition to Ernst and Rheinländer, we have a right bad man in Michael Rieser, who not only treats his wife as the worst servant girl (but very secretly) but also gets into squabbles very easily with other people. God will help us to control such vexation.] Bruckner and Sanftleben are becoming a pair of loyal disciples of Christ and are seriously concerned with the salvation of their souls. The former was able to tell me this and that about the love of the Lord Jesus that he has already experienced, whereas the latter sighs and struggles to attain a certainty and a taste of the forgiveness of his sins, of which he committed many in the years of his ignorance.

Wednesday, the 22nd of December. G [Geschwandel] does not know himself. He considers his external love for God, his zealous singing and reading at home, etc. as signs of his state of grace; and he even complains of his violent temper and chastises himself with rough words. Yet he refuses to recognize that he is mired in selfishness and love of the world. Today we spoke with him a great deal about the parable of the wise and the foolish virgins in accordance with the state of his soul.

The cold, which started last night, is even more severe than in past days. With such a hard freeze we usually have pleasant sunshine, during which everything thaws out and becomes warm; otherwise it would sometimes be as cold as in Germany, where one can protect himself better against it because of the heated rooms and well secured houses.

Thursday, the 23rd of December. Adam Riedelsperger has become very weak again for several days, and it seems to him and others that his release is not far off. His long-lasting sickbed does not make him in the least bit impatient, and he shows an unusual contentment with divine dispensation and tribulation. His heart is entirely full of Jesus and the salvation he has won; and during our visits he puts in our hand the most pleasing matter for profitable discussion and prayer. He is certain of the mercy of God in Christ, so death is his gain and desire. He is very poor, and therefore we help as much as we can in his care. But we must often compel him and his wife with many words to accept something in their need, since they consider themselves too unworthy of these benefactions and believe that there are even needier people in the community.

Mrs. Schweighoffer also registered for Holy Communion. In her eyes she is still the greatest sinner and walks before the Lord with much poverty of spirit. She often looses her confidence, but God again hears her anxious weeping and wailing. Her especial respect for the preaching of the Word of God can serve as an example for many. Although she is lame in her right foot and hand and has other debilities and three small children, she nevertheless visits divine services regularly and the prayer hours often, even though her hut is far from the church and she must cover the distance at night.

Friday, the 24th of December. Several of our dear listeners well recognize how necessary it is to combine zealous prayer with a zealous hearing of the Divine Word; and therefore they would be happy if there were an opportunity for communal prayer in our hut, as in Old Ebenezer. Now, because the space is too small and we cannot maintain a fire in the middle of it in winter time as in the other huts, some Christian neighbors and friends are planning to assemble for prayer in a certain hut, at which meeting one of us would be present, something edifying would be spoken or read aloud, and there would be song and prayer. The good people are in part still too shy to call upon us, and therefore we must often offer ourselves. When the cold has passed somewhat, arrangements will be made in our hut for a few who can and wish to come to us. Such meetings are conducted in a very simple manner, and God does not let them pass without awakening and blessing.

Saturday, the 25th and Sunday, the 26th of December were the celebration of Holy Christmas. To be sure, we had very cold weather during this celebration, yet God mercifully granted that, excepting two [Ernst and Rheinländer], no one let himself be kept from a zealous hearing of the Divine Word. The glorious gospel of Christ, the glorious Savior who was given to us, found good hearts here and there through God's grace, good hearts who applied it to the praise of their dearest Redeemer and to their own salvation. Again and again the huts resounded gloriously with the praise of God and Jesus; and good friends gathered again and again to pass the evening hours with repetition, song, and prayer. Even some previously frivolous young people were awakened to be seriously concerned henceforth about their souls and to honor their so dear Savior better than they used to. In looking at some of them one could almost see that Jesus had taken shape in them and that they had tasted something of His love in their hearts. Thirty-four people went to Holy Communion on the second day of Christmas. May God be heartily praised for everything, and may a fruit of it last into eternity!

About eight o'clock on Dec. 26 Adam Riedelsperger fell asleep blessedly in his Redeemer. I was called from a meeting of some honest Salzburgers in order to pray with him and for him for the last time and to give him a blessing. I found him lying in his last throes, he could no longer speak; but all those present knelt with me and prayed for him and us. After the afternoon divine service he had, at his own request and with a humble heart, partaken of the Body and Blood of Christ in Holy Communion and was thus all the more closely prepared for his important journey into his heavenly fatherland. Our memory of him, as a good Christian, is a blessing for the whole community. I have never heard him speak without receiving edification. His heart was full of love for Jesus and of patience and contentment with his cross. He could truly be called a *Stiller im Lande.*[281]

Monday, the 27th of December. In complaining to me about one of his neighbors, E[Ernst] gave me an opportunity to hold up to him his wanton absence from the prayer hour and public divine service and to reveal to him, according to God's Word, his and his wife's still entirely unbroken hearts. [But even by citing clear evidence of his corrupted condition we can accomplish as little as if we were speaking to a wall. He refers to his praying in secret and says he has enough proof that God hears him and is blessing him. May God be his comfort, if it were not He, then . . . Alas, what should we do with such blind people? One cannot hold back the truth from them; yet, if one tells it to them with love and sincerity, then they believe the preacher either their enemy who hates them, or else a credulous person who likes to listen to false tales.]

On the other hand I was greatly pleased by the words of a pious Austrian, who not only revealed to me the joy of his heart at the private edification that has been begun but also brought me the news from his [otherwise disobedient] wife that the Word of God can now better enter into her and that she wishes to join the prayer hour also, which, God willing, is to be begun in my hut after lunch from one to two o'clock and to treat Pastor Freylinghausen's *Compendium Theol.*[282]

Tuesday, the 28th of December. Balthasar Rieser cannot get rid of his fever yet either, but he seems to be out of danger by now. God is giving him time to prepare for eternity, as he well recognizes and sometimes says very emphatically. Whoever has grown old in the love of the world and temporal things has difficulty freeing himself from them. The example of the late Adam Riedelsperger has, as he says, made a great impression on him. He knew him very well and could say that he prayed diligently, was a lover of Scripture and good books, and was a peace-maker, who, whenever there was about to be any misunderstanding or discord in the communal work, always advised peace and reconciled the parties through gentle words and good admonitions.

This afternoon I went into E[Ernst]'s hut in order to investigate his yesterday's complaint. But he was already satisfied, because his neighbor had given in through love of peace and had stood the loss himself. [As I entered the hut his wife began to moan as if she were seized by fever; and, because this had already happened a second time during my visits, it was probably nothing but pretense so that I could not speak with her. Because I had learned still more about their discord and their dreadful swearing and cursing, I reproved him earnestly for such un-Christian behavior, which could not possibly be tolerated among us any longer. But this time too he not only knew how to justify himself but also used very impudent and wicked expressions about our pious listeners and their preachers, which he contrasted in a clumsy way with the preachers in Regensburg. He does not wish to come into our prayer hours because it is an innovation to assemble in the evening. Such things are not customary in Germany, but only among us here and among the English in Savannah. He could read books as well at home and he could find God's Word in them as well as we could say them to him, etc. At the same time he denounces Mr. von Reck, who persuaded him to come here; otherwise he would have had a good existence in Germany. In short, he is a very miserable man, like the one we had in Rott. Unless some change occurs through God's dispensation, we can fear just as much unrest and trouble from him and his wife as from Rott. I have warned him against continuing his Godlessness, otherwise I will complain of him at the proper place, and he might well remember the sentence that had been passed on him in Savannah. The benefactors would not tolerate scorners of God's Word and other disorderly people in our community. With God's mercy we wish to practice with him the method that the Savior allows, in fact commands, in Matthew 18. [283]

Wednesday, the 29th of December. Christ, the tailor, finds himself incapable for field work, since he is weak and very prone to hemorrhages and must therefore guard himself against hard work and overheating. He is making good progress in his Christianity and gives us much pleasure through his good conduct. We would like to help him in other ways if it were only possible. [He asked my dear colleague to take him into his household as I have taken the English boy Bishop, since he wished to be used for all sorts of things in the housekeeping. But it is not possible to accept him in this way, because there would not only be no work for him and it would not be possible to provide him with clothing and maintenance. I know what it costs me to support Bishop. On the other hand, the services that such a boy can do for me are very poor. I cannot use him for letter writing, for which he was sent to me chiefly: he writes very slowly and unclearly and I would have to dictate everything to him word by word if he were to write something. Also, he takes no pleasure in writing and sedentary occupations but prefers to do something in the housekeeping.[284] At his request and my intercession Mr. Oglethorpe has allowed him a city lot, and in time a field, among the Salzburgers; and he is now busy building a fence around the house lot with the aid of a Salzburger so that something can be sowed for the spring. Through love for the Society, from which he comes as a present, I gladly keep him and will do what I can for him. He is obedient and dislikes the life of the disorderly Englishmen.]

Thursday, the 30th of December. Many circumstances that concern the Salzburgers require us to write to England and Germany again, and this will be done just as soon as some time can be found after the holidays that are still to follow. The most important point that will be presented to the Trustees concerns the gardens surveyed for the Salzburgers, which [according to Mr. Oglethorpe's plan] have fallen in part so badly that the people are losing all courage to work. [To be sure, I have shown this matter in my letters to the Society and to Mr. Vernon; but at the same time I have given hope that Mr. Oglethorpe would have better gardens surveyed in place of the inadequate ones, but he was unwilling to agree to this.] If the people had the two acres of good land for their gardens, then they would be more content with the poor land that will surely be surveyed for them for plantations; and they would be able to help themselves all the sooner. [But giving them nothing but sandy and barren soil for cultivation is against all the promises given to them.] There is enough good land there for gardens on the right side of the city, to say nothing of the cleared out fields on the left side, to which the first and third transports have applied the sweat of their brows and which has not yet been surveyed for them.] The previous cold is diminishing, and after it we have received a warm, fruitful, and, we hope, lasting rain.

Friday, the 31st of December. Today I am finally finished with the task of measuring our people's corn, beans, and potatoes at the request of Mr. Oglethorpe. This has been delayed for several weeks because I have been able to undertake the task only after other necessary business was done and to apply only a short time for it every day. I submit here the catalogue of the crops harvested this year along with the name of the owner so that the benefactors can learn of their current harvest. It is all a blessing of God; and the Name of God is heartily praised, if not by all, at least by most. Nevertheless, this supply is not so large that they could support themselves and their families until the next harvest.

The marvelous and exceedingly merciful God, who feeds the ravens too and provides several times a day for all His creatures as if at His table, will also provide for the needs of our poor people, even if the provisions from the store-house will not be given to the first and second transport next March. That they have received so little corn, beans, etc. is to be ascribed in part to the late removal and in part to the communal work, which was more disadvantageous than advantageous, partly to their sicknesses, and in part to many obstacles, such as that they have had to fetch the provisions. Also, the pigs, horses, and deer have done considerable damage to their crops during their sickness and have especially devoured the beans. Likewise, because some people paid too little attention and could not guard things well, much corn and beans spoiled in the field. If God should grant life, health, and His blessing, those who have received good land should have a better harvest, since they are very eager to cultivate their fields and to earn their bread.

May God be heartily praised for the fatherly goodness and kindness He has shown us again this whole year. In our manifold tribulations He has wrought great things in us and granted many spiritual blessings both to us ourselves and to the members of our dear congregation through the preaching of the gospel, whereby He also used the hard and long-lasting sicknesses as a means of chastisement. Also, He has disposed the hearts of many dear friends and benefactors in Europe to us so that they have helped both us and our entire congregation in our need and want by sending this and the other physical blessing. For all this may His holy Name be praised, from now and into eternity. Amen!

REGISTER

of the Bushels of Corn, Beans, and Sweet Potatoes which the Salzburgers
in Ebenezer in the Province of Georgia harvested in the year 1736

Name of the Proprietor	Corn	Beans	Pota-toes	Name of the Proprietor	Corn	Beans	Pota-toes
Gruber	22	2	10	Landfelder	5	—	—
Gschwandel	19	2	6	Bacher	11	4	4
Hertzog	15	1	7	Christian Riedelsperger	2	—	4
Leimberger	20	1½	6	Sanftleben	2½	1½	2
Rauner	19	2	2	Bach	1	—	2
Simon Reiter	19	2	12	Paul Lemmenhoffer	4½	1½	3
Rheinländer	20	—	4				
Stephan Riedelsperger	5	—	5	Hans Maurer	5	1	2
Schweiger	7	—	3	Gabriel Maurer	4	1	2
Adam Riedelsperger	5½	—	6	Zant	2	1	2
Simon Steiner	6	1½	2	Hesler	4	—	—
Kalcher	6	1	2	Maggitzer	3	—	—
Pichler	5½	1½	6	Bruckner	3	—	3
Rothenberger	4	1	1	Zimmerman	3	1	1½
Burgsteiner	9	1½	1	Kogler	2	1½	2
Rupt. Steiner	12	3	6	Rupt. Zittrauer	5	1	1
Eischberger	4	1	6	Paul Zittrauer	4½	1	—
Brandner	8	1	5	Hans Floerl	2½	—	1
Veit Lemmenhoffer	5	1½	3	Carl Floerl	2	1	3
Balthasar Rieser	3	1	1½	Lackner	3½	—	5

 SUPPLEMENT

Excerpts from the Original Diary

of Johann Martin Boltzius and Israel Christian Gronau
from November 26, 1733 to May 14, 1734,
which having been deleted by Samuel Urlsperger from his
Ausführliche Nachricht . . . provides a welcome
supplement to Volume One of *The Detailed Reports* . . .

Translated and annotated by
WILLIAM HOLTON BROWN

One of the main sources of information concerning the Salzburger emigration to Georgia has been the Rev. Samuel Urlsperger's[1] *Ausführliche Nachricht von den Saltzburgischen Emigranten, die sich in America niedergelassen haben (Detailed Reports on the Salzburger Emigrants Who Settled in America)*, which contains the diaries of Johann Martin Boltzius and Israel Christian Gronau, the Lutheran pastors who ministered to the Salzburger exiles and other German settlers in the new colony. The diaries in their published form, however, had been revised to the extent that, except for reports of illness, they revealed nothing of the adversities the Salzburgers experienced during their voyage and subsequent settlement northwest of Savannah. Consequently, from the *Detailed Reports* (1735–1751) there emanated several misconceptions that have persisted until this day.

Until now, for example, nothing has been known about Captain Fry, master of the *Purysburg* and the person responsible for much of the Salzburgers' hardship during the voyage. Urlsperger even suppressed the captain's name as well as the names of certain members of the pastors' congregation. This resulted in one historian's mistakingly identifying Captain Coram, Trustee and member of the S.P.C.K., as captain of the *Purysburg* and Zwiffler, the apothecary, as commissary.[2]

271

The unaltered account of circumstances and events in the hand-written copies depicts what one would ordinarily expect when two staid clergymen, a group of naive religious exiles, a charming young nobleman, an uncivil sea captain, a malevolent distiller, a school-teacher, and an apothecary are all thrown together for three and a half months on an early eighteenth-century merchantman. Life on board such a ship was extremely harsh even without the dissension that plagued the passengers of the *Purysburg*.

The few clues gleaned from Henry Newman's correspondence indicate that the *Purysburg* was not a very big ship.[3] She was approximately 180 or 200 tons burden and about ninety feet long from stem to stern—very similar in size to the *Mayflower*, which sailed from Plymouth in 1620 with 102 passengers on board. The pastors, however, considered their ship crowded with ninety-one passengers,[4] and they complained of cramped quarters and other inconveniences.

The most distressing circumstances during the voyage were those concerning food and drink. According to the pastors the fare on board the *Purysburg* was atrocious, not only by modern standards but by the standards of early eighteenth-century life on shore. This contrast is evident when the ship arrives in Dover and the Salz-burgers are regaled with sirloins of beef and plum pudding.[5] Eating at sea, however, had been a problem from the time seamen undertook long voyages until well into the nineteenth century. The diet for crew and passengers was unhealthily salty; grain and ship's biscuit tended to become sour or swarm with weevils, and drinking water turned putrid within a short time. The best made wine, beer, or water casks rapidly sprang leaks under the continual lurching of the ship.[6]

The Salzburgers' experiences, then, were not unusual, but because of the parsimony, moodiness, and unreasonableness of Captain Fry, they suffered more want and were subjected to more humiliation than was necessary. During the entire voyage they seem to have subsisted on a meager diet of typical ship's provisions: salted beef, salted pork, ship's biscuit, peas, turnips, oat groats, cheese, flour, butter, a few raisins and almonds, and perhaps an occasional apple. Drink consisted of putrid water, beer that was sometimes sour, and occasionally some wine and brandy. From these provisions, however, they received only one meal each day—usually salty, tough, indigestible beef cooked with unpalatable peas—which actually amounted to semistarvation.

Such circumstances quite naturally resulted in unsociability and irritability even among the pious Salzburgers. An intimation of this is made when the pastors tell of their dependence on the Salzburger Geschwandel as conciliator. One example of the effects of this first brutal month at sea is given when the pastors give an account of the Salzburger Hertzog's giving vent to his frustration —he was "otherwise as gentle as a lamb." Another example is the report on Mr. Zwiffler, the apothecary. Previously he was described as being a sedate and civil person who likes to hear God's word, but on the 15th of February the pastors tell how he at times loses his temper. These symptons of semistarvation, however, can be discerned in their further reference to him on the 27th of January:[7] "Mr. Zwiffler listens diligently to God's word, it is true, but also keeps silently to himself. . . . Concern for earthly matters and what the future may hold trouble him so greatly that at times the furor of impatience and discontent bursts forth quite intensely."

To these outbursts of anger were added the actions of the Roths and Mrs. Ortmann, the schoolteacher's wife. When not fomenting discord among the others, they were bickering between themselves which even on occasion gave rise to violence. Examples are Roth's physically attacking his wife and Mrs. Ortmann's striking the commissary's servant in the face.

Mrs. Ortmann's actions were undoubtedly to some degree the result of the hardship she experienced during the voyage. The Roths, however, seem to have been natural troublemakers and were actually the main cause of vexation among the Salzburgers. Mrs. Roth was quick to take advantage of the Salzburgers' privation and demanded exhorbitant prices from them for her wine and brandy.[8] The pastors complain of her cupidity on several occasions.

However, neither the Roths nor the Ortmanns were Salzburgers. Georg Bartholomäus Roth and his wife Maria Barbara, née Oswald, were Protestant converts from Würzburg. He was forty-five and she was thirty-two years of age. They had two children, who, having been reared as Catholics, were not permitted to join them. Ironically, the Roths had joined the first transport of Salzburgers on Urlsperger's recommendation.[9]

Christopher Ortmann and his wife were Germans who had been living in England for quite some time. They had no children. He was about fifty years old and had kept a charity school in London. She was about forty. They had joined the Salzburgers on the recommendation of Dr. Henry Walther Guerdes, minister of the Swedish Church (actually German Lutheran) in Trinity Lane, London.[10]

In addition to seasickness, some of the Salzburgers suffered from other ailments that usually occurred during long journeys. During the voyage from Rotterdam to Dover, for example, some of the Salzburger children contracted scabies; and, although the pastors state that this was due to salty food and *ex defectu motiones* (lack of movement), this disorder is actually caused by the itch mite, which spreads amidst overcrowding and uncleanliness and is usually transmitted by body contact. Mrs. Ortmann took ill just after the ship departed from Dover, and she remained infirm during the first few weeks of the voyage. Later, an eruption appeared on her neck, and because of this the Roths—both apparently devoid of tact or feeling—refused to eat with her.

Urlsperger, whose main purpose was to edify, inspire, and encourage the Salzburgers' benefactors to make further contributions, naturally deleted all such unpleasant reports from his edited version. In fact, only recent research has led to the discovery of the actual circumstances of the Salzburgers' voyage to Georgia.[11] Leslie F. Church, for example, in his book *Oglethorpe: A Study of Philanthropy in England and Georgia*, states: "The voyage was a happy one, the refugees being under the care of Mr. Commissary von Reck and the Rev. John Martin Bolzius."[12] P. A. Strobel was under the same impression; he gives a rather poetic account of the Salzburgers at sea—apparently all imagined except for his account of their daily worship. The following is a sample from his representation:

> Every day furnished them with new subjects of contemplation. The ocean hushed into repose, or lashed by the winds into furious commotion; the dark and lowering storm howling through their vessel; the gentle breezes wafting them gayly on their course, all supply them with themes of thanksgiving, and awaken in their souls new emotions of gratitude.[13]

It is doubtful that, under the circumstances, the Salzburgers experienced any genuine emotions of gratitude. Human beings, no matter how pious, are bound to feel resentment and discontent when crowded together and deprived of adequate food and drink as were the *Purysburg's* passengers. And they probably spent more time in preoccupation with thoughts of the necessities of life rather than in contemplation of the elements. But on this point Strobel apparently had only Urlsperger's *Detailed Reports* to rely on for his information.

All in all, the pastors' daily records make for a good chronological narrative capable of holding the reader's interest just as they appear in their original form. However, the narrative value of the diaries went unrecognized during the period of the Salzburger colonization of Georgia, and after the reports were edited they were deposited in the Missionary Archives of the Francke Foundation in Halle where they remained dormant for more than two hundred years. Moreover, the edited *Reports* were to be read in the "right spirit" and were intended to afford "ample material and opportunity to praise and glorify God with abundant thanks for His wise and benevolent guidance."[14]

It is interesting to note that these complementary facts concerning the circumstances of the settlement at Ebenezer have only come to light 236 years after the arrival of the first transport of Salzburgers in Georgia.[15] The same length of time elapsed from the year 1620, when the Pilgrims arrived in Massachusetts on the *Mayflower*, until the whole story of their voyage and settlement was published in 1856. In this case it was a manuscript traced to Fulham Palace on the outskirts of London and written by William Bradford, a founder and for many years governor of Plymouth Colony, that supplied much of the present knowledge of the Pilgrims. However, during the first year of the colony, William Bradford and Edward Winslow, another of the original colonists, kept a journal which they sent back to their homeland for publication just as Boltzius and Gronau did more than a hundred years later. This journal in its published form was commonly called *Mourt's Relation*; and much like Urlsperger's *Detailed Reports*, it stressed the great opportunities of the colony but glossed over much of the hardship and disappointment.[16] But just as Bradford's manuscript corrected many misconceptions concerning the Pilgrims, the original diaries of Boltzius and Gronau similarly correct many misconceptions concerning the voyage of the *Purysburg*, and they provide insight into the Salzburgers' actual physical experiences in the Georgia wilderness. P. A. Strobel has already called attention to the other striking parallels in the characters and history of the Pilgrims and the Salzburgers.[17] But this one similarity in the long obscurity of many of the factual details in both histories seems to be the most meaningful, and perhaps it indicates that in time the Salzburgers of Georgia will also parallel the Pilgrims in the memory of posterity.

Urlsperger was, of course, cognizant of the fact that his reading audience would expect the Salzburgers to encounter some adverse conditions. Accordingly, some of the bad news was retained, but this he moderated to some degree by avoiding proper names and by substituting for unpleasant or unseemly words less offensive ones, or he omitted them altogether. In these translated selections a number of such reports are included, but in their original version. Also, for the sake of continuity, a few of the statements that Urlsperger left unaltered had to be retained as connecting links.

A comparison of this original information with the specious reports of Urlsperger's publication will reveal the vast amount of news suppressed or altered. For detailed information on Urlsperger's purposes and methods of editing the *Reports*, the reader may consult this translator's thesis: William Holton Brown, "The Diary of the Pastors Who Accompanied the First Transport of Salzburgers to Georgia, 1733–1734" (Unpublished Master's thesis, University of Maryland, College Park, 1970).

I wish at this time to thank Dr. George Fenwick Jones, Professor of German and Comparative Literature at the University of Maryland, for his valuable suggestions and for making available to me the copies of the original diary made from microfilms kindly supplied to him by the authorities of the University and State Library of Sachsen-Anhalt in Halle, German Democratic Republic.

WILLIAM HOLTON BROWN

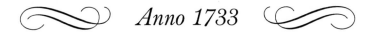

Anno 1733

Thursday, the 26th of Nov.

This morning we called upon the English commissary, Mr. von Ecx, and inquired whether he knew that some emigrants were supposed to be transported with us to New Georgia. But he knew nothing about it. However, he promised to send us word in our lodgings as soon as he hears about the Salzburgers' arrival. Afterwards we went to see Dr. Boynd. A man, whom we asked about his residence, declared him to be a very pious person. He was very friendly to us and conferred with us *latinis verbis*[18] about various things. A few things in the letter, which he could not comprehend, had to be explained to him, for example, the meaning of *novus adjutor, it.,* or *Petrina,*[19] etc. He was suspicious of the seal which the professor[20] had not used on other correspondence sent to him; consequently, he did not trust us, especially since some time ago he was cheated out of a large sum of money *per literas supposititias.*[21] He wanted to write to Halle first, before he would pay out the ducats asked for in the letter. During the afternoon we saw that large crowds of people were taken away by ships; and, when we inquired about them, we found out they were Waldensians, who were to be distributed throughout the country. Much money has been collected up to now for the support of these people.

Friday, the 27th of Nov.

A certain man by the name of Koch, who has an honest and obliging disposition, found his way to us. He gave us the opportunity to become acquainted with some good souls. Among other things, he told us about Mr. Mützen, the Lutheran preacher here, who married an aristocratic merchant's daughter of almost infinite wealth. The father was opposed to the marriage, and he took it so much to heart that he lost his mind. It applies here that children that have attained a certain age can marry against their parents' wishes. This *factum* has caused much vexation.

Today Dr. Boynd invited us to dinner and asked us not to take it amiss that he could not pay out the money to us. As soon as he receives confirmation by mail that it is the professor's wish, he will be genuinely prepared to pay us. We also learned from him that certain pious people of the Calvinist faith would get together. However, he did not want to advise us to go to them because they would soon begin a dispute with us about the *universalis gratia*,[22] and right here this thesis has to be denied by all Calvinists.

This morning our dear Salzburgers arrived and were 37 persons in number. Accompanying them was Mr. Commissary von Reck, the traveling preacher Mr. Schuhmacher, and an apothecary, who has some knowledge in *arte medica*. The ship, called the *Purysburg*, which is to bring us to Georgia, has also arrived; and with her a schoolmaster has arrived, who is going with us to New Georgia.

Saturday, the 28th of Nov.

The commissary is very inconsiderate and frivolous. The poor Salzburgers were received very badly today, since he had given himself up to his feasting and had left them on the ship in much discomfort. We interceded with him for them; he should make arrangements for them to be lodged in a good house where they could get out into the air and sleep more comfortably. But he gave a short answer: "The mayor did not want to allow them to go ashore."

A certain learned man by the name of Kosterus was directed to us, and we conversed several hours with him. He was in America many years ago; he has much experience and insight; and he is an excellent linguist and a great lover of God's work. He told us, among other things, how, not long ago, a Greek priest had visited him who reported that most of the Jews in the Orient were fairly well convinced of the truth of the Christian religion; that many had applied to Greek teachers in order to accept it. This caused the Turkish Emperor to start a great persecution. If, then, God would put an end to the Turkish Empire, the conversion of the Jews would make great progress.[23] Incidentally, this man, through his intelligent discourses, has provided us with some advantage. He wishes to become acquainted with and to correspond with Dr. Michaelis[24] and Professor Callenberg.[25]

Sunday, the 29th of Nov.

Today we began in the name of God to proclaim the Lord's word to our little congregation. The people cannot sing very many songs, and what they know of melodies is very imperfect. Moreover, only a very few can read; however, they have the desire to learn, which pleases us very much. The divine service had to be held in great incommodity on board the very narrow ship, because on this Sunday the commissary had gone out to visit beautiful cities and had, by the way, provided for little or nothing. . . .

Monday, the 30th of Nov.

Today we wrote both to Augsburg and to Halle. At last the Salzburgers have been taken off the ship and lodged in two houses where they can enjoy more comfort. When it was asked why the poor people had not been thus provided for sooner, the following answer was given: The commissary wanted to risk letting the people off the ship although he had no permission to do so. . . . There was also opportunity to remonstrate with the commissary concerning his thoughtlessness and preach to him repentance and faith *modo evangelico.* He does not exactly become indignant when he is told the truth; however, it does not help very much or only as long as he has no opportunity to extravagate. Little by little we prepared ourselves for the trip and purchased all sorts of household goods and victuals, because we were told that we should not be going to London. Of the captain we have been told that he is an atheist—how today with dreadful cursing and swearing he is supposed to have bespoken his villainous heart. He does not understand a word of German.

Tuesday, the 1st of Dec.

Until now we have had summer weather and a drizzle from time to time. A few times there has been a stinking fog, which could be detrimental to health, and from which we try to preserve ourselves as best we can. Since we are not going to London, household goods were purchased yesterday. As a result our money is all gone. We shall do our utmost to induce Dr. Boynd to pay out the ducats. Mr. Schuhmacher departed from here today to return to *patriam.*[26] A Salzburger woman has become ill and she complains very much of languor and asthma. She was given some *essentia dulci,* which soon improved her condition.

During the afternoon we visited the Lutheran preacher, Mr. Mützen, and asked him to supply us with a quantity of wafers, which he was quite willing to do. He told us, however, that for several years now, out of condescension toward the weak ones who have come to them from among the Arminians,[27] they have been using common bread such as the Calvinists use. He said some Wittenbergers had declaimed passionately against this practice, because *secus sentientes*[28] could conclude from this that Lutherans did not know what they were doing. He also averred that not only most of the Salzburgers in Cadzand had died but their preacher Mr. Fischer also.[29]

Wednesday, the 2nd of Dec.

Today we went and fetched the wafers, since the preacher Mr. Mützen sent us news that the Salzburger preacher Mr. Fischer had not yet died as had been assured him previously. A dispute had arisen between the captain and several crewmen so that the latter neither wanted to make ready nor sail the ship, because the captain did not want to give them the money they had earned. After they brought action against him, he had to satisfy them; however, he dismissed them at the same time and took others into his service. They have a nice way here of affording the children a little motion and pleasure by harnessing a big dog to little wagons. A boy walks along beside so that he can guide the dog, which is already used to pulling the wagon slowly and straight. Moreover, they have very small horses here, which are ridden and managed by little boys. When we took our leave from Dr. Boynd, he assured us that he bore great affection for the orphanage, because he owes it so much gratitude; therefore, he would always speak well of it wherever he could. While we were there we delivered a letter we wrote to Prof. Francke, in which we advised him of the receipt of the money. We wanted to buy ourselves a clavichord[30] here for our mental recreation and for learning unfamiliar melodies. We heard, however, that here they think more of taking in money and enjoying themselves than of music and such instruments. If such are to be found, they would first have to be brought from Germany and are therefore very expensive. And for all that they are of inferior or middling resonance. We have been given reason to hope to obtain one from England. Since the Salzburgers were brought aboard ship, one of us remained with them and the other lodged with the commissary in town. Since the commissary has rather come out of his distraction and now takes time to reflect and meditate, one can discuss many good things with him. He has a gentle, flexible disposition. He listens to advice and he behaves very reverently during prayers. At least we hope to be in good peace and love together. Who knows what else God will do?

Thursday, the 3rd of Dec.

Our ship did not leave the harbor until late last night, because yesterday the water was too shallow. We were supposed to continue on our way this afternoon; however, since the captain had not come to an agreement with the crew, we had to remain at anchor. The commissary is much to blame. He could have perhaps satisfied both parties and thus could have hastened our voyage if he had not gone off with the Hanoverian envoy. One of us visited the synagogue, in which everything is much cleaner and more beautiful than was the one in Berlin. A certain merchant by the name of Asten found out that we are going to Carolina. He was very glad about this and showed us much kindness in his home. . . .

Friday, the 4th of Dec.

Indeed, we were supposed to depart today—and all on board the ship wished we would—but the wind had changed, and so again today and the following night we had to remain at anchor in the middle of the river. The commissary came back toward evening and brought along some gunpowder, with which he wished to amuse himself and other worldlings. When the envoy took his leave, he had the cannons, muskets, and pistols fired and had the lackey and others make a violent clamor.[31] And such noise making and unchristian activity took place on two different occasions. Since the Salzburgers were not a little annoyed by this, it was necessary to make mention of this outrage within proper bounds and attempt to save them from all subsequent occurrences. The commissary received a letter from Senior Urlsperger, in which it was again requested that he and one of us travel to London. He was urged to depart as early as the 30th of November; however, he would not comply, because he rather thinks the ship will get there just as fast, and he might otherwise have his reasons.

Saturday, the 5th of Dec.

Until now the weather has been good and the sun has been shining. Last night it started to rain. As soon as there was enough daylight, we departed although the captain was not present. And yet, because of the contrary wind, we could not sail any farther than a German mile. It rained all day. Toward evening the commissary received a visit from the Hanoverian envoy, his two sisters and another young person and departed from us on a yacht. It was inexcusable that he, in addition to the captain, pursued his own pleasure and company and left us alone. In the meantime his servant[32] as well as several sailors carried on in a most wanton manner and committed a most sinful act of using obscene words and gestures, which could not have happened if both had remained here with us and kept order. The commissary returned with the aforementioned persons during the evening prayer meeting. The two maidens had to entertain him with the singing of worldly songs and idle chatter. We absented ourselves. He then dined with them on the yacht and again had the cannons fired in their honor; and, when they departed early in the morning, it happened again. Indeed, we had earnestly remonstrated with him even yesterday evening about yesterday's outrage; and the annoyance caused this transport, of which the least should occur, was pointed out to him. However, he not only attempted to evade the issue, but also indicated by the presently described new disorders that he would no longer heed beneficial suggestions, except when he is without association and opportunity to sin. During the evening a French baker[33] with his sick wife and little children—one of them two years old and the other three weeks old—was brought aboard the ship. The commissary has made a tool of the French preacher, who is supposed to persuade the Waldensians staying here to go to Georgia, because it is said that some silk-weavers are among them. Because of extreme poverty this baker has benefited from the charity of this preacher and the church, of which he will be deprived if he does not agree to go aboard the ship. The man wept on board the ship and said that he had been forced into this decision. This evening the captain finally came on board the ship. He has not once slept in it as long as it has lain here. He has already previously used the harshest expressions in regard to us and the ministry; and, as soon as he came aboard, he gave orders in very harsh words that we should neither enter the great cabin nor eat in it, because he hates preachers as he hates the devil himself, and he breaks out in a cold sweat if he only sees them. However, it was again arranged that we be allowed to make use of this cabin during the day. God have mercy upon the miserable man and strengthen us further.

The commissary's servant is a very wicked scamp, who got roaring drunk recently and again today. While in such a condition, he called one of us a vile name, because he thought we could not hear him. We informed the commissary of this, who, of course, acted with words but not with purposeful energy. Indeed, this Saturday has been full of unrest and vexations; however, nothing could dishearten us. Praise God!

Sunday, the 6th of Dec.

Because only a very few of the Salzburgers have hymn books, and only a few hymns are in those they have, we have decided to recite the songs to them. In our ship, which is not an *oorlogsschip*,[34] but a medium-sized ship, there are so many people and things that we are subjected to many inconveniences. At night we have to sleep under many exhalations and during the day we have to sit and walk with a stoop if we don't wish to remain on deck. We cannot have all the people together during prayer meeting, because there is not enough room. It is not feasible, either, to talk with them diligently in private and to instruct the children. May God in his mercy continue to sweeten all that is bitter such as has hitherto come to pass. Today it was noticed that the Salzburgers were somewhat discontented because of the very miserable fare. The meat is very salty and tough, and the peas that are cooked with it are also bad. Drink is likewise sour. We too partake of such fare—may God let it agree with us! In addition to this, the captain gave to understand that in the future he would give them even less; and it was demanded of them that they accept into their group the Calvinist woman and her fidgety children, and two of them are supposed to lie down in the same place. With God's help this change was not allowed to take place, and the Salzburgers, who live and sleep together in peace, were left alone. One of us had the opportunity to speak *remotis arbitris*[35] with the commissary, and, according to the indications of today's message, to show him what is due true Christians and to recite to him a few *momenta* from the hymn "O Lord! afford a sinner light."[36] He assented to everything but pleaded that it was quite impossible and that one could not live this way with people, for if one did not do as others do, one would be despised. In the evening prayer meeting we pointed out to our Salzburgers the example of the Israelites, how they were not always well off with respect to meat, and God oftentimes allowed them to want in order to test them, etc. It was recommended that they read diligently the first five books of the Old Testament and likewise 1 Corinthians 10.

Monday, the 7th of Dec.

Because of the very bad and indigestible fare, some of the Salzburgers have become rather ill. An attempt has been made to prevent a general malady with good medicine. The captain demands that even the smallest children be content with such unwholesome fare, which has caused much anxiety among their parents. The commissary, however, has taken pity on them and has had butter and flour for mush issued to them, which the children like to eat most of all. Because of shallow water and contrary winds, we still have to remain here on the Meuse. They have even run aground on a sandbar; therefore, it is planned to lighten the ship by putting our things and the water casks on shore.

Tuesday, the 8th of Dec.

Our crew members have been busy all day lightening the ship. Even though they have let all the water out of the casks, the ship will not budge from the sand, because the forward part has gone in too far. The captain has gone to Rotterdam to hire a ship, into which the heavy things are to be loaded. . . . God wants to test his

REPORTS ON THE SALZBURGER EMIGRANTS ...

people by this, too—how they comport themselves in times of distress. May God let none of us become weak in our faith!

Wednesday, the 9th of Dec.

Again today we had to lie to at the same old place. Until now we have been on the lookout for an opportunity to get some exercise but could find none. Now that the water has been let into the bottom part of the ship, we can get lots of exercise by pumping water without worrying about ourselves or our office being degraded by this. The dear Salzburgers are also lending a hand, and they help the crew members in every way they can. Because everything on the ship is in disorder, we are often disturbed in our prayer meetings. But we must go with the times. All are quite content, because the captain is away. All wish that we could get rid of him in Dover and either get another captain or keep our present helmsman, who is quite reasonable and friendly.

We had the opportunity again to discuss at greater length with the commissary and the medico a few points concerning true Christianity, since otherwise this often happens . . . [as in passing][37] and has to happen. Their words, among others, were: no one could call himself righteous (about which different words were spoken, and at the same time 1 John 3: 7 was cited as an explanation). Likewise, no one could be certain of his conversion (to which, among others, the verse 1 John 3: 14 was alleged as an objection). Likewise, they had often had good motives and intentions. (This would incur a responsibility all the more difficult; therefore, Luther said: The way to hell is paved with good intentions.) After this the commissary told us that an aristocratic envoy in Regensburg had come to a very sorrowful end and that he was quite familiar with many of the definite details: On his deathbed the envoy said that he could hear a bell ringing, and he wondered whether it had not been heard by others. As long as he could still hear the sound of this ringing, he still had time to become converted. As soon as it would stop, his time of grace would be over. Not long after that he could not hear the sound any more, and he said that now his time of grace was up. The preachers present were unable to talk him out of these notions. He died not long after that, and this made a deep impression upon all to whom it was known, even upon the commissary himself, who was present in Regensburg at that time. This example was an efficacious refutation of what the medico had just previously brought forward, namely, one would not have to limit divine grace—if only one had these last few hours before death, one could still be converted; but if one were suddenly carried away, then it would be a misfortune. In such a situation one has to take care not to become involved in a debate, or the entire discourse must go astray without having any effect. The truth succintly stated and an efficacious verse of Scripture for careful consideration will often profit the most. A quite pleasing melody of an impressive funeral hymn prepared in Bayreuth was sung to us during the evening hour, and one of us[38] wrote down the music for the edification of ourselves and perhaps of others:

likewise to the melody: "Who knows how near my end is!"[39]
The hymn itself consists of the following verses:

1. I die each day, for life is waning[40]
Continually; my end is near.
No one can promise my remaining
Upon this earth another year.
    The days fly by and death draws nigh.
    Were only I prepared to die.

2. A person burdened with wrongdoing
Is ripe for coffin and the grave.
The apple, in which worms are chewing,
Must fall, for worms like sin deprave.
    The covenant excludes no one;
    The charnel house no man can shun.

3. Death need not always send us visions;
He comes quite often unannounced
And summons us to his dark regions;
A heart prepared is then what counts.
    A single moment can decree
    One's happiness or misery.

4. Lord, master of all life and death,
Disposer of my destiny,
The time when I'll draw my last breath

Is known to Thee but not to me;
 But let each ringing of the bell
 Remind me it will toll my knell.

5. At dawn I wake without misgiving
Of what the evening has in store;
Yet, though I linger 'mong the living,
I may be lying at death's door.
 The way is short to that retreat
 Where worms will gnaw upon my meat.

6. A single stroke brings sleep eternal
When death accompanies decay.
But strike me with thy hands paternal;
Enclose me in Christ's death today.
 And when my body falls like dross,
 The soul will fall at Jesus' cross.

7. Perhaps, then, I shall speak no more
When eyes and mouth and heart are closed.
In days of health I pray, therefore:
To Thee, Lord, I commend my ghost.
 And if my lips are sealed up tight,
 May Jesus' blood call out my plight.

8. If I can't bless friends and relations,
Then Thou canst bless them more than I.
O Savior, be their consolation
When all around me start to cry.
 O listen to their cries of grief,
 And through Thy comfort send relief.

9. Then open up Thy heav'nly portal
When death's last thrust has pierced my heart.
Arrest the pain of this poor mortal,
And let my soul to Thee depart.
 My parting thus will be no pain—
 Though swift, 'tis true—but blissful gain.

Since the dear Lord has made our voyage so difficult and bitter
up to now, the thought occurred to us that we might not see
America but lose our lives on the way. . . .

Thursday, the 10th of Dec.

. . . This morning we used the Gospel of St. John as a point of departure for our prayer meeting. The people read the chapter through beforehand among themselves and bear in mind the *dicta extantiora*,[41] and when we come to them, they read to us those *dicta* which were edifying to them and for which they request an explanation and inculcation. This morning two of Prof. Francke's letters were forwarded to us from Rotterdam. The English agent Mr. Walthers, to whom Dr. Boynd probably handed them over, had them brought by the ship that was brought from Rotterdam to take on the heavy things from our ship. . . . We and our pious congregation had taken our present distress before God, both together and individually. Today He granted our request and led our ship from the sand, upon which it had lodged until now, into deep water, so that we did not need the rescue vessel that had already arrived. Thus the captain's efforts were in vain, since with his grumbling and irreligiosity he had traveled twice to Rotterdam to bring up such a vessel, and his and the irreligion of others came to naught. The poor Salzburgers still must suffer want in regard to food and drink, for which not only the unscrupulous captain but also the commissary is a great deal to blame. He is quite concerned with being complaisant; he exchanges compliments with the captain and does not want to tell him the truth. Consequently, the poor people must suffer. We have already reminded him of his duty. Since he regards this lightly and, at the most, puts the good people off with polite words and promises, we have had to remonstrate with him vigorously about his complaisance and neglect of his duties. He listens to everything we say and makes good resolutions but never puts them into practice.

Friday, the 11th of Dec.

. . . The parents show their children so much fidelity and serve as a fine model for them in their treatment of the Word of God. The most meaningful verses that we teach them during prayer meeting they also attempt to teach their children. We give them guidance for this; and the children are encouraged to learn through gifts such as raisins, almonds, apples, etc. May God help us learn to conform better to weakness and simplicity! Due to the miserable nature of our ship, we have not been able to assist the parents or the children according to our desires, which they probably realize and look forward to better circumstances.

The commissary's wicked lackey fell down the ladder today, and had not God singularly averted misfortune, he would have broken his neck. We quickly seized upon such an opportunity to remind him of this benefit of divine protection and his wretched condition; however, it appeared to make no special impression.

Saturday, the 12th of Dec.

Because we are still progressing very slowly on the Meuse and have sailed hardly two hours today, one of us had a mind to travel on ahead to London, especially since the necessity demands that we confer with the court chaplain, Mr. Ziegenhagen. However, so many difficulties are involved that it cannot be done. For example, it is not only expensive to go from Helvoet-Schleus to Harwich and on to London, but for a stranger it is also dangerous; for hardly a week goes by that some traveler is not attacked and robbed of his possessions and money. Moreover, the commissary would not like it, because he would have to advance us some money, etc. We do not push such external matters, but await our heavenly Father's guidance and disposition. They say that we shall stay in Dover for fourteen days. Perhaps Mr. Ziegenhagen will come there, or we may have the opportunity to travel to him. During the evening hours the commissary introduced the topic on the existence and nature of ghosts. In a few words it was pointed out to him that in this theory one neither sins *in excessu,* as many credulous people do, nor *in defectu,*[42] as many worldly-wise scholars do, and even though it may be established in the Scriptures that there were spirits and apparitions, as were quoted in a few verses. Obj.: Learned and wise people would have liked to find out the truth, and for this reason they traveled to such places where ghosts are supposed to have appeared, so that they might see and believe. When they arrived, they did not see and hear what others alleged to have seen. Thereupon we answered with Spener's[43] words: There is a divine judgment of such people, who believe their reason and five senses more than the Scriptures, that even though they would like to see ghosts, they never do, etc. The ghosts, by the way, were not departed spirits, but devils themselves, etc. He formerly heard something in reference to this theory from Thomasius[44] and Mr. von der Hardt.[45] He affirmed, however, that he had an aversion to the opinions and lives of these men. He himself studied in Helmstedt[46] and therefore knows more to relate of the disorderly life of Mr. von der Hardt than we would care to hear. The abbot Mr. Mosheim[47] is in his good books as if he—notwithstanding his oratorical speeches and far-fetched ideas—had produced much spiritual benefit for him and other people. When he preaches, there is not a person in the city who would not go hear his sermon; however, he meditates upon it for fourteen days. He lives as a pious teacher; his wife, however, who has died, contracted many debts and caused scandal by her extravagance and other irregularities.

Sunday, the 13th of Dec.

Since the commissary intimated this morning that our prayer meeting had been edifyingly arranged, we talked with him about our very important voyage, inasmuch as we intend to entrust our lives and health to a piece of wood—a ship. And because it is not known what danger awaits us, it is absolutely necessary that we betake ourselves to the paternal arms of God in order that we may not perish, but, through death, enter into a peaceful life. He made a few frivolous objections, it is true, but he allowed himself to be corrected. The dear Salzburgers love us and are happy when they can do us some favor. . . .

Monday, the 14th of Dec.

We had much trouble last night from the wife of the French baker, whom the commissary received *de facto* into this transport. She screamed often during the night and exhibited various unusual symptoms. The commissary could readily see that during our intended voyage the woman would not only be a burden, but might even die. He therefore made preparations today to send this mother with her two sick children back to Rotterdam. She consented to her husband's remaining in the ship and continuing with the others to America. If he should fare well, she would make the voyage after him. The man can speak very little German and is also a Calvinist; therefore, he does not fit in very well with our Salzburgers.

Tuesday, the 15th of Dec.

Today our dear Salzburgers were again in want of food and drink. And the good people are anxious about their daily necessities of life, because the captain has resolved to have only four pounds of bread issued daily to five persons. Sometimes the commissary has some of the provisions, which he himself purchased, issued to them. Otherwise their circumstances would be more miserable than they are. But he is too shamefaced to tell the impious captain the truth and to point out to him his injustice and the people's distress. Instead, he jokes, laughs, and curries favor with him. Necessity demanded that he again be reminded of this neglect of his duty and informed that everything is being accurately set forth in the Diary, so that the Senior and others might receive express information. Mr. Zwiffler spoke just as energetically for these good people; however, he accomplished no more than we did. This Mr. Zwiffler is a sedate and civil person, who likes to hear the word of God. He takes the good people's physical welfare to heart and endeavors as far as possible to provide them with medicine for their infirmities. As far as can be observed, he has understanding in *artem medicam*; and, for his part, will probably be useful from now on.

Wednesday, the 16th of Dec.

Just yesterday evening the wind changed to our advantage; therefore, preparations were made at dawn for our departure. Today the commissary was more earnest in his expostulations concerning the hardships of the Salzburgers, and this has already had a favorable effect. It hurts us deeply to see so many people on board ship who live sinfully from day to day, and we cannot bring this home to their hearts and consciences *ex defectu lingua Anglicana*[48] (*sic*) and warn them of God's wrath. In order to work on such very miserable people, we are determined to make the acquisition of the English language very much our business starting now on board ship. Up to now God has also blessed our efforts, because one of us has already made some progress in reading and analyzing. We have elected this method: The schoolmaster Ortmann cannot explain himself properly. This is because we do not take a foreign English book as a basis for reading and analyzing, but the Bible, of which the contents are familiar to us; consequently, the words are easier to understand and remember. From the grammar we become somewhat familiar with the *genius linguae et pronunciationis*[49] beforehand. If a word comes up that we can neither read nor explain, we write down how it is pronounced so that we can repeat it later. The more vocabulary one can get into one's head by diligently reading, the quicker the reading will prove a success; and then one only stumbles over unknown words. If one wanted to read first and then analyze, the reading would progress very slowly, etc.

Thursday, the 17th of Dec.

The captain asked the commissary to lend him 40 Dutch florins. Because his request was denied, he traveled back to Rotterdam to raise this sum, which he has to pay a Dutch navigator, who has been entrusted with bringing our ship from the Meuse out to sea. This Dutch navigator is an old man, but full of spite. We feel so much pity for him, because by all appearances he will probably die in his sins. We are now lying quite close to the sea and are waiting now only for a good wind. Today has been a very nice and refreshing summer day.

Friday, the 18th of Dec.

The captain returned toward evening. Because the wind was good, we went closer to the sea; however, on account of nightfall we did not sail very far. The closer we come to Dover, the friendlier the captain conducts himself, perhaps, for fear of our referring his *vitam ante actam*[50] to the Trustees.

Saturday, the 19th of Dec.

Roth is the most vexatious man among the entire transport. He argues all day about trifling matters; he rails at and torments the Salzburgers and addresses them in a very gruff manner; he shuns the prayer meetings as often as he can. He not only quarrels with his wife, but utters imprecations and shouts oaths at her. Yes, today the two of them even came to blows. The Salzburgers do the captain many good turns on board ship. He does not have many crewmen. If the anchor has to be weighed, or there is any other work to do, he need only beckon to them; thus they are available day and night to bear a hand. But up to now he has shown little gratitude. Toward evening about five o'clock we finally—praise God!— reached the ocean. This morning we had fog so thick that we could scarcely see in front of us, so we lay to. As soon as we had put out to sea, the ship was tossed about so much by the turbulent waves that almost all the Salzburgers began to vomit; and this continued throughout the night. Many good things were discussed with the commissary concerning the hymn "O Lord! afford a sinner light." In other respects he does have a disposition not averse to the good things. He is filled with veneration for God's Word and the Holy Sacraments. He reads the Bible regularly, and he does not take it amiss when we give him good advice. He prays, we assume. His indiscretion, however, is so great that he is quite carried away by a succession of bad examples and ceases completely to be the former.

Monday, the 21st of Dec.

Last night we had a storm, which pitched and tossed our ship about so much that we and others became quite ill. . . .

Tuesday, the 22nd of Dec.

This morning in the midst of a great storm God guided us in a round-about way into the harbor of Dover, which caused great joy among all. The court chaplain Mr. Butienter, who is a colleague of Mr. Ziegenhagen's, also a pious wigmaker, [Junner] Matthiesen, and one of the Trustees [Capt. Thomas Coram] had been waiting for us for nearly three weeks; and they received us with much kindness. . . .

Wednesday, the 23rd of Dec.

A few of our members, particularly women, had become somewhat discouraged by the difficult circumstances up to now and therefore would prefer to remain here rather than continue to entrust themselves to the ship. They are afraid they might become sick and miserable again and even die. But they were strengthened again by not only being cheered up and diverted from their fearful thoughts but also by having good food and drink set before them to fill them up and refresh them—a provision made by the accompanying Trustee and the court chaplain Mr. Butienter. For that purpose they were taken off the ship by us and the commissary and were led in pairs to a certain house where fresh meat was boiled and roasted for them. . . . Food was also prepared for us in the aforesaid house. . . . We were told that we should find Mr. Siron in Pennsylvania, whither he traveled last summer to settle there, because he had to endure much displeasure among his unconverted parents and relatives. They say he is very partial to Count von Zinzendorf.[51]

Thursday, the 24th of Dec.

. . . After the prayer meeting we visited Mr. Butienter, who went over the church agenda of the court chapel with us and showed us how we might arrange our services to best advantage. Praise God for all *monita pastoralia*[52] received from him and from the court chaplain Mr. Ziegenhagen! . . . Mr. Butienter reminded us that the society which has shown the Salzburgers so much kindness is not called *Societas de propaganda Christi*,[53] etc. (which is a different society), but *de promovenda Christi cognitione*.[54] In order that we might obtain an adequate concept of this praiseworthy institution, they have sent us a number of booklets, which we can also distribute among the others.

Friday, the 25th of Dec.

Dear Mr. Butienter and Mr. Matthiesen traveled back to London quite early this morning because their affairs did not permit them to remain here any longer and because they had completed their mission to us very well, to our great pleasure and to the glory of God. Meanwhile, the Trustee will remain here until everything on the ship has been put in order. It has come to pass through their intercession that, since previously we had to sleep in the narrow, damp ship among the colonists, our beds have now been brought into the great cabin. . . . Roth and his wife are a detriment to the Salzburgers, whom they not only scandalize by their disorderly conduct but also put all sorts of vain and unfounded things in their heads. They were urgently admonished today and reminded of the detriment to themselves that will result if they continue this way. A few of the Salzburger children have got scabies *ex defectu motiones*[55] and because of the salty food. For this reason the Englishmen, who are supposed to go with us to America, were difficult about going aboard ship, because they loathe the very sight of such an eruption as they do the plague. However, all has been remedied.

The bill for our expenditures up to now has been sent along to England. It has run somewhat high because of the books purchased and especially because of the household goods, which are very high-priced in Rotterdam.

Saturday, the 26th of Dec.

It has often occurred to us that during these days Christmas is being celebrated in Germany,[56] which moved us all to heartfelt prayer. May God bestow a great blessing upon all preparation classes held and upon the Christmas sermons and also let such thoughts that have previously occurred to us bear much fruit. Today a letter written by Professor Francke was forwarded to us, which overjoyed and uplifted us. Our sea captain, about whom we previously had just cause to complain, behaves extraordinarily friendly in words and actions since our arrival in Dover; and, as to our coming voyage, he promises many good things. They say that he was threatened that if he continues to treat the colonists badly, he would bring on his own ruin. This afternoon he took us up to an old castle, which even Julius Caesar is supposed to have had built. It stands on a high hill close to the sea and seems to have been impregnable. One can find a few old Roman weapons and other *rudera* of antiquity.

Sunday, the 27th of Dec.

Today we explained to our congregation why we had not celebrated Christmas last week, as was done in Germany, and why today is only the third Sunday in Advent. . . . Our question-and-answer lectures show us a great deal in which our listeners are still lacking. God continue to help us! This evening the Lord God of truth drew our attention to the late Abbot's[57] *Ordination Speeches* and a certain supplement from the late Arndt's *Commentary*,[58] which was very edifying and quite appropriate for this particular Sunday. And because we became very eager to read some more of the late Arndt, we also looked up the last appendix in the aforesaid book and were directed by this to an expressive ordination speech contained in Part III, p. 316. No passage could have applied better than this one to our circumstances. May God also be mightily praised for this blessing!

Monday, the 28th of Dec.

On these days just passed we have dined with a few Englishmen, who outwardly appear polite and obliging, to be sure, but show no reverence whatever for God. Even during grace, which by request of the Trustees one of us must say, they occupy themselves with profane things; and by their demeanor they show disgust for it, which cuts us to the quick. . . .

Mr. Purry, a native of Switzerland, who has already led many people to America and erected a city there named Purysburg after himself, has arrived here and will return to Switzerland and the Palatinate very soon to hunt up a number of people for a new transport. He is an old man already. He was very happy to see our Salzburgers and he predicted much benefit for the land to which they are going. He and his people will be our closest neighbors; and, because they don't have a preacher yet, they would, as he said, attend our services. He said that Mr. Oglethorpe—on whom things mostly depend as regards this new colony—is not only very wealthy and receives two thousand pounds sterling every year on revenues alone but that he also loves the Germans very much and, since he himself has no children, had taken them on as though they were his children. Moreover, no one would be accepted among the colonists who would not swear that he is of Protestant religion.

Very late the day before yesterday the commissary received a letter from Mr. Simonds[59] in London, in which he was asked whether there was something in what he had heard about our captain's behaving so badly toward the Salzburgers. But instead of writing the plain truth, he praised the captain and reported that we were very well pleased with him and could not ask for a better captain. Yes, he even had him come to him, read him the contents of his answer to Mr. Simonds, and used such words for him as if the man had never done any wrong, but deserved very well of the entire transport. In this we did not conceal the truth from the commissary. As excuse, he declared that, if he wrote the gospel truth, he would not be displaying Christian charity. We pointed out to him that it was not a question of his troubles but that it was the truth we sought and loved and that it would not be Christian to further the benefit of another with hypocrisy and falsehood.

As we went to sleep our faithful God revived our hearts by reminding us of the spiritual and material benefits we had enjoyed in Halle in the fellowship of the dear fathers and children of God. As often as Monday comes around we repeatedly recall the prayer meeting that we were allowed to attend that last time in the home of Pastor Freylinghausen[60] and which so greatly impressed us. We feel just the same about other services in which we were consecrated for our office and voyage with prayer and many good wishes. Bless the Lord, O my soul, and forget not all his benefits. Hallelujah!

Tuesday, the 29th of Dec.

During our evening devotions the commissary came into our room; and, when he saw that we were both finding edification in the Word of God and in a brotherly conversation about it, it pleased him; and he lamented that he is so often interrupted in his good intentions, and he had sinned particularly and most of all in frivolous talks with other people, since in prayer and during the reading of the Word of God he had after all made up his mind to do better. Moreover, he could not thank God enough that he often had been given so much good encouragement, etc. After dispensing a few admonitions, we then read him a serious passage from *The Salt of the Earth*, Part III, middle of page 156: Rely not upon your good intent and will. Have ye not heard, "The spirit indeed is willing, but the flesh is weak"? What became of the good intentions in the Garden, because the disciples were not faithful in watching and praying? Rely not on the Holy Ghost's good effects and incentives through His Word, for which one should thank God, to be sure, as long as one uses them right; but, on the other hand, if there is not a consequent persevering change in spirit, there will be those *boni motus*[61] accusers and witnesses adverse to such fickle misuse. At the same time he was shown where he was deficient in the outward use of prayer, i.e., he does not combine with prayer the constant battle against a frivolous heart and other enemies. And since he did not understand the sense of these words, it was made clearer to him with examples. His excuse that one could not find many Christian and sedate souls among young people was soon disposed of with a terse rejoinder.

When the medico was told about the fine scholastic arrangements in our cherished institutions and the advantages the young people have there as regards their physical and moral welfare, he was very much surprised and showed his delight and satisfaction on hearing this. A very good thing to do in company, when one notices that the conversation has turned to idle talk, is to start telling about something praiseworthy that will attract attention and cause the previous talk to be forgotten. God is already pointing out opportunity and material.

Wednesday, the 30th of Dec.

It strikes us as very unusual and strange that neither in Holland nor here do we experience much of a cold winter, but have rain now and then and often warm sunshine. Hence the gardens and hills look green and gay even during this time of year. And it is no wonder that in the parlors no stoves can be found to heat them; however, one can make do very well with a fire in an open fireplace.

Our letters, some of which we wrote to London and the others to Halle and Augsburg, left today along with the diary by the London Post. Mr. Hahn wrote from London that, if no one had been found in Halle to go with the Salzburgers to America, he would have had to undertake it.

The commissary asked for an explanation of the scripture 1 John 5: 16. There is a sin unto death, etc. And at the same time he asked for information about the sin against the Holy Ghost. And, because he had some wrong ideas on the subject of Holy Communion, he was set right on this point by a few words from the Bible. At the same time the abuse of this highly venerable sacrament among the healthy as well as among the sick was discussed, and that a true conversion and change of mind would be required if it is to be used for one's salvation. And, because with this his quibbling was cut short and these words were applied to him somewhat further, he began to talk about evil preachers who had led scandalous lives and had not performed the duties of their office. It was pointed out to him that to a large extent unconverted *Politici*[62] would have to share the blame for the corruption of teachers. For example, those who were not well disposed to pious teachers would promote those who complied with their wishes and suggestions. Consequently, patrons and clergymen would welcome their judgment. Alas! one often finds that, when people are discomfited by the Word of God and they have to acknowledge defeat, they hide behind the shallow theory and downright or flagrantly ungodly lives of the teachers and therein seek comfort and protection. One may well say here: Rom. 2. Thou that makest thy boast of the law, through breaking the law dishonourest thou God? For the name of God is blasphemed among the Gentiles through you, etc.

Thursday, the 31st of Dec.

We find that in Holland and here in Dover all things, even the most trifling, are very high-priced. And one has to pay two to three times more dearly for what one can buy in Germany for a few pennies, and yet here it is likely to be more inferior in quality. Therefore, if it should be practicable, those who are wise will bring along the most necessary things such as clothing, linen, household effects, etc.

At dinner Captain Coram, as English Trustee, delivered to us a patent in the English language concerning our church matters, and the words run as follows: The Trustees for Establishing the Colony of Georgia in America to all to whom these Presents shall come send Greetings. Whereas The Reverend Mr. John Martin Boltzius, Minister of the Gospel according to the Confession of Augsburg, hath agreed to Go to the Province of Georgia aforesaid and there to Perform all Religious and Ecclesiastical Offices in the German Tongue for the Instruction and Benefit of the Protestant Saltzburghers and other German Protestants now going to settle in the said Province of Georgia or that shall hereafter Go to and settle there to the utmost of his Ability. Know Ye that We the said Trustees Have authorised and Impowered and Do hereby authorise and Impower him the said John Martin Boltzius to Do and Perform all Religious and Ecclesiastical Offices in the German Tongue that shall be necessary for the better Establishing and Promoting the Christian Religion in the said Colony and all other the Good Ends and Purposes thereby intended agreeable to the Confession of Augsburg and the Tenour of Our Charter In Witness whereof the said Trustees have to these Presents affixed their Common Seal the Twenty-first Day of November in the seventh year of the Reign of Our Sovereign Lord George the Second by the Grace of God of Great Britain, France and Ireland, King, Defender of the Faith and so forth and in the year of Our Lord One thousand seven hundred and thirty-three.

Friday, the 21st of Dec., Old Style[63]

Today our Salzburgers were bound by oath and had to promise with hand and mouth to be subject to the English government, their present authority, and, as subjects, to show obedience in their enjoyment of the rights and freedoms of the land. On this occasion the following ceremony took place: After the morning prayer meeting the commissary came into the room, which had been granted the Salzburgers for their convenience. Captain Coram as Trustee came around ten o'clock along with our ship's Captain Fry and an English merchant. Thereupon the commissary read a brief oration in which he praised the benefits received and urged upon the people gratitude to God and to their benefactors. And after they all had promised obedience with a loud *yes*, he read to them a proclamation written in German, in which the Trustees told them about their future privileges in the land and their duties.

There were many seals impressed at the bottom of this sheet of parchment. The first and last names of the Salzburgers had been affixed to each one of the same. Finally they all had to shake hands with the Trustees and touch the signed sheet, whereby they were asked whether they meant to honor all of this and recognized the signature as their own. They all confirmed this with a yes. In the beginning Roth raised objections to signing his name, because he does not want to be treated as another Salzburger. Nevertheless, having been strongly persuaded, he complied. After this ceremony the commissary wanted to assist the aforementioned Roth in connection with a Guinea that a merchant was supposed to have denied him. Since the merchant continually insisted he had given him the correct money, the merchant had to clear himself with an oath, whereat little formality was exercised. The justice of the peace asked the merchant whether he knew for certain that the former had given him the money and had not got it back. And when he affirmed it, he had to put his finger on the Book of Matthew and say a few words. Toward evening the commissary recalled the many benefits of God and made the resolution to show his gratitude to God with words and with deeds. He also begs to be diligently reminded about his transgressions, which he would regard as the greatest benefit. On this occasion the enemy within himself was disclosed, and it will require much prayer, effort, and vigilance if it is to be overcome. And because association with frivolous people does him the most harm, he must divest himself of their company or, if they cannot be avoided, arm himself well with prayer and always bear in mind what has been promised God. Also the late Professor Francke's rules of conduct, which one would want to have, were suggested to him.

Saturday, the 22nd of Dec.

Mr. Newman sent us a very friendly letter purporting that the Society had learned from the court chaplain Mr. Ziegenhagen that we were anxious to have an English dictionary; therefore, they gave him, Mr. Newman, orders to send us one as a gift. The Society is pleased with our resolution, which we had made in the Name of God, to go to Georgia with the Salzburgers, and they wish us great success there. As soon as the aforesaid dictionary together with the grammar and other little English writings had been handed over to us, we expressed our gratitude for this latest kindness in a reply.[64]

Sunday, the 23rd of Dec.

Today we gave our listeners instruction, partly from the Gospel and to some extent from other edifying sayings, on how to get ready for the imminent celebration of holy Christmas. Therein our faithful God gave us much strength through His grace, and we also hope He will continue to bless what we have preached.

Monday, the 24th of Dec.

This afternoon there arose some anxiety among the Salzburgers, because two of their big chests, in which they kept their belongings, were dashed to pieces so that several more big water barrels could stand in their place. Here in Dover many Frenchmen and Englishmen have been taken aboard ship, who want to go with us to America. Therefore, it is not only very crowded and the people even at night have hardly any place to sleep but we are also worried that we might run short of water unless a large supply is brought on board. It distresses us that these vexatious things have to occur on this evening and perturb our congregation now that we have prepared with them for the festival of Christmas and wanted to make things even better. Nevertheless, we submit silently to God and will turn even these and such like things that come our way to our and their advantage.

During and after supper today God inexpressibly showed us compassion and gave us refreshment. God reminded us not only of His paternal guidance, particularly during and after our occupation with the Salzburgers; but, since we related a few very special tokens of His providence to the commissary and Mr. Zwiffler, they rejoiced with us in the grace of God we have come to know. And, because we have decided with God to mutually make proper preparations this very evening for the festival of Christmas, a passage from the little booklet *Christ's Christmas Gifts*[65] was read, which gave us material for many good talks. Among other things, one of us related the inner-direction[66] of the late Porst.[67] Likewise, through the grace of God, several special circumstances concerning the late Schade, M.A.,[68] made a deep impression on others. In addition to this, we told how our change of heart came to pass through the exigencies of what God let us experience during and after our penitential labor. Together we then possessed our hearts in prayer and left each other in good spirits and with the sincere resolve to be truly and indeed grateful to our dear Lord for the love which He has bestowed upon us. Praise God for His inexpressible mercy.

Wednesday, the 26th of Dec.

On this day, too, the Lord bestowed His favor upon our preaching of the Gospel. In the middle of our sermon a few distinguished

Englishmen and a female came into the room; and, although they may have understood nothing, they were, nevertheless, very attentive. Eventually they gave our listeners some money. The Salzburgers' attention and deference for the Word of God had, without doubt, made an impression on them. We made an additional contribution to this monetary gift, for which a certain customary dish known as pudding was made for everybody this evening. It is made of white flour, milk, large raisins, and butter and wrapped in white cloths and placed in boiling water to cook. Such an offering of a few temporal gifts brings joy to the Salzburgers and their children, which causes them to have all the more faith in us. May God strengthen us further in this connection and protect us from avarice, the root of all evil.

Thursday, the 27th of Dec.

During the morning devotions God granted us mutually much joy and favor through several Christmas carols and the contemplation of the 7th Psalm, and when the commissary heard us singing, he also joined us and lamented among other things that he could not attain the proper sadness for his sins. Thereupon simple instruction was given him according to his situation. We particularly told him how much prayer, vigilance, and effort it had cost us before we had been brought to properly repent of our sins and to recognize the wrath of God, which they sustain; and what great joy will ensue from a little sadness and would at some time take place in eternity if we remain faithful.

One day recently Captain Coram informed us that he had heard that three Salzburgers had begged at several houses, and this would be outrageous and displeasing to the Trustees. When the matter was investigated, it was found that the people were innocent; and to all appearances some Dutch or German beggars, who are stopping here, had passed themselves off as Salzburgers and had gone begging.

Friday, the 28th of Dec.

. . . After the prayer meeting a few asked us whether we knew anything about Tennhardt.[69] Some of his writings had been brought to them in Salzburg, and they had read them and found in them very high-sounding and harsh expressions. We told them about some of his erroneous ideas and how they could thank God that He had kept them from going astray and had held them to the pure Gospel. . . .

Saturday, the 29th of Dec.

God had given us a favorable wind yesterday; therefore, all preparations were made to put to sea. And yet tonight it had become very contrary again so that those ships that sailed away yesterday had to return.

Captain Coram, on behalf of the Trustees, has to the previous kindnesses added yet another by purchasing for us four dozen bottles of Spanish wine, to which we may help ourselves in case of need on the way. We have also been provided with a large supply of brandy, tobacco, and pipes, which we will let our listeners have, because we don't use them and can't give them back either.

Wednesday, the 2nd of Jan.

The commissary told us that he had tried out a pistol today and that the bullet had rebounded and had flown past very close to his head. He said divine protection had kept him from losing his life. We pointed out to him how important it is to be penitent and to have faith in order to prepare in time to die as a Christian and not to delay conversion until one is on one's deathbed. Moreover, he should acknowledge that God is a holy and just God; with a disastrous shot He could have punished *jure talionis*[70] those sins in which he engaged by shooting and screaming on board the ship as it was leaving Rotterdam. True, he is often moved and prompted to reflect on his actions by such conceptions, only it does not last very long. In this evening's prayer meeting we had much cause for patience and sighing, for in all the rooms of our quarters there had gathered a large crowd of citizens engrossed in the harangue of a man, who, through their votes, hoped to become a Member of Parliament. Not only did they just rudely scream but they also called a large number of street urchins together, who, by shooting and yelling, made a great *strepitum*.[71] A preacher was also present in one of the rooms.

Thursday, the 3rd of Jan.

For eight days now Boltzius has been troubled by a severe toothache, and he has not been able to get rid of it although many medicaments, externally and internally, have been tried. And since no one would even undertake the risk of pulling the tooth, it was packed with softened mastic, after which the pain subsided. Oh, what a real blessing it is when two are together who can help each other, not only in temporal affairs but also in the performing of official duties. The commissary searched through his letters this evening and found one that Senior Urlsperger had written him, and which he should have read to us at that time, because in it were various topics that concerned us and would have done us a great deal of good if they had been made known to us. Owing to his many distractions at that time that he himself created, he did not find time to do it; and we remonstrated with him once again about this.

Friday, the 4th of Jan.

. . . During the prayer meetings we often have opportunity now to teach them about adiaphorism,[72] and the way will be prepared for us to arrange our church establishment in the future for the edification of all in common and to leave out *consentiente ecclesia*[73] the ceremonies at which the others might perhaps take offence.

Owing to Captain Fry's delinquency, the Salzburgers have not been given their allowances for several days, and this has brought on much mental distress. However, as soon as Captain Coram was told about this, he indicated his displeasure and made definite preparations to have meat cooked once more for them this very evening. The Trustees try hard to be kind and helpful to the good people, and they have had a great deal purchased. Whether the ship's provisions are properly administered according to their intentions and will be later, only time will tell.

Sunday, the 6th of Jan.

. . . Roth has applied to Captain Coram, as well as in writing to the Trustees in London, for permission to remain here with his wife, who is heavy with child. Otherwise there would be danger that under the miserable circumstances on board ship mother and child could suffer injury, and otherwise much inconvenience could be caused during her travail and after childbirth. It appears, however, that the Trustees are not consenting to his petition; but for his wife's sake they will perhaps make the best possible arrangements on board ship.

Tuesday, the 8th of Jan.

After the north wind started blowing it began to freeze rather hard here, for until now we have had mostly summer weather and occasionally rain. With this wind we sailed away from Dover to-day in God's name, and we praised the Lord for all the kindness that was bestowed upon our bodies and souls in the English harbor.

Friday, the 11th of Jan.

We can make good use of the Salzburger Geschwandel in the performance of our duties. Things go on sometimes among our listeners to which we can't and don't want to call attention, at least not as plainly and individually as necessity often requires. We need only drop this man a hint and he tries to correct such disorder, and with good results at that.

During prayer meeting the 24th Psalm was very edifying to one of us, especially in the beginning: The earth is the Lord's, etc. Our listeners participated also in this.

Saturday, the 12th of Jan.
One of our group had taken some water from a battered barrel, at which the captain became very angry again. He probably did it in all innocence; therefore, we did not concern ourselves about it further, as was asked of us, other than to admonish them to use caution and patience.

Sunday, the 13th of Jan.
Even now there is no lack of sorrowful circumstances, but for the listeners' part divine solace is not absent either. . . .

Monday, the 14th of Jan.
. . . During these past days the wind has indeed been strong and very favorable to us, but at the same time it has been rather cold, yet not nearly as cold as it is in Germany around this time of year.

Roth fell into a terrible fit of anger with his wife on account of a little mistake. They say he pushed and struck her, although he denies the latter in spite of the fact that two crewmen appeared as voluntary eyewitnesses to testify against him. After he had calmed down, one of us attempted in the spirit of love and gentleness to bring home to his heart and conscience his transgression, the annoyance caused, and his wretched condition. Not much can be done about him.

Thursday, the 17th of Jan.
The wife of the schoolmaster Mr. Ortmann has lain sick ever since we have been at sea. This has made her quite weak. One notices that through this sickness God is working diligently on her heart, and she promises to devote herself completely to the Lord when she is well again. May God grant that this turns out to be true so that she will not be detrimental to us but will be able to be useful in several ways in God's work.

Friday, the 18th of Jan.
. . . The captain's treatment of our listeners as well as other people on board is again irresponsible, for he does not have issued to them what has been purchased for their sake. Every day they receive salted beef, which cannot be eaten because it is so tough and salty. They can eat only the peas, with which it is cooked. They receive very little table beer—it is almost sour anyway. And the water in several of the casks stinks, and of this they can't even get

enough! The commissary is sighing with us over this privation of the poor people; however, he doesn't have the heart to act with energy and point it out to him. It would not be the proper thing for us to do, because otherwise we would entrench upon another's office. In the meantime we shall take pleasure in serving our listeners according to our ability with the things that were given to us in Dover for our use. The commissary will do the same.

Saturday, the 19th of Jan.

. . . The commissary asked the captain to give the people cereal and soup along with a little butter or cheese instead of the tough and indigestible meat. He offered the same old excuse: The flour, butter, etc. were packed away so that he couldn't get to them.

Today we had to speak earnestly with Mrs. Roth and remonstrate with her about her cupidity and profiteering in wine and brandy, which she carries on at the expense of the Salzburgers. . . .

Tuesday, the 22nd of Jan.

On this day, on which we embarked two weeks ago, God permitted us to see a beautiful rainbow at sea for the first time, and we made good use of it to strengthen our faith. Today, after the spectacle was over, the captain had oat groats cooked for the people; and, even though nothing more than a little butter was given them to make the groats tasty, they were nevertheless much more cheerful than when they had the salted, indigestible meat, because they did not have to suffer so much from thirst. At Dover we were given a considerable supply of brandy for our own use, which would have lasted us for several years. Now we realize that even in this respect God guided our benefactors correctly so that with it we could be of service to our listeners in their present need. As they say, amidst all this bad treatment it is a real tonic; and they don't know how to thank us. Thanks to our Heavenly Father for this kindness. The captain also received brandy for the people but he has not given them a drop of it yet.

Thursday, the 24th of Jan.

This day again was as lovely as a summer day in Germany. When it sometimes rains, then the rain is very warm and it soon passes away.

Friday, the 25th of Jan.

. . . The sailors informed us that we had crossed the tropic of Cancer last night and had arrived in a region where the wind blows steadily for six months from an easterly direction and will take us directly to our destination.[74] . . . In this region the first quarter of the moon appears other than in Germany. The so-called horns are not at the top and bottom so that the curve would be seen at one side, but the curve is on the bottom and the two horns at the right and left are turned straight up and in such a way that one can even perceive the entire circle quite clearly. The form is thus: [75]

Saturday, the 26th of Jan.

Because the dear Salzburgers get only one meal a day—and poor and scanty at that—and the hard ship's biscuit is so dry that they can't put it in their stomachs, they buy cheese from the helmsman, a pound for six stivers, whereupon they show themselves as grateful as if it were being given to them. We have offered to share gladly some of our salary with them if their money should not suffice, just so they don't injure their health. It is highly inexcusable that the captain does not serve out when necessary the provisions taken on board for the benefit of these poor people. Since that evil Roth continues to carry on his profiteering at the expense of these poor people, we have done everything possible to put a stop to this evil. . . .

Sunday, the 27th of Jan.

. . . Mrs. Ortmann has once more started to go on in her own frivolous and unchristian way, and even her husband is incapable of keeping her under control. Consequently, it was shown him in privat what is incumbent upon him to do in this emergency, viz: he himself must find salvation in God so that with an exemplary life he can serve as a model for her. And in this order he should pray diligently and lay this marriage difficulty before the Lord, who restrains all evil and guides the hearts of men. At the same time he was given to read the edifying short treatise, page 953, from the seventh contribution to *The Fabric of God's Kingdom*.[76] We sincerely wish he would let himself be saved, because in the opposite case he would be more hindering than beneficial in our ministry. He gladly accepts good suggestions.

Mr. Zwiffler listens diligently to God's word, it is true, but also keeps silently to himself. However, he won't go so far as to concern himself with the spiritual approach to life. Concern for earthly matters and what the future may hold troubles him so greatly that at times the furor of impatience and discontent bursts forth quite intensely.

Monday, the 28th of Jan.

The captain declares he has orders that during the voyage he is not to break into the ship's provisions given him to take along such as brandy, cheese, potatoes, etc., but he is to bring them to Georgia, and there they are to be given to the people for their sustenance. Captain Coram, on the other hand, told the commissary in Dover that everything on board ship is supposed to be used during the voyage. Time will tell.

This afternoon around two all of us on board ship had a terrible scare, which made a deep impression upon our hearts and the hearts of our listeners (and, God grant, upon all on board), and effected much good through God's mercy. The captain was having his dinner cooked; and because as is his custom he bumped into the cabin boy, who was supposed to be preparing it, and frightened him so that he spilled the broth from the meat into the fire so that the steam penetrated throughout the ship and into the cabins. Since some of the sailors were in the powder magazine at the time, it seemed to the commissary, who was there, that the powder had been ignited. He immediately called for water and came running on deck in great fear. Thereupon the captain and everybody ran to the bow of the ship and everyone believed to be face to face with death. It is impossible to describe what a wretched sight this was and how miserably the old and the young were screaming. . . .

Tuesday, the 29th of Jan.

Today the people received pork for a change, which pleased them very much, because it is not as tough and salty as the beef. Tomorrow he wants to give them pudding, for which he has had flour and raisins sought out.[77]

Friday, the 1st of Feb.

There are several sick persons and two nursing babies among the Salzburgers for whom a soup of water and flour has to be made from time to time because the indigestible fare does not agree with them. When they come to the fire the captain not only rails at them but taunts them by saying that a single Salzburger gulps down more than three Englishmen and there would not be enough victuals for them in Georgia. This is all a rude untruth. Only once during the entire day does he give them food and then for five persons only a little piece of meat, a little soup, or, when this is lacking, three of four turnips and throughout the whole day a quart of beer and two quarts of water—with this so many persons must content themselves on top of this salty food. Yes, the captain often has to be urged to give them this small quantity of beer and water. If God did not specially strengthen the people they could not subsist. . . .

Monday, the 4th of Feb.

The people thank God because the captain has started to issue pudding, oat groats or pork sometimes instead of beef, for such food agrees with the people better. We regard as an answer to our humble prayer that the man now does the poor people this kindness.

Thursday, the 7th of Feb.

Because the water in several barrels is stinking and hardly drinkable, the people were advised to pour some brandy into the water and in this way give it a different taste. The captain has also offered to grant them some. However, because it was pointed out to him that the people are in need and that the Trustees would not be opposed to it if he gave up some of the brandy that he is supposed to take to Georgia, he let himself be induced to have a small barrel distributed among the colonists. It seems then to be true after all that he is not supposed to break into the victuals taken on board. When the captain is in high spirits he doesn't find it so difficult to give up something very necessary, but then one mustn't ask often.

Friday, the 8th of Feb.

The Salzburger Hertzog, in whom the fear of God can be perceived, became rather emotionally upset over these miserable circumstances and poured forth very desperate words. This caused us much sorrow. He is otherwise as gentle as a lamb, but till now he has not been without temptations. Yet, in this respect he has always let himself be shown the right way. He regrets very much that he ever let himself be persuaded into coming along. May God look with favor upon our efforts to comfort him and our prayer for him. In the evening prayer meeting God was merciful in that the aforesaid Salzburger was stoutly heartened and strengthened in his faith in God. . . . We were amazed to hear how powerfully and impressively they spoke to poor Hertzog about his anxiety and harsh expressions.

Sunday, the 10th of Feb.

. . . They are glad that God has heard their prayer and has made the captain much kinder and more friendly toward them. They have resolved to continue setting a good example and praying for him. We reminded them of the words of Solomon: When a man's ways please the Lord, he maketh even, etc. He is now not only peaceable and friendly but continues to give them alternately good pork, pudding, oat groats and butter instead of beef. Also, the water is now much cleaner and more palatable than usual.

Tuesday, the 12th of Feb.

Wrangling has broken out between the Ortmanns and the Roths, whereby scandal has been stirred up again. An eruption has appeared on Mrs. Ortmann as if she has a very disgusting disease on her neck, on account of which Roth and his wife not only refuse to eat with her (for they take their meals together), but they have shouted all sorts of insults and abuse at each other. In the beginning this matter was brought before the commissary by Roth and then by Mrs. Ortmann, since so much contention and sin arose. May God put a stop to all evil.

Wednesday, the 13th of Feb.

Today, on account of a trivial matter, the captain fell into such a rage that he not only talked of beating and stabbing, but even struck a Salzburger with a cane, who till now has been one of the most cheerful ones and has comforted others. The reason was that five persons, who had received much too little meat, desired some more meat. Someone else, to all appearances, seems to have put before the captain a wrong construction upon the words and gestures of this person, as if he had scolded and threatened. This is not the way of these good people, but they strive to imitate the patient Savior and David, whose example up to now has been demonstrated in the Psalms. Accordingly all the Salzburgers testify that the accused is completely innocent. In this violent rage he threatened to give neither beer nor meat any more, because he has been obligated to do this for only three weeks. At the same time he wanted to make sure right now in advance that they would have even less to eat in Georgia.

Thursday, the 14th of Feb.

Today the captain is friendly again to the Salzburgers and again had beer and meat given to them as previously. Just as one cannot rely much on his friendliness, his wrath does not last long either; however, it is often so great that one must be terrified. . . .

Friday, the 15th of Feb.

. . . We have clear evidence that our dear Saviour has blessed our efforts with the medico. He formerly had great aversion to true Christian conduct, and once in a while showed signs of great emotional upset over this or that. Because we noticed that he could not bear to be told about his defects under these distressful circumstances, we found it advisable to take up his various excuses in our prayer meetings and to show the inevitable necessity of re-birth. We also did this in private and applied it directly to him. By and by this served to convince him and to make him resolve to become not only a mere hearer but also and active doer of the Word, through the Grace of the Holy Ghost, as he acknowledged today with tearfilled eyes. . . .

Monday, the 18th of Feb.

. . . The place where our prayer meetings have to be held is ex-tremely small and irksome, yet this has not prevented us or our congregation from gathering mornings and evenings to pray and study the Word of God. Roth, his wife, and Mrs. Ortmann are the only ones for whom this has been too bothersome.

Towards noon a strong south wind arose, which developed into a violent storm about four o'clock and caused great consternation everywhere, especially since the wind sheared the one big sail from the main mast, which is supposed to hold the ship on course. . . . In his great fear the commissary made solemn vows, and after we had pointed out to him the unfaithfulness and sin to which he was still subject in his heart, he promised with hand and mouth to work for his salvation with fear and trembling if the Lord would save us from this mortal danger. . . .

Thursday, the 21st of Feb.

. . . Two Salzburger men have fallen sick due partly to the great shaking of the ship and partly to the miserable circumstances in which they find themselves. The water is so evil tasting that it would be no wonder if all got sick. Mr. Zwiffler is a very useful man in the practice of medicine who cares earnestly for all the sick on the ship. . .

Sunday, the 24th of Feb.

Even yesterday they started to deprive the people of the little beer in which they had found some relief up to now from the hor-rible water, and they are giving them water instead. This and other privations impelled us to pray even more earnestly to our most compassionate Father for the hastening of our voyage. . . .

Tuesday, the 5th of March

. . . After sunrise one of the sailors called from the mast that he had sighted land and not long afterwards we could recognize it clearly from the deck below. . . .

In the Lord Very Esteemed Court Chaplain,[78]

In great haste and in praise of God I am sending you word from Charleston—whither together with the captain and the commissary I have departed in a boat from our ship, which has dropped anchor at sea—that all who embarked at Dover are still alive, although some had to suffer a great deal. In our diary, which we are enclosing, there are several sorts of *laeta & tristia*[79] to be found. I daresay you will know how to make use of it all according to your wisdom. From here a pilot will be taken on board, who will steer our ship the rest of the way. We have been at sea for eight weeks and two days. Mr. Oglethorpe has provided us with many good things for our refreshment. As soon as we have arrived at our destination, we will write more. Please send this diary to Halle at your earliest convenience. Commended to the Lord and His mercy, I remain,

Your Reverence,
Most obliged in prayer and service to my
Very Esteemed Court Chaplain in the Lord,
Joh. Martin Boltzius.
Charleston,
the 7th of March, Old Style,
1734.
My dear colleague sends his most cordial greetings.

Thursday, the 7th of March

. . . This city of Charleston not only looks good from the sea but is also well built, though not expensively, and has no walls. We have especially noted the following:

.   .   .   .

(6) That we have met here also a few Germans who were very happy at our arrival and who will visit us for Holy Communion. The printer, named Timotheus, is also a German. He is the publisher of the local newspaper. He has also been in Halle. One of the Germans, who had lived in Pennsylvania at first, told us about many things but especially many bad things about a preacher from Ansbach named Schultze. After he had first caused much annoyance, he eventually journeyed on from here in complete secrecy. People had gathered from miles around to hear a sermon. But instead of preaching the Word of God, he sent them word that he would not preach until he had first received his money. Even this, which they wanted to give him, seemed to be not enough for him. Therefore, the Anabaptists and the Quakers have reproached the Lutherans with many things because of their doctrines and their teachers and have even won the simple folk over to their side.

(7) That three weeks ago a ship with a rich cargo was burned completely right in front of the city due to the negligence of a cabin boy.

(8) That a sick woman desired that we administer Holy Communion to her. Because we had not known her previously and our own circumstances did not permit it either, we could not bring ourselves to a decision on this. Meanwhile, we showed her in brief the way to the spiritual benefit of Christ and recommended to her chapter six of John's Gospel for diligent reading and practice.

(9) That it is a great convenience to have many slaves to do the work; but this convenience is coupled with great danger, for the blacks, who are said to number thirty thousand in Carolina alone, are not faithful to the Christians and are very malicious. A respectable gentleman assured us that about two months ago on the two islands of St. Thomas and ————,[80] which are said to belong to the Swedes and Danes, the Negroes had got together and killed all the white people that were their masters, because they were far superior to them in numbers.

. . . .

Monday, the 11th of March

Our ship has struck a sandbar; and for this reason the drinking water, which will no longer be needed, will be let out of the casks in order to lighten the ship. Previously the captain was so frugal with the water that the people had to suffer from thirst, and now he has to empty so many of the casks.

Today Mrs. Ortmann again gave us a sample of her very bad temper. She not only picked an annoying quarrel with the commissary's servant, but struck him in the face for no reason at all and caused altogether a great disturbance. Her husband is a slave to her and can't govern her, and she won't listen to other people at all.

In Charleston a German carpenter, who wanted to go with us to Georgia, came aboard our ship. Having heard how badly the captain had treated the people during the voyage, he told several on board that he considered this an unreasonable and inexcusable action. His words were repeated to the captain, who, for this reason, fell into a terrible rage and hurled abuse at him and even wanted to fall upon him with blows, which seemed outlandish and frightful to all on board.

Tuesday, the 12th of March

... Through God's wonderful direction the captain's atrocious behavior yesterday even had to serve to our advantage. The captain hectored the aforesaid carpenter with harsh words and threats for such a long time that he decided to go ahead of us in a small boat to Savannah, which he reached yesterday evening . . . He announced that our ship had struck a sandbar . . . This caused an experienced navigator to come to our aid who quickly brought our ship to its destination at high tide. . . .

Wednesday, the 13th of March

. . . This ill-bred Roth has asked and even received permission to settle in this place. We looked upon this as an answer to our prayers, because these people would breed much mischief in our congregation. We have strenuously admonished him often, but with no effect. They frequently shunned our prayer meetings, during which, as well as at other times, they caused scandal by their words and action. God have mercy on their poor souls! The commissary and Mr. Zwiffler had a terrible falling-out with both of the Ortmanns, after which the latter are absolutely implacable and so enraged that they not only utter many threats but also want to go back to England. She is a veritable termagant, has an evil, lying and slanderous tongue and is full of other abominations. Owing to her, he too got very angry. . . .

Thursday, the 14th of March

Mr. Oglethorpe arrived here today and received us and our Salzburgers in very friendly fashion. . . . We dined with him at noon. After dinner Mr. Ortmann came with his wife to Mr. Oglethorpe and accused the commissary of using some harsh language. The commissary then lodged several points against the woman, and, contrary to our expectation, summoned us in addition to the Salzburgers to appear as witnesses. Although on examining these matters many distressing things came up, God attended everything with his blessing in that we all came together in a room, prayed together, and with great emotion we became reconciled with one another and also formed the earnest resolution to lead Christian lives in the presence of God and man.

Saturday, the 16th of March

. . . Mrs. Roth, who has been sick for several days due to her approaching childbirth, is given just everything she desires from the storehouse or magazine. . . .

In spite of the fact that up to now we have taken great pains to put an end to Mrs. Ortmann's hitherto existing wicked conduct and put her on the right path (which she herself earnestly promised to follow), we had to learn today that she continues in her bad habit of setting people at variance, slandering them, lying to them, quarreling, etc., because these actions have already become second nature to her. And because today's outrages are so palpable that she can't even prevaricate, as is usually her habit, we looked upon this as divine judgment in which God even better reveals the wickedness in her heart, since she has refused to utter a word of repentance. Our listeners intimated to us that they would like it if she were not allowed to live among them at all. It is also dangerous to take her along, since she does not earnestly repent and has not publically apologized to the congregation she previously and currently offended and promised them to mend her ways.

Tuesday, the 19th of March

.   .   .   .

Roth and his wife caused us much anxiety yesterday and today on account of their worldly intentions. When we were still on board ship and it was learned how he always asked princes, counts, etc. to stand sponsor to his children, it was intimated to him that this time he should not look around for prominent people but for true children of God who, with their prayers, could obtain a blessing for him and his child. He made many promises but now keeps few of them since, for the sake of superficial advantages and favors, he has asked Mr. Oglethorpe, the wife of the mayor[81] and vice governor of this place, and the commissary to stand sponsor. We pointed out to him in charity and earnestness that we do not find fault with these persons; however, it would not be reasonable to elect them for this, 1) because the first two are not of our religion, 2) they do not understand our language and therefore cannot answer the questions, 3) none of the three is going to remain in this country and therefore could not take care of the child in place of parents. But they paid no attention to any of our expostulations. And, although Mr. Oglethorpe will not be returning from his trip for several days, they want to wait that long until he comes, even though his return should be protracted to four weeks. God, however, heard our prayer and ordained that today this holy ceremony would be undertaken and it was quite edifying. . . .

Friday, the 22nd of March

To the pleasure of everyone, Mr. Oglethorpe returned here today. Since he will go from here to Charleston tonight, and from there immediately to London, we have given him the continuation of our diary along with some letters to Court Chaplain Ziegenhagen, Professor Francke, Senior Urlsperger, Pastor Klein in Cleves, Secretary Newman, Adj. Baumgarten,[82] Pastor Mischke,[83] and to both of our mothers.

The helmsman and most of the Englishmen came to Mr. Oglethorpe today to bring charges against the captain who treated the people like dogs. Since the commissary is not taking sides with the unscrupulous captain, it might look bad for him. Mr. Oglethorpe is strict in regard to law and justice.

Sunday, the 24th of March

. . . Although the Roths had asked Mr. Oglethorpe that they not be required to go with the Salzburgers and their request was granted, they have now changed their minds and would rather travel with us after all than live among strangers whose language they do not understand. The reason they give is the preaching of the Gospel, which they would have to do without if they separate from us. As usual they gave little or no thought to this, yet it was precisely this point that we had tried to impress upon them.

Monday, the 25th of March

Today an execution of judgment was held here in Savannah. A man from this place had been accused and convicted of sodomy and inciting others, for which he was to receive three hundred lashes under the gallows. . . .

Tuesday, the 26th of March

A trial was conducted today and the captain was called to account for his harsh methods aboard ship. The commissary, who himself presented several important points against him, related that the mayor and assistant judges were astonished at the captain's iniquity and wretched treatment of the people, and they had prophesied to the captain that nothing good would come of this. The reports are supposed to be sent to the Trustees in London. The helmsman will bring action against him tomorrow. . . .

Wednesday, the 27th of March

. . . This afternoon an Indian husband cut off both ears and all the long hair, which widows customarily wear, of an Indian widow[84] who lives in Purysburg, because she had been sitting with a white man and was said to have been quite familiar in her conduct with him. . . .

Monday, the 8th of April

. . . Everybody who is able is working with great enthusiasm, except Roth and Ortmann who, it seems, will separate from us.

Tuesday, the 9th of April

. . . The Salzburgers have pitched themselves two tents, which, however, do not protect them enough against frost and heat. We, on the other hand, live with two English families in a cabin, where at present we cannot even keep dry and which in other respects has many incommodities, because everything is very narrow, low, unclean, and constantly open at both ends where one is supposed to enter. Yet, through God's fatherly providence, all of this does not impair our health, although it does prevent us from accomplishing very much if anything. One must be amazed that, after being here for four months, the people of this place have made no attempt to either build houses or till the soil, but make shift to live and eat up their provisions with idleness.[85] Perhaps the Salzburgers' unflagging diligence will induce them to reflect a little and emulate them. . . .

Friday, the 12th of April

. . . Roth leads the same vexatious life here as before so that even the Englishmen, with whom he and his wife live, have complained to us about his malevolence and are surprised that, since both of them are included in our number, they don't attend any prayer meetings. Again we reproached him severely for his unchristian conduct, but without effect. He often carries on the most horrible and reckless discourses, because God does not let him prosper, but obviously works against him due to his carnal-mindedness. He lays all the blame for his misfortune (as he calls it) partly on the commissary, partly on other distinguished people in Regensburg and Augsburg for promising him many advantages in America that are now nonexistent. He does not want to do any work, but instead act as lord and master. Because we have declared to him that in the future we will vigorously stop his disorderly and shameless conduct, he now wants to separate from us again and intends to ask the mayor in Savannah to let him remain here in Abercorn.

Monday, the 15th of April

. . . Mr. Ortmann, the schoolmaster, wrote me a lengthy letter in which he complained about persecution, disregard for his talents, unkindness, etc., about which he frets so much that he is declining very much in strength and is coming closer and closer to his grave. He asks that we be compassionate enough to administer the Holy Sacrament to him before his death, which may be fast approaching. We should also see to it that his wife is provided for, etc. This confused letter gives evidence of his mental disorder. Consequently, I asked him to walk with me a little in the forest, since otherwise we haven't the slightest opportunity to talk with anyone in private. Here I refuted the contents of his letter and showed him in all friendliness the reason for his suspicion and assured him of constant sincere love. His spirits were exceedingly raised and he even promised to faithfully continue his admonitions to his wife, to set her a good example in prayer and in his way of living, and not to be taken in so much by her smooth and deceitful words. And love was indeed shown him, which put even more emphasis on what was said. . . .

Wednesday, the 17th of April

Gronau arrived again here in Abercorn today. He will stay with us from now on because he is no longer needed in Ebenezer, also because he might risk his health if he lives any longer all alone in such wretched circumstances without care, properly prepared meals, etc. . . .

Thursday, the 18th of April

. . . If one loses sight of the blazed trees by which one can recognize the way to some extent, one runs the risk of getting completely lost as happened recently to two German men in Purysburg, who went so far into the forest that nothing was ever seen of them again.

Saturday, the 20th of April

Since there is no beer to be had in this country, the Salzburgers have learned from the Englishmen how to cook a half-beer which they prepare from time to time for themselves. They take a few pieces of sassafras, a little syrup, and, instead of hops, some green pine-tops, which are boiled in a kettle of water. . . . The inhabitants of this land praise this beer as being very good for the health;[86] conversely, they consider water harmful, implying that it is responsible for dysentery, from which many people here die. For ourselves, we prefer water to this mishmash and feel quite well drinking it, although occasionally we mix in a little wine. . . .

Sunday, the 21st of April

Roth handed over a letter to the commissary and us, in which he greatly humbles himself, acknowledges several matters concerning his previous wicked conduct and earnestly requests us to take him back and allow him to live and work in Ebenezer among the Salzburgers, from whom he has already separated twice on account of evil intentions. We reminded him of his hitherto existing disorder and the scandal he has caused, admonished him to repent, and cautioned him against avarice and taking advantage of his fellow-man, to which he is singularly inclined. And because he has lived in enmity with the schoolmaster Mr. Ortmann and his wife for several weeks, we urged both parties to become reconciled with one another, which they, in fact, willingly did. . . . There is a great need here for preachers and teachers; for parents and children go along in a manner which grieves one's soul. Perhaps the very laudable Society would consent to appoint a general catechist as was introduced in the county of Wernigerode and who provided the people with the Word of God during sickness and health. Toward evening another storm arose with much rain. It became very violent about ten o'clock and stayed that way for a long time. We and the Salzburgers were very much inconvenienced by the rain, which leaked into the cabins. But, because of God's blessing, it harmed no one.

Monday, the 22nd of April
. . . We are all very happy that God will soon get us out of these restless and unpleasant circumstances. . . .

. . . .

. . . Every day God gives His blessing to the commissary for the growth of his Christian spirit, for he uses the Means of Salvation, the Word of God, and prayer in all seriousness. In the beginning he was disposed to levity and complaisance, his principal enemies, which he will steadily overcome even better in the strength of Christ. Then certainly God will also assign him as a blessing to others. He has already begun to increase the talents entrusted to him, especially with some French people, because he speaks their language; and this afternoon, to our surprise, he again gave beautiful testimony. It hurts his soul very much to see that so many bad people are being sent to the New World, people who insult God in the worst manner; and he has made the firm resolution that, when God will have further need of him as commissary, he will bring none here except those who are true converts to God or those of sound purpose and principles.[87]

Tuesday, the 23rd of April
. . . Several people who have come from Ebenezer report that yesterday large hailstones, as long and as thick as a middlefinger, fell there. They say that they have never had such heavy rain before as they have now, and this then is something unusual.

Wednesday, the 24th of April
. . . Wagons are not to be had in this region, and until they can build one, the people are using a sledge, which cuts deeply into

the ground and delays progress, especially since the horses that have been sent us are very lean and ineffectual and aren't at all accustomed to pulling.

By order of the commissary a Salzburger by the name of Mittensteiner was supposed to ride after two cows that had wandered into the forest, and he has not returned yet. He is a very simple man; and, because there are no paths in the forest, we have been seized with fear and apprehension as to whether he will find his way out. They have sent others after him, who, by shouting and shooting, are supposed to signal to him what place he should ride to if he wants to come out of his confusion. They have also fired the cannons four times, but they still have not seen him again. May God Himself seek this lost sheep and answer our prayer for him! He is an honest Christian and a diligent worker. The worst is that he has eaten neither breakfast nor dinner and has left his hat and coat behind.

Thursday, the 25th of April

. . . Today an Englishman died in the very cabin in which we are staying with the commissary and Mr. Zwiffler. He left his wife and two very small children in great poverty. The people in this entire province are in a bad way with their sickness, for certain people, whom they call doctors here too, have got their hands on them and are torturing them to death with blood-letting and all sorts of absurd home remedies. The man who died was bled the day before yesterday, although in his state of languor he could hardly move a foot or hand. . . .

Friday, the 26th of April

The horse on which Mittensteiner had ridden into the forest came back this afternoon. He himself is not back yet. The horse itself would have brought him back to us again if only Mittensteiner had given it the reins. May God have mercy on him and let this example serve as a warning to others to use more caution. Since the horse returned without reins, we suppose that he fell from the horse and kept the reins in his hands, for he is too awkward and simple to ride horseback.

Saturday, the 27th of April

The dear Salzburgers cannot become accustomed to the air and water, which they have to drink in the heat. Nor can they become inured to so much toil and hardship. Consequently, some complain terribly and must be sustained with medicine. . .

Sunday, the 28th of April

. . . It has not pleased our dear Lord yet to grant our prayer for our lost Mittensteiner, which we have said in public and in private. We have not yet been able to learn anything of him at all or of his circumstances. The Lord's will be done!

Wednesday, the 1st of May

Because of the accumulation of water and the softness of the road, the transportation of our belongings and provisions is proceeding very slowly and with much difficulty. In addition to this, the horses that were miserable to start with, being exerted to do a little work, are becoming even more wretched and useless. It is a harsh existence for the good people. During the day they work till they are tired and exhausted and at night their sleep is greatly disturbed by so many noxious insects, because they still have to lie in the open tent. Moreover, they can find little relief from the food supplies of this country. They are bearing everything patiently and praise God for everything.

Thursday, the 2nd of May

. . . A young Salzburger man fell into a dispute with a carpenter who has spoiled one of his axe handles. It was such that the one threatened the other with the stick. . . .

Friday, the 3rd of May

. . . Because Mrs. Roth has offended other Englishmen by her cupidity, which she practices at the expense of her hostess, who has shown her so much kindness in her cabin, the truth had to be told her in all earnestness. God let it be of use!

Saturday, the 4th of May

.   .   .   .

Mrs. Huber, an old woman with four children, caught dysentery very unexpectedly and is suffering greatly. The people cannot yet become accustomed to the food, drink and air. For this reason many an anomaly arises in their bodies.

Sunday, the 5th of May

Today some of our congregation who are not Salzburgers caused grief and other scandal by their desecration of the Sabbath. We reproached them severely for this sin against God's commandment and admonished them to repent. Braumberger, who is from Bavaria, is an obstinate and spiteful person. May God give us the wisdom and energy to handle him correctly. On this day, while in the forest, a carpenter from Abercorn found the neckerchief that belongs to the Salzburger who is lost and gone astray. Till this day we have not been able to find out where he has gone. The neckerchief was found close to the swamp, which is full of reeds and brushwood. It is very likely then that he may have run into it after the horse, which, lacking a rope, he had perhaps previously hitched up with the neckerchief. He was a man of poor resolve and deliberation.

Wednesday, the 8th of May

In Ebenezer as well as in Abercorn the people are greatly troubled by diarrhea—some even by dysentery—and are somewhat enervated. We suspect the unusual air, which is otherwise quite clear and appears to be healthful, but especially the salty food, lots of drinking in the heat, and catching cold during the frosty nights are to blame. On account of modesty they do not tell anyone right at the beginning, since the one great evil could be easily prevented by divine blessing. Our medicine has done incomparable service for some, since the malady had not already gained the upper hand, and, thank God, has revived the people. Not being able to stand aloof from their difficulty, we have hastened to their aid, for during this time Mr. Zwiffler has not always been present, and besides, a few have no confidence in him. It would be desirable if we could serve more of them in the future, but our few provisions, which we may need for our own feeble bodies, prevents this. The river water is not good for us or our people, because it has not yet been cleaned of the many trees, bushes, and filth. . . .

Thursday, the 9th of May

The cabin constructed for us as an interim dwelling is detrimental to our health and office. Our dear commissary probably realizes this and is intent on making an improvement. And, because we must also have a place where we can hold prayer meetings and services until the church is built, a roomy cabin of boards will be built for this purpose at a healthy place. . . .

Sunday, the 12th of May

One of us called on Mrs. Ortmann, who had reported to go along to Holy Communion, and sought to awaken her conscience. However, nothing could be done with her and she tried to hide behind the evasion of the Old Adam and other empty excuses; and we therefore invited her husband to supper. He seems to have honestly given his heart over to God, so we asked him to assist his wretched wife vigorously. This has been done with good results. Roth and his wife, whom we also called on, are almost past amending; however, exhortations help enough to temper their malevolence and they attend church services more assiduously.

Tuesday, the 14th of May

The commissary, who has set out on his return voyage, took along letters to the following persons: Senior Urlsperger, Professor Francke, Pastor Freylinghausen, Mr. Ziegenhagen, Mr. Butienter, Pastor Meier, Mr. Semmler, M.A., Mr. Lauen, Mr. von Burgsdorff, Inspector Betticher, Preacher Müller, Mrs. Arnold, Mr. Siron in Pennsylvania, Mr. Schumacher, Mr. Costerus in Rotterdam, Mr. Wachsmann.

Notes

1. See *An Extract of the Journals of Mr. Commissary von Reck* . . . (London, 1734). An echo of von Reck's enthusiasm can be heard in a pitifully optimistic letter from a certain John Henry Labhart (Johann Heinrich Lebhart?) of St. Gall, who took his reports all too seriously. See George F. Jones, ed., *Henry Newman's Salzburger Letterbooks* (Wormsloe Foundation Publications No. 8. Athens, Ga., 1966). Hereafter cited as *Newman Letterbooks*.

2. See George F. Jones, ed., *Detailed Reports . . . Edited by Samuel Urlsperger* (Wormsloe Foundation Publications No. 10. Athens, Ga., 1969).

3. *Ibid.*, 156–61 *et passim*.

4. Samuel Urlsperger, ed., *Ausführliche Nachricht von den Saltzburgischen Emigranten* . . . (Halle, 1735 ff.). Cited hereafter as *Ausführliche Nachricht*.

5. George F. Jones, ed., "The Secret Diary of Pastor Johann Martin Boltzius," in *Georgia Historical Quarterly*, LIII (1969), 78–110. Cited hereafter as *Secret Diary*.

6. An obviously expurgated edition of this journal appears in the *Ausführliche Nachricht* (2nd continuation, Halle, 1739), 803–76. The chapter concerning Ebenezer and Frederica has appeared as George F. Jones, ed., "Von Reck's Second Report from Georgia," in *William and Mary Quarterly*, XXII (1965), 319–33. Cited hereafter as *Reck's Report*.

7. William Holton Brown, "The Diary of the Pastors who Accompanied the First Transport of Salzburgers to Georgia, 1733–1734" (M.A. thesis, University of Maryland, 1970).

8. An exception is seen in his entry for 19 June, by which time he was in practical rebellion, as the *Secret Diary* shows. See entry for 12 June also.

9. See his letter in *Newman Letterbooks*, 578–83.

10. See entry for 23 June.

11. See entries for 25 March and 14 April.

12. See entry for 19 June and 14 April, also *Secret Diary*, 95.

13. *Newman Letterbooks*, 188

14. See entries for 17 and 20 June and 7 and 28 Dec.

15. See entry for 12 June, also *Secret Diary*, 104–105.

16. A German translation of this charter, which was granted on Oct. 13, 1735, appears in the *Ausführliche Nachricht*, 2nd Continuation, 809–14.

17. See Newman's letter of Dec. 3, 1734 to von Reck (*Newman Letterbooks*, 145–47).

18. See Adelaide L. Fries, *Moravians in Georgia* (Winston-Salem, 1905).

19. See note 59.

20. See entries for 13 May, 1 June, and 1 Aug.

21. See entry for 3 May, also *Detailed Reports*, II, 186.

22. See note 6, above.

23. Easter was the occasion for the great Buchmessen or Book Fairs in Frankfurt, Leipzig, and other German cities.

24. See note 6.

25. The appendix has been omitted from this edition for reasons given in the Introduction.

26. Ebenezer Creek.

27. Writing as a British subject, Boltzius used the Old or Julian Calendar, whereas Urlsperger and other Germans used the New or Gregorian.

28. Among these were the Anglican ministers John Wesley and George Whitefield, founders of Methodism. The orphanage at Ebenezer inspired Whitefield to found Bethesda near Savannah.

29. Some of the first transport were recruited as they were passing through Memmingen on their way to East Prussia (*Newman Letterbooks*, 319). Some of the second transport had sojourned in Lindau (*Detailed Reports*, I, 193, note 14). Free Imperial Cities were cities subject directly to the Holy Roman Emperor, not to any territorial lord.

30. A medicine manufactured at Augsburg by Johann Caspar Schauer, a benefactor of the Georgia Salzburgers.

31. The Protestant Body, an organization of Protestant deputies at the Imperial Diet at Regensburg.

32. Roman Catholics, especially at Augsburg, resented the emigration to Georgia and the propaganda derived from it.

33. See note 28.

34. On the Savannah River, some seven miles through swamps and pinebarrens.

35. To the eastern Mediterranean, as a galley slave.

36. The Society for Promoting Christian Knowledge had sent German missionaries from Halle to the Danish mission at Fort St. George near Madras. See *Der Königlichen Dänischen Missionarien aus Ost-Indien eingesandter Ausführlichen Berichten Erster Theil . . .* (Halle, 1735).

37. George II was also Duke of Hanover, Brunswick, and other German lands.

38. See *Detailed Reports*, II, 114–17.

39. It is not always clear what Boltzius means by *unerzogen*. Sometimes it seems to mean "badly brought up, naughty," and sometimes it just means "not yet educated" or "not yet reared" and therefore still a responsibility for the parent.

40. *Gib dich zufrieden, und sey stille.* Opening verse of a hymn composed by Paul Gerhardt (1607–1676) in 1666, music by Jacob Hintze, 1670. It is still in the Lutheran hymnal.

41. Boltzius omitted the names of the weekdays from 11 Jan. through 14 March.

42. *Sammlung auserlesener Materien zum Bau des Reiches Gottes. Der I. Beitrag* (Leipzig, 1731).

43. Gotthilf August Francke, spiritual father of the Georgia Salzburgers, son and successor of August Hermann Francke, founder of the Francke Foundation in Halle.

44. All references to the "late" Prof. Francke are to the father. See note 43.

45. All references to Prof. Francke as still living are to the son. See note 43.

46. August Hermann Francke, *Christus der Kern Heiliger Schrifft Oder Einfältige Anweisung . . .* (Halle, 1702).

47. Boltzius consistently used the word "teacher" (Lehrer) for ministers. Here it refers to A. G. Francke.

48. Johann Anastasius Freylinghausen, *Schriffmässige Einleitung zu rechter Erkäntnis und heilsamen Gebrauch Des Leidens und Sterbens unsers Herrn und Heilandes Jesu Christ* (Halle, 1715).

49. *Der Feind*, a common German designation for the devil.

50. Since Mrs. (Maria) Schoppacher was still alive at this date, then the Maria whom Mr. Vat reported as dying on April 4, 1735, must have been one of the two daughters. See *Newman Letterbooks*, 580, 482.

51. Added by Urlsperger.

52. See note 46.

53. From the Savannah River up Ebenezer Creek, which was navigable only during high water.

54. Red Bluff, a high bank on the Savannah River at the mouth of Ebenezer Creek, site of New Ebenezer. Indian Hut, a bluff a short distance down the Savannah River where someone had built a hut in the Indian manner.

55. According to the King James version, these would be the sixth and seventh commandments. Like the Vulgate, Luther's Bible combines the first two commandments and divides the tenth, thus changing the numbers of all the intervening ones.

56. Very small German coins.

57. Johannes Arnd(t), *Vier Bücher vom Wahren Christenthum*, probably the edition of A. H. Francke.

58. Added by Urlsperger.

59. This is one of the many passages in which Boltzius preaches his Pietistic tenant that man cannot be redeemed by his own works but only by Jesus. Because good works, bourgeois respectability, etc. may delude people into thinking themselves saved, they are actually a snare of the devil. To be saved, one must acknowledge his own depravity and throw himself on the mercy, not the justice, of God. See entries for 6 May, 16 Aug., 7 Oct., 15 and 26 Nov., 12 Dec.

60. See note 55.

61. Johann Samuel Carl (1676–1757), Pietistic professor of medicine at Halle.

62. Friedrich Eberhard Collin, ed., *Das Gewaltige Eindringen ins Reich Gottes* ... (Frankfurt/Main, 1722).

63. See note 42.

64. Added by Urlsperger.

65. Added by Urlsperger.

66. See *Detailed Reports*, II, 143–44.

67. See note 57.

68. *Ach treuer Gott, barmhertzigs Hertz*. Words by Lutheran hymnist Paul Gerhardt (1607–1676). Hymns of this century show a distinct transition from the confessional to the devotional type.

69. *Gott, den ich als Liebe kenne*. Unidentified.

70. Added by Urlsperger.

71. *O es kostet viel ein Christ zu seyn*. Words and music by Christian Friedrich Richter (1676–1711), Pietist hymnist in Halle.

72. Thou shalt not steal. See note 55.

73. Spanish moss.

74. He was building the City of Frederica on St. Simons, also settling Highlanders at Darien. Boltzius should have said "down" instead of "up."

75. Joseph Schaitberger, *Neu-Vermehrter Evangelischer Send-Brief* ... (Nürnberg, 1733). Schaitberger was an early exile from Salzburg.

76. These colorful metaphors were dearly loved and liberally used by the Pietists.

77. This was Oglethorpe's most patent fabrication.

78. Ernst Ludwig, then only about 17 years old.

79. "Out of kindness," i.e., not because it was deserved.

80. *Ewiger Vater im Himmelreich*. Words ascribed to A. Reusner, probably the same as Adam Reissner of Mindelheim (1496–1575). It was an old song well known in Salzburg, where people were forbidden to sing it.

81. The King James version says, "For here we have no continuing city, but one to come." (Hebrews 13: 14).

82. Carl Heinrich von Bogatzky, *Güldenes Schatz-Kästlein der Kinder Gottes* (Halle, 17??).

83. A slightly germanized form of the Latin name of the Society for Promoting Christian Knowledge.

84. The Stone of Help. See *Detailed Reports*, I, 67.

85. Bartholomäus Zauberbühler, Bartholomew Zouberbuhler, later the head of the established (Anglican) church in Georgia.

86. A case of necessity.

87. The seven requests in the Lord's Prayer: 1, Hallowed be Thy name; 2, Thy kingdom come; 3, Thy will be done; 4, Give us this day our daily bread; 5, Forgive us our trespasses; 6, Lead us not into temptation; 7, Deliver us from evil.

88. By words and deeds.

89. Oglethorpe's two ships were still detained near Tybee Island at the mouth of the Savannah River because their captains refused to take them through the unchartered waters to Frederica.

90. The great Lutheran hymn of faith, whose tune is definitely attributed to Martin Luther, was based on Psalm 46. The Pietists did not usually encourage the singing of old orthodox Lutheran hymns.

91. *Ach, treuer Gott, barmhertzigs Hertz*. See note 68.

92. One of the many complaints against the Trustees' insistence on inheritance by tail-male only.

93. Johann Joachim Zubly, later to play a major role in the religious and political history of Georgia.

94. Boltzius says they bore no *Strapatzen*, which literally means no hardships; but he must have meant that they did not share in the hard work of hauling the provisions. In this passage Boltzius' grammar is clear, but his logic is not.

95. Whosesoever sins ye remit, they are remitted unto them; and whosesoever sins ye retain, they are retained.

96. This was a cardinal tenet of the Pietists in contrast to the orthodox Lutherans.

97. Most of the Salzburg exiles had emigrated to East Prussia, where the Elector, Frederick I, offered them good conditions.

98. And forgive us our debts. . . . Matthew 6: 9.

99. See note 82.

100. This remarkable letter shows Boltzius' quick mastery of English despite his isolation and lack of English contacts.

101. you.

102. claims.

103. our.

104. These were reserved for the common good, not for the selfish or personal use of the Trustees, as Boltzius seems to have assumed. In Savannah the trust lots eventually became city parks.

105. hitherto.

106. tithingman, a citizen responsible for nine others.

107. Their life on this earth.

108. The Book of Common Prayer of the Episcopal Church calls this "The Sunday called Sexagesima, or the Second Sunday before Lent." The epistle selected by Boltzius is the one used in the Anglican liturgy, a fact that might attest how well the church agenda of the Salzburgers was accommodated to English usage. See *Detailed Reports*, I, 34.

109. A gentle medicine for the eyes.

110. *Jesu, Du Wurzel des Lebens Zum Leben.* Composer unknown.

111. These verses show the impact of the more exaggerated expressions of Pietism on the girl's mind. There were no hymnbooks for children in the 18th century.

112. King James version: "But where sin abounded, grace did much more abound" (Romans 5: 20).

113. King James version: "and him that cometh to me I will in no wise cast out" (St. John 6: 37).

114. Boltzius always distinguished between the religious exiles of the first two transports and most of the motely group brought by von Reck with the third transport.

115. See note 103.

116. Luke 10: 16.

117. *Herr Jesu Christ, ich schrey zu dir aus hochbetrübter Seele.* Words by J. Schindler, pastor at St. Andreä and senior minister at Braunschweig. Jeremias Weber added verses 11–14.

118. Deliver us from evil. See note 92.

119. *Gertrudenbuch*, a Catholic devotional book.

120. "Words of the institution (Holy Communion) from the mouth of Christ." Above the line Urlsperger has translated it as *Worte der Einsetzung, die Christus beym Nachtmahl gesprochen.*

121. Added by Urlsperger.

122. Added by Urlsperger.

123. Protestants since Luther had looked upon the Pope as the Anti-Christ predicted in Revelations.

124. For feeding silk worms. The Salzburgers were the only group in Georgia to succeed in producing silk, which had been a major goal of the Trustees.

125. St. Thomas and St. Croix in the Virgin Islands, now owned by the United States.

126. With words and deeds.

127. Georg Bernhard Bilfinger (1693–1750), professor at the University of Tübingen, composed an edict incorporating the Württemberg Pietists into the established Lutheran Church. Apparently he must have also recognized Count Zinzendorf and his Herrnhuters. Christoph Matthäus Pfaff (1686–1760), a colleague of his there, was one of the world's most celebrated scholars at the time.

128. Johann Spangenberg, *Postilla. Das ist Auslegung der Episteln* . . . (Nurnberg, 1582).

129. *Meine Seele senket sich.* Words by Johann Joseph Winckler (1670–1722). The page number may refer to Freylinghausen's hymnal. See note 164. This hymn expresses a cardinal tenet of Pietism—the ultimate goal of a mystical union of the soul with God.

130. Apparently Charles Wesley. See entry for April 15.

131. The *Secret Diary* (p. 92) states that Helfenstein had six and Müller had five. The names of the children are given in the Earl of Egmont's list of settlers in Georgia (pp. 83, 123). The *Secret Diary* (p. 93) calls Ernstdorf a Palatine but does not give his Christian name. He is probably the J. Peter Armsdorf listed, without dependents, by Egmont (p. 11).

132. Boltzius seems to mean false judgments or conclusions.

133. Kiefer may have wished to keep his Carolina holdings not only because they were extensive (500 acres as opposed to a maximum of 50 for the Salzburgers) but also because he could own slaves there.

134. This was a French-Swiss woman of the Reformed Church, mother of the second Mrs. Schweiger.

135. This was a complaint against the unpopular stipulation of inheritance by tail-male insisted upon by the Lord Trustees.

136. Jerg Schweiger's second marriage is related in *Detailed Reports*, I, 117, 143–44, 164, 173, 175, 183–84.

137. Results contrary to those desired.

138. Remember the Sabbath. See note 55.

139. Boltzius must have heard, not read, this name, for he wrote it phonetically as Tzerrickey.

140. Boltzius is implying that some of the Trustee's decisions were designed to punish the Salzburgers for leaving Old Ebenezer.

141. It is not clear whether he is referring to John or Charles Wesley. See entry for March 22. The younger brother, Charles, had come only as Oglethorpe's secretary; but, when John went to Frederica, he assumed the position of minister in Savannah.

142. That is, to Old Ebenezer. It is not clear why Boltzius wrote this sentence, or why Urlsperger deleted it, unless it implies that the person in question came from Purysburg for worldly reasons, or perhaps he got drunk in Old Ebenezer.

143. Matthew 26: 40.

144. Also written Schomansgruber and Schönmansgruber.

145. See note 135.

146. Devices for frightening birds.

147. John Perceval, Earl of Egmont. Georgia Trustee and benefactor of the Georgia Salzburgers.

148. Boltzius seems to have used the word *Hochteutsch* to refer to all Germans except the Salzburgers, whose Bavarian dialect he must not have considered High German.

149. Boltzius and Gronau were relieved of this onerous and dangerous duty when it was brilliantly performed by Heinrich Melchior Mühlenberg, who visited Ebenezer on his way to Pennsylvania and again some thirty-five years later.

150. The *Secret Diary* reveals that von Reck had wished to take even more men, whom he wished to employ on the fortifications at Frederica in order to ingratiate himself with Oglethorpe.

151. It is not clear what Boltzius meant by this clearly written English word.

152. *Liebster Jesu, wir sind.* Words and music by Tobias Clausnitzer (1619–1684), primary pastor at Weyden in the Upper Palatinate. This hymn is still in the Lutheran hymnal.

153. For Boltzius' belief in the importance of names, see entry for 10 August.

154. *Guter Hirt, wilt du nicht deines Schäfleins.* Words by Angelus Silesius (1624–1677), Catholic mystic. His name was Johann Scheffler before his conversion to Roman Catholicism.

155. *Girrendes Täublein,* d. i. *Gebundene Seufzerlein eines mit Gott verbundenen Hertzens, wodurch dasselbe bey allen äussern Umständen das Feuer seiner heiligen Liebe zu unterhalten Suchet* (Leipzig, probably second edition of 1731).

156. *O Jesu Christ, mein schönstes Licht.* Words by Paul Gerhardt (1607–1676). See note 68. This hymn is still in the Lutheran hymnal.

157. Turkeys were introduced by the Spaniards to Europe, where they were usually called Indian or Calcutta hens (cf. French *dindon*). The English, who knew them as turkey fowl, applied the exotic name to the native American bird.

158. August Hermann Francke, *Christus der Kern heiliger Schrifft Oder Einfältige Anweisung* (Halle, 1702). English translation, *Christus Sacrae Scripturae Nucleus:* or *Christ the sun and substance of the Holy Scriptures in the Old and New Testament* (London, 1732).

159. Many words, much speaking.

160. For the sad story of Rott and his wife, see *Detailed Reports,* II, 32, 33, 90. Boltzius had previously spelled the name Roth. Rott was a Bavarian distiller.

161. First Sunday after Easter.

162. This entry and that of May 31 are eloquent encomiums of private enterprise.

163. See note 160.

164. Johann Anastasius Freylinghausen, *Geistreiches Gesang-Buch* (Halle, 1704). Boltzius probably used the 3rd edition of 1725.

165. Noble Jones was then laying out Savannah Town far up the Savannah River, as a trading post for Indian traders who bought deer skins.

166. Rauner was a Swabian from Ulm.

167. By "junior" Boltzius means "younger." Charles Wesley was substituting for his older brother, John, who was in Frederica. See note 11 for April.

168. As a Freemason, Noble Jones probably took a dim view of Boltzius' tight little theocracy.

169. Compare this with his statements in entry for 23 June.

170. Imperial dollar, originally coined of silver from Joachimsthal in Bohemia.

171. Von Reck described these hardships in his journal. See *Reck's Report.*

172. Usually written Ossenecker, sometimes Ossenegger.

173. Boltzius confused the name Jones, which he heard but did not see, with Jonas, the German form of the man swallowed by the whale.

174. Jones obviously had orders to survey the land according to maps in London, not to the realities of the terrain. Once Americans were freed of British restrictions, homesteaders by-passed infertile areas and staked their claims where they wished. The land around Ebenezer was and is largely swamp and pine-barrens, with only infrequent oases of relatively fertile land.

175. Boltzius did not wish his parishioners corrupted by contact with English indentured servants.

176. Boltzius is describing slabs, or outside boards with one side still covered with bark.

177. See note 173.

178. This hardly concurs with what he said in entry for 12 June.

179. One of Boltzius' many encomiums of private enterprise. See entries for 29–31 May.

180. August Herman Francke, *Vorbereitung auf das heilige Pfingst-Fest/den 3. Junii 1713* (Halle, 1715).

181. Mrs. Zwiffler followed the first transport to marry Zwiffler in Ebenezer, where she seems to have arrived in December, 1734.

182. The MS has *Stack,* which must be a scribal error for Stanck.

183. Probably Capt. Eneas Mackintosh, commander at Palachacolas. See entry for 26 August.

184. Spangenberg and Nitschmann counted as freeholders, the others as their servants. This enabled them to avoid military service.

185. *Eile, errete deine Seele, stehe nicht stille, und siehe nicht hinter dich.* The King James version reads very differently: "Escape for thy life; look not behind thee, neither stay thou in all the plain." Genesis 19: 27.

186. Von Reck seems to have advised his people wrongly about the exchange rate. See entry for 21 Sept.

187. *Ich hoffe darauf, dass du so gnädig.* Psalm 13: 6 in Luther's Bible. King James version, with different tense: "But I have trusted in thy mercy."

188. *Weg, mein Hertz, mit den Gedanken,* hymn by Paul Gerhardt (1607–1676). Most gifted and popular Lutheran hymnist after Luther. See note 68.

189. He caused the firing of farewell salutes. He had previously offended Boltzius in Rotterdam by firing firearms and firecrackers at the departure of the Hanoverian ambassador. Urlsperger deleted this from his *Ausführliche Nachricht.*

190. Von Reck described the busk in his journal. See *Ausführliche Nachricht,* 2nd Continuation, 866–67. If Boltzius was correct in saying of the busk at Palachacolas that "nothing came of it," then von Reck's account must have been based on hearsay or a written source.

191. See note 158.

192. This was apparently Samuel Everleigh. See entry for 12 Jan.

193. Christian Schweikert, von Reck's lackey on his first trip, died on 20 Nov. 1735. Sebastian Glantz was "sick unto death" on 14 Jan. 1735, immediately after his arrival; but neither Boltzius nor Egmont gives the date of his death.

194. John 11: 40.

195. *Der Herr hat nicht Lust an der Stärcke des Rosses,* noch. . . .

196. As assistant chaplain of the royal (Lutheran) chapel in London, Heinrich Butjenter had played host to the first transport in Dover and to the second transport in London and had taken up collections on their behalf.

197. See entries for 13 May, 1 June, 7 Aug. For Rott's fate, see *Detailed Reports,* II, 32, 33, 90.

198. Friction was most often caused by rivalry in the Indian trade and by rum-running from South Carolina to Georgia, where rum was illegal.

199. *Sey Lob und Ehr dem höchsten Gut,* hymn by Johann Jacob Schütz (1640–1690), friend of Jacob Spener, founder of Pietism.

200. Urlsperger's footnote: "This is caused by the spiritual kinship that the Catholics claim, because of which kinship such people cannot intermarry. Therefore, they limit themselves to one so that the kinship cannot grow too large."

201. Boltzius means, of course, without a spiritual significance, as is usually found in Biblical names. See entry for 9 May.

202. Isaac is usually interpreted as "laughter." Boltzius, who never laughed, must have accepted some more edifying etymology.

203. Genesis 13:7.

204. *O dass ich könnte ein Schloss an meinem Munde legen.* Syrach 22: 23. This does not appear in the King James version.

205. Apostles' Creed.

206. The nature of the disease.

207. There was no escaping the anopheles mosquito anywhere in the fresh-water regions of the Georgia coastal plain.

208. Eneas Mackintosh. See entry for 1 July.

209. See note 59.

210. See note 75.

211. Boltzius used the word *Vorspann,* which designated an auxiliary team of horses added to pull a heavy load.

212. The negative must be an error on the part of the Halle scribe.

213. One wonders whether Boltzius did not really enjoy his authority.

214. This heavy load consisted of a ten gallon wine cask containing six hundred-

weight of copper farthings and 158 pieces-of-eight weighing 137 ounces (*Newman Letterbooks*, 192).

215. *Durch Adams Fall ist gantz verderbt menschlich Natur und Wesen*, hymn by Lazarus Spengler, chief town clerk at Nürnberg (1479–1534).

216. *Wer nur den lieben Gott lässt walten*, hymn by Georg Neumarck of Langensalza (1621–1681), archivist-secretary of the Fruchtbringende Gesellschaft, a language society at Weimar. The hymn is still in the Lutheran hymnal.

217. *Wer Gott dem allerhöchsten traut, der hat auf keinen Sand gebaut*. This hymn by Georg Neumarck is based on *Wer Gott vertraut, hat wohl gebaut*, a hymn by Joachim Magdeburg (ca 1525–after 1583).

218. This helps explain the Salzburgers' "heap of baggage" complained of by Mr. Peter Simonds, the owner of the Prince of Wales (*Newman Letterbooks*, 503).

219. See note 176.

220. Johann Goebel, the Prussian representative in Salzburg, had been trying to collect moneys owed to the emigrants who sold their property before leaving Salzburg. This may have been from that source.

221. A Protestant charity collected to aid the distressed expulsees from Salzburg, Carinthia, Upper Austria, and other areas.

222. By "Austrians" Boltzius means Upper Austrians (*Oberösterreicher*), the Salzburgers' neighbors on the east.

223. *Meine Hoffnung stehet fest*, hymn by Joachim Neander of Bremen (1650–1680).

224. See note 42.

225. Those on low bushes are chinkapins (chinquapins), or dwarf chestnuts.

226. Reck or Röck.

227. Before marrying the girl from Purysburg, Schweiger was admonished to much prayer on 6 Aug. 1735. See *Detailed Reports*, II, 117. She was apparently Swiss Reformed.

228. This was the kind of cotton first known to the Germans, whose word for cotton (Baumwolle) means "tree-wool."

229. *hat wenige äusserliche Sitten*. Boltzius means he lacks social polish.

230. Gotthilf August Francke, the son.

231. The majority of Salzburger exiles had emigrated to East Prussia.

232. Probably Capt. Eneas Mackintosh of Palachacolas (see note 183) or else Capt. MacPherson of Fort Ogeechee (see *Detailed Reports*, II, 106, 110).

233. The Zwifflers married on 24 December 1734, apparently soon after her arrival at Ebenezer.

234. Urlsperger underlined the previous five sentences to indicate that they should be deleted, but the printer failed to do so.

235. Volmar, see entry for 19 March.

236. John 1: 29; Matthew 11: 28.

237. District governor.

238. The last word of this and the next dozen lines have been partially lost in the microfilm and have been reconstructed through analogy.

239. This number, which seems high, is clearly written.

240. South to Frederica to work on the Fort.

241. Apparently the time for which they were indentured, although the more usual term was seven years.

242. Matthew 6: 33; Hebrews 13: 5.

243. pulvis antispasmodicus, a remedy against paroxysms; essentia dulcis, a sweet medicine.

244. It would appear that Boltzius is combining the symptoms of other ailments with those of malaria.

245. Happy ending: she and her children later established a tannery; and her descendants, known as Helvenstone, became prominent Georgians in the mid-nineteenth century.

246. Boltzius had implied that Oglethorpe was breaking his promise, but Urlsperger added two words to soften the sentence.

247. Probably from the area of Mobile, but possibly from the Ohio region.

248. It is a moot question whether Boltzius' parishioners have really taken his sermons to heart or whether they are merely ingratiating themselves.

249. Pious joining of souls.

250. A portrait now lost or unknown.

251. Benjamin Ingham. See *Newman Letterbooks*, 178, 204, 214.

252. This method of pulling the boat is explained in the entry for 28 August.

253. Ortmann was 55, a ripe old age at the time.

254. The word *Sie* here could mean "it," but it seems to refer to Mrs. Ortmann, who was a worldly influence.

255. For Boltzius' views on "natural honesty," see note 59.

256. See note 174.

257. The second two verses: *Wirf dein Anliegen* and *Befiehl dem Herrn deine Wege* are from Psalms 55: 22 and 37: 5. In the King James version they read: "Cast thy burden upon the Lord" and "Commit thy way unto the Lord."

258. Boltzius believed that Oglethorpe was punishing them for not going to Frederica. Vat shared this view. See entry for 22 February.

259. The name usually appears as Hermsdorf. For his activities, see *Reck's Report*, 328.

260. See note 257.

261. See note 59.

262. Matthew 11: 28, a favorite of Boltzius.

263. A large dugout, pirogue. Boltzius used the Spanish form of the Carib word.

264. The Bible does not say that this servant was named Eliezer, which name must be deduced from Genesis 15: 2.

265. English has no word for a bride-seeker or marriage intercessor. Here it means ministers who seek new souls (brides) for Christ.

266. Boltzius must be referring to the four lepers in 2 Kings 7: 3.

267. Later we learn that this was the versatile Swiss, Theobald Kieffer. See entry for 6 Dec.

268. Urlsperger changed this to read "Since Nov. 31st."

269. Boltzius is too delicate to explain his condition, which may have been prostate trouble.

270. But Boltzius should remember that Volmar was seventy-three, some eighteen years older than the "old" husband!

271. Boltzius wrote *harricane*, which is probably the way he heard it.

272. See note 263.

273. Expectorate, to speak fully, to speak from the heart.

274. Zwiffler's successor was Christian Ernst Thilo, a doctor from Halle.

275. John 5: 14.

276. This list is found on p. 270.

277. Boltzius confronted a dilemma. If he minimized the yield, he would prove that the removal had not helped and he would diminish the subsidy paid on crops. If he exaggerated the yield, he would imply that the Salzburgers no longer needed support.

278. Johann Anastasius Freylinghausen, *Compendium, oder Kurtzer Begriff der ganzen Christlichen Lehre. . .* (Halle [probably 7th ed. of 1734], unless Boltzius was using a Latin version, as his title suggests).

279. This clearly shows the break between Pietism and Orthodox Lutheranism.

280. Matthew 18: 6.

281. *Stiller im Lande*, "a quiet person in the country," a derisive term for the Pietists, later accepted by them.

282. See note 278.

283. "Wherefore, if thy hand or thy foot offend thee, cut them off, and cast them from thee" (Matthew 18: 8; cf. v. 9).

284. The German word *Haushaltung* was broader than our word "housekeeping" and designated the entire economy, including the farmyard.

Notes for Supplement

1. Samuel Urlsperger (1685–1772), pastor of St. Anne's Church in Augsburg and senior Lutheran pastor of that city, made most of the arrangements for the Salzburgers' emigration to Georgia. In 1712, while pastor of the Savoy Chapel in London, he had become a corresponding member of the S.P.C.K. (Society for Promoting Christian Knowledge) and was therefore able to interest the members of that organization in the plight of the Protestants expelled from the Archbishopric of Salzburg in 1731. He was also author of *Amerikanisches Ackerwerk Gottes*, a continuation of his *Ausführliche Nachricht*. See *Die Religion in Geschichte und Gegenwart* (Tübingen, 1962), VI, cols. 1194–95.

2. Carl Mauelshagen, *Salzburg Lutheran Expulsion and its Impact* (New York, 1962), 135–37.

3. One clue in particular is an indication of the *Purysburg's* size—her draft of $12\frac{1}{2}$ feet mentioned in a letter to Henry Newman from the Rev. Richard Lowther in Rotterdam: George Fenwick Jones, ed., *Henry Newman's Salzburger Letterbooks* (Athens, 1966), 387.

4. Hermann Winde, "Die Frühgeschichte der Lutherischen Kirche in Georgia" (dissertation, Martin-Luther-Universität, Halle-Wittenberg, 1960), 265, No. 75.

5. Jones, ed., *Henry Newman*, p. 84.

6. In their entry for March 8, the pastors report a shoemaker's account of a storm he had experienced during his voyage to America which had broken all of the ship's water barrels except one: George Fenwick Jones, ed., *Detailed Reports on the Salzburger Emigrants Who Settled in America . . . Edited by Samuel Urlsperger*. Vol. I, 1733–1734. (Athens, 1968), 57–58.

7. An elaborate experiment begun in 1944 at the University of Minnesota produced strikingly similar symptoms during a twenty-four week period of semistarvation: Floyd L. Ruch, *Psychology and Life* (Chicago, 1958), 128–30.

8. Roth, being a distiller, probably brought along his own private supply.

9. Jones, ed., *Newman Letterbooks*, 371, 413.

10. *Ibid.*, 60.

11. Dr. George Fenwick Jones, Professor of German and Comparative Literature at the University of Maryland, has performed considerable research in this area.

12. Leslie F. Church, *Oglethorpe: A Study of Philanthropy in England and Georgia* (London, 1932), 145.

13. P. A. Strobel, *The Salzburgers and Their Descendants* (Baltimore, 1855), 58.

14. Jones, ed., *Detailed Reports*, I, xxi.

15. *Newman's Letterbooks* supplies much additional information; and "The Secret Diary of Pastor Johann Martin Boltzius" edited by George F. Jones, *Georgia Historical Quarterly*, March, 1969, pp. 78–110, brings to light the deplorable conditions at Old Ebenezer, the difficulties and officialism involved in the removal of the settlement to the bank of the Savannah River, and the disagreements between the pastors, von Reck, Vat, and Zwiffler.

16. Frank R. Donovan, *The Mayflower Compact* (New York, 1968), 17–18.

17. Strobel, *Salzburgers*, 23–24.

18. In Latin.

19. *Novus adjutor* means "new assistant" and probably refers to Gronau; *it. (item)* means "likewise"; *Petrina* refers either to Petrine or Petrinism.

20. Gotthilf August Francke (1696–1769), son of August Hermann Francke, became chief professor at the University of Halle when his father died in 1727. He continued his father's work with foreign missions by sending missionaries to Pennsylvania (e.g. H. M. Mühlenberg) and India. It was he who selected Boltzius and

Gronau to accompany the Salzburgers to Georgia. See Urlsperger, ed., *Die Religion in Geschichte und Gegenwart*, II, cols. 1016–17; Winde, Dissertation 160, 171.

21. Through counterfeit letters.

22. Universal grace as opposed to the Calvinistic doctrine of God's *predestination* of some men to salvation.

23. Urlsperger made this news item a footnote to the entry for December 30, 1733, and he changed the last line to read as follows: "and it appears that, if God would give the Turkish Empire another blow, the conversion of the Jews there would make great progress."

24. In 1733 there were two professors in Halle by the name of Michaelis: Johann Heinrich Michaelis (1668–1738), professor of oriental languages and senior inspector of the theological seminary, and his nephew Christian Benedikt Michaelis (1680–1764), professor of theology: Samuel Macauley Jackson, D.D., LL.D., ed., *The New Schaff-Herzog Encyclopedia of Religious Knowledge* (Grand Rapids, Michigan, 1952).

25. Johann Heinrich Callenberg (1694–1760) was educated at Halle, where in 1727 he was appointed associate professor of philology. His deep interest in Protestant missions among the Jews and Mohammedans of the East led him, in 1728, to found the *Institutum Judaicum* for the education of missionaries: Jackson, *Encyclopedia*.

26. To his native land.

27. The Arminians were followers of the sixteenth-century Dutch theologian Jacobus Arminius (real name Jacob Harmensen or Hermansz). They did not attempt to form a sect but viewed themselves as members of the Reformed Church, simply differing in opinion on points of Calvinistic doctrine. They argued mainly that Christ died for all men and not only for the elect. After a period of intense theological controversy at the beginning of the seventeenth century, the Arminians were slowly assimilated by existing Protestant churches.

28. Those feeling otherwise.

29. These Salzburgers were the Tirnberger (German, *Dürrnberger*) miners and their families, and they were the last large group (780 persons) of Protestants to leave Salzburg. Accompanied by their young preacher Johann Gottlieb Fischer, they arrived on the island of Cadzand in March, 1733. Despite the sincere promises made by the Dutch ambassador at Regensburg, these people were dispersed throughout the island and maltreated by the inhabitants. During the summer of 1733 a fever epidemic broke out, to which more than a hundred of the Tirnbergers fell victim. In despair, many families began to return to Germany. Although Fischer himself was enfeebled by the sickness, he nevertheless traveled from place to place, exhorting them to stay. However, only 42 families, a total of 216 persons, resolved to remain: Gerhard Florey, *Bischöfe, Ketzer, Emigranten* (Graz ,1967), 231–34.

30. The original German word is *Clavier*, which is translated today as "piano." Formerly it meant clavichord or harpsichord. In 1733 the piano was only in its early stages of development and did not become popular until the 1750's. The harpsichord was a much more elaborate instrument than the clavichord and therefore out of the question for Boltzius' purposes.

31. Von Reck annoyed Boltzius again with a noisy farewell on July 15, 1736.

32. Christian Schweikert remained in New England when von Reck returned to Europe. Later, he returned sick to die in Ebenezer.

33. His name was Gilbert Beque and he is mentioned for the last time in the entry for the 14th of December.

34. Dutch for "man-of-war."

35. Removed from witnesses or listeners.

36. This is the title of T. Bird's translation of the hymn "Erleucht mich, Herr mein Licht!" by the North German theologian E. W. Buchfelder (1645–1711). It is No. 245 in Freylinghausen's *Gesangbuch*, 1704, and, in the aforesaid translation, No. 290 in the *Moravian Hymn Book*, 1826: John Julian, D.D. ed., *A Dictionary of Hymnology* (London, 1892), 191.

37. Translation of Greek phrase in the diary.

38. This refers probably to Boltzius, since he was very interested in music and had taken part in establishing the College of Music of the Francke Foundation.

39. "Wer weiss, wie nahe mir mein Ende!" by Ämil. Juliane, Countess of Schwarzburg. It is No. 678 in Freylinghausen's *Gesangbuch*, 1714, and No. 458 in Philipp Schaff's *Deutsches Gesangbuch* (Chambersburg, Pa., 1860).

40. This is this editor's own translation of the hymn "Ich sterbe täglich, und mein Leben" by the Silesian theologian Benjamin Schmolck (1672–1737), the most popular hymn-writer of his time. It was translated as "Both life and death are kept by Thee" (fourth stanza), by J. Kelly, in the *Family Treasury*, 1868, p. 689: Julian, *Dictionary*, 1013.

41. More prominent sayings.

42. . . . *excessu* . . . *defectu* . . . This seems to mean that neither believing in nor doubting the existence of ghosts is sinful.

43. Philipp Jacob Spener (1635–1705), German Protestant theologian from Alsace, was the founder of Pietism. In 1666 he became first pastor at the Lutheran Church of Frankfort on the Main, where he organized his *Collegia Pietatis* (meetings for Bible study and religious inspiration) and published, in 1675, his *Pia Desideria* and, in 1680, his *Allgemeine Gottesgelehrtheit*, in which he set forth mystical religious views advocating emphasis on conversion and regeneration. In 1686 he became court preacher at Dresden: *The Universal Standard Encyclopedia* (New York, 1956), 7969.

44. Christian Thomasius (1655–1728), German philosopher and jurist, became professor of law at the University of Leipzig in 1684, where three years later he substituted the German language for Latin in his lectures. The caustic wit with which he criticized educational methods and religious topics of the day, together with his advanced views, on theology in particular, aroused a storm of opposition, and he was forced to leave Leipzig. In 1690 he became one of the founders of the University of Halle, where, from 1694 until his death, he was professor of jurisprudence: *Encyclopedia Americana*.

45. Hermann von der Hardt (1660–1746), German orientalist, exegete, and historian, spent a year in Dresden with Spener and, through him, resolved to become an expounder of the Scriptures. In 1688 he received a professorship at the University of Helmstedt, which opened an avenue to him for an extensive literary activity. At the same time, however, his attitude changed in regard to the Bible and Pietism; and under the influence of Thomasius his rationalism became so pronounced that he was censured by the official visitors to the university, and in 1713 forbidden longer to deliver exegetical lectures on the Old Testament. He disregarded this order, however, and complications followed which ended in his retirement as professor (1727), although he was permitted to act as sublibrarian for the university: Jackson, *Encyclopedia*.

46. Helmstedt in the *Land* of Lower Saxony, Federal Republic of Germany, is now a frontier post on the main railway and *Autobahn* to Berlin. In 1576 Julius, Duke of Brunswick, founded a university there, and throughout the seventeenth century it was one of the chief seats of Protestant learning. It was closed by Jerome Bonaparte, King of Westphalia, in 1810: *Encyclopaedia Britannica*, 1966.

47. Johann Lorenz von Mosheim (1693–1755), German Lutheran theologian and founder of the pragmatic school of church historians, was a popular and influential professor at Helmstedt from 1723 to 1747: *Encyclopedia Britannica*, 1966.

48. Due to a lack of knowing the English language.

49. Nature of the language and its pronunciation.

50. Previous way of living.

51. In 1722 Count Nikolaus Ludwig von Zinzendorf (1700–60), godson of Spener, granted refuge on his estate in Berthelsdorf, Upper Lusatia, to a group of Moravians of the persecuted Bohemian Brethren. Their community, called Herrnhut, became a refuge for the Brethren from other lands and for members of other persecuted Protestant sects. For more information see the *Encyclopaedia Britannica* or *The Universal Standard Encyclopedia*, 9457.

52. Pastoral warnings.

53. Society for the Propagation of Christian Knowledge.

54. Society for Promoting Christian Knowledge.

55. Lack of motion.

56. As a German, Boltzius used the Gregorian calendar, which, by 1733, was eleven days ahead of the Julian calendar used by the British. On the first of the year he changed to the British reckoning.

57. Abbot Breithaupt—the name was included in Urlsperger's *Detailed Reports*. Along with Paul Anton and A. H. Francke, Joachim Justus Breithaupt, senior of the theological faculty at Halle, was regarded as one of the three pillars of Halle Pietism. He was greatly admired by Boltzius, who experienced both Breithaupt's and Anton's death in 1732: Winde, Dissertation, 158, 164–65.

58. Arndt's *Postille*. Johann Arndt (1555–1621), German mystic and theologian, was the author of *Vom wahren Christentum (Of True Christianity)* and *Paradies-gärtlein aller christlichen Tugenden (Little Garden of Paradise of all Christian Virtues)*. The appearance of the *Wahre Christentum* gave rise to a violent controversy. Steeped in the mysticism of the Middle Ages, Arndt asserted the insufficiency of orthodox doctrine toward the complete attainment of the true Christian life, and upheld the necessity of a moral purification made possible by righteous living and by bringing the soul into communion with God. Though he held fast, formally, to the doctrine of the Lutheran Church, he nevertheless became thus the great precursor of Pietism: Jackson, *Encyclopedia*.

59. Peter Simonds was owner of the *Purysburg*.

60. Johann Anastasius Freylinghausen (1670–1739) assisted A. H. Francke in Halle; and when Francke became pastor of St. Ulrich's in 1715, Freylinghausen became his colleague, and in the same year married his only daughter. He became pastor of St. Ulrich's and director of the Francke Institutions after Francke's death in 1727. He was a hymn-writer of the highest rank, but his importance in the history of spiritual song depends principally on the hymnals which he edited and in which the melodies of the hymns were often replaced by his own compositions.

61. Well-meaning.

62. Men in public office.

63. On this day Boltzius adopted the Julian calendar. See note 56.

64. On the 28th of December, 1733, Henry Newman, secretary of the S.P.C.K., wrote Urlsperger, "I have by order of the Society sent Ludowig's Grammar and Dictionary in 2 Volumes each to Messrs. Bolzius and Gronau . . .": Jones, ed., *Newman Letterbooks*, 91. Christian Ludwig (1660–1728), born in Eilenburg near Leipzig, lived in New England and England for many years. Eventually he returned to Germany and settled in Leipzig, where, in addition to teaching English, he published his *English-German, German-English Dictionary, Introduction to the English Language*, and *Rudiments of the English Language*. His *Thorough Instruction in the English Language* came out in Leipzig in 1717: Christian Gottlieb Jöcher, *Allgemeines Gelehrten-Lexikon*, Vol. II (Hildesheim, 1961), col. 2585.

65. This is Johann Caspar Schade's *Ein Herrliches Geschenck oder schöne Christ-Bescherung, in einem Einfältigen Gespräch Zwischen Lehrer und Kindern Von der Geburth des lieben Jesus-Kindleins unsers Heylandes (usw.) (A Magnificent Present or Christ's Beautiful Bestowal of Gifts in a Simple Talk between Teacher and Children about the Birth of the Dear Baby Jesus, Our Savior, etc.)* published in Leipzig in 1694: Winde, Dissertation, 223.

66. The German word is *Seelen-Führung* and the subject is probably related to one of Porst's smaller works, *Göttliche Führung der Seelen (Divine Guidance of Souls)*.

67. Johann Porst (1668–1728) was won over to Pietism through the reading of Spener's penitential sermons. For several years he was second preacher of the Friedrichswerdersche und Dorotheenstädtische Kirche in Berlin, and in 1709 he became the chaplain of Sophie Louise, the second wife of Frederick I. In 1713 the king offered him the office of provost of Berlin, which Porst accepted. In 1715 he aided Boltzius' uncle, Johann Müller, in finding a pastorate. Porst wrote a number of religious works, but he is best known for his hymnals: Winde, Dissertation, 157.

68. Johann Caspar Schade (1666–98), German theologian and hymn-writer and friend of A. H. Francke, was Spener's deacon in Berlin. He is best known for his opposition to absolution too routinely granted after private confession, which eventu-

ally resulted in the abrogation of obligatory confession by Frederick I, then Elector of Brandenburg: *Die Religion in Geschichte und Gegenwart*, V, col. 1381.

69. After the death of his wife and in response to a visionary calling in 1704, Johannes Tennhardt (1661–1720), Pietistic mystic and religious fanatic, devoted himself to writing prophetic tracts and open letters allegedly dictated by God, which were disseminated from his home in Nuremberg. His zeal, however, brought him into conflict with ecclesiastical and civil authorities, resulting in his arreset in 1710 and 1714: *Die Religion in Geschichte und Gegenwart*, V, cols. 689–90.

70. *Jure talionis* is the same as *lex talionis*, the principle or law of retaliation that a punishment inflicted should correspond in degree and kind to the offense of the wrongdoer.

71. A loud noise.

72. Adiaphorism is the theory that certain doctrines or practices in morals or religion are "indifferent matters." The first adiaphorist controversy in Germany arose over the religious compromises contained in the Augsburg and Leipzig interims (1548), which sanctioned the jurisdiction of Roman Catholic bishops and observance of certain rites. The second adiaphorist controversy arose in the field of morals in 1681. Whereas Luther had maintained the right of temperate enjoyment of secular amusements, the Pietists held that actions not bidden of God are necessarily actions which profit not and are therefore collectively wrong. For complete information see Jackson, *Encyclopedia*, 41–44.

73. With the approval of the church.

74. From Spain to the West Indies ships followed the arc of the northeast trade wind which blew them from the Canaries to the Lesser Antilles in about a month. In January, however, the trade wind boundary begins just north of the Cape Verde Islands.

75. The pastors actually observed a thin crescent, since new moon was two nights earlier.

76. *Sammlung Auserlesener Materien zum Bau des Reichs Gottes (Collection of Choice Materials for the Fabric of God's Kingdom)*. Der I. Beytrag (Leipzig, 1731); Winde, Dissertation, p. 223.

77. Even a hundred years later this was considered as something special: "To enhance the value of the Sabbath to the crew, they are allowed on that day a pudding, or, as it is called, a "duff." This is nothing more than flour boiled with water, and eaten with molasses. It is very heavy, dark, and clammy, yet it is looked upon as a luxury, and really forms an agreeable variety with salt beef and pork. Many a rascally captain has made friends of his crew by allowing them duff twice a week on the passage home.": R. H. Dana, Jr., *Two Years Before the Mast* (New York, 1969), 23.

78. This letter is for the Rev. Friedrich Michael Ziegenhagen, Chaplain of his Majesty's German Chapel at St. James's.

79. Joy and sadness.

80. Either the pastors did not understand the name of the island or they had forgotten it when they made this entry; consequently, they left this blank. However, the other island is probably St. John, since it is quite close to St. Thomas.

81. Mrs. Thomas Causton.

82. Siegmund Jakob Baumgarten (1705–57) studied at the Halle Orphanage, of which his father had been first inspector, and at the University of Halle. He became inspector of the Halle Latin School in 1726, assistant preacher to the younger G. A. Francke in 1728, associate on the theological faculty in 1730, and ordinary professor in 1743: Jackson, *Encyclopedia*.

83. Mischke was inspector of the German School at the Orphanage in Halle. He died shortly after Boltzius and Gronau arrived in Georgia.

84. In Urlsperger's version there is no mention of the widows' custom of wearing long hair, and the words "an Indian widow" were changed to "his Indian wife."

85. This was written from Abercorn, a settlement on the Savannah River.

86. The beer was healthful because it was boiled.

87. According to Boltzius' many complaints in Volume III of the *Detailed Reports*, this is just what von Reck failed to do in collecting his third transport.

Index

Bruckner, Georg, Salzburger, a loyal disciple, 264; total crop, 270

Buchfelder, E. W., hymn by, 333 (n. 36)

Burgsdorff, Landeshauptmann von, letter to, 224, 321

Burgsteiner, Matthias, Salzburger, total crop, 270

Burgsteiner, Mrs., wife of above, churched with baby, 22

Busk, Indian festival, 177, 329 (n. 190)

Butienter (Butjenter), Heinrich Alard, court preacher at London, letter from, 184; letter to, 224, 321; meets Salzburgers at Dover, 291; arranges church agenda, 292; returns to London, 292. See 329 (n. 196)

Butter, Mr. Vat will not distribute, 66, 91; lack of, 96, 215, 223, 228, 260; Oglethorpe provides, 179, 183, 202; Mrs. Schweighofer needs, 214; Boltzius distributes, 231; part of 1st transport's diet, 272; used in mush, 283; used in pudding, 300; inaccessible, 304; given to Salzburgers, 308

Calendar, Gregorian (New) and Julian (Old), 3, 335 (n. 56)

Callenberg, Johann Heinrich, theologian at Halle, 278, 333 (n. 25)

Calvinists, 278, 279

Cardo-benedicten herbs, 213

Carl, Johann Samuel, medical professor, his religious tractate read at prayer meeting, 28, 325 (n. 61)

Carpenter, Nicolas, English boy at Ebenezer, unsuited for duties, 126; sent back to Savannah, 156

Catechism, method of teaching it, 18, 22. See Luther, Martin

Cattle, calves destroyed by wolves, 15; cows, lost in forest, 25; a great benefit, 36; brought from forest, 55; devoured by wolves, 85; produce butter, 202; donated to 3rd transport, 204, 247; cattle brand requested, 233; Oglethorpe to raise cattle at Old Ebenezer, 40; guarded by Salzburgers, 157, 165; oxen, some run away, 55, 221; donated as fresh meat, 144, 154, 204, 205, 216

Causton, Thomas, mayor of Savannah, scapegoat for Oglethorpe, xv; disapproves Vat's behavior, 19; aids Zubly brothers, 55; writes friendly letter, 93; very helpful, 105, 120; sends provisions, 136, 241; receives petitions, 141, 164; promises to send up provisions, 208; fails to do so, 214, 223; refuses to give

boards, 213; charges for provisions, 219; very friendly, 219, 253

Causton, Mrs., wife of above, chosen as godmother, 313

Charleston, S.C., Salzburgers reach, 310; description of, 310 ff; Negroes in, 311

Cherokee Indians, friendly to English, 102; description of, 102

Chinkapins, found at Red Bluff, 216, 330 (n. 225)

Christ, converted Jew from Frankfurt, a serious Christian, xv; has hemorrhages, 98; gives much pleasure, 113; conducting himself well, 249; incapable of field work, 267

Christ the Core of the Holy Writ, religious treatise by A. H. Francke, Boltzius to send translation to Eveleigh, 17, 328 (n. 158)

Christ the Sun and Substance of the Holy Scriptures, same as above

Christ's Christmas Gifts, religious treatise, read, 299

Church, Leslie F., historian, quoted, 274, 332 (n. 12)

Church discipline (penance), 57, 59, 90, 111

Churching, 22, 37, 214

Clapboards, used for building, 133

Clausnitzer, Tobias, hymn by, 328 (n. 152)

Coleman, Benjamin, clergyman of Massachusetts, his letter deleted, xxi, 1

Collin, Friedrich Eberhard, pietist writer, his treatise cited by Boltzius, 325 (n. 62)

Commandments, Ten, 324 (n. 55)

Communal work, performed by Salzburgers, 127; ineffectual, 148, 151, 165, 171, 235

Compendium Theologiae, see Freylinghausen

Contribution to the Building of the Kingdom of God, devotional book, read at prayer meeting, 16, 22, 28, 216, 324 (n. 42)

Cooing Dove, devotional tract, used in Sunday school, 130, 328 (n. 155)

Copper money, most useful, 218

Coram, Capt. Thomas, Trustee and member of S.P.C.K., meets Salzburgers at Dover, 291; presents patent to Boltzius, 297; donates wine, 301; provides meat, 302; not captain of *Purysburg*, 271

Corn, flourishes on fertilized ground, 210; subsidy paid for, 245, 260, 268; register of crop, 270

Cornberger, Johann, Salzburger, has scur-

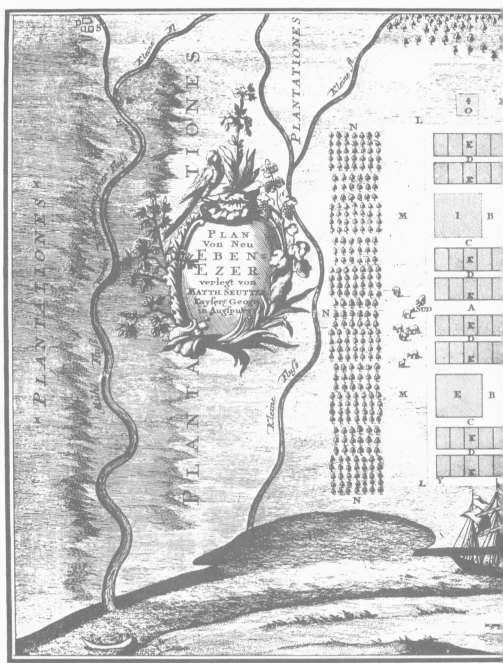

A. *Haupt Straßen.* B. *Marckt Plätz.* C. *Mittle Gaßen.* D *kleine Gäßlin* .E. *Store Hauß.* F *Pfarr-Wohnungen* . G *die Kirchen u̇*
rer ein jeglicher Zehen Wohnungen faßt; so in einem Hauß Hof u̇ Garten bestehet. L *ein Schindel zaun Sechs Fuß hoch we*
welcher ebenfals eingezäunt. P *Holtz.* Q *Eigenthumlichs Land einer kleinen Nation Indianer.* R *die Mühl.* S *Kübricorn e*
Land wo die Saltzburger ihre Vieh Ställe haben. Y *Sind 20 Hauß Plätze zwischen drey Straßen. so Hr. General Oglethr*

This Plan of Ebenezer first appeared in Urlsperger's *Ausführliche Nachrichten, 13te Continuation, Ers*